The More Things Change

The More
Things Change

WHY THE BABY BOOM WON'T FADE AWAY

(Previously published as *My Generation*)

MICHAEL GROSS

Cliff Street Books
An Imprint of HarperCollinsPublishers

The Library of Congress has catalogued the hardcover edition as follows:

Gross, Michael.
    My generation: fifty years of sex, drugs, rock, revolution, glamour, greed, valor, faith, and silicon chips/by Michael Gross—1st ed.
        p.   cm.
    Includes bibliographical references and index.
    ISBN 0-06-017594-X
    1. Baby boom generation—United States. 2. United States—Social conditions—1960–1980. 3. United States—Social conditions—1980– 4. Gross, Michael. I. Title
    Hn58 .G77 2000
    305.24—dc21

                                    99-055384

ISBN: 0-06-093124-8 (pbk.)

00 01 02 03 04 05 ❖/RRD 10 9 8 7 6 5 4 3 2 1

In Memory of Milton Gross (b.1912)
and for Estelle Gross (b. 1915)

And you may ask yourself
What is that beautiful house?
And you may ask yourself
Where does that highway go to?
And you may ask yourself
Am I right? . . . Am I wrong?
And you may tell yourself
MY GOD! . . . WHAT HAVE I DONE?
Same as it ever was . . .
Same as it ever was . . .
Same as it ever was . . .

—*Talking Heads, "Once in a Lifetime"*

Contents

Preface to the Paperback Edition

"Our generation has a rendezvous with responsibility."
—Hillary R. Clinton, at the 2000 Democratic National Convention

"Our generation has a chance to reclaim some essential values, to show we have grown up before we grow old."
—George W. Bush, at the 2000 Republican National Convention

THESE TIMES TRY a baby boomer's patience if not the generational soul. Having survived the moment when the first boomers turned fifty, this should have been our moment in the sun; we should have been settling down, comfortable with power, at ease and in control, but instead the turn of the millennium has turned into a winter of free-floating disillusion. We worry whether our minds are going, along with our eyesight, our hearing, our knees, our cherished position in the cultural vanguard. We find ourselves looking over our shoulders, wondering who's gaining on us. We joke nervously about suffering senior moments. Our generation's first president turned himself into a sex joke. We're not sure our jokes are funny anymore. But wait; there's hope. The story that follows offers a score of examples of baby boomers who've found ways to grow, to change, to evolve, to age with grace and good humor.

Why, then, does it seem that as a generation, the baby boom is suffering a mass midlife crisis? Or, at least, a midlife blip of sufficient significance that it stands out even in our already stormy story? Quite likely because, as so often before in our collective biography, a vocal minority has hijacked a generation's image and taken it for a ride. Admittedly, boomers are self-important, self-righteous, and self-aware to a fault. But in the year since this book was first published, the media has been filled with an orchestral surge of generational self-flagellation that is just as extreme in its way as were the extremes of our youth.

"The Summer of Love is descending into the Night of the Living Dead," reported *Time* magazine (edited by a baby boomer) in an article (written by a baby boomer) entitled "Twilight of the Boomers" that called us preening, self-congratulatory and smug. Reviewing a book about the latest generation, our children's, in the *New York Times Book Review*, another Boomer called his generation "insufferable." Which was kind compared to what appeared in *Esquire*, also edited by a baby boomer. In an article called "The Worst Generation," the author, another boomer of course, literally trashed his fellows as a "garbage barge of a generation."

These pundits are acting as if our storied great expectations—for a re-creation of American society, for continuing cultural centrality, or just living as well as we can as long as we can—have been blown away like so much dust. Why? I can't help thinking it's because we're growing older and some of us can't face it yet. We haven't had to deal with the inevitability of aging because middle age is coming upon us later than ever before in history. And the nattering negativists fear that when it does come, it will close minds that were once wide-open and stiffen spirits that were once as flexible as our limbs. They assume the worst about their fellow boomers—and not without good reason.

Ever since our parents started expanding schools and suburbs to make room for us fifty years ago, American society has constantly adjusted to the needs of our particular demographic. For a long time, we were the youth in the Youthquake; youth culture was invented for us, if not by us. Problem is, we've continued to worship youth even as we've ceased to be young. As Alphonse Karr, a French journalist and satirist, wrote more than 150 years ago, the more things change, the more they stay the same. And so a new young have asserted themselves. We are hoist with our own petard, caught in a cultural paradox, an aging majority in a society we constructed to revolve around youth.

Almost all of us have fought this inevitability for twenty years, by going to either the health clubs or rock concerts—until the rock stars started going gray, too, and the truth got harder to avoid. So now, some of us see in the mirror a rebuke to our self-image, a negation of our self-definition, a nuclear bomb dropped on our self-worth. (We're still rather *self*-ish.)

As a generation, we've reached a crossroads. So much of our identity is grounded in the importance of youth, but where does that leave us, now that we're aging? Nostalgic wallowing in sex, drugs, rock and revolt is as annoying to today's youth as their cultural markers are to many of us. And some of us don't want to be reminded of our pasts at all; the old war stories, whether of world-changing victories or humbling defeats, make the disconnect with the present too powerful. Those amnesiac boomers don't want to be reminded of what they once were; it's too far from what they've become. They've mistaken moving on for selling out.

Jim Fouratt, one of those whose story is told in the pages that follow, says that the self-loathing boomers now dominating the debate about our generation are suffering from a pernicious new social disease he calls "internalized ageism." True, many of us find technology and tattoos, Eminem and *South Park* just as alien and offensive as our parents found the extremes of our youth. Yet secretly we yearn to understand and be part of them—just as we have yearned to be friends to our children instead of the parents they need. Youth culture, which once pandered to us, now mocks us by reflecting the contempt we injected into it for everything associated with maturity: wisdom, prudence, experience, history, memory.

The generation gap is a chasm—again. We (again, most of us) don't talk the same language as do kids. At last, they have a music we can openly despise, though we only do so in front of our age peers because we want to be *down* with the little ones. They understand those damn computers; many of us still think of them as a cyber-nuisance. And, I've heard way too many boomers say, *what's with the TV shows and movies they watch?*

Who can blame Generation X for pouncing on the corpse of its predecessor—even though we're still moving—and reveling in our passage from cultural centrality? We stole their youth; we were so overwhelming that we sucked all the air out of the room. They never had a culture of their own—only the chaotic ruins we left behind. As American capitalism focuses on the next generation, the first of the new millennium—the one some clever marketer has already dubbed Generation Why Not?—Gen X'ers can at last relish our comeuppance. They got the power that matters to us most of all: They can still pass as young.

Soon, people will be writing books about our lurch toward decrepitude. We've done it all. Nothing left to do but die. No haircut, no piercing, no pair of phat shoes will help a boomer be anything other than what he or she is fast becoming: old.

Today's youth, we're reminded via multiple media, have knowledge, skills, attributes and attitudes we don't have. They not only see a new world, as we once did in our halcyon days, but also consider themselves its natives—leaving us to bring up the rear. ("No, no, we're not the AARP group," we assert brightly. "We're with those gel-haired cyber geeks over there!") The fact is that we are tired to death of the struggle to stay au courant—but are wracked with fear about what will come of us if we're not. Are we now . . . *then?*

With these kinds of issues, it's no wonder we're resorting to fakery and quick fixes—diets and nutritional supplements for anti-aging, Viagra for sexual vigor, liposuction for those unsightly reminders of lives well lived. Plastic surgery has become the new norm, a cure for time. "The effect of decades of the advertising machine is to tell us, it's fine," says Kathy Peiss, professor of history at the University of Massachusetts and author of a history of the cosmetics business. "Baby boomers always had the attitude we could make our lives come out the way we wanted. Now, years of chipping away at the negative moral value placed on artifice has finally led a generation to say, 'I'll do what I want and it doesn't matter.'"

Or does it? Susan Bordo, a professor of women's studies at the University of Kentucky, has made the impact of media on culture and the individual her life's work. "We no longer learn how to live with the inevitable weakening and deterioration of our bodies," she says. "Advertising, entertainment, medicine, technology, each in its own way, is telling us we don't have to get old. It's a lie. People may die a little later, but they die. Learning to accept that is an education that happens in a more productive and beneficial way if we absorb it bit by bit. I don't feel good about wrinkles and sags, but I look at them as little opportunities to think about my life."

So, despite our midlife jitters, despite our best efforts at turning back the clock, we've reached a turning point. An unavoidable realization: Others have passed this way before us. We can't fight the inevitable forever. After all, we are the generation that has overseen America's evolution from an old economy to a new one, from an intolerant society to an inclusive one, from the industrial age to the information age, from the second millennium to the third. We hardly need to skulk around with paper bags over our heads. But we do need a new way of looking at the next fifty years of our time on this planet. "Old Age" doesn't quite cut it as a descriptive anymore.

"God knows, baby boomers are not the first generation to get old—why did Ponce de Leon go to Florida?—since its inception, mankind has tried to remain young," says Joe Coughlin, head of the Age Lab at the

Massachusetts Institute of Technology. "But boomers are the first with the money, the education and the numbers to demand that the experience be different. What we need to determine is the nature of older adulthood. We've yet to experience it, so we're trying to maintain what was yesterday instead of striking out for the new frontier. Old now means ill, poor and alone. But in the next twenty years, we will craft a new vision of aging and all of a sudden an older face will represent a new vision of life."

Coughlin speaks truth. But until we make peace with our pasts—until we connect again with who we once were, reconcile that with who we are and try again to live up to the impossible promise of our youth—we cannot move forward. Why *not* look in the mirror and see wrinkles as something more than signs of degradation and decay? Rather, let's see them as what they are: badges of honor, marking the times—both good and bad—of our lives.

Cast of Characters

CYNTHIA BOWMAN—Runaway hippie turned PR executive.

STEVE CAPPS—Nerd turned software superstar.

JIM FOURATT—Hippie turned Yippie! turned gay activist and new music impresario.

MICHAEL FUCHS—Media maven turned multimillionaire retiree.

JOHN GAGE—Free Speech Movement activist turned computer-evangelist.

NINA HARTLEY—Red diaper baby turned bisexual feminist porn star.

VICTORIA LEACOCK—Second-generation celebrity turned AIDS activist.

BARBARA LEDEEN—Marxist turned right-wing conspirator.

DAVID MCINTOSH—Eagle Scout turned conservative maverick.

DOUG MARLETTE—Southern racist turned Pulitzer-winning political cartoonist.

MARK RUDD—Radical bomber turned vocational school teacher.

TIM SCULLY—LSD chemist turned software designer.

CAMERON SEARS—Environmental activist turned Grateful Dead manager.

RUSSELL SIMMONS—Ghetto pot dealer turned urban entrepreneur.

LESLIE CROCKER SNYDER—Radcliffe preppie turned hanging judge.

KATHRYN BOND STOCKTON—Jesus freak turned Queer Theorist.

DONALD TRUMP—Military school cut-up turned Ur-Yuppie.

THOMAS VALLELY—Vietnam War hero turned Asian redevelopment expert.

MARIANNE WILLIAMSON—Wild child turned spiritual celebrity.

The More Things Change

Bethel, New York

AUGUST 14, 1998: I'm driving along a back road in rustic upstate New York when a *déjà vu* of an intensity I've experienced only once before overwhelms me. That time, en route to a meeting in Dallas, I drove into an open expanse called Dealy Plaza and didn't understand why it felt so eerie until I was alongside the Texas School Book Depository, approaching a triple underpass imprinted in my memory from repeated television news broadcasts. I sensed more than saw that I was driving where John F. Kennedy was killed in 1963.

This is different. I've been here before. In front of me is a huge natural amphitheater full of people arrayed before a great wooden stage, amassed for a three-day rock and folk concert called A Day in the Garden. This "garden," once a farm belonging to a man named Max Yasgur and long ago an Indian gathering ground, was also the site of a gentle, auspicious music and arts event called the Aquarian Exposition, better known as Woodstock, where at age seventeen I spent three near-sleepless days in August 1969.

Never trust anybody over thirty, people used to say in the years after Kennedy was killed. So this, the twenty-ninth anniversary of Woodstock, may be the last chance to trust in the Age of Aquarius.

In 1969, the bacchanal of 400,000 people was front-page news. "HIPPIES MIRED IN SEA OF MUD," sneered New York's then-conservative *Daily News.* Perhaps we were. But we were also enjoying the biggest coming-out party ever for America's biggest generation ever, the Baby Boom. And everyone wanted to be there.

Our youngest member was about four and a half that day. The oldest participants were gray-haired bohemian-era precursors and young-at-heart boomer pretenders. We were all caught up in the excitement of the moment when a window of opportunity—for drugs, for sex, for "liberation"—opened up and about 76 million of us scampered through before it slammed shut. It's no wonder the generation that followed resents us. Youth ruled, and if it still seems to, that's largely because we cannily repackage our youth and sell it over and again. But there's a lot of gray hair at Woodstock 1998, onstage and off.

Don Henley (b. 1947) of the 1970s band The Eagles is playing an age-appropriate, elegiac song, "The Boys of Summer," as I park my car and wade into the crowd past concession stands emblazoned with peace symbols. "Everybody knows the war is over," Henley sings. "Everybody knows the good guys lost." But did they? Here they are, grown up into wrinkled, happy people, in neat rows of beach chairs, lawn furniture, Mayan cherry-wood chairs ($20 a day, $120 if you want to take one home), and Indian-print bedspreads scattered with Beanie Babies for their brood.

It's a generational Rorschach. You can see what you want here.

Hippies? Woodstock '98's got 'em, even if some are a little shopworn. Head shops still line the road, and beatific teenage girls with daisies in their hair dance waving tinsel in the hay fields. Everywhere are tie-dye, suede, and patchwork clothes that look as if they just emerged from ruck-sacks circa Woodstock '69.

Drugs? Occasional wisps tell you marijuana is still around, but far harder to find (and of far better quality) than it used to be. "We went *hmmm*," says young mother Susan Kaufer, eyeing her three kids, six, eight, and eleven, and the cloud of pot above their heads. "They haven't said anything, thank god."

Yuppies? There's a BMW 733i passing a Jaguar with a vanity plate that says INTRNET on Hurd Road. The only psychedelic Volkswagen in sight is a New Beetle painted with the logo of a local radio station. The satellite ATM van is as busy as the Port-a-sans. The concession stands offer pasta caprese, focaccia, mixed baby green salads and cappuccino alongside the burgers and beer. Henley launches into a song called "The End of Innocence." There are Woodstock '69 and Woodstock '98 T-shirts for sale, Woodstock license plate frames, Woodstock mouse pads, even Yasgur's Farm Ice Cream.

"My wife brought me," says Ken Adamyk, who was nine years old the first time around and didn't go to Woodstock '69. "My older brother went. He doesn't have hair now, but he did." A couple in their fifties walks by with laminated backstage passes marked FOH, for friends of the house, I assume. I ask them what the initials mean anyway. "Fucking Old Hippie," he says. She laughs. "Old hippies fucking," she says brightly.

But we've grown up. Really, we have. Even if Jim Farber (b. 1957), who's covering the event for today's more sympathetic *Daily News*, complains that every time he asks a boomer his age the answer is thirty-seven, most people I talk to are glad to proffer their birthdate.

"I'm one of the people who held onto the beliefs, and some of the products—I don't have to go into specifics," says Stephen Biegel (b. 1950), a builder from Hoboken, New Jersey. "I'm still proud we stopped a war. But you have to go with the flow. I grew up, had children; you have to support them. That's not a contradiction. The contradictions are either dead or wandering the streets."

Bill Lauren, a Woodstock '69 veteran wearing Oakley sunglasses and a gnomic red hat, is selling those Mayan chairs. "The first time, I liked the mud," he says. "Been there, done that."

At the first Woodstock, drugs were in everyone's eyes and the scent of sex was in the air. "You can get away with a lot of things in a cornfield," Don Henley is saying onstage. Not anymore, though, not in this cornfield. Overnight camping is banned. There are no drug dealers in sight. Visible skinny bra straps have replaced visible bralessness as the women's fashion. The lake where people skinny-dipped is fenced and posted PRIVATE LAND.

On day two, one of the performers, Joni Mitchell (b. 1943), will note another change. "Free love?" she asks from the stage. "There's no such thing now." She lets out a high, wild laugh. "Pay later," she adds wryly before hitting the first notes of "Woodstock," the song that gave this day in the garden its name.

Stevie Nicks (b. 1948), a former singer with Fleetwood Mac, performs after Henley and sings the lyric, "Thunder only happens when it's raining," just as it starts to rain—to general mirth. I remember the rain from 1969, how it turned the grassy bowl into a muddy tangle of blankets, sleeping bags, food wrappers, underground newspapers, discarded clothes and filthy, half-awake teens. In 1998 I glance down. At my feet is a trampled copy of *Seventeen*. Lying nearby, a *Harper's Bazaar*. Otherwise it could be a New York Philharmonic concert on the great lawn in Central Park, so polite and well-ordered is the crowd.

It starts to rain harder, though, and people leave in droves. "We're going to the Hamptons," a friend from the music business says as he heads for the parking lot. "We're going to shop the outlets," adds another who flees, a one-time hippie with a teenage daughter in tow. I didn't know anyone who walked out of the first Woodstock, rain notwithstanding. But a couple of my friends were there and escaped it anyway, they were so high on LSD.

Woodstock '98 is aimed at two separate audiences. Friday and Saturday are for baby boomers. Sunday will be Generation X day; it will feature a much bigger crowd of much younger people, traffic jams, an all-day mosh pit, more than a dozen drug arrests, the sudden appearance of designer labels like CK, lots more piercings, tattoos, and dog collars, a much-remarked-on beer ban, and newer musicians such as Janis Joplin-style belter Joan Osborne and several pop bands: Goo Goo Dolls, Third Eye Blind, and Marcy Playground. That last band's lead singer mentions LSD—indeed, he admits taking it. Hardly anyone cheers.

Acid flashes aside, Day Two is the real nostalgia day, starring three Woodstock '69 veterans: Melanie (b. Melanie Safka, 1947), Richie Havens (b. 1941) and Pete Townshend (b. 1945), along with Donovan (b. 1946) and Mitchell, who wrote "Woodstock" even though she wasn't there. Lou Reed (b. 1942)—the former Velvet Underground leader who probably wouldn't have been caught dead at Woodstock '69—is the swizzle stick in the day's mixed drink.

By this time in 1969, the first Woodstock's fences had been torn down and the concert officially acknowledged to be free. So I go up to the main gate and find it fully operational. State troopers are everywhere, as they were the first time around; this time, though, they seem to be running things. A rumor has swept the press tent that Michael Lang (b. 1945), an organizer of the first Woodstock, is on site and furious at Allan Gerry, the sixty-nine-year-old cable television millionaire who now controls the thirty-seven-acre site and acreage around it through a charitable foundation. Gerry has turned it all into a Baby Boom Disneyland with three miles of gravel roads, five miles of freshly cut split-rail fences, and, of course, focaccia. Protesters from the Woodstock Nation Foundation are angry with Gerry, too. They've filed lawsuits and committed acts of civil disobedience against what they consider the illegal taking of a sacred piece of public land. But is this site really sacred anymore? In 1998 Lang was planning a thirtieth-anniversary concert, aimed at the young rock audience, not boomers; it took place a year later on a decommissioned air force base in Rome, New York, and by the end, degenerated into an orgy of burning, looting and rape that left concertgoers and nostalgia buffs alike declaring the Woodstock ideal dead.

That concert, as it happened, took place just a few days after John F. Kennedy Jr. (b. 1960), his wife and her sister died in a small-plane crash off Martha's Vineyard. For the youngest boomers, the tragedy was an opportunity to experience the sort of mass mourning via media surrounding the 1963 assassination of President John F. Kennedy.

With their picture-perfect parents, John Jr. and his sister, Caroline (b. 1957), were idealized symbols of the Baby Boom. And in strange synchronicity with the Kennedy progeny, our generation has proved to be as tragic as it was blessed, as late-blooming as it was prematurely admired, as reckless as it was adventurous, as pitiable as it was enviable.

The young Kennedy's death and the retread concert that immediately followed had the impact but not the import of the originals they so eerily echoed. The thirty-nine-year-old was not yet the man his father was, and Woodstock '99 was more *Lord of the Flies* than the event on which it was based. It is the peculiar curse of the baby boom that the shadows of its youth often seem brighter than its present.

I MISS DONOVAN'S show because I head to the rock-and-roll mall, a high-tech tented pavilion full of merchandise and memory at the rim of the concert bowl. You can buy a lot here: photos of Jimi Hendrix (b. 1942) and Janis Joplin (b. 1943), hippie bags, handmade brooms, Catskill Mountain Farm goat cheese. Cornelius Alexy (b. 1943) sells peace symbols made from pieces of the storm fence that surrounded the site in 1969. Farmers had carted most of it away, but Alexy kept the gate.

"It's funny," says Cindy Beno Persico (b. 1953). "I was standing right next to that fence. I had a ticket. I walked to the gate and four hundred people knocked it down. Now I'm back with my eight-year-old daughter. I've met a lot of people who were there. We've changed—we're maybe not living in communes—but we've still got the spirit of youthfulness."

"I was here for the first one too," John Sharp chimes in. "I had a blast. I was fourteen. This was all woods. This was Gentle Way and Groovy Path," the intersection where people bought and sold drugs. "I've changed, too," he says. "I'm married. I have a son. I work every day, but I still love adventure." I ask whether he's finding any here. "It's a lot more organized," he says. "It's a lot more commercialized."

Want peace in the world? Buy a badge or a bumper sticker. Want to chill out? Get a massage for a dollar a minute. Want to wave your freak flag? Have your hair braided with beads for a dollar an inch, or, for something more permanent, get pierced.

"It's the new thing, a tribal, instinctual thing," says Lisa Sampson, who's working the piercing booth. "The pierced people are the children of the freaks," piercer Danny Domino says. "They don't do it for a reason. Reasons go away. This doesn't."

"A fifty-five-year-old just pierced his belly button," Sampson adds.

Next door, you can buy books by boomer heroes like Ken Kesey and Allen Ginsberg, and videos of druggie idols like Timothy Leary and Neal Cassady, the star of Jack Kerouac novels and Kesey's traveling Merry Pranksters troupe. The Grateful Shed is selling hemp (marijuana plant) clothing, twine, hats, sandals, and even hemp "Aware Bear" teddy bears. John's Rocking Ride, based in Dayton, Ohio, is hawking tie-dye Jerry Garcia posters and Cuban cigars at $20 each. "The government's gone berserk," the salt-and-pepper-bearded proprietor storms. "We do business with butchers in China, but poor Castro can't get toilet paper!"

A few stalls away, Marcia Weiss (b. 1948) is one of several people selling original Woodstock ephemera. "Every generation had a best time of its life," is her explanation for why people buy it.

"They want to stay in touch with who they are, how it used to be," adds a browser, Greg Packer (b. 1964). Randy Smith (b. 1955) overhears him. "I drive a '69 Dodge Charger," Smith says. "I still have an eight-track tape player." He buys tapes for it on the Internet.

A copy of the programs given away at the first Woodstock will run you $125. Unused three-day tickets are $100. For some, these things mean more than money. "Money is a drug," says one man selling old tickets, Bill Burnham (b. 1943). "Most people can be bought. But it wasn't bullshit, it was real." By *it*, he seems to mean the Woodstock spirit. "It'll come back. There'll be a resurgence. We meant it and we've survived."

THE GENERATION THAT lived the Who lyric "Hope I die before I get old"—sung at the first Woodstock—has on the whole opted to do neither. And let people jokingly refer to the event as Geezer Woodstock; boomers are the backbone of this production, running not only the 1960s-style rock show, but also the very 1990s live Internet broadcast. Now that they finally control the culture they once merely dominated, boomers are determined to stay on top of it. Educated, worldly, raised on breached barricades, broken rules and new paradigms, they—we—are uniquely qualified to deal with the new global society we were instrumental in creating. So we've become the aging rulers of a culture of youth.

When the first demographic boomers turned fifty in 1996, far closer to their sixties than to the 1960s, as many have said, the media portrayed a generation still dancing away from maturity, and mortality, as fast as it could. "Sales of skin creams, suntan lotions, hair coloring, cosmetics, vitamins, and nutritional supplements are surging as millions of boomers join the battle against aging," said *American Demographics* magazine, which invented a new stage of life just for us—Mid-Youth, "a new and vibrant midlife marketplace"—and pointed out that boomers would not comprise the majority of Americans over age fifty until 2005.[1] *Life* printed a special edition honoring the generation, but its list of the fifty most influential boomers rang curiously hollow beyond the childlike arenas of sports, computers and the arts.

Some journalists pointed out that the boomers, just reaching their peak earning years, were poised to begin inheriting what economists refer to as a "$10 trillion legacy," history's largest transfer of wealth from one generation to another. Much of that will be spent by the boomer elite on power toys (from tiny cell phones and Palm Pilots to huge sport utility vehicles), travel and entertainment. But average boomers earn less than their parents in real dollars and will soon become financially responsible for those parentson top of mortgages and college tuition for children, and without a solid base of savings to rest on—so they will likely defer retirement and continue to work and create wealth well past retirement age, whether they want to or not.[2]

The shaky state of Social Security only adds to our social insecurity and desire to stay vital as long as possible. As Peter G. Peterson pointed out in *Atlantic Monthly* that year, by 2030, when the last boomers turn sixty-five, the country won't be able to afford them. "We deal with aging and mortality as reluctantly as the Victorians dealt with sex," Peterson said.[3]

I may get old, but I'll never be old.

The new siren song of the generation is sung by many of the musicians who visit the press tent to answer questions. "I don't think it's about giving up being young," says Melanie, whose treacly "Beautiful People" was one of the songs of the summer of '69. She's pudgy now in her embroidered velvet hippie frock, a shock of white hair sprouting above her still little-girl face. "They're not ever gonna grow up," she continues, gesturing out at the crowd. "They grew up with Peter Pan. It's too late."

"You have to look at the sixties as a renaissance thing," says Donovan Leitch, whose namesake son, a sometime model/rock musician, was quite appropriately one of the visual symbols of the 1960s revival in the 1990s. "Woodstock was symbolic of the way ideas that came out of jazz clubs, bookstores, and bohemia took over the arts. What we are seeing here are the consequences. We're not reliving but continuing what began then. This tradition, whatever you want to call it, should continue."

Guitarist and songwriter Peter Townshend (b. 1948), formerly of The Who, is next up to the microphone. Slightly stooped, with a pouchy face and sad eyes, he's no longer the guitar-smashing firebrand of Woodstock '69; he looks like a Dickensian clerk. Why return to Woodstock? "What brought me back was a sense of wanting to look at the reality of the whole thing," he says. "It was the single most important concert in our career. I'm fifty years old now. I know what makes the world go 'round. History is fucking important."

He recalls arriving at the first festival. "There were people everywhere, wandering in the woods like ghosts on drugs," he says. Doesn't it bother him, someone asks, that this latest Woodstock has no unifying theme, no politics? "The very fact that somebody has bought this land and wants to make music here says a lot about what really was important about the original occasion," he replies. "That's what the festival was really about. Everything else turned out slightly flawed."

Like his creation the pinball wizard Tommy and his one-time guru Meyer Baba ("Don't Worry, Be Happy"), Townshend is often treated like a seer, even though his rock star status and sudden, early wealth effectively separated him from his peers. Now he's asked to comment on the encampment just up the highway that includes local Woodstock Nation purists and members of the Rainbow Family, a band of caravaning vegetarian pacifists who come to the area every summer and are boycotting the concert. Townshend's answer is short and sweetly sensible. "I know what paid my rent," he says. "It was my father working."

Someone tells him Joni Mitchell is about to go onstage, and he excuses himself to go listen. I follow him out and ask one more rushed question.

Earlier, Townshend had said that after the first Woodstock, the kids who attended realized they had to take destiny into their own hands. "It was no longer about drugs or the generation gap," he'd said. "It was, 'What do we do?'"

So what did they do, I ask, all those Baby Boom kids? "What actually happened was, people took responsibility," he says. "They got jobs. They had families. And they started to live."

Conception

THIS IS THE story of the Baby Boom generation, the 900-pound gorilla of twentieth-century America, of how it grew up, and of its profound impact on the culture and history of its times. The Boom is usually defined as the 75 million-odd people born during the American fertility explosion from January 1, 1946, to December 31, 1964. That strict demographic excludes Americans born in the second trimester of the 1940s, after Pearl Harbor but before V-J Day, those members of the Silent or Swing generation whose beliefs, experiences, and cultural references formed the cutting edge of the Baby Boom.[1] And that definition also includes early 1960s babies closer culturally to the *next* generation, the spiky-haired kids snickering in the back of the Boom room, the so-called Generation X.

This book focuses on the lives of nineteen quintessential boomers, each of whom embodies or epitomizes a moment, idea, accomplishment, trend or tendency intrinsic to the larger narrative of this extraordinary, controversial generation. In order to single out these individuals, more useful generational cutoff dates had to be set. Clearly, a person born in 1942 has as much or more in common with someone born in 1946 than with the children of the late 1930s. So the day the Japanese bombed Pearl Harbor—December 7, 1941—seems as good as any to mark the start of the boom, and November 22, 1963, the day of John Kennedy's assassination, is an equally appropriate end.

The loose shoe fits. Many back-end members of the preceding Silent Generation were anything but silent and prefer, indeed demand, to be identified with boomers, their younger brothers and sisters. Though some late boomers look on the generation with disdain, many children born in the early 1960s grew up relating more to their immediate elders than to the often disaffected, cynical group that followed.

The oldest people in this book, New York State Supreme Court Justice Leslie Crocker Snyder, and John Gage, the chief science officer of Sun Microsystems, both born in 1942, are hardly silent types, and the youngest, filmmaker and AIDS activist Victoria Leacock (b. 1963), is anything but disaffected. All three identify themselves as Baby Boomers.

WE ARE NOT what you think. Although often referred to interchangeably, the Baby Boom is not the self-styled counterculture that flowered in the 1960s. The groupings do overlap, often to the detriment of the boom in general, which is more diverse and accomplished than the sex, drugs, and rock 'n' roll-driven counterculture it ushered in. Conventional wisdom has it that the Baby Boom peaked as a social force in summer 1969 with Woodstock, and began a descent into drug-induced paralysis and irrelevancy that winter, after the famously murderous Rolling Stones concert at Altamont, California. In fact, it was only the counterculture alliance of anti-establishment radicals and freaks that ended in those eventful months. And radical youth were a tiny—if highly visible—minority.

At the close of the century most of the counterculturalists' revolutionary pipe dreams have been overturned or co-opted. The agents of that overthrow, it now appears, were the generational majority, who turned out to be vastly different than anyone expected. Like First Baby Boomer Bill Clinton (b. 1946), we are not so much committed moralists as morally flexible, ambition-driven pragmatists far more like the parents we rebelled against than we may care to admit.

This distinction eludes many boomers, as well as those who pontificate about them, which has kept discussions of the generation mired in misconception. Ask an early (b. 1942–1949) or middle (b. 1950–1957) boomer to cite generational heroes, and you'll likely hear the names of political figures like Gloria Steinem, Tom Hayden and Abbie Hoffman, or of musicians like Joan Baez, John Lennon and Bob Dylan. In fact, these folks' birthdates precede even a loosely defined start of the boom. Steinem was born in 1934, Hoffman in 1936, Hayden in 1939, Lennon in 1940, and Baez and Dylan (then Robert Zimmerman) in 1941. Indeed, none of the major figures of the civil rights, antiwar or feminist movements were boomers. But this stands to reason. Youth typically admires and makes role models out of slightly older trailblazers.

Despite their constant evolution, those six icons remain tethered to the past. Though Hayden moved off the political fringe and became a Democratic party politician and officeholder, and Hoffman an environmentalist, they will always be remembered as the firebrand leaders of the 1968 youth revolt. The popular image of Steinem is freeze-framed in 1972, the year she founded *Ms.* magazine. And Baez, Dylan and Lennon will be forever linked to the mid-1960s. In truth, theirs is not the story of the generation that followed. If the boom was forged in the fires of the 1960s, its true and lasting accomplishments came later.

Baby boomers have reinvented themselves time and time again. When the hookah-smoking caterpillars of the 1960s turned into butterflies in the early 1980s, our flight patterns were informed by strong recollections— accepted or rejected—that affected everything we've done since. "If you remember, you weren't there," we say. But we were there, and loath as we are to admit it, we remember plenty.

I WAS BORN smack in the middle of the Baby Boom, in 1952, and grew up in one of the Levitt-built neighborhoods of Long Island, just outside New York City, that sprang up after the war to house new families of returning veterans. My parents—a former nurse and a newspaper columnist who served in the World War II Coast Guard—were both born in the second decade of the century. I was raised in the relative prosperity and surface calm of the Eisenhower-era economic boom, when abundance and upward mobility seemed assured. My first pair of baby shoes was bronzed. The Beaver and Eddie Haskell, Clarabell, the Mouseketeers, Mr. Wizard, Princess Summerfall Winterspring, Howdy Doody and Topo Gigio were beamed to me from the tiny, flickering screen of a huge wooden-cased black-and-white television set. I wore a Davy Crockett coonskin cap and carried a Roy Rogers lunchbox, and lived amid the ceaseless wonders of the American century.

I studied science and "new math" because we were lagging behind the Russians. The Cold War and its deadly symbol, the Bomb, which we'd created to end World War II, were constant threats. I was regularly forced to crouch under my desk in elementary school during air raid drills because the Russians were supposedly coming (they'd developed their own bomb in 1949, and though only we had dropped one, *they* couldn't be trusted). At age eight, I wore a Kennedy for President button and worried about Francis Gary Powers, whose U-2 spy plane had been shot down over Russia. At nine, I faked a stomachache to stay home to watch Alan Shepherd become the first American in space; at ten, I was sure the world was ending during the Cuban Missile Crisis; and at eleven, I spent four days watching the aftermath of Kennedy's assassination on television. Like millions of others, I saw Jack Ruby shoot Kennedy's alleged killer, Lee Harvey Oswald, live on TV, a defining moment at the Baby Boom family hearth—the end of the last generation's America, the beginning of ours.

Three short months later, the Beatles arrived and the world began to change at an ever-accelerating clip to a subversive soundtrack of Top 40 hits. Two years later, I discovered Bob Dylan, the first pop musician to tie high-minded ideas like peace, justice and surrealism to the lowest form of music around. By 1967, I was wearing bell bottoms, boots and protest buttons, listening to Malcolm X speeches at the local Economic Opportunity Council office, and marching for peace in Vietnam on Fifth Avenue in New York City. I read about Timothy Leary in *Life* magazine, tuned in to FM radio, bought Mothers of Invention, Jefferson Airplane and Jimi Hendrix records, and smoked my first marijuana, shortly after finding a pack of Zig Zag rolling papers in the street while hitchhiking. When I brought home the exotic little folder and asked my father what it was for, he knocked it out of my hand. Needless to say, I found out, fast.

In summer 1968, my concerned parents refused to let me go to the Democratic party convention in Chicago, so I watched on TV as Hubert Humphrey defeated Minnesota Senator Eugene McCarthy, and Chicago's Mayor Richard Daley and his blue-clad police force beat back the children's crusade behind McCarthy's peace candidacy, destroying any lingering belief my friends and I and thousands like us had in traditional electoral politics. Chicago clarified the curious disaffection that had lingered in the psyche of the Baby Boom ever since those shots were fired in Dallas in 1963. We were now in open opposition, and anyone our age who didn't agree was excommunicated, demonized, *not young*.

The following summer, in July 1969, mankind—American mankind, in fact—set foot on the moon. But I didn't watch; I didn't care. And neither did my new friends. By fall my suburban peers were taking everything from LSD to speed to Seconol, occupying the high school auditorium to protest the National Guard's shooting of students at Kent State University, and putting out an underground newspaper full of innocent poetry, protest and four-letter words. Though I took my share of drugs, politics was still what got me high—until the day a fellow marcher pulled an apple out of my hand at a demonstration, yelled, "Don't waste it!" and tossed the fruit through the window of a stock brokerage. That was the moment I realized the counterculture might be moving farther and faster than I wanted to go.

Still, in one of the first college classes defined by affirmative action goals, I managed to become a sort of pioneer. Of course, only at a formerly all-women's school could a relatively but not spectacularly intelligent white male from Long Island be a member of a minority. When I arrived at Vassar College in 1970 as a member of its first coeducational freshman class, the sexual revolution was nearly a decade old. I made it my business to catch up. Luckily, in those days, the worst thing you could catch from promiscuity was a shot of penicillin.

My freshman year ended with another building takeover—this one inspired by the school's decision to deny tenure to Vassar's more vocally left-wing faculty members and to open a technology school on our Poughkeepsie, New York, campus, in concert with the local computer giant, IBM. Like savage little latter-day Luddites, we dubbed it V.I.T.—the Vassar Institute of Technology—and drove a spike through its cyberheart. But we couldn't save the radical faculty. Their day was done.

We'd lost the war in the streets. Richard Nixon was president, and his Silent Majority had routed our ragtag troops of wannabe revolutionaries, sending the most radical among us underground to blow things up in increasingly futile gestures against a powerful state that could not win the war it was waging but knew how to kill students and Black Panthers. The rest of us began an unorganized retreat into the self. Tom Wolfe's Me Decade had dawned, and though some called it spiritual awakening, we were actually putting our former selves to sleep.

Midway through 1971, whatever was left of the "Movement" at Vassar began to disappear. Our politics weren't so much repudiated as simply left behind like so many Herman's Hermits records. We took drugs and had fun, instead. The campus soon split between two types of "heads." On one side were fans of Quaaludes, the suddenly fashionable soporific both renowned for enhancing sex (before delivering users into a near-coma) and disparaged as a CIA plot to quash opposition. Then there were the speed freaks and acidheads, whose edgy disdain for those who took downs knew no bounds. In between were a small core of if-it-feels-good-do-it experimenters who were up one night, down the next, bedding boys, girls, and both if they had the chance. If we had a movement, it was hedonism. In the words of the politician George Washington Plunkett, "We seen our opportunities and we took 'em."

Within a matter of months, I'd evolved from head of the New Student

Union—the successor to the Vassar chapter of the radical group Students for a Democratic Society—to rock critic for the school newspaper. Like all good college sophomores of the time, I'd discovered decadence. I read Huysmans, Baudelaire and Rimbaud; listened to T. Rex, David Bowie, the New York Dolls and Patti Smith; made my first pilgrimage to Max's Kansas City, the New York City bar where bohemia blended into glam rock; and had my first taste of cocaine and first—and last—of heroin. (I'm not running for president, so I can just admit it.)

Through the rest of the 1970s, I worked but mostly played as a rock writer and magazine editor, extending my adolescence by making a living out of what was once an enthusiasm. By the end of the decade, when corporate rock and disco made music mechanistic and soulless, it was time to get serious. I cut my hair, bought a suit, and began a series of nine-to-five jobs. Though I affected to despise Yuppies, the materialistic back-end boomers who'd come of age well after the economic expansion of the 1960s, I was in training to become one.

The transition wasn't easy. Others used communes, eastern religions, or self-actualization movements like *est* as their way out of the 1960s. Sex and drugs had been my escapes, rock music my refuge. Now I began to repudiate them all. In 1980, I made a portentous move from a loft downtown to an apartment on the edge of the canyons of midtown Manhattan. I started to care about a career and making money. I still spent time with druggies, but now saw their pathos. I kept playing the field, but worried about herpes, a new sexually transmitted disease with no cure. I began seeing the woman I would later marry; my penultimate lover went on to contract AIDS.

By 1984, at age thirty-two, I'd finally begun to focus. I'd identified a journalism beat—fashion and society and celebrity—that suited my taste for the prevailing *Zeitgeist*, found a job, joined a gym, bought some stocks and a co-op apartment, and sold half my record collection. As "dinks"—double income, no kids—my wife and I were financially stable. Like Madonna (b. 1958), whom I soon interviewed for *Vanity Fair*, I was living happily in the material world. And that November, in what seems in retrospect a significant rite of passage, I voted for my first Republican presidential candidate, Ronald Reagan (although I hedged my bet by writing in *my* dream ticket of Reagan and the Democratic candidate for vice president, Geraldine Ferraro).

I bought my first personal computer, a Kaypro 2, in 1984. A year later, I found myself, to use a 1960s phrase, in the belly of the beast when I went to work as a fashion columnist for the *New York Times*. Clothing

designers, the new imagicians, had replaced rock stars as cultural locomo-
tives. Many were baby boomers, as were most fashion photographers and
editors and the bulk of their market. And now, the same techniques that
once sold us records were being used to shrink-wrap us all in name-brand
products from underwear to perfume. By the 1990s, when a new fashion
market from the next generation emerged, we were ready to sell them
our youth—the swinging Anna Sui 1960s! the glam Gucci 1970s!—cannily repackaged and emptied of bothersome social and political meaning.
Our sacred signifiers—sex, drugs and rock songs—had devolved into sales
tools for Detroit car makers and Seventh Avenue jeans manufacturers. As
long as we could dress the new youth up to look like us, we could sustain
the illusion that we were still young ourselves.

This book was born about six years later. I'd moved to *New York* magazine and discovered that what I loved was deconstructing the carefully
cultivated images of the seemingly superficial people and worlds I covered. Then I was asked to write a profile of the lawyer representing Ivana
Trump in her divorce from her boomer billionaire builder husband,
Donald. Though ten years too old to be a boomer, attorney Michael
Kennedy was a true cultural curiosity—and one of those members of the
preceding generation who had set the tone for those of us who followed.
An officer in the army training troops bound for Vietnam at Fort Knox,
he left the service, left his wife and ran off with his best friend's, and
ended up remarried and radicalized in 1960s San Francisco. There he
gained fame as a leftist lawyer representing the Chicago 8 and Los Siete
de la Raza, then defended drug dealers in the 1970s and gained underground renown for purportedly helping LSD guru Timothy Leary break
out of federal prison. Michael Kennedy re-created himself yet again in the
1980s, moving to New York, where he had a grand Manhattan apartment
and a beautiful Hamptons beach house, and made a move on
Manhattan's high society with Ivana as his vehicle. Examining his journey, I somehow saw my own reflected in it—and wanted to deconstruct
that feeling.

How had he gotten from there to here?

How, for that matter, had any of us?

THE STORY OF a generation's cultural impact is best told not through
the lives of average members but through those who achieved or failed or
both, extravagantly. So a portrait of this generation necessarily focuses on
the affluent, the well-educated, the accomplished and the lucky, the bulk
of the group that sets the generational agenda.[2] For this American genera-

tion, that group was generally, though not exclusively, white and, to a lesser extent, male. Boomers perfected the notion of politically correct colorblindness, but they were not raised with it; other races didn't mix much with the white boomers. Only for back-end boomers like hip-hop impresario Russell Simmons was a truly integrated society a fact of life, not a preacher's dream.[3] This, then, is unabashedly the story of an elite, a story of the city, not the country, of the coasts, not the core, of public life, not quotidian existence, of the coming things, not where they ended, of the ambitious, not the content, of the culturally noisy, not the silent majority.

"Donald Trump isn't a baby boomer," an editor friend balked when I said I planned to include him. Others were surprised at the selection of Simmons, who is responsible for so much of the hip-hop rage that cut the Baby Boom off from the cultural cutting edge. And Republican Congressman David McIntosh of Indiana is not typically associated with the generation whose excesses he eschewed. The point is, not all boomers came from the suburbs, grew their hair long, protested, smoked joints, listened to folk and rock, were sexually promiscuous and wound up in *est*. The differences between the individuals who comprise the generation are as significant as the similarities.

YOUNG ADULTS TODAY still dance to the boom's tune. Obvious stylistic differences (from piercing to rap) aside, their music and dress are about rebellion—kinder and gentler, perhaps, but rebellion nonetheless.

Celebrated by a now all-pervasive media as the prime movers of American culture in our youth, my generation continues to seduce the young with an adolescent solipsism clung to throughout our failures, maturing tragedies brought on by an awesome and sometimes awful self-centeredness. Told from birth we were special, unique, a bit above it all, we've come to believe it. As we move through middle age toward the end game, our sense of importance remains self-fulfilling.

It is no surprise to find baby boomers behind movements like postmodernism and hip-hop music. We relish making once-"subversive" notions mainstream and have certainly institutionalized the notion of our defiant, alienated adolescence. Yet we've now acquiesced to precisely those things we railed against in our youth: labels, brands, corporations, celebrities, the establishment, the machine.

In a world where war has been reduced to the third or fourth item on the network news, boomers are preternaturally inured to the low-level chaos. The first generation to grow up with remote controls, we invented channel-surfing and attention-deficit living. That taught us to be infinitely adaptable, even in the face of the Baby Boom cliché of "diminished expectations." We expect a lot. Which is why it is our hands and brains behind Microsoft, Apple, online trading and Web surfing. In an act of stunning cultural jujitsu, we have turned those diminished expectations into a thriving new economy. Or, at least, we want to believe we have.

Experts in imagery, we sometimes grant those illusions more value than we do actual substance—which partly explains why we fall for quixotic movements and false idols, intensely marketed charlatans, rock stars and fashion designers offering instant gratification of desire. We were raised on instant oatmeal. We want what we want when we want it, and generally speaking, we want it now. To a great extent, we've gotten it.

Despite growing older, settling down, marrying, having children, and giving up some if not all of our youthful indulgences, our absolute unwillingness to be middle-aged still marks us. Finally, we're at the point when we must translate experience into wisdom. And it's likely we will, if only because most of all, we intend to keep history's stage as long as we can.

THE NIGHT AFTER Woodstock 1998 ended, Bill Clinton, our "Rock-and-Roll President," as the *New York Times* referred to him in 1997[4], went on television for four closely watched minutes two nights before his fifty-second birthday. The man who'd let the good economic times roll finally admitted, after seven months of heated denials, that instead of saving Social Security, let alone establishing a new moral order, he'd been letting his own *bon temps roulez* by engaging in adulterous, one-way oral copulation in the White House Oval Office with a woman less than half his age—Monica Lewinsky (b. 1973), the pulpy, sexually adventurous daughter of two Baby Boomers. The seamy affair seemed an apt representation of something larger, for here was youth fellating the man chosen to symbolize the generation that became the very font of Youth, reinforcing that he and those he stood for ("We elected Bill Clinton, and he is us," wrote Rob Morse in the San Francisco *Examiner*[5]) are still potent, attractive, vigorous—*young*. Boomers could forgive Clinton a last burst of selfish stupidity. But they regretted it in the morning, disgusted by his weakness and their need to defend it. We are often graced with guilt over the advantage we have taken.

Clinton was hardly the first president to engage in extramarital sex during his term, but he was the first to be pursued by a pack of radical fundamentalists intent on repudiating the last fifty years of American history and returning us to Puritanism. The first to have his private life made so brutally public (ironically via an instrument, the Internet, that in many ways embodies the liberation ethic of his generation). The first to be forced by an inquisition to confess to his adulterous sexual escapades. Pundits of all ages leapt on that admission and used it to tar Clinton and everyone his age, declaring that he represents the worst traits of the Baby Boom, a generation that, in the prophetic words of Clinton's future wife, Hillary Rodham (b. 1947), at her college graduation in 1969, has spent its lifetime "searching for a more immediate, ecstatic, and penetrating mode of living."[6]

Here was proof, they said, that by defying all tradition, by letting it all hang out, the Baby Boom has been responsible for a plague of generally agreed-upon modern pathologies, notably drug abuse, promiscuity and lawlessness, and other subjects of debate: abortion, alternative sexual behavior, the coddling of criminals, political correctness, the cults of grievance and victimization, identity politics, declining standards of decency, discourse and education, and general incivility.

Whichever side of these battles boomers are on, one thing is sure: they are absolutely certain they're right.

Boomers, who now form the bulk of the country's adult population, chose to support their good-times guy. We sent out a clear message about using Baby Boom foibles as fuel for the politics of personal destruction and saved Clinton's presidency, even if many of us had to hold our noses to do it. That's how the generation has usually dealt with its overripe past. It wants forgiveness, not reminders. Jann Wenner (b. 1946), the publisher of *Rolling Stone*, whose drug-taking and carousing are the stuff of legend, and who celebrated his midlife crisis by leaving his wife for a younger man, neatly summed up the Boom's attitude toward Zippergate in an editorial.

"It's been fun," Wenner snickered. "Enough."[7]

Deny or dodge: that's the way we've done things. "I didn't inhale," Clinton claimed. I did inhale and remember anyway. We did drugs, had sex, dodged the draft, and indulged in oedipal fantasies of a bloodless "revolution" fought to the beat of The Rolling Stones record *Beggar's Banquet*. We lived like libertarians while supporting social engineering— for everyone else but us. We had a thoroughly irresponsible blast. Sure, we did good—a lot—in opening America up in a hundred different ways, creating a more inclusive and tolerant society, but that was counterbalanced by, as Neil Young (b. 1945) put it, "the damage done." Along with the rules, we shucked too many standards and hard-earned lessons of history.

So Clinton's lowly acts attained the status of generational apotheosis. "Suddenly," wrote Maureen Dowd (b. 1952) of the *New York Times*, "Baby Boomers realize that, despite a buzzing economy and a passel of luxury goods, we are going to die without experiencing the nobility that illuminated the lives of our parents and grandparents."[8]

If the president did not represent the best of us, he was a fair approximation in 1996, when we reelected him, and again in November 1998, when, though ambivalent about it, we punished the Republicans and, reaffirmed our allegiance to the president.

The Clinton-Lewinsky scandal hovered in the background of all the conversations contributing to the story that follows. They began just after Woodstock 1998 and ended in February 1999, just after the impeached president was found not guilty by the U.S. Senate. Some characters in the story know the Clintons personally. Some support them. Others hate them passionately. All found their situation symbolic. And none seemed terribly surprised that our First Boomers had ended up in such an unholy mess.

It hasn't been easy for the Baby Boom to grow up.

Childhood

JOHN GAGE (B. 1942), chief science officer for the Palo Alto, California-based computer giant Sun Microsystems, is driving through the warehouse district of San Francisco in his used Volvo. As he makes his way to an appointment with a startup software company, the evangelist for this $10 billion manufacturer of networking computers talks to me on his cell phone about Sun customers, "people who are creating brand-new things, making orchestras play inside the computer," he says. "They need tools, and they don't just want them to work; they want to know how they work."

Gage parks his car. "I'm going to walk in, and there will be six people who are writing software to make smart cards to move money around the world," he tells me. "This small company will develop the software, and then they will deliver it on a really tiny embedded consumer device that costs fifty cents. Here's the loading dock. I'm going in." And with that, he snaps his cell phone shut like postmodern punctuation.

Gage's father, a Texan prodigy, graduated from UCLA at nineteen, served as a lieutenant in the World War II navy and then became head of logistics for California-based Douglas Aircraft (later McDonnell-Douglas), moving his wife and son to Hollywood. In 1950s Los Angeles, pop music drove the city's tawny youth, and songs like "Sh-boom" told of worlds beyond the manicured lawns and perfect facades of Beverly Hills, where Gage had a paper route. L.A. was a blenderized city. Someone from Ohio lived next to someone from Massachusetts who lived next to someone from Mexico, creating a strange new sense of freedom. Like many his age, Gage got the feeling anything was possible.

Just as Gage was about to enter Hollywood High, his father moved the family to Newport Beach, a center of America's new space program, where he was building a factory to manufacture the McDonnell-Douglas Atlas rockets that would carry America's first astronauts into space. The space program symbolized modern American civilization, and its soul, Gage says, resided in Southern California—before the population explosion crunched the place under loop-de-loops of freeways.

Young Gage was Big Man on Campus: student body president at Newport Harbor Union High School and a three-time all-American swimmer. He also worked as a lifeguard at a body-surfing beach, and at night ran the parking lot at the Rendezvous Ballroom, where Jan & Dean played and beach music like "Wipe-Out" and "Pipeline" poured from tinny dashboard radios. "Swim, surf, study, sail—I had a rich life," Gage recalls. Not much different from any prosperous white war baby growing up in a nation of victors.

Despite superficial homogeneity, Newport Beach had its divisions. The school Gage attended attracted students from rich coastal towns, adjacent working-class neighborhoods and agricultural areas; the 4-H Club crowd was as big as the surfer clique. Yet Gage's family were Texas Democrats amid the conservative Republicans of Orange County who felt that their riches meant they were never wrong. Watching his father operate with calm and reason in that six-martini right-wing world, Gage grew curious about what lay beyond. The conjunction of popular culture and technology fed that desire. Gage listened to the radio deejay Wolfman Jack broadcasting rock 'n' roll that was out of control from somewhere below the Mexican border; it was out of control of advertisers and of the mechanisms of power that had run the country for almost 200 years.

By the time Gage graduated from high school in 1960—just before John F. Kennedy was elected president—he wanted out of Orange County. That fall, he entered the University of California at Berkeley, planning to follow in his father's footsteps; Berkeley was a national center for mathematics and physics, home of Nobel laureates, the place to be if you were inspired by Kennedy's can-do optimism about new frontiers in science and space.

After a year, though, Gage dropped out. He was restless, tired of school. He ended up in a beach town—he knew beach towns—only this time it was St.-Tropez, France, where he ran a seaside concession for a time. He was back in Berkeley when Kennedy was killed in Dallas, Texas, a year later, on November 22, 1963. That moment riveted his attention. It seemed like the death of something far greater than one man.

* * *

"IT WAS EXHILARATING," Jim Fouratt (b. 194?)[1] says breathlessly. "This twenty-one-year-old, five foot-two gay boy gets murdered and the cops say it's not a hate crime—they have yet to admit it's a hate crime. But to feel all that energy and youth excitement, and all those older people there, and running in the streets . . ."

The night before, Fouratt, a professional trend-hopper who's been everything from a Yippie! to an AIDS activist, had gone to a demonstration protesting a gay-bashing murder in the Midwest. He'd brought an Indian drum and beat it, just as he did in the 1960s. "Last night meant to me that no matter how many times the homophobes, the right wing, the Republican party, the Democrats and the liberals abandon the expression of freedom, people are not going to roll it back," he says. "It's this thing in the human spirit. For all the decadence, the depression, the Prozacing of our culture, there's still a vibrant energy that's about transformation. Could I debate some of those young kids with their tattoos and their anger? Of course. But I knew which side I was on."

He pauses a moment. "I'm not a relic."

Fouratt is the oldest offspring of an unmarried teenage mother and a wealthy man twenty years her senior who left soon after their third child was born. When Fouratt was three, his mother moved to Washington State, where *her* mother lived, and shuttled her children back and forth before marrying an Irish World War II veteran working as a short-order cook in Rhode Island, a widower with a child of his own.

Fouratt remembers spending a lot of his youth taking care of his mother. But he was sickly himself, between the ages of six and ten suffering from rheumatic fever, leukemia and polio. ("I'm one of the first cases cured through massive doses of cortisone, a wonder drug at the time," he says.) He missed third through fifth grade and watched television instead—everything from soap operas to the hearings of red-baiting Senator Joseph McCarthy, whose search for Communists in every nook and cranny of American life created national hysteria and intrigued Fouratt. When the boy heard about a Committee of One Million Americans supporting McCarthy, he toted petitions for the cause around the neighborhood. "Nobody would sign, and when I told my mother, she ripped them up."

Fouratt was enrolled in a Christian Brothers private school. A good dancer and a member of the Rhode Island chapter of Junior Achievement, he ran for class office but failed, he thinks, because his fellow students knew before he did that he was gay. Fouratt finally realized he was attracted to boys when he was thirteen. His sexual experience was limited to fleeting encounters while hitchhiking. ("You can do it to me," as he puts it.) His mother and stepfather, highly permissive, took him to a strip club for his sixteenth birthday. The boy was mortified.

But Fouratt's interests were catholic for a Catholic: he admired Dorothy Day, the Berrigans and other religious antiwar activists, and was fascinated by the outsider culture of beatniks and bohemians. College didn't interest him, so at sixteen he entered a Paulist seminary to become a priest. His motivation, he now thinks, came from "being a gay kid who wanted to feel good about himself and didn't quite know how."

Fouratt spent eighteen months in the seminary. Toward the end he went to a beatnik reading in nearby Baltimore and was instantly attracted to one of the poets. They had sex, and three weeks later, Fouratt contracted crab lice—a mystery to him but not, unfortunately, to the head of the seminary, a former Marine chaplain, who quickly deduced how he'd gotten them. The timing couldn't have been worse. Two other students had just been discovered as lovers and thrown out of the seminary. In the inquisitorial atmosphere that followed, one of Fouratt's classmates searched his dresser drawers, where he found photos of nude men Fouratt had clipped from magazines—for an art project, he says. He was given six hours to pack and a bus ticket home. He got off the bus in New York and headed straight to Greenwich Village. It was 1961. He was still a teenager and looked years younger.

When he stepped off the Greyhound bus, Fouratt headed to Sheridan Square, where the bohemian demimonde shaded imperceptibly into New York's still-secretive homosexual underground. "When I came to New York, like many young artist types, it wasn't to be gay," he says. "It was to be a bohemian, a beatnik, those were code words." Fouratt stayed in the city through the summer, and then moved to Cambridge, Massachusetts, where a friend had a dorm room at Harvard. The following spring, New York's experimental Phoenix Theater set up shop in Cambridge. Fouratt fell in love with one of the actors.

Unfortunately, when he followed the fellow back to New York, Fouratt discovered his love object was otherwise engaged. Since theater folk nonetheless gave him the sense of community he craved, he got a job at the Phoenix, decided to become an actor, lived on Coca-Cola and pizza, and joined the Village social scene, hanging out in West 10th Street bars like Julius and The Knight's Inn, where the artistic clientele could not care less who went home with whom. "Julius wasn't a gay bar," he says. "Everybody was gay and yet nobody was gay, you know?"

Fouratt's new friends provided entrée to New York's thriving underground theater scene. Jim began performing in minor roles at Caffe Cino, a legend on the Off-Off Broadway circuit, and with the Living Theater, an avant-garde operation known for its radical political agenda, interracial company and experimental productions. "Being in that world was exciting," he says. "People smoked marijuana, and there were black people and jazz musicians and poets, and the poets were attracted to the folk music scene, and there was all this crossover going on. We didn't want to be mainstream. It wasn't about politics. It was about other kinds of values."

Fouratt soon became a minor player in major events. He scored heroin for the comedian Lenny Bruce. In 1963, when the Internal Revenue Service seized the Living Theater's performance space commune on 14th Street, Fouratt was sent to get bail money from Mickey Ruskin. Ruskin owned Les Deux Megots, a Beat poet coffeehouse, and had just taken over The Knight's Inn and turned it into a jazz club.

Fouratt met Communists, anarchists and Beatniks committed only to antimaterialism. Saul Gottlieb, a radical and Living Theater fund-raiser, invited Jim on a cross-country drive to San Francisco, where Fouratt got a taste of North Beach bohemianism. In November 1963, back in New York, studying at Lee Strasberg's Actor's Studio, he was en route to class in an elevator in Carnegie Hall when someone boarded and said, "The President has just been shot." The elevator got stuck between floors. By the time it started moving again, it was confirmed that Kennedy had been killed, "and one of the women in that elevator had slept with Kennedy," Jim says with impish pride.

"SHE'S GREAT STUFF, she really is," a New York City detective says as she heads into Acting Supreme Court Justice Leslie Crocker Snyder's heavily guarded courtroom. The guards are necessary; Snyder (b. 1942), a soft-spoken blonde with fine features, brown eyes and pale pink nails, has gained a reputation as a hanging judge in her sixteen years on the bench. She's been nicknamed "Ice Princess" and "213," for the total years in jail she gave the leader of a drug gang called the Jheri Curls. In 1998 glassine bags of heroin stamped with her picture and the brand name "25 to Life"—after the maximum sentence for drug dealing—went on the market. It is a condition of her cooperation that I not give details about her family. She's about to demonstrate why.

Judge Snyder is sentencing a drug gang leader, Carl Dushain, and his chief enforcer, Danny "Cash" Green, who murdered a Harlem building superintendent as he begged for his life because they thought, mistakenly, that he'd snitched on them. They'd kidnapped and hung another victim from a pipe in a rat-infested dungeon, all in the course of running a multimillion-dollar crack and PCP trade in New York's slums. The slogan of their Dushain's Crew, gangsta band, was "Drugs, Sex, Murder."

Dushain stands before Snyder in chains. He has recently ripped a steel door off its hinges to smash a window in a failed escape attempt. He claims he was framed. Quietly, in a tone as sharp as a stiletto, Snyder calls him a monster, "grotesquely deviated from the norm." He stares back coldly. Decrying Dushain's release from jail in 1991, a mere three years after he shot his seventeen-year-old girlfriend in the head, Snyder catalogues his crimes: intimidating a witness with a photograph of a dismembered body, turning young girls into drug accountants-cum-sex toys while claiming to be helping them with penmanship. "I don't know whether you are sociopaths or psychopaths or if you had deprived backgrounds and *I don't care!*" Snyder nearly spits. "You've set a subhuman standard that's hard to achieve. Listening to you has made me sick." She gives Dushain a minimum 150-year sentence and Green 91 years in prison.

Snyder grew up in a family of scholars; her father was a professor of eighteenth-century French philosophy and literature. Leslie spent her infancy in the Virginia countryside, then at age eight moved to Baltimore, where she attended a private country day school on full scholarship. Their academic lifestyle—hopping from school to school, grant to fellowship—made their lives rich but kept them relatively poor. Summers were spent in Europe, where relatives owned hotels in Monte Carlo and London.

Snyder's father was usually immersed in his work. Her mother, who had a master's degree in French literature, was her inspiration. Though she worked as her husband's editor and assistant, she made sure her daughter understood that wasn't the only way for a woman. "My mother was a feminist before her time," Snyder says. "She would say to me, 'You can do anything you want. Aim high.' She was frustrated and wanted me to have a more satisfying existence."

Snyder's childhood was insular, "almost a time warp," she says. Her parents were New Deal Democrats, beliefs they expressed only in the voting booth. On trips to New York, where her family had more rich relations, she was cosseted, dining in posh restaurants and attending the theater. In Baltimore, she often felt like the odd girl out, the only Adlai Stevenson supporter among the young Eisenhower-era elite, a *New York Times* reader in a school full of debutantes. So though she acted the all-around girl, playing lacrosse every afternoon and cracking the books all night, Snyder always felt different. "That made me even more determined to have my own career," she says. In 1954, Snyder's parents moved to France while her father wrote a book. She attended a lycée, learned to speak French, Greek and Latin, went to museums, and lived in a bubble. Back in New York at fourteen, her protective shell cracked. She saw Elvis Presley on *The Ed Sullivan Show* and "absolutely flipped," she says. "I had a little inexpensive record player and I started collecting forty-fives, so I associate that music with sexual stirrings, real adolescent feelings." Snyder had another secret vice, one fewer of her contemporaries shared. On Sunday nights, she would go to bed early and tune her clock radio to a weekly show about the FBI's Ten Most Wanted List. "I'd take notes," she says. "Very strange." But very real. "As opposed to the eighteenth century," she says with a laugh.

Her family got a television in 1950 and Leslie was allowed to watch for fifteen minutes a night. "But on Friday and Saturday we could watch half an hour," she says. She chose a show called *Man Against Crime*. And when her parents asked what she wanted to be, she had a ready answer. "At five, I was saying, 'I want to be a lawyer.'" By eight, she'd chosen a specialty: criminal law.

By the time Snyder was a teenager, she'd skipped two grades, "although I would say socially I was not particularly mature." She liked boys and harbored secret crushes. But they never got very far. When she started dating a college boy, her father cross-examined him "to the point that was totally inappropriate," she says ruefully. Not until she'd graduated first in her class and headed to Radcliffe at sixteen, in 1958, could she indulge those interests. The school's association with Harvard—sharing everything except dormitories—made it virtually coed. In 1961 the birth control pill first became available and caused a sea-change in sexual attitudes and behavior, drastically lowering the potential price of sex just as the first baby boomers reached puberty.

Snyder was young, very young, and essentially unsupervised. "I went a little boy-crazy," she admits. Then she found a smart, good-looking Harvard jock boyfriend who represented everything her parents disdained. They got engaged. Her Bachrach portrait ran atop a *New York Times* engagement announcement.

Her fiancé had competition of a sort: John F. Kennedy—the Elvis of politics—who while speaking informally at Harvard would look the Cliffies over, Snyder recalls. "I was just totally smitten," she says. "He was so handsome and charismatic. I started getting a lot more interested in politics."

* * *

THE TALL, THIN man has a long graying beard, distant eyes, and a pixilated smile. "I was born in Berkeley; I wasn't one of those outside agitators," says Tim Scully (b. 1944). He's still in Berkeley, or near enough, working at the Alameda-based software company Autodesk, where he runs design teams. He's lucky to be here. In 1974 he was sentenced to twenty years in a federal penitentiary. Asked to sum up his life, Scully quotes the Grateful Dead, for whom he once built sound equipment.

"It's been a long, strange trip," he says.

The Scully family came to the Sierra foothills in the 1840s Gold Rush. Scully's father married young and unhappily the first time, and his Irish Catholic parents wouldn't recognize the divorce. So when as an engineering student at Berkeley he married Tim's mother—an English Protestant and the daughter of a major in the Philippine constabulary—he was disinherited and had to drop out and work in a gas station.

Scully was raised in the northern California countryside. His mother was a clinical lab technician, and his dad, after the war, went to work at an oil refinery and later became a federal firefighter. "He felt he was underusing his intelligence," Scully says. "So the family script was, 'Get your Ph.D., get your security clearance, do government research. Don't join any organizations, don't dig girls, because you might get sidetracked.'"

As a child, Scully liked to visit his mother at the lab where she worked, and was fascinated with electronics, flashing lights and lit-up dials. He read science fiction writers Robert Heinlein and Arthur C. Clarke and *Amazing*, a magazine filled with short stories that projected future problems readers would solve. Realizing he'd only get to a good college on scholarship, Scully entered science fairs and in the eighth grade built a small computer that won him a summer job at the University of California's Lawrence Radiation Lab in Berkeley; he stayed in the attic of his grandparents' shingled house there. Back at school, Scully set out on a two-year project he hoped would get him to the University of Chicago: the construction of a linear accelerator designed to bombard mercury with neutrons and create gold. "It's good physics, but it's also alchemy," he says, laughing. His teachers gave him a spare classroom to work in and forgot about him. Their mistake. "I'm sure I was wiping out radio reception for miles around when I turned the thing on," he says. He was about to start making radiation—what a linear accelerator does—when his teachers abruptly called a halt to the project and encouraged him to apply to Berkeley for early admission. He didn't mind moving on. "I was a real wiseass twerp, too obviously smart and socially inept," Scully says. "I hadn't learned how to get along with people." He was too busy dreaming up ways to harness thermonuclear power, although he did make a few friends selling time-delay stink bombs to fellow students.

"They never proved it was me," he says, smirking.

MICHAEL FUCHS'S GRANDFATHER was an immigrant butcher on East 12th Street in lower Manhattan. Today Fuchs (b. 1946) lives a mere block away, but in a multilevel penthouse of glass and dark wood, surrounded by pre-Columbian and modern art and scrapbooks and photos commemorating a stellar career as a corporate maverick in what has come to be called convergent media. Though trained as a lawyer, Fuchs spent nineteen years, most of them as a top executive, at Home Box Office (HBO), the prototypical cable television brand. Named its chairman in 1984, he turned it into the first modern independent movie studio before being forced to resign in 1995 in a corporate shakeup that left him retired and rich, thanks to a multimillion-dollar "golden parachute"—the last in a lifetime of holy grails for aging baby boomers.

Though his name still comes up for top jobs at movie studios or television networks, he says he's having too much fun to take them seriously, driving race cars one day, flying off to Hawaii with his latest flame the next. At the start of an interview in his retirement office on 57th Street, Fuchs paces restlessly before settling in. Though his office is massive and has a drop-dead view of Central Park, it is somehow still confining.

The youngest of three children, Fuchs was born and raised in the Bronx, where his father managed the family business—real estate holdings like the Concourse Plaza Hotel, accommodation of choice for the New York Yankees. So young Fuchs gleaned not only the confidence born of being your own boss but a lifelong devotion to sports.

A precocious child, Fuchs read his first newspaper headline, TRUMAN FIRES MACARTHUR, during the Korean war, when he was four years old. Fuchs's brother, four years his senior, frightened the little boy by telling him that invading Communist Chinese soldiers had spread to Yonkers as a result. Politics seemed important; by age ten, Fuchs was handing out literature for Adlai Stevenson in his second run against President Dwight D. "Ike" Eisenhower.

Although Fuchs was to become a cable TV pioneer, the pioneering days of television—"the fakeness of the sets" of programs like *Captain Video*, which he watched on the family's five-inch black-and-white

Dumont—held little interest for him. Plus, he notes, "television didn't babysit kids in those days. They said, 'Go outside and play.'"

Early on, Fuchs decided he was part of a different generation than his older brother. "His generation expected to go to a good school and just fit in, and the sixties changed all that," he says. "We experienced an enormous amount of volatility, and it became part of our lives. We didn't expect things to just turn out normal."

One thing he and his brother shared, was rock 'n' roll. "I was there at the beginning," Fuchs says. The boys were listening in 1954 when Alan Freed, the Ohio radio disc jockey who gave the sound its name, first broadcast on the New York radio station WINS. Three years earlier in Cleveland, Freed had aired previously banned rhythm and blues "race records," sending record producers across America on the hunt for a white "crossover" artist who sounded black.

That act emerged from Chester, Pennsylvania, led by a hulking singer with a spit curl in the middle of his broad forehead. Bill Haley and the Comets were a modest success until 1955, when their song "Rock Around the Clock" was used in the film *The Blackboard Jungle*. Rioting ensued in movie theaters when it played over the title credits. Soon rock 'n' roll was everywhere. Fuchs and his brother would bring a transistor radio to the dinner table, claiming school news was being broadcast, until their father caught on and put an end to their ruse. But Mr. Fuchs could not stop rock from rolling. Pop music would never be the same. And neither would his teenage sons, who now had a sound entirely their own.

Fuchs entered high school in Mount Vernon, an ethnically diverse, middle-class town on the New York City border, in 1960. Though "the sixties sort of kicked in" while he was there, he says, "there was nothing like what you read about now, with kids and drugs and weapons." Though a good student, Fuchs was no academic star, "because I really didn't work at it," he says. "I used to short-cut everything and was hardly ever prepared." The only place he shined was on the basketball court. Mount Vernon was a basketball town, his high school a local athletic power, and Fuchs practiced and played almost every day. When his parents offered to send him to a private school in New York City, he declined. Young Fuchs had met the privileged kids on the basketball court. He thought they played "like girls."

Fuchs carried his competitive spirit into the realm of current events. "I was disappointed when the Sputnik beat us into space," he says. "I had a public school education that taught us America was the biggest and best at everything." He chuckles. "We were really so provincial."

Fuchs began to think about going into politics. "Kennedy lit it up for me," he says. "He was the president and a movie star and he said the right things." In spring 1963, Alabama governor George C. Wallace tried to stop two black students from entering the state's university. "I remember Kennedy sending [Attorney General Nicholas] Katzenbach down South to face Wallace. They seemed much more activist than the Eisenhower administration. I traveled overseas at that age—I was in Israel the summer of 1962, when I was seventeen—and everyone loved Kennedy. That was the last time working in Washington seemed glamorous." Curiously, Fuchs doesn't remember the Cuban Missile Crisis as anything out of the ordinary. "We grew up having air raid drills, so it was in our mental DNA. I remember many times hearing noises that would make me say, 'Could that be . . . ?'"

Fuchs finished high school in June 1963, and headed to Union College in Schenectady, New York, that fall. He'd wanted to go to Cornell but wasn't admitted. Aiming to be a professional athlete, he was "very casual about college," he says. "I filled out my application on the last night. Everything came to me pretty easily. And coming from a family with a family business—not that I wanted to go into that business—I knew I would be okay."

Years after the fact, Michael Fuchs had a fresh take on Kennedy's assassination, which took place just three months after he started college. He was supervising an HBO documentary on violence when he realized that before JFK's death, random, senseless killing was a rarity in America. By July 1966, when Richard Speck killed eight nurses one night in Chicago and Charles Whitman climbed a tower at The University of Texas and went on a ninety-four-minute shooting rampage that left sixteen dead and many more wounded, these events had begun to seem the eerie norm.

"Something was unleashed that year that was never put back in the bottle," Fuchs says. "It's not a theory that stands up to a lot of questioning, but post-'63 these things happened, and pre-'63 they didn't. If you could kill the prince, anyone could die."

GAZING DOWN FROM where Donald Trump lives and works, New York's Central Park looks like a doormat. In the 1980s, Trump (b. 1946) became a symbol of the small but highly visible group of young men and women who garishly displayed their awesome, often leveraged new wealth. Many have since learned to curb their egos and keep their consumption inconspicuous, but Trump has never been one to hide or be humble.

His office is full of trophies and testimonials—framed magazine covers, keys to cities, sports memorabilia, autographed photographs and drawings of his many properties, some bought, some built, some still in planning. "Take a look at that," the blond, blue-eyed tycoon instructs as I try to begin our interview. "That's my new building opposite the U.N." He doesn't mention that it has so outraged its neighbors, they have launched a public campaign against it.

Trump's career builds on his father Fred's, who before and after World War II constructed millions of lower- and middle-class dwellings in New York's outer boroughs that now house people likely to live their entire lives without seeing the New York Donald Trump inhabits. Like Abraham Levitt, the Russian-Jewish immigrant who built much of nearby Long Island, Fred Trump, the son of a Swedish immigrant, developed the brick pillbox houses many veterans moved into with their families when they came home from the war.

"My dad went down to Newport News, Virginia, where they had the biggest shipyard, and built some quite low-income housing for sailors coming home," Trump says. Then he developed single-family houses and some apartment houses in New York's boroughs. "It was a niche, and he did it really well."

Fred Trump owned about 20,000 rental units and was worth $20 million by the time Donald was born. Fred and his wife raised their five children in a twenty-three-room house in Jamaica Estates, an unusual 500-acre tract of large private residences in New York City that was developed at the beginning of the century and was home to doctors, lawyers, and politicians.[2] "But I didn't view us as out of the norm," Trump says, "and I think that's the way my parents wanted it."

Even as a child, Trump wanted to go farther faster. From the roads and rooftops of the outer boroughs, he would stare at the glittering Manhattan skyline. "I didn't like my father's business; I wanted to be over here," he says, gesturing out his window. "Brooklyn was a rough way to make a buck. If you raised the rent a dollar and a half you'd have people leave buildings. I'd rather sell an apartment for six million dollars."

Trump started going to building sites at age five, drove his first bulldozer at thirteen, and began working as a rent collector for his father soon thereafter. "Building is still my greatest asset," he says. "I get more credit for promotion and finance, but the truth is, what I do best is conceive of something and get it built."

He was a better student on construction sites than at Key Forest, the school he attended in Kew Gardens, Queens. "I was bored in school,

understimulated," he says. "I wanted an energy release." He found it
harassing his teachers, even punching one,[3] though he'd rather talk about
throwing chalk at blackboards when they'd turned their backs. "It used to
explode if you'd throw it hard," he recounts with glee.

In 1960 young Trump was sent to New York Military Academy, on the
Hudson River near West Point. He still remembers a drill sergeant who
brooked no nonsense. "This wasn't like school, where a teacher would say,
'Now, Donald, that's not very nice to do.' This guy would go crazy. He
would grab you and throw you out a window. This was a rough group.
And I don't say it in a negative way. I thought they were great. This was
before you had prohibitions on stuff. Today, he couldn't do that." By the
time he graduated, Trump had been made captain of cadets, "rather hard
to believe for anybody that knows me," he concedes.

"TODAY IS THE anniversary of the Cuban Missile Crisis," Mark Rudd
(b. 1947) tells me from his home in Albuquerque, New Mexico. It's been
almost twenty years since he's given an interview about his life. And he's
been waffling about whether to do one ever since I tracked him down at
the junior college where he teaches math. But Rudd has a sense of history—and a new wife, his second, who says that since he likes shooting
his mouth off so much at home, he ought to do it for a larger audience.
"Fire away," the former firebrand of the Weather Underground finally e-
mails. "No, better do that nonviolently."

Rudd's father was brought to America at age eight during the great
wave of Jewish migration from Eastern Europe at the start of the last century. He grew up in Elizabeth, New Jersey, two houses away from his
future wife, then studied to be an electrical engineer. After graduating
college in the depths of the Depression ("the fear of poverty really
defined them," Rudd says), Rudd's father couldn't find a job, so he joined
the Civilian Conservation Corps and ended up in Utah working with the
Navajo. Serving in the infantry in World War II, Jacob Rudd was stationed
in the Philippines, preparing to invade Japan, when America dropped the
first atomic bombs in 1945. "So I guess Hiroshima saved his life and
brought me into the world," Rudd says.

Rudd grew up in a Newark neighborhood shared by blacks, Irish and
Jews. They all mixed at his grandmother's candy store. "I was there almost
every day behind the counter," he says. Rudd's grandmother worshipped
the liberal hero Franklin Delano Roosevelt, and his parents were New
Deal Democrats, but the family wasn't political. Neither were they religious. Though they attended services at a Conservative synagogue, the

priority was education, based on the principle that "it's necessary to know what's going on because there's always danger lurking," Rudd says.

The upwardly mobile family soon moved to Maplewood, a suburb. Rudd's father ran his own real estate business, so Mark got whatever he wanted. "But they weren't nouveau riche conspicuous consumers," he says. "And I defined myself not as wealthy but lower-middle-class. I always worked odd jobs, mowing lawns and stuff." Rudd was overweight, a loner—"I didn't fit in; I thought I was more mature than the other kids." He preferred his ham radio to sports and read constantly. "That really was my passion," he says. "History. Biographies. Novels. I remember being thirteen or fourteen and my mother saying, 'Don't read Dostoyevsky. It will make you depressed!'" He read the multivolume *World Book* encyclopedia for fun. Years later, he saw himself in the hero of Phillip Roth's *Portnoy's Complaint*, "who was from Newark and knew all the names of the president's cabinet," he recalls. "I didn't know all the names, but I knew a lot of them."

He also knew he didn't like them. As a teenager, he already had a radical bent. He was reading Allen Ginsberg, Lawrence Ferlinghetti and the *Village Voice* by the time he went into Manhattan alone at twelve to take the ham radio operator's exam. By high school, Rudd had like-minded friends. They were all in their school's advanced classes, and none of them worried about college or careers—unthinkable today. When the young teenager heard that John Kennedy had been killed, he was unmoved. "I can't explain it, but I recognized that he was ultimately an American militarist," Rudd says.

The Cuban Missile Crisis had scared the Maypo out of him. And he was worried about Vietnam. There had been only 1,000 American advisers there in January 1961, but within a year that force had tripled. Then it tripled again. Then came June 11, 1963, the day Alabama's Governor Wallace blocked the door of the state's university, President Kennedy announced his support of a civil rights bill, and a civil rights worker named Medgar Evers was shot dead by a sniper in Mississippi. That same, momentous day, a Buddhist protester burned himself to death in Saigon. Copycat self-immolations followed. Rudd was more shocked by the distant events than those closer to home.

He took no pleasure from the Beatles, thinking them trivial compared to American rock, Motown, rhythm and blues and the new protest song movement. He'd started listening to folk musicians like Woody Guthrie and Pete Seeger in junior high. A few years later, he and his first girlfriend started taking the train into New York to see foreign films. Rudd decided that they were a release valve for America's simmering discontent, as were the Beats; James Dean and Marlon Brando; Norman Mailer; the phony-hating protagonist of J. D. Salinger's *Catcher in the Rye*, Holden Caulfield; the incendiary books published by Grove Press; and the "sick" comedy of Lenny Bruce and *Mad* magazine.

Rudd enrolled in Columbia University—mostly because his girlfriend would be close by at Sarah Lawrence, but also because he'd first tasted hot-and-sour soup at a Chinese restaurant near the campus, he says. Through his girlfriend, he'd already met his future: people like Michael Neumann, son of a German philosopher, Franz Neumann, and the stepson of another, Herbert Marcuse, the writer whose synthesis of Freud and Marx would soon make him a hero of what would be called the New Left.

BARBARA LEDEEN (B. 1948) works in a tiny warren of Formica-floored basement offices in a townhouse in Washington, D.C. All around the blowsy, frizzy-haired fifty-one-year-old are political buttons, signs and stickers—almost all bearing slogans making fun of President William Jefferson Clinton: "O.J. Clinton." "Don't Blame Me—I Cooperated with Ken Starr." Then there's a cartoon of three members of the National Organization for Women, with little Willy Clinton sucking his thumb, a brassiere sneaking out of his pocket, over the caption, "You leave our Billy alone . . . the little pervert's strengths outweigh his flaws."

Ledeen, executive director of the Independent Women's Forum (IWF), has been called a Judas wife and a she-wolf by feminists outraged over her opposition to affirmative action, which the IWF refers to as "feminist pork," part of the "victimhood industry." Ledeen embodies what's been called the Second Thoughts movement—a loose agglomeration of former members of the New Left who have rediscovered patriotism after deciding that American democracy not only tolerated but incorporated aspects of their radicalism. That made Ledeen part of what First Lady Hillary Clinton called the "vast right-wing conspiracy" aimed at bringing down her husband's administration.

Ledeen returns the compliment, excoriating feminists and the First Lady for supporting Clinton despite his affair with a White House intern. "Hillary Clinton represents that part of the Baby Boom that dug in for the long march through [America's] political institutions," Ledeen says. "Hillary Clinton is now where she was in 1968. We were wrong then, and they're wrong now."

Ledeen's father was an Orthodox Jew whose family had left Russia and settled in Rochester, New York. Her father spent World War II in uniform, erecting telephone poles along the Northwest coast, building infrastructure to guard against a Japanese invasion. "He loved the army, the heroism, the telephone poles; he loved the West and the mountains and how majestic and beautiful they were," his daughter recalls. "He loved America. Love it or leave it; that was my dad."

Back in Rochester after the war, he worked for his father's painting business and courted his future wife, the daughter of a wealthy German-Jewish doctor. "So obviously this is not a marriage made in heaven, right?" Ledeen says. Shortly after she was born, her mother's parents moved in with them when the doctor, who'd conducted X-ray experiments on himself, developed cancer and had a stroke. An already tense household became "miserable." Her father couldn't support them all, let alone in the style to which her mother's family was accustomed.

Her grandparents had kept some trappings of wealth; Ledeen's grandmother had a concert piano, and Barbara first watched television on a huge Dumont set with a tiny screen in her grandparents' apartment, upstairs in the duplex house they all shared. Though he could hardly speak, as they watched the Army-McCarthy hearings, in which the right-wing senator's accusations that the military was harboring communists led to his own downfall, her grandfather muttered, "Shame. Shame."

After inheriting the family painting company, Ledeen's father, a Stevenson-style liberal, became anti-union and entrepreneurial, and joined one of the Jewish country clubs in the area, "the nouveau country club, which was orange and chartreuse," she says. Ledeen had become a tightly wound coil of resentment. She was the only Jewish girl in her school. She seethed because her parents were always fighting, because they were stuck living with her grandparents. Looking at Jacqueline Kennedy, who accompanied her husband on a Rochester campaign stop in 1960, all she wanted was "to grow up and look like her and not like a Jew," she recalls. "I was a behavior problem; I didn't respond well to people telling me what to do," she adds. "Some things don't change."

An explosion was inevitable. Although she was secretary of her seventh-grade class in 1962, she got expelled for organizing a demonstration against enforced curfews. Her mother promptly took her to her own alma mater, the local private school. When the headmaster asked why she wanted to come there, Barbara said she didn't. "You're just a bunch of rich, spoiled kids," Ledeen snapped.

"You're accepted," the headmaster shot back. "We need you to liven this place up." The world outside only added to Ledeen's melancholy. The Cuban Missile Crisis that fall was "scary as hell," she says. "We used to sit under desks and wait for a nuclear bomb." Then Kennedy was killed. "That was *our* day that would live in infamy."

Private school wasn't easy. Ledeen's family was looked down on by the rich kids. "Dad wasn't a professional man, and I was a wild animal," she observes. "I get to this school and they had expectations about work and intellectual achievement, which I had never been exposed to before." Her parents were called in but couldn't change her behavior. So the school imposed a schedule: "From four to six, do your homework, from six to seven, set the table and eat, from seven to eight you'll be in your room, no telephone calls, no visiting, no radio, no TV," she recites. "And they said to me, 'We don't care if you don't do your homework, but you will not leave your room.'"

For a month, she refused to work. Then, while her friends were discovering the Beatles, she stumbled on *Beowulf*, the Old English epic poem about the adventures of a Scandinavian warrior. "I had never seen a poem," Ledeen says. "I did not know meter or rhyming or rhythm; I didn't know anything about the beauty of language. And I was totally seduced. I could not stop reading and writing. I wrote one poem and then another and another, and eventually I became the star student in literature. I was civilized by this."

"YOU KNOW, THE problem is, they don't remember things," Cynthia Bowman (b. 1949) says of her old friends who once called themselves Jefferson Airplane. The Airplane's singer, Grace Slick (b. 1939), has just released an autobiography. Bowman dismisses it as "mostly fantasy."

"She can't remember," Bowman insists. "She had to call all of us to be reminded. I had to reconstruct her wedding for her entirely. And they're all the same. Marty Balin, Jack Casady, Paul Kantner—they were at the same place at the same time, but the interpretation is entirely different."

Bowman remembers more than they do because it was long her job to be on top of things when the Airplane and its successor group, Jefferson Starship, were flying high. Although the tall, slim, well-coiffed blonde drives a slick sport utility vehicle and wears a tailored black-and-white nailhead suit appropriate for a woman running a million-dollar public relations business, her ragged voice hints at a raffish past. So does her office in the rickety wooden building that once housed The Black Cat, one of San Francisco's legendary bohemian bars, a hangout for homosexuals, artists and writers. She landed here by accident, having once told an employee to find her a new office just before taking off on a trip to Mexico. "I never made a plan in my life, but I end up where I'm supposed to be," she says.

Bowman's parents divorced when she was five. Her father, a radio operator in the Air Force during the war, fled to New York. She, her brother, and their mother moved from their middle-class Ohio neighborhood into a housing project in the Cleveland flats. Their descent from postwar prosperity was abrupt. "Sometimes we had Cheerios for breakfast, lunch and dinner," she recalls. Bowman's mother waited tables and finally moved the family to a better, if still impoverished, neighborhood in 1960.

Meanwhile, her father remarried and prospered, scaling the heights of corporate public relations at Mobil, where he worked on the oil company's sponsorship of public television, and later ran a similar program at United Technologies. Cynthia and her brother spent several weeks each summer in New York. "I remember seeing *Peter Pan* with Mary Martin on my sixth birthday and just being mesmerized," Bowman says. Although she recalls feeling "completely out of sync with that lifestyle," it became her own in fall 1963, when the kids moved in with Dad.

Cynthia was enrolled at St. Hilda's and St. Hugh's, a prestigious Episcopal private school near Columbia University. Bowman wasn't prepared for its rigors or for students far better educated and richer than she. "One girl's father was a vice president at NBC and she'd be delivered to school in a limousine," Bowman says. "I was schlepping on the subway. My experience was so different." She felt unattractive, too. "Very tall, really thin. Everybody had a flip in their hair, a Patty Duke thing. My hair wouldn't do that at all."

No love was lost between Bowman and her stepmother. "She couldn't have any kids of her own and certainly didn't want two miscreants from Cleveland, but she was stuck with us," Bowman recalls. And though he'd eventually stop, her father drank too much. Trouble was all around. Her brother, also in private school, hooked up with a member of the Vanderbilt clan, who introduced him to heroin; he was soon thrown out of school. "Having grown up in the projects, I'd always thought the *solution* was money," Bowman says wryly.

Though she found ways to fit in to her new environment—"I wasn't academically successful, but I was socially successful because I was pretty funny. And I didn't mind being made fun of, either"—she adds that she "was as dysfunctional as a kid can be." By ninth grade, she had become disruptive. One morning, when the girls were having a giggle over a nun with a stutter who was conducting the daily mass, the joke wound up being on Bowman. "I started laughing so hard I peed," she says. "And I got thrown out of St. Hilda's for disrupting chapel, for urinating."

AS SOON AS I tell Doug Marlette (b. 1949) I'm writing a book about the Baby Boom, he starts slamming Bill and Hillary Clinton. He's known them almost twenty years, both as a fellow southerner and as a Pulitzer Prize-winning political cartoonist. "Reptilian," he calls them. "Calculating. Cold-blooded. Astonishing."

Like Garry Trudeau (b. 1948), the Yale graduate who introduced "Doonesbury" in 1970, Marlette brought liberal Baby Boom politics into the funny pages—first as an editorial cartoonist, then through his "Kudzu" comic strip. But unlike Trudeau, a native New Yorker and a full-fledged member of the media elite, Marlette was born southern Baptist and raised to be a racist. He began his career in the Deep South and stayed there after attaining professional prominence, commuting between North Carolina, where he lives with his family in an 1833 farmhouse, and New York, where he's a syndicated editorial cartoonist for *Newsday*.

Marlette is surprised by his own ambivalence about his generation and its first American president. "I'm embarrassed by my younger self," he says that first time we talk. "I'm appalled by the glib, facile narcissism of Bill and Hillary. I've known, liked and identified with him, but what his self-absorption has done to this country is deeply depressing. He doesn't feel anyone's pain. He doesn't even feel his own."

Marlette was born in Greensboro, North Carolina, to a family of yellow-dog Democrats ("if a yellow dog ran as a Democrat, you voted for him"). His grandparents worked in the local cotton mills. "Lint was in the air," Marlette says. "So my people were called 'lintheads.' It's like 'nigger.' My father escaped the mill cycle by the grace of Adolf Hitler." A hospital corpsman in the Marines, Marlette's dad was among the first onshore in the invasions of Anzio and Salerno, carrying morphine instead of a rifle into the carnage and winding up with shrapnel in his forehead. Still he stayed in the Marines, "a lot better living than working in the mills," Marlette says. "So I was a military brat."

In his thirties Marlette learned his family's hidden history. His grandmother "Mama Gracie"—whom he remembers as an overpowering eccentric who chewed tobacco and carried a .38 in her purse—had been assaulted by a National Guardsman during the Uprising of 1934, when a half-million mill workers from Massachusetts to Alabama went on strike, their hopes raised by an early New Deal law granting them the right to unionize. Within three weeks they were defeated. Many went to prison, others were blacklisted. Though it led to the 1935 Wagner Act, which strengthened the right to organize, the uprising was a huge defeat for labor. "All across the South there was a mass amnesia about it," Marlette says.

As a child in Durham, he was taken to Burlington after church on Sundays to visit Mama Gracie and her husband, who lived in a back house and never spoke to his wife, mother of his eleven children—"Tennessee Williams stuff," Marlette says, laughing. On the hour-long drive home, the family would listen to the radio. "That had a huge impact, listening to Jack Benny and the Theater of the Mind," he remembers.

He first saw television at a neighbor's in 1953 and was captivated by Oswald Rabbit and *The Milton Berle Show*, *I Love Lucy* and Edward R. Murrow. Far less pleasurable was a broadcast he saw at age five, "something about the effects of nuclear war—everyone dying," he recalls. "I couldn't shake this thing; it was the first time I had the feeling things could spin out of control and the world could end and my parents couldn't do anything about it. But I was a sensitive lad."

As a first-grader he watched Mary Martin play Peter Pan on TV. "I remember sitting there weeping, weeping. My parents couldn't understand it. And I was too embarrassed to tell them: Wendy had grown up. I was devastated."

Television also gave him affirmation. "I remember, in '57, the University of North Carolina played Kansas in the national championship, Wilt Chamberlain played for Kansas, but we won in triple overtime, the beginning of the North Carolina legacy of great basketball. I remember the beginning of Andy Griffith's career, a North Carolina thing, too. It was the first time I heard someone who talked like us on national television."

Marlette had the foresight to preserve the cadences of his grandfather, interviewing him on tape when he was in his eighties and allowing him to give his southern-fried politics full vent. They talked about his birth in 1890, about his first vote—for Woodrow Wilson—and about his favorite President, F.D.R., "the only president who cared anything about the poor man," the old man told him, leaving Marlette "all dewy-eyed with sentimentality," he recalls. "And then he said, 'The only mistake he ever made, he should've let Hitler kill them Jews.'

"That's the contradiction that lies at the heart of the Southern Populist, the prideful need to feel that we may be bad off, but at least we're better off than somebody," Marlette says. "What was so interesting about that is that my grandfather was very kind to black people, to Jewish people. But he had these abstract notions that were obscene and had nothing to do with the reality of how he behaved, which was pretty decently, whereas in the North, people have all the correct ideals but behave horribly to other people."

Marlette's parents had the same inheritance; cultural segregationists, they were hostile toward the civil rights movement, quite active in largely black Durham under the leadership of Floyd McKissick, who would later head the Congress of Racial Equality (CORE). When the news broke about the 1954 Supreme Court decision *Brown* v. *Board of Education*, which mandated school desegregation, Marlette's family wasn't happy. And although the Marlettes voted for Kennedy in fall 1960, they weren't reconciled with that, either, Marlette recalls. "Catholics were like Jews. Other. Different. Foreign."

The Marlettes were devout Baptists. "Hellfire and brimstone, pulpit-thumping for Jesus: You'd go to church more than anybody on the face of the planet," he says—except for other Southern Baptists, that is, for whom it was a common experience. "Bill Clinton, Al Gore, we all know the same hymns."

Uncommon was Marlette's talent. As soon as he could hold a pencil, he started copying cartoon characters from ads for *The Mickey Mouse Club.* Once he traced a character, he could do it again and again; his visual memory was superb. By the time he started school, he could astonish friends by drawing Mickey Mouse and Donald Duck. "They would give me desserts and marbles to reward me," Marlette says. A teacher suggested his parents enroll him in a summer painting program. "But I wasn't serious. They said, 'Paint what you see out the window,' and I would paint Popeye." Every day, he'd read the "Peanuts" and "Steve Canyon" comic strips in the newspaper. Every week, he'd spend his allowance on Archie and Jughead, Batman, Superman and Caspar the Friendly Ghost comics. "I could get two comic books and a nickel's worth of gum, or a Cherry Coke and a comic book," he says. "I had my twenty-five cents figured out every week."

In 1962, Marlette was an eighth-grader. "I'd been doing well in school—I'd gone to my first dance and danced the Twist with a girl, was selected president of my class—and then we moved," he says with a sigh, to Laurel, Mississippi, a hotbed of racial unrest. A young man named James Meredith, the grandson of a slave, had sparked a riot when he became the first Black student at Ole Miss, the University of Mississippi, that November (with a little help from the Kennedy administration and the National Guard). A year after that, when Kennedy was killed two states away, Marlette walked home from school, listening to the reaction of his fellow Southerners. "I remember vividly kids cheering," he says. "The Kennedy brothers were Antichrists. It was much more interesting and complicated than the national media portrayed it. It's the Civil War, states' rights, and it's tainted with racism." Marlette headed to a field where he and his friends gathered. "It was a cold November day, gray and overcast, and I had that same feeling I had when I saw the nuclear war thing on television: *The adults are not in charge; you can't count on them.*"

The next February, Marlette, along with millions of others, watched The Beatles on *The Ed Sullivan Show.* "I was embarrassed by how much I liked it," he says. "I was not a hip kid. I was emotionally immature, because I'd started school early. I was behind my friends in going through puberty. They were dating and I was terrified. The next morning, in Algebra, I'm drawing John Lennon, I'm drawing Paul McCartney, and giving them to these cow-eyed adolescent girls who would pay me to draw one of the Beatles. It wasn't until I got older that I realized it was the first time we were all seeing the same things and listening to the same music." Late at night he and his older brother would sit in the car and tune in rock stations from Little Rock and Chicago. "I Want to Hold Your Hand" was number one. "She Loves You" was number two. "Please, Please Me" was number three. The Beatles—and the boomers—had taken over the charts, if not the world.

THE FIRST TIME Thomas J. Vallely (b. 1950) was in Vietnam, there was no such place as Ho Chi Minh City; it was called Saigon. A lance corporal in the U.S. Marines, Vallely won a Silver Star for conspicuous gallantry in combat. Thirty years later, he's finally succeeding at what he and his fellow soldiers so conspicuously failed to do all those years ago: He is making Vietnam a better place.

The bookshelves in Vallely's office off Harvard Square spill over onto tables stacked high with hardcovers about Vietnam, the war that defined the Baby Boom's youth as surely as World War II formed its parents'. As the Vietnam program director of the Harvard Institute for International Development, Vallely helps run the six-year-old Vietnam Fulbright program, which recruits Vietnamese students and professionals for scholarships and graduate study in the United States and offers a bilingual program in applied economics in Ho Chi Minh City for the all-American purpose of preparing Vietnamese managers for an open market economy.

Vallely was born in Boston and grew up in its suburbs, the fourth of eight children of a man who after World War II worked as a lawyer for James Michael Curley, the Boston mayor and political boss fictionalized in the novel *The Last Hurrah*. When Curley left office in 1950, Vallely's father lost his job. But a few years later, he became counsel to the state's then-governor, Foster Furcolo, and finally a judge.

"Someone in Vietnam once asked me, how did you get to know so much about communism?" Vallely says. "I said, 'It works almost the same as the party machine.'"

The Vallelys encouraged their children's curiosity. Their mother was a college graduate and a student of history. When Tom was a boy, the family lived in West Roxbury, an Irish Catholic community "where everyone was a bigot, in her mind," Vallely says. "And she was probably right. She was smart, worldly, and knowledgeable, so we did not get stuck thinking we were superior to other people." She wanted out of the neighborhood, and soon they were living beyond their means in a big, book-filled house in upper-middle-class Newton.

Like most boom-era parents, the Vallelys encouraged their children to follow current events and their own stars. "No one turned out particularly traditional," Vallely says of his siblings. Vallely thought himself the most normal among them. He played Little League baseball, loved electric trains, and wanted to be mayor of Boston. Politics suffused his childhood. Vallely remembers his father wearing Stevenson buttons and renting a television set at their summer house on Cape Cod to watch the 1960 Democratic Convention that nominated John F. Kennedy. "We were not a Kennedy family," he says. But when the president was shot three years later, "we watched the whole thing. I remember my dad crying. I had never seen my father have a tear in his eyes."

For Vallely, who had a bad stutter and undiagnosed dyslexia, school was a place of embarrassment. "I was a good observer but I was not a participant," he says. "Getting through school dominated my childhood." He was the worst student in the family, he adds, "which is basically how I got to Vietnam."

ARRANGING AN INTERVIEW with Marianne Williamson (b. 1952), the spiritual notable, is such an arduous process that at one point, *she* compares it to the Paris peace talks that ended the war in Vietnam. So when we finally begin, I say, "Le Duc Tho is at the table, is Mr. Kissinger ready?"

"Well, I don't know," she answers, "what shape is the table?" She laughs. "Are we dating ourselves, or what?"

The beautiful and celebrated Williamson has sometimes suffered from the side effects of fame, so her cat-and-mouse game, though annoying, is understandable. There are questions that may not be asked (I will ask them anyway) and nicknames that may not be repeated—a potential deal breaker I vow to forgo.

"Deal" language is appropriate. The distilled rap on Williamson is that she's a spiritual snake-oil salesman, more Hollywood than Kingdom of Heaven. She herself has said she wanted to be the Lenny Bruce or Aretha Franklin of the spiritual world.[4] And her agents and publicists do little to dispel the show-biz impression left by a career that began in a Houston New Age bookstore. Williamson's populist preaching, in lectures based on *A Course in Miracles*, a metaphysical tract that proposes belief in God as a sort of psychotherapeutic treatment for sickness, fear and other human failings, led inexorably to the *People–Vanity Fair* circuit, through which so many boomers had already planted roots in the shifting sands of celebrity. In a 1993 article that posited her as "a hustler of happy feelings and intellectual meringue," *Washington Post* sketched out Williamson's "sphere of influence": Barbra Streisand (b. 1942), Oprah Winfrey (b. 1954), Cher (b. 1946), Billy Crystal (b. 1948), and "Hollywood super-player" David Geffen (b. 1943).[5] Shortly thereafter, she added Bill and Hillary Clinton to her flock. In August 1998, she was part of an ad hoc spiritual healing team that ministered to the humiliated president.

Williamson was raised in Houston, where her father, Sam (née Vishnevetsky), a Russian Jewish Socialist, was a lawyer and her mother, Sophie Ann, a housewife. They were Depression-bred Conservative Jews who were also political progressives. A peripheral figure in the leftist Group Theater of the 1930s, Sam Williamson was kicked out of the American Communist Party for being too intellectual, his daughter says. He served as a major in the Philippines under General Douglas MacArthur, and afterward became a leading immigration lawyer, renowned as much for his longshoreman's mouth as his mentoring skills. "He was like a cross between William Kunstler and Zorba the Greek," Williamson says. "True characters are rare these days. Not as in a man with character but just a character. The modern world has become so homogenized that truly unique people—" She stops herself. "Let's just say that he was a very unique person."

Though the family lived in Eisenhower-era affluence, Sam Williamson didn't like the 1950s President, considering "gee" and "golly" the most profound things Ike ever said. His daughter has come to a more positive conclusion, recalling the former general's nobility, his warning against the military-industrial complex, and his admonition that politics should be the part-time profession of every American.

A Brownie and later a cheerleader, Williamson took piano, ballet and acting classes, idolized Eleanor Roosevelt, got good grades, and at her father's urging, read Marx, Lenin and Aquinas. But she had a self-esteem problem. "I shudder at the way children today are slapped so easily with labels of pathology like learning dysfunctions," she says, "because I'm sure if I were growing up now, I would be. The system of education under which I labored did not cater to my kind of intelligence." Williamson took an early interest in religion. "Go away, Mommy, I'm talking to God," she said at age three. But Hebrew school "was not one of the things that fired my religious imagination," she says. "Its superficiality did not make me reject God. But I, like millions of others in my generation, did not receive the spiritual sustenance we perhaps should have. If I had, I would probably be a rabbi today. The idea of being a religious facilitator was in my psyche." Instead, she thought it would be cool to be a priest.

Like so many her age, Williamson was wowed by John Kennedy's performance at his inauguration and, later, at televised press conferences in which he dazzled with his grace and wit. She was eleven and in sixth grade in November 1963. The day before Kennedy died, she'd been in the crowd at his speech at Rice University in Houston. When the news of his assassination came, she ran from classroom to classroom, telling all the other students and teachers.

Every summer, Williamson's father would take her away—to India, the Orient, even behind the Iron Curtain. "When you travel as a child, you become someone not easily susceptible to the illusion of differences," she says. "So when some spin machine tries to project guilt or blame or judgment or anything less than the full respect and honor due all children of God onto any group or nationality, I have a gut sense of rebellion. Because I learned very early we're all the same."

In summer 1965, she went to Vietnam because her father wanted "to show us what war was." Her social studies teacher had told the class that if Americans didn't fight in Vietnam, they would soon be fighting on the shores of Hawaii. Hearing that, her father stood up and pounded the table, roaring, "I'm going to sue the school board! Get the visas! We're going to Saigon!" In their hotel there, he showed her the telephone with buttons marked not A-B-C but Fire—Bomb Squad—Police. Then he took her outside and showed her bullet holes. "These are signs of war," he said. "Don't let anybody ever tell you it's okay."

Though their politics were liberal, her parents' cultural outlook was conservative. Her mother was controlling and frequently disapproving. "I was supposed to lead the revolution, but in white gloves and organza," she says. In tenth grade, she joined a sorority.[6] "I'm not someone who got it in 1965 or 1966. I was still a cute cheerleader, a student council type— but falling in love with the boys with long hair."

If mama didn't like it, so much the better.

I FIND STEVE Capps (b. 1955) in cyberspace. A friend tells me about him and sends me the e-mail address of his wife, Marie D'Amico, a lawyer specializing in intellectual property in cyberspace. She forwards it to Capps, who e-mails back to me. He tells me his office is thirty feet from his wife's at their home in Seattle, but they never speak during the day; they only e-mail.

Capps is a software architect for Microsoft, but because he's a star— working for Apple in the early 1980s, he co-authored the revolutionary Macintosh graphic user interface and still retains some fifty patents on which Apple products are based—he needn't report to the office. In the world of the wired, Capps rules. No mere hacker, he writes computer code for a very good living and is known among his peers as the fastest, most artistic coder on the planet, capable of designing everything from artwork to type fonts, willing to fight right down to the last pixel for what he believes consumers want.

It's best to e-mail Capps because his phone is usually lost under the mess on his desk. When he's in the coding zone, he doesn't answer it anyway. The focal point of the room is his computer, no longer an Apple but a Pentium PC. Around it chaos spills off the desk, off the monitor, off the windowsill, into piles on the floor. Atop the monitor are a screwdriver bit, the word *random* from a magnetic poetry kit, a toy ball that plays Spike Jones riffs when you jiggle it, a lead soldier crouched to fire a mortar, a stack of frequent-flier membership cards, 6 CDs without cases, and a thin layer of dust. His wife keeps a to-do list. Even though he is the spiritual father of the handheld computers known as Palm Pilots, Capps jots notes on scraps of paper. Apparently my phone number winds up on one of them, because eventually we get to talk.

Capps was born in Fort Wayne, Indiana. His mother, an artist, is the child of college professors. His father became an engineer for General Electric after serving stateside in the World War II army. "I was a GE brat," Capps says, moving every couple of years as his father rose from designing air conditioner motors into management. Finally, when Capps was in second grade, they landed in Schenectady, in upstate New York, where his father ended up running the company's turbine division. Filled with upper-middle-class scientists and engineers, Schenectady supported a school system so good that though he consistently scored in the top 10 percent of his class, "I didn't think I was anything special," Capps says.

Schenectady was special; it was home to the Knoll Atomic Research Power Lab, a government nuclear research facility run by GE. "There was a reservoir right near my house surrounded with high-security barbed wire, and so of course we all assumed it was a missile site. I'm sure it was a figment of our Cold War kids' imagination." Nonetheless, a friend's father, who headed the psychiatric department at a local hospital, kept a stock of the diet drink Metrecal in the basement. "That was their bomb shelter," Capps says. "My father didn't either fall for that, or he was right-wing enough that he didn't care." Capps's father was a Nixon Republican, "but it was never explicit," Capps says with what sounds like a sigh of a relief.

Though his family was well-to-do, Capps grew up without many of the modern conveniences most boomers took for granted. "We were a media-deprived family," he says. "We didn't have a color TV until my mother won one. We had a record player made of fiberboard." As a youngster, Capps "was essentially anti-social," he says. "I had one good friend and that was about it." He loved photography and film and would make movies with the family's super–8 camera. "We played music and we'd make tapes," he says. But he wasn't listening to the Beatles or the Stones. Inspired by Herb Alpert's Tijuana Brass, Capps formed a band in which he played snare drum and a homemade xylophone. "We were kind of weird," he says. "And we sucked, we absolutely sucked."

RUSSELL SIMMONS (B. 1957) is enduring some serious disrespect in the hallway of Rush Communications, the New York headquarters of his multimedia hip-hop empire. Simmons, a baby-faced mogul in oversize clothes, smiles fondly at a young producer telling him he's too old to have ears and too rich to be street anymore. With a string of curses and an endearing lisp, Simmons snaps that he was making hits when the whippersnapper was still sucking from a bottle. The producer backs off, but the curses continue, fading slowly as the young man wanders off and Simmons breaks into a proud smile. As long as his employees dis him, he's still one of them.

Russell Simmons is more often held in awe than derision. Though he didn't invent hip-hop, or its rap soundtrack, he is generally acknowledged as the man who brought urban entertainment into the mainstream, the baby boomer who killed off the boom's beloved rock and replaced it (on the charts, if not in their hearts) with a sound aging 1960s types regard with the same scorn their parents heaped on Bob Dylan's nasal twang and Mick Jagger's dirty desires. Rap, the latest voice of rebellious youth, beat of multicultural America, agent of change, has made Simmons a very wealthy man. He summers in the Hamptons, winters in St. Barthèlèmy, dines at the best restaurants, trades in old Bentleys for new Mercedes, rubs elbows with Ronald O. Perelman and Donald Trump, and gets written up in business magazines. And though he hasn't made the *Forbes 400* yet, only a fool would bet against him. His curriculum vita barely contains his ambition.

Simmons was born in a lower-middle-class neighborhood in New York's borough of Queens, near the South Jamaica Houses, twenty-seven brick buildings built on the site of a squalid slum for "colored people" in the 1940s that became a model for public housing developments. Simmons's father was a war vet who supervised school district attendance for the board of education and went on to teach black history at Pace University. His mother, an artist, taught preschool classes as a social worker in the Department of Parks. But their son was not big on academics.

"Music and sports mattered, and that was it," he says. He cheered for the underdog New York Mets and listened to "all the stuff that didn't cross over into mainstream: the Delfonics and the Dramatics and the Moments, the Spinners and all that kind of shit was hot. Bobby Womack and Al Green." Motown, the first black music most white boomers heard, was too polished, too pop; of its acts, only the gritty Temptations were in Simmons's pantheon. "But James Brown was the hottest," he says. "Every fucking week he'd have eight records on the Soul Sixteen. I remember shit like that."

Simmons didn't idolize President Kennedy, but his parents did. "My father had this letter sent to him by Kennedy thanking him for his support, and being aware of his struggle." Years later, his parents would hang a picture of Kennedy and the martyred black leaders Malcolm X and Martin Luther King Jr. on their wall after all three were dead. "Every black household in America had that picture," Simmons says. "Those three people and a flag behind."

Simmons doesn't remember Kennedy's death, but has a clear recollection of Malcolm X, the fiery black nationalist, being shot early in 1965, just after Russell's family had moved to a better neighborhood. Simmons's father, a civil rights activist, often went to hear Malcolm speak. "My father was a fighter," Simmons says. "He organized picket lines in Jamaica where they'd sing, 'Can't let nobody turn me around, turn me around, glory'. . . Sing that shit and be on the line." Russell rode on his shoulders.

In America's ghettos, some were already haters. But Simmons's parents were integration-era exemplars. They'd taken some steps up the ladder, thanks to the war, the push for equality it inspired, and the opening of civil service jobs to minorities. And they gave their values to their son. "We were conscious of racism and conscious of what our duty was as individuals to rise above it," Simmons says.

WITH HER SPIKY, two-tone hair—blonde with a black diamond in the back—computer chip earrings, leggings and black jacket with badge-laden lapels, Kathryn Bond Stockton (b. 1958) looks nothing like an academic as she and her girlfriend enter the Marriott in Trumbull, Connecticut, near her parents' home. Yet the attire is perfectly appropriate for a hotel lounge or a lecture hall. Neither academics nor academia looks the way it did when boomers went to college, and Stockton personifies the change.

An English professor and director of graduate studies at the University of Utah in Salt Lake City, Stockton is also a leading light of the new academic specialty called Theory. This matrix of new thought, ignited in the questioning counterculture of the 1960s, was "a sudden illumination of how our unexamined habits of mind perpetuated an unjust status quo," the critic Richard Bernstein noted in his book *Dictatorship of Virtue*. "Out of the burning wish for betterment grew what has now become a kind of bureaucracy of the good."[7]

Theory combines comparative literature, the study of culture, and connected philosophical ideas like poststructuralism and deconstruction with innovative academic specialties like new historicism, Afrocentrism, and gender and ethnic studies. It challenges the preeminence of objective truth, rational discourse and logic, among other tentpoles of traditional Western thought, deriding them as oppressive constructs that oppress everyone but white heterosexual males. Though conceived by members of the preceding generation, Theory found a ready audience in students like Stockton, searching for a way to be gay in academe.

A descendent of Richard Stockton, a signer of the Declaration of Independence, Stockton hails from Columbus, Ohio, but grew up in Connecticut, where her family settled in 1961. Her father was born wealthy, but his family was impoverished by the 1929 stock market crash. He met his wife in college, where he studied to be an economist. A Socialist then, he was a strong believer in the civil rights movement, had political aspirations—he lost a race for the Ohio state legislature—and served stateside in the Air Force during the Korean War. Their daughter, a sickly child, spent most of her time with her mother, an early bonding experience she thinks might have encouraged her sexual orientation.

Stockton was three when the family moved to Bloomfield, Connecticut, an island of ethnicity surrounded by "lily-white, absolute Protestant towns," she says. Her father worked as an economist at United Technologies; her mother, who'd studied to be an artist, ran a nursery school. The Stocktons were Unitarians, but most of Kathryn's friends were from Jewish or Catholic families. Politics was a constant subject of dinner table conversation. Her father, a Kennedy supporter, "was very much a young Kennedy type, dashing, attractive, a charismatic presence," she says. "He and my mom went to Kennedy's inauguration, a very big deal for them." Among Stockton's earliest memories is watching the young president speak on television.

In awe of her brother, who is four years older, Stockton became a tomboy. She shared his enthusiasm for the space race. "Your parents would get you out of bed and you'd watch countdowns on TV," she recalls. She was also a sports fanatic. "That was the most important thing in my young life. Football, basketball, baseball, tennis, skiing."

In 1962 one of her neighbors built a backyard bomb shelter, and she and her friends would stage plays and mock weddings on its raised roof. "The bomb didn't seem very real to me," she says. "It was part of life. It just seemed like a remote possibility." She was in kindergarten the day Kennedy was assassinated. "They just dismissed us. I came home and my mother was watching TV and crying. I remember watching the funeral, and my parents bought books about it and saved all the clippings. The day Lee Harvey Oswald was killed, I remember Dad saying, 'The world is falling apart.' That seemed momentous," Stockton says. "If my parents were strongly moved by things, I felt it as a kind of second-order effect, never really feeling them forcefully."

What she did feel forcefully was that she had been born the wrong sex. "In my head, I thought I was a boy," she says. "I was the Dutiful Girl by day, a model straight-A student. I don't think I've ever gotten a B in my entire life." But as soon as recess was called, she says, "I would go out on the playground and play with the boys. Then, after school, I would imme-diately change out of those clothes and get into my tomboy clothes. For quite a long stretch in childhood, children really are allowed to be strange or different. I think that's what's interesting about being a proto-gay child. There is this problem, and you don't yet know what it means. "

Stockton was "interested in girls like other boys," and even perceived the Beatles through the lens of her sexual orientation. "I have very conscious memories of an attachment, watching them on Ed Sullivan. And then of course we played the Beatles in the neighborhood. Everybody was a Beatle. I was Paul, of course, trying to attract the girls."

IT'S THE DAY after Lincoln's Birthday, 1999, and David McIntosh (b. 1958), a Republican congressman from Indiana and chief ideologue of its Conservative Action Team, has just returned home to Muncie after one of the stranger episodes in American history—the impeachment of President William Jefferson Clinton.

Though McIntosh is a leader of House conservatives, his role in the process was limited. He'd made his position clear, both as an avowed Christian and a highly partisan Republican. "We have to send the message in everything we do that those . . . fundamental moral values that make a society work—honesty, integrity, keeping your word—are important to us," he'd said on *Meet the Press*, shortly after winning reelection in a season that saw many fellow House Republicans go down to defeat. Now, dandling his seventeen-month-old daughter, Ellie, on his knee, the boyish but gray-haired congressman returns to the subject that has consumed him and his colleagues for months. "A whole generation of people who have children have been forced to think about this because their kids have asked, 'What's going on?'" McIntosh says. This Christian conservative had been inspired to enter politics by a fellow Hoosier, George Bush's vice president, Dan Quayle (b. 1947), and by summer 1999 would announce a run for governor of Indiana. Though he is a fierce partisan, he admits partisanship probably isn't an effective means for reaching moral consensus. But he insists consensus must be found nonetheless.

"There have got to be some standards," McIntosh says. "And we have to find a way to establish them. The role of people who believe that the Bible is the source of moral values is to reach out to those who have never experienced it, or have done something that they feel ashamed of and so feel they have to reject it, and say that the ironic message Christ brought was that you have to love the sinner while you hate the sin. Yes, there are values, but above that, there's love, and whatever has happened in your life you're welcome.

"And that is very hard to do in a public discourse."

Public discourse has interested McIntosh for as far back as he can remember. Born in Oakland, California, he grew up in the suburbs of San Francisco, where his father opened a steak house with a partner in 1962. The restaurant was successful enough that the next year, just before McIntosh entered kindergarten, the family moved to a better house in a town closer to the city.

One of McIntosh's first memories is John Kennedy's death. "I remember my mom and dad crying," he says. His mother was a Kennedy Democrat. "Her views were shaped growing up in a small town, then moving to San Francisco, the big city. Before she met my dad, she lived in the Haight-Ashbury area and enjoyed being part of that culture and picked up a lot of postwar modern thought. She was a libertarian liberal. Very strong on equal rights. Racism was wrong, everybody was the same, the color of your skin didn't matter."

McIntosh doesn't know much about his father's politics because he died of stomach cancer in January 1964. At the end of that school year, the family moved to Kendallville, near his mother's hometown in northeast Indiana, where her brothers, both doctors, lived; one hired her as a nurse. Equidistant between Chicago and Detroit and surrounded by lakes, Kendallville, population 7,000, epitomized white, small-town America. First inhabited in 1832, it grew from a single log cabin into a blue-collar town named for a Civil War–era postmaster general and filled with Protestant churches. Many people worked at the Kraft caramel plant, a refrigerator factory, and several foundries that made auto parts. In the 1950s and 1960s, the foundries had recruited coal miners from Kentucky to come north for better pay, and the town filled with yellow-dog Democrats. Mostly, though, there were farmers. "If it was a bad year for farmers, everybody in town talked about it," McIntosh recalls.

Everybody knew everybody else's business in Kendallville, and nobody thought there was anything wrong with that. McIntosh walked the four blocks to school each day, "and if I strayed off the beaten path, immediately my mom knew because three or four neighbors would call," he recalls. "So it was a very sheltered place, a good place to raise a family, especially for a single mom. You didn't see a lot of the social turmoil that was happening in other parts of the country."

NINA HARTLEY'S HOTEL room is getting crowded. She's in Atlantic City for a videocassette dealer's convention that ended a few hours ago; as a superstar of pornographic films and producer of her own line of sex instruction videos, she was a featured attraction. Now she's bouncing around her room with two chirpy young women with unnatural breasts barely covered by T-shirts cropped to show their pierced belly buttons, and lips plumped so full of collagen they look ripe to pop. Their names are Shiloh and Tammi, and they've come with Dr. Phil Good, their boyfriend (the three live together), and a guy named Dave, who is setting up a camera to tape sex tips for something called *Sex Drive Video Magazine*.

Hartley (b. 1959), a petite, blue-eyed blonde, sits on one of the beds, shoeless, dressed in a black and red polka-dot flirt dress, a charm bracelet festooned with a gold vagina, a tiny crystal phallus, a crouching female figurine—a miniature of the Venus of Willendorf, a Paleolithic carving thought to be a prehistoric matriarchal goddess—and a pair of linked female symbols. On the other sits Bobby Lilly (b. 1942), a husky woman in aviator glasses with blonde hair streaked with gray, whom Hartley calls her wife; they share a husband named Dave (b. 1948).

They all talk about life in the three-way world ("Tripods are very stable," says Hartley) and Bill Clinton ("I'd push Bill out of the way to get to Hillary"), before Nina offers up impromptu sex tips for the camera ("A clitoris is not a doorbell; don't lean on it") for an hour. Then, as soon as the lights go off, she strips off all her clothes, poses for good-bye snapshots with her interviewers and, still in the nude, one hand plucking absently at her pubic hair, reveals that Nina Hartley is the nom de porn of a nice Jewish girl from Berkeley, California, a third-generation feminist and child of Communist Buddhists, a Jew-Bu, as she puts it, whose real name is Mitzi.

Mitzi is two years older than Nina. Her mother's family came from a small town in Alabama, where her great-grandfather built the synagogue. Mitzi's maternal grandparents were both professors at the University of Alabama until her grandfather read *Foundations of Leninism* by Joseph Stalin, declared himself a Communist, and promptly got fired. "He became a Jewish pinko nigger lover," Hartley says with a laugh, and went to work for an organization that defended political prisoners. Her grandmother quit her job, and joined him in the state of pariah.

Crosses burned on their front lawn, and her grandfather was beaten and left for dead by a mob that, family legend has it, included one T. Eugene "Bull" Connor, who would come to national attention years later as the chief of police and chief defender of racism in Birmingham, Alabama. By then, though, Mitzi's family was long gone. In the 1940s they moved to California, where Mitzi's mother earned a double degree in statistics and chemistry and tested airplanes during World War II. Her older sister, Mitzi's aunt, realized she was a lesbian and later came to family functions with her husband and their respective girlfriends.

Mitzi's father was Pennsylvania Dutch and German, the grandson of a turn-of-the-century art dealer who raised the boy in strict religious fashion in a mansion in Flushing, New York. A childhood visit to Germany, just as the Nazis began their rise, made him anti-fascist. A sensitive young man, he escaped an unhappy first marriage and moved to California to act. He tried but failed to enlist in the Army during the war, moved to Berkeley, joined the Communist party, and met his future wife when she auditioned for a part in a play a friend of his had written about the Spanish Civil War.

Kindred spirits—"not ideologues at all; they really wanted to make the world a better place," Hartley says, the pair married and quickly had three children. In 1949, Mitzi's dad began hosting a program called *This Is San Francisco* on local CBS radio as Jim Grady. Disillusioned by the 1956 Soviet invasion of Hungary, the couple abandoned communism, but that didn't help "Grady" when a process server from the House Un-American Activities Committee came calling the next year, said he never missed *This Is San Francisco*, and handed him a subpoena.

"He did the honorable thing, didn't name any names, and it ruined his career in[nbs]broadcasting," Hartley says. "And that severely affected my personal life, because it caused anger and resentment. My mother, whose father's politics were a burden on her, married a passionate, idealistic young man who ruined her life. You know he's doing something heroic, you hate him for it, but you can't get mad at him, and that gets buried for, oh, thirty years."

Grady got a series of low-paying jobs. But he'd get fired when, as Hartley says, "the guys in the suits come, knock-knock, 'It's about your employee.'" He was found guilty of contempt for refusing to say if he was a communist.[8] Desperately in need of an escape, the couple took a camping trip to the Samuel P. Taylor Regional Park in northern California in June 1958. "They made love under the moon and the trees and the tent, and Dad hadn't brought the condoms, and my mother's a Fertile Myrtle," Hartley says. "They took a chance, because I'm sure it was a romantic, wonderful moment." Nine months later, their youngest child, a daughter named Mary Louise, whom they called Mitzi, came along. "My mother calls me a purposeful accident," she says. "Which was a nice way of putting it. The emotional reality was, they really had no business having another child, and my mother had to go back to work when I was six weeks old, so I'm put in the care of a competent, caring stranger, but not a parent who really gives a shit." Seven years later, they could no longer afford help. Mitzi's father became a house husband while his wife worked at the California Department of Public Health.

Though she never cried between age six and twenty, Hartley hastens to add that Mitzi wasn't consciously unhappy. "I certainly have happy memories of childhood," she says, "but I was very shy, very malleable, terribly insecure about my worth as a person. I stayed to myself. I had a treehouse. I got lost in books very easily. I loved Prince Valiant and Captain America comics. I remember watching *The Love Boat*, Jackie Gleason, Lucy, *Gilligan's]Island* and *The Brady Bunch*. And I also remember I was one of those incessant talkers. My father called it radar. Keep blipping out until you find someone who'll respond."

CAMERON SEARS (B. 1960) arrives at a Mexican restaurant in Novato, California, near the Grateful Dead's office north of San Francisco, wearing a plain T-shirt over trekking shorts and climbing boots, his brown hair bowl-cut, his beard touched with gray, clutching a cell phone that rings several times as we dine on refried beans and burritos. The Dead is dead. Its days as an active band ended with the 1995 death of its front man, Jerry Garcia, but the Dead as an enterprise lives on. In 1998, Sears was president of Grateful Dead Productions.[9] He seems a little too clean-cut to be the man behind the band that inspired a generation of acid heads and three generations of Dead heads, but then, even the Dead grow up.

Sears was born in Boston, grandson of an Andover professor and the oldest of three children of a real estate executive and his wife, a classical musician. Well-educated and cultured, Sears's father, a sailor in the Korean War-era navy, was stationed in San Francisco when he met his wife, a University of Michigan graduate, waiting on line at the box office of the San Francisco Opera. After he earned his own degrees at the universities of Kansas and North Carolina, the couple moved to Boston. They summered in East Dennis, Massachusetts, on the elbow of Cape Cod, where Sears' ancestors, all seafarers, had built a house 200 years before. Sears' grandmother, who is in her mid–nineties, still lives in the beautiful bayside homestead that inspired her grandson's lifelong passion for the outdoors.

Sears moved to Washington, D.C., when he was an infant, and lived there until he was ten. His childhood was "very conventional," he says. What stands out was going backpacking with his father. And he can't forget the day his parents took him to a downtown office building to watch the cortege to John Kennedy's funeral. The slain president's flag-draped casket was carried out of the U.S. Capitol, loaded on a caisson drawn by six matched gray horses and a seventh mounted horseman and escorted by nine honorary military pallbearers and one riderless horse to St. Matthew's Roman Catholic Church, as an unprecedented gathering of world leaders followed behind. Though he was only three, says Sears, "it made a definite impression."

VICTORIA LEACOCK (B. 1963) keeps a bottle of fortified amber-colored wine called Leacock Madeira on a shelf in the living room of her townhouse apartment in the Chelsea section of New York City. Her family created the brand on the Portuguese island of Madeira, in the North Atlantic Ocean, in 1741. The label tells of her ancestor, Thomas Leacock, and his tenacity in overcoming a vine disease that wiped out many vineyards. Generations later, Victoria would play a small but crucial role in the battle against a disease that wiped out vast numbers of Baby Boomers.

Leacock was born on the fringe of America's celebrity culture. Her mother, Marilyn West, a Midwesterner, had been captivated by the Andrews Sisters when she was fourteen. After sitting in the front row through six straight concerts by the World War II-era harmony group in Chicago, she was invited backstage. With the encouragement of one of the sisters, Maxene, she interviewed them, sold the story to the *Chicago Tribune*, and then moved to California to become a fashion model. Years later, when Leacock learned that her red-haired, blue-eyed mother had been bisexual, she wondered if that explained the attraction. "I think Mom and Maxene were sort of enamored of each other," she says. "Whether it was requited, I never got a word out of either of them."

Back in New York after college, Leacock's mother continued to model (becoming the face of Toni Home Permanents) and had a love affair with France Burke, the daughter of Kenneth Burke, a philosophic and linguistic critic and niece of Catholic activist Dorothy Day. One of France's sisters was married to a filmmaker, Richard Leacock. Raised on a banana plantation in the Canary Islands and educated in English schools, Leacock came to America when the Spanish dictator Francisco Franco nationalized his family's business in 1937. He'd already made his first documentary, which caught the eye of a schoolmate's father, Robert Flaherty, director of *Nanook of the North*. Flaherty and such other family friends as Bertrand Russell wrote letters of recommendation that won Leacock admittance to Harvard.

War broke out in his third year there. Leacock got his American citizenship and enlisted in the U.S. Army, where he served for four years as a filmmaker. When he got out, Flaherty hired him to shoot a film called *Louisiana Story*, which promptly won a British Academy Award. By the late 1950s, Leacock was an unhappily married father of four when his sister-in-law's lover asked him to teach her how to use a darkroom. "Marilyn," he told her, "I am never going in a dark room with you."

In 1959, Leacock's wife left him for another man. Fortunately, his career as a documentarian was just taking off. He'd gone to work for Robert Drew of Drew Associates, home to many of the future stars of documentary filmmaking. In 1960, Leacock, Albert Maysles, and D. A. Pennebaker took off for Wisconsin, where Drew was making *Primary*, about the presidential campaigns of Democratic candidates John F. Kennedy and Hubert Humphrey. They had just developed a way to synchronize sound to motion pictures without cables, creating the raw, spontaneous films that became known as cinema verité.

In 1963, Leacock made *Crisis*, a film about Robert Kennedy's battle with Alabama Governor George Wallace over school desegregation. Between shoots in the South, he would return to New York where, early one evening, he ran into Marilyn West and Maxene Andrews at the Algonquin Hotel. "Who is that man?" Maxene demanded of Marilyn afterward. "You're all red. I've never seen you so flustered."

"That's the man I'm going to marry," she replied. Leacock was enjoying the sudden coincidence of bachelorhood and success. At the end of 1962, "Dad had three girlfriends tell him they were pregnant, all in one month," Victoria Leacock reports. "And my mom was apparently the only one telling the truth." She and Leacock both swore off other women and were married in February 1963. Victoria was born six months later. Maxene Andrews was her godmother. She was barely three months old when John F. Kennedy and an era of high hopes died.

IN JANUARY 1964, Bob Dylan released his third record, *The Times They Are A-Changin'*. Its title was prophetic. That month, Lyndon Johnson, the new president, declared a war on poverty and a military junta took over South Vietnam. The next, Cassius Clay (b. 1942) won the world heavyweight boxing crown and promptly changed his name to Muhammad Ali. Also in February, Dylan and his girlfriend Joan Baez played a concert together in Berkeley before heading to Europe, where legend has it he introduced the Beatles to marijuana.

That spring, crosses and churches burned across Mississippi as a warning to young white radicals from the North who were planning an action

called Freedom Summer, a series of civil rights protests and voter registration drives. Three of the Freedom Riders, James Chaney (b. 1943),
Andrew Goodman (b. 1944) and Michael Schwerner (b. 1940), were
murdered on their arrival in late June by the Ku Klux Klan. Six months
later and fifty miles north in Laurel, Mississippi, the father of one of
Doug Marlette's classmates was arrested in connection with those murders, just as the school year was ending. Laurel was also home to Sam
Bowers, Grand Dragon of the White Knights of the Ku Klux Klan and
one of Marlette's neighbors, who set up wiretaps on civil rights workers.

Marlette had been born in Greensboro, North Carolina, the city where
the modern civil rights movement began in 1960, when four black students sat down at a whites-only lunch counter. More than a dozen years
later Doug was still drinking from "Whites Only" fountains, going to segregated schools, attending racist rallies, and sitting up front in buses
where black people were forced to the back. "*This* is embarrassing," he
says. "My very first cartoon was anti-Martin Luther King." It questioned
how King could win the 1964 Nobel Peace Prize when so much violence
followed in his wake. "I wish I could say I'd had more insight and compassion," says Marlette, "but I sensed the party line. I was a good boy, a par-
ent-pleaser."

Marlette's mother was crippled; she'd contracted polio before the Salk
vaccine and walked with a stiff leg. "So I felt a great responsibility," he
says. "And part of my deal with my mother was to be her agent in the
world—emotionally. I was still in the thrall of my raising, expressing their
views, on the wrong side. But when I went with my dad downtown one
day when there was going to be a demonstration, I had that feeling in the
pit of my stomach again that the beast wasn't far from the surface."

From age nine, Marlette had been reading and collecting *Mad* magazine. Founded in 1952 by William M. Gaines (b. 1922), a diet-pill-gob-
bling grown-up child who'd inherited a company that published comic
books based on the Bible and begun churning out horror and war comics,
Mad was a profound influence on boomers. Parodying everything from
movies and films to its own staff ("the usual gang of idiots"), it fostered an
attitude of irreverence toward authority—any authority. In 1955, when
Mad introduced its gap-toothed mascot, Alfred E. ("What, me worry?")
Neuman, and switched from comic book to magazine format in order to
skirt the Comics Code, a law instituted to protect boomers from corrupting cartoon influences, its corrupting influence increased. By the time
Marlette bought his first issue in 1958, *Mad*'s satire was a well-planted
thorn in the side of mainstream culture.

Marlette perfected his drawing by copying caricatures and cartoons from *Mad*'s pages. In 1964, at fifteen, he wrote a letter to one of the cartoonists, including a satire he'd drawn of television's *The Man from U.N.C.L.E.* A form rejection letter promptly came back to Laurel. "My mother was furious," Marlette recalls. "She wrote them a three-page letter."

A mere year later, "Like a Rolling Stone," Bob Dylan's first rock single and the first six-minute song ever to top the charts, was played in a hamburger joint, where Marlette heard it and was stunned by Dylan's verbal fireworks. He worked his way backward through Dylan's oeuvre. Despite the way he'd been reared, he says, "Bob Dylan got under my skin." Dylan had been in Greenwood, Mississippi, not long before, singing for civil rights workers. "That had a huge impact on me. Because until then, they'd been the enemy."

LYNDON JOHNSON SIGNED the Civil Rights Act in the summer of 1964, as what were still called "Negro" neighborhoods seethed with protests and uprisings; in August the Democratic Convention in Atlantic City refused to seat delegates from the Mississippi Freedom Democratic Party, and America's troubles spanned the globe after U.S. forces attacked the North Vietnamese in the Gulf of Tonkin. Congress authorized escalation of the undeclared war in Southeast Asia, and America began drafting its young in numbers unheard of since the Korean War.

In the late 1950s, Beat culture—which gave America Jack Kerouac and Allen Ginsberg, and mass culture counterparts like Maynard G. Krebs, the bongo-batting beatnik on television's *The Dobie Gillis Show*—found a home in the cafes of the North Beach neighborhood of San Francisco. The Bay Area in general, and the University of California at Berkeley in particular, became magnets for progressive young people. A decade of protest began in May 1960, when students from Berkeley demonstrating against House Un-American Activities Committee hearings being held there were literally washed out of San Francisco's City Hall by police with fire hoses.

By 1963, students had begun emulating the civil rights activists of the South, picketing, committing acts of civil disobedience, and getting arrested at San Francisco car showrooms and hotels that discriminated against nonwhites. In July 1964, the Republican party held its convention in San Francisco's Cow Palace and nominated Arizona Senator Barry Goldwater, whose archconservative stance was summed up in his acceptance speech. "Extremism in the defense of liberty is no vice," he said.

"Moderation in the pursuit of justice is no virtue!" His call was soon to echo on the left.

That fall, Berkeley's dean of students announced that students could no longer use a stretch of sidewalk in front of the campus for political organizing. When students from across the political spectrum disobeyed, several were hauled before deans and suspended. In response, a coalition of student groups set up tables on the steps of Sproul Hall, the Berkeley administration building. Just before noon on October 1, university officials began citing them. One, a graduate student, Jack Weinberg of CORE, was arrested and tossed into a squad car. Before he could be carted off to jail, a crowd of students surrounded the car, launching an impromptu sit-in.

Returning home from a class in his varsity jacket and zebra-striped swim team sweater, John Gage caught sight of the 2,000 people who'd gathered in the plaza. "Everyone who had watched news coverage of the civil rights movement knew precisely what to do: sit down so the police car couldn't move," he says. Students began climbing on the car's roof and giving speeches, including Mario Savio, a twenty-one-year-old philosophy student Gage recognized from a math class. Savio, president of the Berkeley chapter of the Student Non-Violent Coordinating Committee (SNCC), had just returned from Freedom Summer.

Gage watched astonished as Savio, who stuttered, turned into a compelling orator. Even more surprising, the brainy jock found himself sympathetic. He believed universities should be free forums, and though he knew it wasn't rational, he realized, standing there, that he'd break the kneecaps of anyone who ever tried to stop him from speaking—or listening. At dusk, when a group of drunken students looking forward to a football weekend started pushing into Sproul Plaza to free the squad car, Gage was among the gang of crew men and football players who pushed back.

He didn't stick around that night—"It was dinnertime," he says with a laugh. By the next day, the university had dropped charges against Weinberg and the students dispersed, but the Free Speech Movement was just getting started. It was Weinberg who coined the phrase "Don't trust anyone over thirty" when the university appointed a man in his early thirties to negotiate with the students, thinking he'd be seen as a peer. When administrators still wanted to discipline the eight students cited in the plaza, Gage was among the growing number who decided the school wasn't playing fair.

In early November, students set up tables in the plaza again, and the university's position hardened. On November 20, about 3,000 students marched on a meeting of the university's regents. The school's policy on political activity was being debated, and the decision to suspend Savio and seven other students was upheld. When Gage returned home to conservative Orange County a few days later for Thanksgiving, family friends wondered if he wasn't turning Communist.

Back on campus, students announced a strike. Savio gave the speech that made him famous. "There comes a time when the operation of the machine becomes so odious . . . you can't even passively take part," he said. "And you've got to put your bodies on the gears . . . And you've got to indicate to the people who run it, to the people who own it, that unless you're free, the machine will be prevented from working at all."

When Savio finished, his audience of 800 occupied Sproul Hall again. This time, the police were ready. Beginning at 4:00 A.M. and for the next twelve hours, led by a deputy district attorney named Ed Meese—later Richard Nixon's Attorney General—they made 814 arrests. Television reports showed limp students being dragged down long flights of stairs to paddy wagons. Though faculty raised bail and the students were released from jail, Berkeley was paralyzed. Many began wearing IBM computer punch cards marked I AM A STUDENT. DO NOT FOLD, SPINDLE OR MUTILATE.

A compromise was worked out: amnesty for arrested students and a reversal of the ban on sidewalk tables. The school still insisted on the right to punish students for "illegal advocacy" on- or off-campus, a clear attempt to hobble civil disobedience. Four days after the mass arrest, 18,000 administrators, teachers and students gathered at Berkeley's Greek Theater for an "extraordinary" convocation. "There I was, wearing my striped zebra sweater again, and Mario sat down about two seats away in clogs and a long overcoat," Gage recalls. School president Clark Kerr announced the "compromise" couched with pointed remarks about reason and respect. Furious, Savio got up from his seat and moved toward the podium, where he was intercepted by university police and dragged off. Gage tried to follow, "yelling at various administration people," he says

In short order, Savio, released, was declaring victory at another rally as the school's chancellor was replaced. Still, Savio eventually was expelled and sentenced to four months in prison. His followers lost only a semester, but they—and the bulk of the Baby Boom just behind them—got the message. Having realized that authority could lie, Gage, like many others, now saw lies everywhere. Ironically, this seismic shift occurred just as *Time* magazine declared the boomers to be "a generation of conformists."

Gage quit the swim team and started doing things athletes didn't do. For middle-class, law-abiding, churchgoing kids like John Gage, marijuana had been the marker of the good child gone down the dope fiend path. Yet millions of them went to pot in one way or another during the next five years. A girlfriend gave Gage his first puff of the magic dragon. "It seemed like a good idea at the time," he says.

Suddenly, school seemed less interesting, even as student concerns increasingly set the national agenda. Lyndon Johnson had been elected to a full term as president in fall 1964, a peace candidate against the supposed warmonger Goldwater, but by spring 1965, the United States was sending ground troops into battle and bombing North Vietnam. Antiwar protests began. In May, Berkeley was the scene of a "teach-in"—a massive consciousness-raising symposium on the escalating war in Vietnam.

That summer, "Eve of Destruction," an anti-war song, topped the Top 40. In September Gage walked into the headquarters of an insurgent congressional campaign. Robert Scheer (b. 1936), an activist and journalist at a leftist magazine called *Ramparts*, was running in the Democratic primary against a Johnson-style pro-war liberal. Hired on to the campaign by its manager Alice Waters (b. 1944)—who went on to found the landmark Berkeley restaurant Chez Panisse—Gage took over two precincts and won them for Scheer. Unfortunately, the candidate lost almost everywhere else. His brand of radicalism had not yet entered the mainstream—even in Berkeley.

A Scheer win wouldn't have changed what happened next: Gage was drafted. And like most smart, white, privileged baby boomers, he promptly looked for a way out, joining a National Guard unit, then spending four months at Fort Ord Truck Driving School. He can still wax nostalgic about watching white, black, and Latin boys having their heads shaved and their identities and distinctions stripped away. "It's America at its best," says the self-described Jeffersonian Democrat. "You think I'm un-American? I'll show you who's American."

ACCEPTED AT BERKELEY, Tim Scully moved in with his grandparents again. In 1963, he wandered into and became a design consultant at Atomic Laboratories, a company nearby that made equipment to measure radiation. By 1964, he was doing so well he'd dropped out of school, bought a house of his own, and rented out rooms to fellow students. While many their age were marching for civil rights and disarmament, Scully was designing a fuel gauge for space rockets. "I had bottles of liquid Cobalt–60 in the attic," he says. Another chemical was about to set his future.

In 1943 Albert Hofmann, a biochemist at Switzerland's Sandoz Laboratories, accidentally ingested a minute amount of a material he'd first synthesized during medical research in 1938. He ate some more a few days later, on purpose. "I experienced fantastic images of an extraordinary plasticity," Hofmann would later say.[10] That compound, known as LSD or acid, after lysergic acid, its base material, soon became a subject of considerable interest in several separate but connected communities: the worlds of psychological research, the military, and espionage.

The foremost psychologist studying LSD was a Harvard lecturer named Timothy Leary (b. 1920). A roguish Irish Catholic, he was the son of West Point's dentist and went to the military academy himself. Accused of drunkenness by upperclassmen, he was asked to resign, but demanded a court martial instead. Though found not guilty, his bad form led to his being silenced—shunned—by his fellow cadets. He finally quit and continued his schooling in Alabama. During World War II, he served as an army psychologist in a veterans' hospital. After the war, he married, had two children, Susan (b. 1947) and Jack (b. 1949), earned a Ph.D. from Berkeley, and became a specialist in personality assessment and behavioral change.

Leary's own behavior changed profoundly after his wife asphyxiated herself in their garage on his thirty-fifth birthday. He quit his job, sailed to Spain, and returned to lecture at Harvard about a rebel movement then challenging behaviorism and psychoanalysis: existential-transactional psychology, which treated all behavior as a set of games. In August 1960, Leary rented a villa in Cuernavaca, Mexico, for the summer. Curious about the "divine mushrooms" of the Aztecs, just written up in *Life* magazine, he took some and was transformed.

Back at Harvard that fall, Leary learned that Sandoz had synthesized the active ingredient in psilocybin mushrooms. He started giving it to test subjects and graduate students as part of a psychological study. Leary quickly hooked up with Aldous Huxley (b. 1894), author of *Brave New World*, whose lifelong quest for higher awareness had led him to first take mescaline, another psychoactive drug, in 1953.[11] Huxley suggested it was Leary's responsibility to enlighten the elite about psychoactive drugs. Soon Allen Ginsberg arrived in Cambridge, where he took psilocybin and wandered Leary's house naked with his lover, Peter Orlovsky. Ginsberg then introduced Leary to Jack Kerouac, Robert Lowell, Dizzy Gillespie and William Burroughs, and psychedelics quickly became the secret vice of New York's hip elite. Leary began taking psilocybin every three days.[12]

Leary's closest colleague was Richard Alpert, the child of a great railroad fortune and a graduate of Tufts and Stanford. Alpert had tried marijuana in graduate school. While working for Harvard's Center for Research in Personality, he took psilocybin and signed on to Leary's project. Together, they started giving the drug to prisoners in a state penitentiary. The results were positive. Leary believed he'd found an agent that could alter consciousness and change people for the better.

His superiors weren't so sure. In February 1962, the Harvard *Crimson* began writing about Leary's mushroom experiments. The story broke nationally within a month.[13] Harvard asked Leary to turn over his psilocybin. Unknown to the school, he'd just tried LSD, provided by a Briton, Michael Hollingshead, who'd fallen in with a tiny circle of beats and psychedelic devotees in New York City and had convinced a friend who worked in a hospital to get some LSD from Sandoz's U.S. office.[14] After turning up at Leary's door with his stash in a mayonnaise jar, Hollingshead quickly turned Leary on and became Jack and Susan's babysitter.

That summer, Leary went to California. LSD research had been going on there since 1959. Several Hollywood psychiatrists and psychologists had experimented with the stuff, testing its effects on patients, including Henry and Clare Booth Luce (of the *Time* and *Life* Luces), Anaïs Nin, Cary Grant, James Coburn and Jack Nicholson.[15] LSD parties were becoming a phenomenon in Hollywood.[16] Beatniks, who had been "expanding their consciousness" with drugs for years, were also eager to try the new thrill.

Several hundred miles north, Tim Scully was still following his family's careful script. When Berkeley's Free Speech Movement began, he kept his distance. He'd read the riot act to a friend who'd smoked pot. But one of his tenants, a student of Oriental philosophy whom Scully knew from kindergarten, went to work on him after Tim showed interest in his talk of consciousness. "Don finally talked me into smoking marijuana while I was reading the *Tao Te Ching*. It certainly bends your thoughts in the right direction." The notion that marijuana and other drugs led to reefer madness was wafting out windows all over the world.

TIMOTHY LEARY WAS at Harvard during Leslie Crocker Snyder's senior year at Radcliffe. "Now, I never had anything to do with Timothy Leary," she says. "I heard that he was involved with some Radcliffe students and drug experiments, but I was a pretty straight kid. My crowd was fairly straight. Drugs were just not a part of our existence."

Still, Snyder felt the mood that encouraged drug use—even if she didn't go that far. By her junior year, "I was losing all interest in academia, unfortunately," she says. Aware of the student movement, Snyder admired civil rights workers, wanted to help, and knew she would one day. She also knew people in the thriving Cambridge folk music scene, but was more likely to be found on the banks of the Charles watching her boyfriend race crew. The day she broke out she found herself on the periphery of the Harvard Latin Diploma riot. When the school decided it would no longer issue diplomas in Latin, students gathered in Harvard Square, "and the police gassed us," she recalls. "I still remember the tears pouring down my face. And feeling outraged." Her fiancé, "a guy all the girls loved," was mean and unsympathetic. Luckily, just before they got married, she met someone she liked better, and she and the jock called it quits.

Snyder had lost direction. At huge Harvard, there was no one to turn to for advice. Both she and her fiancé had planned to go to law school, one at a time—he would have been first, of course. She was slated to enter a one-year program at Harvard Business School that would funnel her into a good, high-paying job in the interim. It was too late to change course.

Then there was the undeclared war in Vietnam. To most Harvard students, it was a vague, amorphous conflict, certainly no cause for concern. Snyder heard that a Harvard friend had been killed there, one of the first hundred American casualties. "And then," she says, "we started thinking and talking a lot more about Vietnam."

Snyder's first brush with discrimination came when she entered Harvard Business School. Radcliffe graduates were not considered full-fledged business students until their second year. Though they were taught by Business School professors, they were segregated into classes of their own. She decided to forgo a second year and, thanks to her fluency in French, got a job in Paris as an executive trainee. But her parents demanded she return home. "This is not a constructive thing to do," her mother told her. Snyder had desperately wanted to go to law school. But her parents wouldn't pay. Even if she could have gotten in—she'd been a B student at Radcliffe—loans for women law students were unheard of. Her father offered a deal: if she would come home, she could go to law school for free at Cleveland-based Case Western Reserve, where he was teaching.

"I was horrified because, god, to go to Cleveland for three years—and Case Western was a mediocre law school," Snyder says, but it did accept her and was, in essence, free. She agreed. First, unbeknownst to her parents, she hitchhiked across Europe with a young man. She even thought about staying. "I could have gone off course," she says, "but it just wasn't in me. I wanted to go to law school more than anything else."

In September 1963, Snyder moved in with her folks and enrolled as one of only two women in her law school class. If feminism was part and parcel of Radcliffe culture, it was nowhere to be found at Case Western. ("I hear you went to Radcliffe," a student said to her after her first class, "so obviously you believe in free love.")

Snyder was in class when she heard her idol Jack Kennedy had been killed. "I started weeping and went to find my father," she says. Like many around her, he was equivocal: "Well, he isn't that great a man or a president," he said.

Cleveland offered one consolation, the rock 'n' roll Snyder loved. She saw the Beatles play there on their first American tour, and she saw James Brown, too. This was still Middle America; it would be years before coastal craziness hit the banks of the Cuyahoga River. But it was coming. A neighbor's nephew, whom Snyder had a crush on, died of a heroin overdose. An unmarried couple she'd befriended who shared her taste for poetry got stoned when she wasn't around. "They were from New York," she says. "I had never heard of people smoking marijuana. That's how isolated I had been. I was never interested in drugs but was fascinated by people who were."

Fascination never led to experimentation, though. "I get upset if I'm not in control," says Snyder. She'd nearly made a wrong turn in Europe. Now on the right track, she was determined to stay there.

IN 1964, JIM Fouratt got a job as a page at New York's new Four Seasons restaurant. "I took people to their tables and got huge tips with little notes saying, 'We'll pick you up at eleven.' These gentlemen would pick me up in limousines. And I wouldn't put out. I didn't know that was the deal!"

He'd recently smoked pot for the first time, but hated the stuff. Fouratt preferred speed. Having first tried the bootleg Benzedrine pills known as white crosses that were sold in Washington Square Park, he graduated to pharmaceuticals when the poet Allen Ginsberg introduced him to one of New York's Doctor Feelgoods, renegades who gave "vitamin" shots laced with amphetamines to the elite (President Kennedy among them).

If Fouratt has trouble keeping his memories ordered, the breadth of his experience is a likelier reason than his drug use. For example, having met Brian Epstein when the Beatles manager, a closeted homosexual, had first come to New York, Fouratt was comped to see the band at Carnegie Hall, their second American concert, on February 12, 1964. Escorting the hottest girl he could find, Jill Haworth, an actress who'd just appeared in the movie *Exodus*, Fouratt went backstage afterward, met the Beatles, and took them to the Peppermint Lounge in Times Square to see the Ronettes, and then went back to the Plaza Hotel, where they were staying. "Jill wound up with Paul and I was pissed off," Fouratt remembers. "I didn't think she was going to leave me to go fuck a Beatle."[17]

Another example: On August 8, 1964, he met a fellow acting student in Duffy Square, to rehearse a scene. Instead, he got caught up in New York's second demonstration against the Vietnam War and wound up one of seventeen people arrested, in his case for breaking a window and resisting arrest. He was innocent, he says, but was convicted by a judge who solemnly informed him that police officers do not lie. "We'd all grown up in the fifties with everything nice on the surface, no one talking about what's underneath," Fouratt says. Some were, though. In summer 1965, Fouratt was there when Bob Dylan, inspired by the Beatles, strapped on an electric guitar and scandalized the Newport Folk Festival by playing "Like a Rolling Stone."

In December 1965, Mickey Ruskin opened a bar that became the Underground's clubhouse and Fouratt's new hangout, Max's Kansas City.[18] Fouratt had a $20-a-month duplex loft just off the Bowery near a neighborhood then becoming known as the East Village. Fouratt's new boyfriend was a Chilean poet and playwright named Claudio Badal who knew Andy Warhol, the Pop artist who'd emerged in 1962 and became the king of Max's, going there almost nightly in 1966. Max's was the place "where Pop Art and pop life came together," Warhol wrote, "Everybody went to Max's and everything got homogenized there."[19] It was also okay to be homosexual there—a matter of some import to Fouratt.

The fast lane finally caught up with Fouratt in early 1966. He came down with hepatitis—from Dr. Feelgood's speed shots, he thinks. Without insurance, he ended up in Bellevue, a public hospital. While there, his short hair grew longer, almost to his shoulders. By the time he got out, he had the latest look among the young: hippies had come onto the scene. The values the longhairs espoused (peace and free love), the drugs they took, which encouraged sexual experimentation, and the androgynous style they adopted were right up Fouratt's alley.

Never one to stay on the fringe of a fringe, compelled to propel himself right to the red-hot core, Fouratt began a noisy public career that has made him a figure of some controversy in boomer circles for three decades. Out of the hospital, he returned to San Francisco, where he met some of the leaders of the new hippie scene—members of the San Francisco Mime Troupe. The troupe, a politically progressive guerrilla band of actors that performed commedia dell'arte in the city's parks, had come to national attention the year before, when denied permission to perform a play San Francisco's parks commission considered obscene.

A few months later, several members of the mime troupe broke off to form a street theater and cultural action group called The Diggers, which became known for ladling free stew in Golden Gate Park's Panhandle. Fouratt was particularly taken with the Diggers' public information arm, the Communications Company, which published a stream of mimeographed communiqués and manifestos for the new community of hippies taking over the Haight-Ashbury section of San Francisco, a working-class neighborhood full of Victorian houses bordering Golden Gate Park. Ideas were free, too. When Fouratt returned east, he brought that one with him.

BARBARA LEDEEN'S SOCIAL consciousness was awakened in 1964 by the murders of Freedom Riders in Mississippi. She'd always had an inchoate sense of fairness. Her family situation was unfair. So was the curfew that got her expelled from school. Being a Jew instead of a Jackie Kennedy was unfair. So was being mistreated because you were a Jew. And now Jews were being killed for trying to cure the awful incivility Negroes faced in the South.

She burned to go South, but didn't. Still, she turned up the heat. She was seventeen, a junior in high school and president of her class, when she discovered the opposite sex. "I had a boyfriend, lovely guy," and so did her best friend. "We were the only four in the class who would have sex. Other people had more self-restraint. So the four of us would double date all the time." She played "bingo" with spermacides she bought herself.

When it came time for college, Ledeen wanted Barnard, but her parents vetoed her choice of a school in dangerous New York City. So she went to Syracuse University, close to home, where "everybody was Jewish except my roommate, the daughter of a Missouri Synod Lutheran minister who believed the Jews killed Jesus," she says. Ledeen took an instant dislike to Syracuse. She was horrified when she realized some of her fellow students didn't know how to use a library and cared more about football and sororities than poetry and philosophy. She'd escape when she could to visit her boyfriend at school in Wisconsin. By November, she had decided to transfer. The latest thing in college was work/study programs. Few colleges had them, but Beloit, an experimental school near her boyfriend's in Wisconsin, did. "It was me, because I didn't want to be in school anymore. I wanted to go do stuff."

AT COLUMBIA UNIVERSITY, Mark Rudd quickly hooked up with the campus radicals. "The guy who introduced me to what you might call an anti-imperialist analysis was John Jacobs," Rudd says. Jacobs (b. 1947), known as J.J., was a Russian revolution buff who'd worked for a leftist newspaper before entering the class of 1969 and joining the May 2nd Movement that summer. Named for the first antiwar demonstration in New York in 1964, May 2nd was a front for Progressive Labor, a breakaway faction of the Communist Party that followed the teachings of Chinese Communist leader Mao Tse-Tung. It had sponsored the Duffy Square protest in which Jim Fouratt had been arrested the year before.

J.J. was in thrall to revolutionary rhetoric. By the end of that school year, Rudd, in thrall of J.J., was organizing his first antiwar protest. Furious over the escalation of the war, he'd started seeing himself as an outsider in his own culture, and when he began smoking marijuana that year, it reinforced that feeling. "It's thirty-three years later, and I haven't stopped," he says. "The entire time, it's been illegal. That's made me an outlaw. I like that. Maybe if they made it legal, I'd stop."

In March 1966, Rudd and other members of the Columbia Independent Committee on Vietnam joined a crowd of about 40,000 people who marched down Fifth Avenue against the war. "We had snotty signs that read, 'READ BOOKS!,'" he says. That month, Buddhist monks in Vietnam kept the pressure on and demonstrators burned the U.S. Consulate in Hue before the new prime minister, Nguyen Cao Ky, used troops to end the rebellion. "I remember distinctly being moved by this," Rudd says.

After a summer spent hitchhiking solo through Europe, Rudd returned to school, where he first heard of Students for a Democratic Society. SDS was a descendent of the Intercollegiate Socialist Society founded in 1905 by Clarence Darrow and Jack London. It was reborn shortly after one of its leaders, Tom Hayden, visited San Francisco in the wake of the 1960 protest against HUAC, and made a Lourdes-like pilgrimage to the steps of City Hall.

In 1962, just after John Kennedy called for the nation to build fallout shelters, SDS was among the groups that drew several thousand anti-nuclear protesters to Washington. That June, Hayden wrote a document for the group's convention that would become known as the Port Huron Statement. "We are people of this generation, bred in at least modest comfort, housed now in universities, looking uncomfortably to the world we inherit," was the stirring start of the otherwise interminable manifesto. That December, Bob Dylan, whose antiwar song "Blowin' in the Wind," recorded by the folk trio Peter, Paul and Mary, had just hit the Top Ten, turned up at the annual SDS convention. Protest had gone pop.

Inspired by SNCC and Martin Luther King's stirring March on Washington, SDS devised an earnest program to organize the urban poor. The following summer, as hundreds of college students flooded rural Mississippi, SDS was operating in northern slums. Then, in April 1965, SDS drew 20,000 students to Washington, D.C., for the largest antiwar demonstration in U.S. history.

SDS began attracting more recruits, becoming a refuge for members of the May 2nd Movement, which disbanded early in 1966. That June, James Meredith returned to the headlines when he began a one-man voter registration march, and was shot and wounded just as he crossed the Tennessee-Mississippi border. In response, civil rights leaders like Martin Luther King Jr., Whitney Young of the Urban League, Roy Wilkins of the National Association for the Advancement of Colored People, and Stokely Carmichael (b. 1941), leader of SNCC, took over Meredith's march for him. When Carmichael was arrested in Greenwood, Mississippi, something changed. He emerged from jail with a new battle cry: Black Power. Carmichael and another SNCC leader, H. Rap Brown (b. 1943), picked up the torch of the slain black nationalist leader Malcolm X. So did the Black Panther Party, born in Oakland, California, after Bobby Seale (b. 1936) met Huey Newton (b. 1942) at junior college in 1966. With their fiery rhetoric and threats of violence, these new-guard black activists split the civil rights movement in half. White radicals in awe of the black radicals' authenticity, but expelled from their organizations, also found a new home in SDS. That fall, a group of them formed a chapter at Columbia. It would soon overshadow its parent—and outrage parents across America—by igniting a revolutionary impulse in the crowded, roiling ranks of the nation's young.

Adolescence

IN FALL 1962, with his Harvard teaching contract about to expire, Timothy Leary set up the International Foundation for Internal Freedom (IFF), a commune based on one of Aldous Huxley's novels, *Island*, about a druggy utopia. At IFF, LSD was being served far more than science. Trouble loomed. In spring 1963, the first adverse reactions to the stuff were reported. People never came down, had their personalities shattered. A new anti-amphetamine law had just given the FDA control of experimental drugs, and it began cutting off the supply of LSD. But Leary had his own supply and agenda: to turn on America.[1] On Good Friday 1963, he gave students LSD in Boston University's chapel. The publicity—in the Harvard *Crimson* and then in the national press—was explosively negative. Harvard fired Alpert on May 27, 1963. Leary was relieved of his duties.[2]

Leary's next project, the establishment of psychedelic communities in Mexico and Dominica, did not bear fruit. He was rescued by Peggy Hitchcock (b. 1933), a grandchild of the founder of Gulf Oil and a descendent of the Pittsburgh Mellons and Long Island's polo-playing Hitchcocks. She'd come into Leary's psychedelic orbit after hearing about Alpert's psilocybin experiments from a fashion model friend.[3] Hitchcock had introduced Alpert to one of her brothers, William Mellon Hitchcock (b. 1939), a broker at Lehman Brothers. "Billy," who was married to a Venezuelan fashion model, was a rising financial star who had recently become acquainted with numbered Swiss bank accounts.[4] Alpert gave him books by J. D. Salinger and Thomas Mann, his sister convinced him to try mescaline, and Leary gave him LSD. Fascinated by his psychedelic experiences, he rented Leary a sixty-four-room Bavarian house on his family's 2,500-acre private shooting reserve in horsey Millbrook, New York, for $500 a month.[5]

When, on the very day John F. Kennedy was killed, Aldous Huxley also died of cancer, high on acid, Leary took the King of Psychedelia's throne and moved his court to Millbrook. At the end of 1963, he dissolved IFF, started Castalia, named after a colony from a Herman Hesse novel, *The Glass Bead Game*, and began proselytizing. In a *Playboy* interview, he claimed LSD improved sex. Soon seekers filled Millbrook's many bedrooms. In summer 1964, the future arrived on a bus that proclaimed it was going FURTHUR in front and warned, CAUTION: WEIRD LOAD, in back.

The man behind the wheel, Ken Kesey (b. 1935), had lived in the late-1950s bohemian academic community of Palo Alto, California, in which drug experimentation was ritual. Kesey tried psilocybin and LSD at a veterans hospital where CIA-sponsored drug experiments were being done, went to work there, and was inspired to write his first novel, *One Flew Over the Cuckoo's Nest*, published to great acclaim in February 1962. That summer, Neal Cassidy turned up at Kesey's door. Cassidy, who'd grown up surrounded by pimps and hobos, was a car thief and a sex-and-drug-charged improvisational speaker who became a hero in the novels of Jack Kerouac. Just out of jail for marijuana smuggling, he helped inspire Kesey and his friends to form the Merry Pranksters—a band of on-the-road consciousness explorers based on Robert Heinlein's science fiction novel about a mystic cult, *Strangers in a Strange Land*.

When Kesey finished a new book, he bought his bus and decided to paint it psychedelic and drive it to New York for his publication party. Later, Tom Wolfe, a reporter from *New York* magazine, would write about it all, and *The Electric Kool-Aid Acid Test* would become one of the most influential books of the decade, captivating impressionable teenagers as late as 1969, when it was published in paperback, spreading the story of how LSD crossed the line from property of Apollo to plaything for Dionysis. "LSD, peyote, mescaline, morning-glory seeds were becoming the secret new *thing* in the hip life," Wolfe wrote. ". . . and in the heart of even the most unhip mamma in all the U.S. of A. instinctively goes up the adrenal shriek: beatniks, bums, spades—*dope*." [6]

Millbrook proved too stodgy for The Merry Pranksters, who left quickly, declaring the East Coast acid academics constipated. As they drove away, they took the cutting edge of drug use with them.

In summer 1965, Kesey and the Pranksters held the first "Acid Test," a huge private party featuring LSD, Allen Ginsberg, strange sounds and a light show—a multimedia experience. Soon afterward, they did it again in San Jose, for the hip public, after a Rolling Stones concert. The band that night was the Warlocks, soon to be known as The Grateful Dead— led by Jerry Garcia (b. 1942), a guitar player who'd crashed Kesey's Palo Alto parties.[7] The Acid Test uncovered how many people were secretly taking drugs. Encouraged, Kesey decided to do it again and again—until these legal acid-rock parties made the papers. Then Stewart Brand (b. 1939), a post-Beat San Francisco biologist (who went on to found *The Whole Earth Catalog*), organized a commercial elaboration of the Acid Tests—the three-day Trips Festival, held at Longshoreman's Hall in January 1966. Three days before, Kesey, already arrested for marijuana possession in April 1965, was busted again, and forthwith jumped bail and disappeared. The Trips Festival made a nice profit, anyway, and *Time* magazine trumpeted the advent of the acidhead.

Kesey wasn't the only frontier scout in legal jeopardy. When Leary returned to Millbrook in spring 1965—a giddy marriage to a fashion model ended abruptly after a sobering honeymoon in India—things were a mess and the money was running out. That April, he and Alpert began commercializing their crusade, giving lectures with sound-and-light shows in a Greenwich Village theater he rented with Billy Hitchcock, selling LSD T-shirts and charging visitors for drug-free weekend "trips" to Millbrook.[8] He was becoming *too* visible. That Christmas, Leary, his kids and a new girlfriend took off for Mexico to meet Hitchcock. Leary was arrested at the border for a stash of drugs found in daughter Susan's underwear. Incensed, Hitchcock set up a legal defense fund to which he was the primary contributor.[9] Nonetheless, in March, Leary was sentenced to thirty years in Texas state prison. In April, while free on bail pending appeal, he was arrested again in a raid on Millbrook, led by a Duchess County district attorney named G. Gordon Liddy (who would later come to national attention as a Watergate burglar). Liddy was running for Congress "on a plank which was largely Throw Hitchcock Out of Millbrook," Billy later told a family biographer.[10]

The legal lashing was accompanied by a media campaign. Accounts of bad trips flooded the press, three congressional subcommittees announced hearings, and anti-LSD legislation was quickly drafted. That July, legal LSD research officially ended. A new Bureau of Drug Abuse Control began to root out underground supplies. By October, LSD was illegal in every state of the union.[11] All around the country, Baby Boom kids began to wonder, What was the fuss about?

The counterculture, the Youthquake, had overtaken America. Miniskirts were the new fashion. Ronald Reagan was elected governor of California in 1966, in part by running against the "insolent, ungrateful" students of Berkeley, but he couldn't hold back the tide. There was more and more crossover between radical culture and the rebel young. A writer in the *San Francisco Examiner* had coined the term "hippie" in September 1965 to describe the 15,000 long-haired young people who'd taken over Haight-Ashbury. Groups promoting marijuana and sexual freedom flourished in San Francisco. So did the new psychedelic rock culture. That summer and fall, groups like The Jefferson Airplane, The Great Society and Country Joe and The Fish emerged. In October, The Family Dog, a hippie collective, began promoting concerts at Longshoreman's Hall. Bill Graham, manager of the San Francisco Mime Troupe, promoted his first concert, starring The Jefferson Airplane, the Warlocks, Lawrence Ferlinghetti and the Fugs, in November 1965, as a benefit for the troupe featuring a tinfoil-lined garbage can full of LSD-infused Kool-Aid.[12] Astonished at the crowd, he promoted another the following month, starring the Airplane and the Grateful Dead, at the soon-to-be-famous Fillmore Auditorium. A month after that, Ken Kesey and the Merry Pranksters pulled into town for another of their Acid Tests.

The counterculture wasn't monolithic. While groups like the Diggers were giving away free food and clothes to the hippies, Graham was a prototype of the hip capitalist, promoting rock shows for profit. Despite the legal problems facing Leary and Kesey, their drug promotion schemes had also spawned commercial elaborations. In January 1966, The Psychedelic Shop opened on Haight Street and became the prototype for the head shops selling drug paraphernalia that sprouted like magic mushrooms nationwide.

That summer, as ghettos exploded again, the hip found common cause with political hotheads. Anger about a curfew on the Sunset Strip in West Hollywood boiled over into a riot, inspiring a hit song by a new band, Buffalo Springfield, that began, "There's something happening here/What it is ain't exactly clear." Increasingly clear was that a culture of opposition was rising—and it had a visual symbol. Despite a new ban on burning draft cards, they were going up in flames at demonstrations coast to coast.

IT WAS 1966. The Marlette family had just moved to a Navy air base in central Florida, where their younger son spent his last year in high school as his father prepared to ship out to Vietnam on the *U.S.S. Enterprise*. Doug Marlette had no idea there was a peace movement. He believed what he was told: we were winning and the undeclared war would be over soon.

The sudden move to Florida had stunted his social life again. He didn't date. Back in Laurel, he would have started on the basketball team. Instead, he drew for the high school paper and was taken with a hippie teacher who spoke of Bob Dylan and death-of-God theology. When Marlette went back to Mississippi to visit friends, he found he was "leaving them behind," he says. "I made them uneasy. I was asking questions about things nobody had thought about." In Florida, he started asking his father the same questions, just to get under his skin. He'd talk about a black person he'd met. "I smelled him, but I didn't smell anything," he'd say.

Marlette's mother had an emotional breakdown after her husband shipped out. With Doug's brother in college, at sixteen, he became the man of the house. He got a job at the local paper, the *Sanford Herald*, drawing cartoons of local sports figures for a couple bucks a pop. In short order, he graduated to the art department of the *Orlando Sentinel*. He enrolled at the local community college. Though he still sometimes fantasized about working for *Mad* or becoming a political cartoonist like Pat Oliphant, an Australian then making cartoon waves, Marlette's ambitions stayed small. Drawing decorations for church socials had given him the idea he might one day become a sign painter. He met his first girlfriend at church, the daughter of a local attorney whose family offered the stability his no longer had.

Marlette was simultaneously being pulled out of his cocoon by cartoons like those of Jules Feiffer, whose "Upper West Side, Jewish, intellectual sensibility spoke to a fifteen-year-old towheaded Mississippi Baptist," he says. In 1968, Doug discovered *Zap Comix*, R. Crumb's wildly outrageous sex-and-dope-filled underground comic books. "I felt woozy, like I'd entered someone else's dream," he says. People would try to get him to draw underground comics and he refused. "I considered it preaching to the converted. Hippies already knew. I wanted to sow seeds of sedition among the straight and comfortable."

AUGUSTUS OWSLEY STANLEY III (B. 1935), like his grandfather, a Kentucky governor and U.S. senator, felt called upon to serve his fellow Americans. Expelled from prep school for rum-running for his classmates in the ninth grade, he arrived at Berkeley in 1963 and got into the drug business by cooking up a batch of methedrine in his girlfriend's school lab. After a failed attempt to make LSD, Owsley moved to Los Angeles and embarked on a quest to make it with pharmaceutical purity. Though he produced less than half a kilo in his entire career, that was a substantial amount, and he knew how to share with others.

Acid was still legal, so Owsley was able to buy 460 grams of lysergic acid, the material LSD is made from, stored half of it in safe deposit boxes under false names, and whipped up the rest. Soon, people all over the West Coast were asking for Owsley and his acid. Moving to San Francisco, he became part of the Pranksters' scene, survived a serious acid freak-out, and spent what profits he made on equipment for the Grateful Dead.[13]

Across the Bay, Tim Scully and his tenant Don continued their quest for enlightenment. Scully read *Heaven and Hell* and *The Doors of Perception* by Huxley. Finally, the pair set out to find some LSD. "We were doing it in search of a mystical experience," Scully recalls. As they came down from their first trip, one of them said, "You know, we could make this stuff and give it away."

Scully's first trip, on April 15, 1965, was taken on acid Owsley had made in L.A. that spring. In the months that followed, as Scully failed to find a source of lysergic acid, he kept hearing about Bear, as Owsley was called by friends. Scully was looking for the chemist when the man himself turned up in Berkeley that fall, having met a girl at Kesey's who was renting a room from Scully. Owsley had gotten wind of Scully's interest in LSD manufacture and his appreciation for alchemy—now turning toward the transmutation of consciousness into cosmic gold. Owsley was also interested in Scully's knack for electronics, so Scully helped build sound equipment for the Dead, hoping to pass an acid test of his own and getting to make acid with the master. "Bear thought that we were almost certain to go to jail," Scully says. "He didn't want to end up feeling guilty for getting this naive kid sent away for a long time, so he tried to make it hard for me."

Midway through his junior year at Berkeley, Scully dropped out and moved to Los Angeles, where the Pranksters (minus Kesey, but with the addition of Hugh Romney, a Beat poet and comic who would later join a commune called the Hog Farm and take the name Wavy Gravy) were running Acid Tests. Scully built a mixing board for the Dead that would allow them to record their shows and practice sessions. Then he ran the board at the Pranksters' second L.A. event, the Watts Acid Test, which took place on Lincoln's Birthday, 1966, in a vacant warehouse in Compton, California, later the birthplace of gangsta rap.[14] At Romney's urging, two garbage cans full of Kool-Aid were placed on the floor, one pure, the other laced with LSD. Despite cryptic warnings, some attendees drank the drugged batch by accident. When one girl freaked out, several Pranksters filmed her and broadcast her wails. Behind his mixing board, Scully was upset by their callousness, but he stayed with the troupe through several more events in the next few months.

Scully wasn't *on the bus*, as Tom Wolfe famously put it; the band traveled and lived separate from the Acid Test crew. The fun of playing roadie for the Dead, renting a house and buying groceries for its extended family, setting up and tearing down equipment, not to mention losing his virginity and doing lots of acid and pot, more than made up for Scully's discomfort with the Pranksters' approach to psychedelia. "It felt a lot like running away to join the circus," he says. Meanwhile, Owsley pressed the last of his processed acid into 2,000 primitive tablets in the attic of the house Scully had rented for the band in East Los Angeles.

Scully wanted to make enough acid to turn on the world before the government's inevitable crackdown. "I had the fantasy that people who took psychedelics might produce a culture that was less likely to trash the planet, less likely to have wars," he says. That Owsley sold half his production and gave away the rest was a turn-on, as was the chemist's aim to make acid purer than that manufactured by Sandoz or Eli Lilly.

Finally, Owsley decided to set up a new lab and go back into production. He had to be more careful, since possession of LSD had become a misdemeanor in California that August, so he found a house in Port Richmond, near Berkeley, where emissions from an oil refinery would camouflage the smell of a lab. Though he had Eli Lilly's LSD formula, it didn't describe how to make a lot of acid in very pure form or how to stabilize the compound so it wouldn't decompose. Scully remembers countless conversations about purity and yield, and believes he contributed improvements to the process, which finally produced twenty grams of the purest LSD ever made. Scully had passed the acid test.[15]

Owsley was an instinctive marketer. They began naming their product—one batch of white tablets was called White Lightning. Then they made up five batches of 3,600 doses each and dyed them five different colors, hoping to confuse authorities as to the source. An unintended side effect: Buyers thought each color had different effects, and by and large preferred the pills they called Blue Cheer and Purple Haze.

AT UNION COLLEGE, Michael Fuchs was a political science major. As a freshman, he supported the war in Vietnam. By 1965, he'd grown skeptical. But Fuchs was no radical, politically or culturally. He remembers being unimpressed upon seeing the Beatles for the first time. "Their music was cutesy, they were foreign, a novelty. I didn't feel that they were taking me anywhere." Neither was basketball. He went out for the freshman team, but after realizing that "Union was not a great athletic power," he quit to play lacrosse. He couldn't commit to a fraternity, either. After living in a frat house his sophomore year, "I de-brothered," he says. "I have an enormously independent streak, and I didn't find any terrific benefits in fraternity life." Union was a party school, and he took advantage. "College in those days was alcohol; marijuana had just come in," Fuchs says. Skidmore, an all-girls college, was nearby, "so we were on the road a lot."

Despite his surface straightness, Fuchs embodied several clichés about the baby boom. Defiance was already his posture. He's been fired from every single job he's ever held, beginning with one at a summer camp in the early 1960s. "I was very outspoken," he says, "and it took me a while to understand I didn't deal with authority very well." He had no interest in SDS or in going to Mississippi, either. "I'm not a joiner," he says. He wasn't worried about making a living. "I wasn't anxious to get a job," he says. "I knew I was going to have to work the rest of my life. I thought this was the time to have fun."

EXCELLING IN SCHOOL, Leslie Crocker Snyder was named to Case Western's National Moot Court team and made an editor of the Law Review in 1965. She met a Cleveland criminal lawyer who let her work on cases. Then she applied for a summer job at one of the city's top firms. The interviewer didn't look at her when she walked in. "Sit down, Mr. Crocker," he said. Then he winced. "I'm sorry, but we don't hire women." Furious, she flew to New York and found work there, but the experience rankled.

In 1966, after graduating at the top of her class, Snyder returned to New York and became one of two new women hires at a large law firm that put her to work doing research and writing briefs. In the little spare time she had, she made some friends, visited the Village, went to Bill Graham's new Manhattan concert hall the Fillmore East, and sniffed around the New York scene. Briefly, she worked for Robert Kennedy, then a New York senator, in 1967. "I was still hung up on John Kennedy, Camelot and all that," she says.

A partner in her firm invited her into a contract conversation with one of the Rolling Stones, who then asked her to join him for a long weekend in London. "I was so straight, I said no," she reports. (And so unimpressed, she can't recall which Stone it was.) Snyder thinks skipping grades and always being two years younger than her peers put her at a social disadvantage that wound up a plus. "Because I was ahead of myself, I just missed it," she says wistfully of the 1960s. "It's like a train that's coming toward you; you're aware of it, but you're not hit by it."

Late in 1967, bored with her job, Snyder decided to apply for a new one as a criminal prosecutor with the United States Attorney's Office. But women weren't allowed in the federal prosecutor's criminal division. That same day, she applied for jobs with Legal Aid and the New York District Attorney, Frank Hogan. Though he was hardly a forward-thinker—he was the DA who prosecuted Lenny Bruce for obscenity—Hogan was willing to hire women. The interviewer at Legal Aid told her right up front how unhappy she'd be there; Hogan saw fit to ask repeatedly if she'd ever been married. "Mr. Hogan, I really think if I'd been married I'd remember that," she replied. He regarded her oddly and offered her a job working on legal appeals. She explained that if she was going to take a 50 percent pay cut, she wanted to do criminal work. He was offended. "I decide where my people will go," he huffed. "Women do very well in the Appeals Bureau." In that case, she told him she'd stay with her law firm. He asked her to sit outside for a few moments.

To this day, Snyder isn't sure what happened then. "He was a great DA, but he was a patriarchal moralist," she says. "Was he worried I was gay? Aberrant? Living in sin?" Hogan finally offered her a job trying misdemeanors—low-level criminal prosecutions. Snyder was a natural; she quickly blossomed in her job—and pleased Hogan by getting engaged.

WHILE DONALD TRUMP was in the military academy, "the world changed a lot," he says. "When I first went up there, the military was like God. In my last year, 1964, it was almost looked down on. It was the beginning of twenty years of turmoil."

Those changes stayed outside the walls of the school. Cadets were only allowed to see television on weekends. They weren't taught about *Brown v. Board of Education*, or the civil rights movement, or the Buddhist revolts in Vietnam. "They were teaching me how to march," Trump says. "You marched to meals, to class, to almost everything." Trump was marching when President Kennedy was shot.

He feels lucky to have been so sheltered. "Because it could be that I would have gone very strongly the other way, very, very strongly the other way. But you see, I didn't have a lot of exposure to it; I knew people who would just as soon shoot a beatnik as talk to him—literally. I mean, if they had the opportunity and were guaranteed not to get caught, they'd shoot as many as they could."

In 1964, Trump enrolled in Fordham University, a Jesuit school in New York City. After a year commuting from his parents' home, he got his first apartment in Manhattan, but he was still under close scrutiny. "The Jesuits had an almost militarylike grip over that school," Trump says. In 1966, rejecting the alternative of film school, he transferred to the Wharton School of Finance at the University of Pennsylvania. "Ultimately, I decided that real estate was a better business, and that maybe I could put show business into the real estate business," he says, "which I've done."

Trump noticed hippies, of course. "They were very idealistic, and I thought that was good. But I didn't look favorably upon them because they were always very dirty." He agreed with them on one point; he was opposed to the war in Vietnam. Trump "saw it as a terrible deal," he says. "The tremendous conflict at home, while well-intentioned, gave the other side an incentive to keep going, because they knew this country was being ripped apart from within."

Trump wasn't much for rock 'n' roll. "I was never somebody that liked watching the game; I liked to play the game," he says. Which partly explains why CBS founder William Paley's commencement speech at Wharton in spring 1968 made a bigger impression on him than the killings of Martin Luther King and Bobby Kennedy in the weeks just before. The next year, he would not be among the throngs at the Woodstock festival, either. "I thought they were crazy!"

Trump had fun, though. "I don't think anybody had more sex than I did," he boasts. "I didn't do drugs. I wasn't a drug guy. But there was a lot of sex. Sex was all over the fucking place. At Penn it was wild. And after I got out, it was even wilder."

He was already making deals, too, making money. While he was still at Wharton, he and his father bought a townhouse development in Cincinnati, fixed it up, got rid of old tenants, raised rents, and made a big profit.[16] He did the same with a series of small properties in Philadelphia, renovating and selling them. When he arrived back in Manhattan in summer 1968, his net worth was already $200,000. "I was always able to make a lot of money, for whatever reason," he says. "It's like a kid, three years old, sits down and he's playing Mozart. I was doing deals, and they were really cool deals."

Donald outshone his brother, nine years his senior and his father's designated heir. "Fred Jr. was a great guy, a nice guy, too nice," Donald says. "He had a great personality. He was very handsome. I learned a lot from him. But he wasn't somebody who enjoyed business. Which taught me one thing: if you're not into something, don't do it. Fred was a really good pilot. That's what he liked doing, and that's what he should have done. Instead, he went into the business, and he didn't like it. If you don't love it, you're not going to be good at it; he didn't, and it was very tough on him."

Fred Trump Jr., an alcoholic, died in 1980.

WHEN RUSSELL SIMMONS'S family moved to Hollis, Queens, it was a middle-class neighborhood of small businesses and homes with basements and neat front lawns. Simmons was in a fifth-grade class at P.S. 135—his parents had moved so he would be eligible to be bused to the better, integrated school—when Martin Luther King Jr. was killed.

Influence flowed to new leaders. In the fourth grade, Simmons saw his first speech by the separatist Nation of Islam's Louis Farrakhan (b. 1933). "I think everybody my age who is black and came from the lower middle class or any ghetto in America saw Minister Farrakhan speak." But Simmons was multicultural. At home in Hollis, he had black friends; at school he hung out with Jewish kids from nearby Queens Village.

Simmons played baseball with the Hilltop Little League. "It was all white except every team would have two or three black guys," he says. "They were mostly all Jewish, but the funny thing is, the All-Star Team was all niggers—except there was a great Italian pitcher, and Ricky Farina, who I'd always thought was white. I find out one day he's Puerto Rican."

Simmons gives thanks for busing "every fucking day," he says. "I had a lot of white friends, more than most people, because I was integrated, and it did affect my whole life. All of us got something out of being bused, because you learned to feel better about being in the white world. A lot of times I'm still the only black guy in the room. But I'm not aware of it, because I've been that a lot."

IN 1967, JOHN Gage was back in school, and running the math section at Cody's, a Berkeley bookstore. He smoked dope and drove a yellow Volkswagen convertible, but didn't get caught up in the new counterculture. His was not a Summer of Love. His girlfriend, a childhood polio victim, was an organizer for the rights of the disabled and was busy demanding wheelchair access to the Bay Area Rapid Transit subway system, then being built. They thought the hippie world was kid stuff. Local politics and poverty were more serious and had a grimmer edge. "I tried to keep a thin, continuous stream of hedonism, but not sink in it," Gage says.

There was more than enough to sink into. If the myriad events of 1967 and 1968 have been shorthanded to a Baby Boom mantra, consider how in any other time each one would have stood out as extraordinary.

At the First Human Be-In in San Francisco on January 14, 1967, Timothy Leary told the crowd to "tune in, turn on, and drop out"—facilitated by free Owsley acid. On March 26 another "be-in" was held in New York, and on April 15, 400,000 protesters marched on the United Nations, protesting the Vietnam War. Half a million marched in San Francisco.

On May 2, the Black Panthers gained national attention by invading the California Legislature, carrying M1 rifles. On May 20, the New York Diggers, a local version of San Francisco's free soup troupe, dropped dollar bills gathered from drug dealers, disco owners, and liberals from the spectator's gallery of the New York Stock Exchange (which was glassed in shortly thereafter).[17] Twelve days later, the Beatles released their psychedelic magnum opus, *Sergeant Pepper's Lonely Heart's Club Band*. On its heels, Paul McCartney told television viewers worldwide that the Beatles had taken LSD. Acid never got a better endorsement.

A race riot consumed Newark, New Jersey, that summer, leaving 20 dead and 1,500 injured, and another in Detroit lasted a week, resulting in 43 deaths and $400 million in property damage; there were more eruptions nationwide.

Congress ended draft deferments for graduate students on July 2. Then in short order and nearly the same breath the Beatles endorsed legalization of marijuana, and then promptly renounced the drugs and the hippie culture they'd helped create and took off on a pilgrimage (along with Mick Jagger and his girlfriend Marianne Faithfull) to hear transcendental meditation guru Maharishi Mahesh Yogi at a retreat in Wales. There word reached them of their manager Brian Epstein's death from an accidental overdose of sleeping pills. In October, the San Francisco Diggers sealed the coffin on the Summer of Love with a piece of street theater called "Death of Hippie, Loyal Son of Media, Birth of Free Man."

On October 22 national antiwar demonstrations culminated in the Exorcism of the Pentagon, a wacky attempt to levitate the building, which led to 647 arrests. Among those detained was author Norman Mailer, who parlayed the experience into a Pulitzer Prize with his book *The Armies of the Night*. On New Year's Eve, Berkeley activist Jerry Rubin joined with civil rights worker Abbie Hoffman, publisher Paul Krassner, acticvitst Robin Morgan and others to announce the formation of Yippie!, the Youth International Party. On Vietnamese New Year, January

30, 1968, the South Vietnamese liberation movement, known as the Viet Cong, launched the Tet Offensive—a mass attack on the South and American troops that snowballed American public opinion against the war. On March 8, students rioted in Warsaw. On March 12, antiwar senator Eugene McCarthy won 42 percent of the vote in the Democratic primary in New Hampshire. Four days later, Robert Kennedy announced that he, too, would run for president.

On March 31, a bitter, tired Lyndon Johnson announced a bombing halt in Vietnam and his decision not to seek reelection. Five days later, the Rev. Martin Luther King was shot and killed in Memphis, Tennessee, engendering riots nationwide.[18] On April 23, students occupied buildings at Columbia University in New York. May ushered in the Southern Christian Leadership Conference's Poor People's March on Washington, and student and worker uprisings in Paris, across Europe, and behind the Iron Curtain, where Prague Spring was under way.

Between mid-May and mid-June, H. Rap Brown, Catholic activist Phillip Berrigan, Baby Boom baby doctor Benjamin Spock and Yale University chaplain William Sloan Coffin were all sentenced and/or convicted for political activities. Andy Warhol was shot by Valerie Solanis, leader of a one-woman proto-feminist group she dubbed SCUM (The Society for Cutting Up Men). Two mornings later, on June 5, moments after he won the California primary, Bobby Kennedy was killed by a Palestinian named Sirhan Sirhan. In August, 10,000 demonstrators disrupted the Democratic Convention in Chicago, chanting "The whole world is watching," as it did—on television.

NEW YORK'S HIPPIE scene coalesced around Saint Mark's Place in the neighborhood newly dubbed the East Village, where rents were bottom-dollar. On October 6, 1966, the day California banned LSD, a group of young people held A Psychedelic Celebration in nearby Tompkins Square Park, burned incense and chanted "Hare Krishna" with a swami.[19] Swamis were suddenly everywhere, along with yogis, Buddhists,, and psychedelics, which were either illegal, like LSD, or too new to have attained that status, like DMT and STP. If people weren't taking drugs, they were likely still breaking some law or another. Ed Sanders, who ran a beat bookstore in the neighborhood, and Tuli Kupferberg were singing obscene songs at the Player's Theater with their ragged parody of a rock band, The Fugs. At the Dom, on Saint Mark's, Andy Warhol's Exploding Plastic Inevitable, starring the Velvet Underground and Nico, was a regular freak scene. Upstairs at the Balloon Farm, a New York version of the

Trips Festival briefly came down to earth. In February 1967, Timothy Leary's League for Spiritual Discovery opened a headquarters in the West Village attended by Leary, his Harvard colleague Alpert, and a batch of beats: Allen Ginsberg, Gregory Corso and William Burroughs.

Ginsberg felt New York needed its own Be-In. "Somebody has got to do it," he said. "I'm not going to."[20] Jim Fouratt and his boyfriend stepped into the breach, proposing an event on Easter Sunday. "I had learned that how you live your life is politics," Fouratt says. "You find similar people who share your values, and you conspire." Artist Peter Max, another prototype hippie entrepreneur whose psychedelic paintings became the Hallmark cards of the counterculture, agreed to create and pay for 40,000 Day-Glo notices, which a pack of private school kids plastered all over the city. The organizers had agreed the event would embody the hippie values of peace, love and ego transcendence, so when Max put his name on the notices, they made him reprint them—"the only time the proprietary yogi took his name off anything," Fouratt says, chuckling.

That spontaneous Sunday, Central Park played host to about 10,000 hippies, dressed in the finest thrift-shop regalia, faces painted, fists filled with kites, balloons and daisies. They danced in the meadows, climbed the trees, and cavorted with bemused refugees from the city's Easter Parade. "A lot of people think it was about LSD, but that was not the point, in my mind," says Fouratt, who now views it as the last completely uncorrupted moment of the era. The only time police threatened the action was when two men took off their clothes. A crowd quickly gathered, chanting, "We love cops," and the men in blue turned back.[21]

The Be-In gave Fouratt a sense of purpose—a way to stay in the spotlight and do good simultaneously. He quit the Actor's Studio. "The theater is in the streets," he says. "It's not on Broadway. I was really upset when I didn't get an Obie Award for it. I thought it was the most theatrical thing that happened that year."

More followed. They called them "goofs"—little pieces of street theater meant to befuddle the straights and attract new recruits to the hippie thing. They were often staged by New York's Group Image, a media-savvy Digger-like band specializing in cultural agitation and propaganda. Papers like the *Village Voice* spread the word, and Fouratt played his hand among the new media cropping up all around the movement: underground newspapers like the *East Village Other* and the *Berkeley Barb*; sexually explicit underground comics like *Zap*; "progressive" radio stations broadcasting on the FM band; the rock press, led by *Crawdaddy* and *Rolling Stone*; and mass-market magazines like *Cheetah* and Hearst's *Eye*, for which Fouratt wrote up happenings he would then create, so his New York column looked current when it ran three months.

Outside New York City and San Francisco, this new medium hit like bolts from the blue. Boomers poured into the hippie centers, the East Village and the Haight, to see for themselves, providing ready clientele for more long-haired capitalists, who opened countless psychedeli-catessens selling posters, black lights, hippie clothes and buttons bearing assorted slogans as well as random obscenity, beatnik books, rock records and drug paraphernalia—and often the drugs themselves.

Getting along just fine on extra work, odd jobs and unemployment insurance, Fouratt, armed with his trusty Gestetner mimeograph machine (donated by a *Voice* journalist prior to the Be-In), opened a Communica-tion Company of his own, aimed at disseminating information the way the Diggers did in San Francisco. It got put to use fast when on Memorial Day seventy policemen and more than two hundred hippies clashed in Tompkins Square Park over the right to play music and sit on the grass. Within hours, Fouratt was printing out directions to the night court where beaded, barefoot kids were being arraigned. The next day, the Communications Company spread the news that a section of the park had been declared a troubadours' area. All charges were eventually dropped. "The Tompkins Square riot really galvanized the politicization of the hippie movement," Fouratt says.

He acknowledges that he had multiple agendas to fulfill—his progres-sive Catholic's need to do good, his ego's need to lead and his desire for sexual and cultural freedom. "I became a hippie leader," he says. "I mean, it was cloaked in all kinds of feel-good stuff, but I didn't play unless I could be in charge."

The New York hippies had ties to radical groups around the country, which were moving toward larger antiwar actions. In June 1967, a faction of SDS held a national meeting called "Back to the Drawing Boards" at a rustic camp in Michigan to rethink its agenda. Diggers and hippies crashed it, "trying to get them to take acid, essentially," says Fouratt, whose overt homosexuality didn't go over well with the self-serious macho men of SDS. He, on the other hand, admired them "because they really wanted to not adjust," he says. "They wanted to change the world." Fouratt also admired the butch Digger King Emmett Grogan and his out-rageous band of renegades, who had visited New York in March.

New alliances were forming all over, like the one linking Fouratt with civil rights activist turned hippie organizer Abbie Hoffman. Hoffman (b. 1936) was a graduate of Brandeis who'd worked as a pharmaceutical drug salesman until the early 1960s, when, inspired by both the civil rights movement and drugs, he became a full-time activist. Asked to leave SNCC along with other whites, he moved to the East Village and met Fouratt when both briefly worked as youth liaisons for New York's liberal Republican mayor, John Lindsay. "Abbie was trying to figure out how to co-opt the energy for his agenda," he says. "A lot of the hippie kids trusted me. They did not trust Abbie. And Abbie was smart enough to recognize that."

Suddenly, they were New York Diggers; emulating their San Francisco counterparts, they ladled out free stew and opened a store where everything was free. Fouratt renamed himself Jimmy Digger. Hoffman printed a guide to street survival called *Fuck the System*, using city Youth Board funds.

Homosexuality clearly put him off. Abbie wouldn't even acknowledge Fouratt's boyfriend. Though his lover warned him not to trust Hoffman, Abbie struck Fouratt as a cross between Lenny Bruce and Groucho Marx, and he got more involved with the older radical. "Abbie was always trying to fix me up with some hippie chick," Fouratt says, laughing. They began planning actions together. A huge disco, the Electric Circus, had just opened on Saint Mark's Place, with a big dance floor, bands, and a foam rubber room. George Plimpton attended the opening night party; the East Village and hippies were becoming chic.[22] The Diggers planted a tree in a mound of dirt out front.

That spring and summer, the Diggers tossed soot bombs outside the headquarters of Con Edison, New York's electric and gas company; formed the Committee of Concerned Honkies to deliver food to riot-torn Newark ("Diggersareniggers," Hoffman wrote under the pseudonym George Metesky; Fouratt was detained by police for refusing to specify his gender); shot off cap pistols at conferencing Socialists; and staged their invasion of the New York Stock Exchange. "War is profitable, and we wanted to show that," Fouratt says. "They stopped the clock, and people bent down and picked up the fucking dollars!" Hoffman and Fouratt were fired from their city jobs a few days later.

IN 1965, WHEN Cynthia Bowman was a rebellious sixteen, her father got her an apartment of her own and said that if she'd get a job, he'd pay for her to finish school at night. She started modeling at Bloomingdale's, the New York department store. "It really wasn't right," she says. "I was too young to be on my own." By summer 1967, her father had decided she was out of control and threatened to cut her off. Like the heroine of the Beatles song "She's Leaving Home," Bowman and thousands of others her age were hunting hard for freedom, fun, and "something inside that was always denied for so many years."

That and all the other songs on *Sergeant Pepper's Lonely Hearts Club Band* cast a mesmerizing spell on boomers. In the year since the Beatles' last LP, *Revolver*, the moptops had lost any lingering taint of cuteness when John Lennon told a reporter the band was more popular than Jesus—inspiring bonfires of their records in the Southern Bible Belt—and abruptly quit touring. Fueled by pot and acid, the twentysomething millionaires wrote and recorded their drug-soaked masterpiece.

Now it was out and had changed the world, immediately and indelibly. One day, as her father raged that he would no longer subsidize her lifestyle, Bowman nonchalantly flipped through *Time* magazine's new cover story, "The Hippies: Philosophy of a Subculture," while blithely inquiring how he expected her to pay for school. "If you're so smart" he yelled—she looked at a picture of the Grateful Dead, then of the Jefferson Airplane—"you figure it out!"

Bowman had an older girlfriend, Lexy, who'd "turned me on to pot and told me all about sex," she says. Lexy had just agreed to meet a guy in San Francisco. Cynthia took her to the airport in a taxi. At check-in, Lexy begged her, "Please, please come with me. What do you have to lose? You know you are going to die here by yourself." She didn't even have her purse. But tickets weren't expensive then. Late that night, she called her father from California. "I'm in a commune at Six-Thirty Lyon Street," she said, "and you need to go feed my dog and clear out my apartment. And could you send me my purse?"

"He was probably relieved," Bowman says now. "All he had to do was clean out an apartment and take a dog to the pound. Instead of having to deal with me anymore."

THE STUDENTS WHO joined SDS in the mid-1960s were different from the earnest radicals who'd started the organization. These new recruits saw radical students as the vanguard of a much larger movement. As an original SDS leader, Todd Gitlin, would later write, they were "breaking out of the postwar consensus . . . of complacency, good behavior and middle-class mores," allowing themselves to "break with adults, be done with compromises, *get on with it* . . ."[23]

In Mark Rudd's sophomore year, these impatient young radicals began confronting Columbia over its secret affiliation with the Institute for Defense Analyses (IDA) and its policy of allowing Marine Corps and

CIA recruitment on campus. Rudd spent the Summer of Love in an antidraft project in city summer schools. Stationed in a downtown SDS office, he planned rallies in front of high schools and offered draft counseling. And he started hanging out on the Lower East Side, "going to hear Country Joe and the Fish on Tompkins Square and dropping mescaline," he recalls.

That August, Rudd hitchhiked to California, stopping at the SDS National Office in Chicago, where the leadership gave him a book by Regis Debray about the Cuban revolution. The Americans were impressed by Debray's theory of the *foco*, a small vanguard band that could start a revolution when "their exemplary actions won over people ready to become radicalized," Rudd says. "You start doing it, you don't just talk about it, and that starts the revolution. We began to see ourselves as guerrillas within this country."

Rudd continued on to Haight-Ashbury at the tail end of the summer, when "the love had turned to hate on Haight, and there was a lot of drug-dealing and squalor." Then he went on to Los Angeles, where he stayed with SDS friends, and to San Diego, where he bunked in Herbert Marcuse's house, although the great man wasn't there at the time.

Back at school, Rudd skipped the Exorcism at the Pentagon, and was furious with himself afterward. A new friend, Jeff Jones from the SDS Regional Office, had gone and come back with wild stories. "I instantly realized that I had been on the wrong track; militancy and action was what was needed."

An argument began at Columbia that would split SDS there into two factions, dubbed the "praxis axis" and the "action faction." The former, led by the group's older founding chairman, was concerned with education and discussion, the latter with splatter. Like the Yippies and the Diggers, the action faction, younger students led by Rudd who'd seen the wisdom of Abbie Hoffman's ways, wanted to use street theater, massage the media, and turn on anyone who tuned in.

A month after the march on the Pentagon, Secretary of State Dean Rusk was set to give a speech to a Foreign Policy Association dinner at the Hilton Hotel. One of the peace groups had planned a legal picket, but the SDS Regional Office publicized a huge, unsanctioned street action— "Dine with the Warmakers"—and attracted a crowd of thousands. Deliberately provocative (they were armed with animal blood, red paint and eggs) and predictably provoked by charging police, they started a bloody riot that ended with forty-six arrests, Rudd's very first arrest among them.[24] Abbie Hoffman was one of his cellmates. "I don't think he paid any attention to me," Rudd admits. "I could see he had a lot of energy, but I also disagreed with him; I was more serious."

OWSLEY, THE ACID king, had finally decided to retire and train Tim Scully to take his place as the gourmet chef of LSD. Early in 1967, just after the San Francisco Be-In, Scully headed to Denver to find a lab of his own, where he expected to finish his training in the art of acid-making by processing the rest of Owsley's raw material. He also redesigned the lab equipment and tinkered with the Eli Lilly recipe so they could produce LSD on a grander scale. But when he came back to Berkeley for supplies, he discovered their success had a price. The authorities were on to them. Federal agents had been pressuring their suppliers for evidence against Owsley. "They didn't want to turn in their friend, so they turned me in," Scully says. When he came to pick up his order in the Sunshine Cookie truck he'd used as a Grateful Dead roadie, a Fed helped him load up and followed him.

He got away—and quickly learned evasive driving techniques. But the Feds always found him again. "It was terrifying until we realized they weren't about to swoop down and bust us, what they wanted to do was follow us," Scully says. "Every time I came back to California, they had my house staked out. So we had to lose them every time."

Then came another glitch: Owsley started playing cagey about the remaining raw materials. "I don't think it's the right time," he told Scully, handing him a 3-by-5 inch card with another recipe, for another psyche-delic drug, a mescaline derivative with an amphetamine kick, that would soon be named after the automotive additive STP. Thinking this yet another test—making LSD was complex, STP easier—Scully worked months refining the recipe. "I spent a lot of time in the library," he says.[25]

While Scully made STP in Denver, Owsley took off for New York, where he visited Leary and *his* master chef: Nick Sand of Brooklyn, a teenage bathtub chemistry prodigy who'd made batches of DMT (a fifteen-minute hallucinogen) and synthetic mescaline. Owsley also met Billy Hitchcock, who gave him financial advice and provided contacts to help him set up an offshore account for the $225,000 he'd stashed in a safe deposit box.

Under government surveillance, too, Hitchcock, Leary and Sand left Millbrook one by one and headed west. Leary showed up in San Francisco spouting megalomaniacal nonsense about buying land with money he didn't have and setting up his own country, based on freedom of mind, body and drug ingestion.[26] Scully knew Leary and didn't think much of him. "Thinking you're doing something that's saving the world is totally addictive," Scully allows, "but he was strident and flamboyant in promoting acid, which felt wrong to me." Leary was a media personality hurtling headlong toward martyrdom—and taking a lot of people down with him.

AFTER THE SUMMER of Love, the bloom quickly came off Flower Power. Converts and tourists crammed the tiny enclaves of the Haight and Saint Mark's Place, driving crime rates up and the original colonists into the country, where they made news again by forming communes, most of which did not last very long. Panhandlers replaced street theater. "You no longer had middle- and upper-class kids being hippies," Jim Fouratt says. "You had all these kids coming in who had no safety net and no place to stay. Then the Mob took over LSD distribution, and started mixing it with speed. Amphetamine is a great street drug, because you don't have to go to sleep."

It wasn't only the Mob. Nick Sand had arrived in San Francisco in July 1967 and set up an STP lab. Owsley had been handing out Tim Scully's version, which he'd turned into high-dosage tablets. STP was sold as better, stronger acid, but even after they taste-tested it and cut the dosage in half, the market didn't like it. Luckily, just as word hit the streets that Scully's new product was too strong and causing lots of bad trips, Owsley finally came up with the second half of his stash of lysergic acid. It turned out that his girlfriend had locked the stuff in a safe deposit box, but forgotten the bank branch where the box was.

By fall 1967, the tide had turned, perceptibly. After the Diggers had declared hippiedom dead in San Francisco, New York Diggers including Fouratt and Hoffman appeared on *The David Susskind Show* flailing a toy duck Groucho Marx-style each time Susskind said the word *hippie*. On that show, Fouratt pulled off another first, announcing his homosexuality on national television. "I was all dressed in white, Indian cotton shirt, blond hair, the sweetest thing you could possibly find," Fouratt recalls. "I said things you weren't supposed to say on television—I might have been on acid; I don't remember. We were just trying to shock David, because he was the ultimate sort of liberal."

In New York that month, a wealthy blond art student from the New York suburbs, Linda Rae Fitzpatrick (b. 1949), and James "Groovy" Hutchinson, (b. 1946), two kids who'd lived in a crash pad commune on East 11th Street and loved amphetamines, were found with their skulls bashed in by bricks in the boiler room of a tenement on Avenue B. "The flower thing is dead," an East Village neighbor told the *New York Times*. In December, the New York Digger Free Store closed down after it turned up at the center of a mess of drugs, informants, violence, Puerto Rican gangs and hippie factionalism, and the police started busting apartments full of runaways. The hippie moment passed quickly in the places where it was born, but rippled out across the country for two more years.

Even among the hippie activists, the mood had changed. Tussles ensued between Fouratt and Hoffman, by then heavy into drugs, Fouratt says. Hoffman and Robin Morgan (b. 1941), a former child star who'd married a leftist poet and become a civil rights worker, appropriated the Communications Company's mimeograph machine. Hoffman also absconded with a bail fund Fouratt had raised, but Fouratt was undeterred. "There was a movement going, and I wasn't going to be left out of it," he says. Hoffman's magnetic energy had attracted the Bay Area antiwar activist Jerry Rubin, an organizer of Berkeley's first Vietnam Day who'd come in second in a run for mayor there. When Rubin came to New York in late summer 1967, he and Hoffman became fast allies and were photographed together burning money.

Rubin had been invited to New York to help plan a peace march in Washington. It was decided that the protesters should encircle the Pentagon, perform an exorcism, and attempt to levitate it. By injecting surreal fun into the serious work at hand, Hoffman, Rubin, and their fellows captured the imagination of America's young. They made national news, too, when Hoffman said that police use of Mace would be countered with demonstrators' use of "Lace," an LSD-infused skin-penetrating compound that when sprayed on cops and soldiers would cause them to rip off their clothes and start having sex. Unfortunately, Lace was a fiction, the Pentagon did not fly, and Hoffman and his new wife, Anita (whom he'd married in a Be-In–like media event in Central Park), were arrested. They gave their names as Mr. and Mrs. Digger.

CYNTHIA BOWMAN LANDED in San Francisco just after the Summer of Love ended. Her first day in town, she steered her friend Lexy to the Jefferson Airplane mansion, a Greek Revival house with seventeen rooms facing Golden Gate Park. The Airplane were already stars of the Haight-Ashbury scene. Marty Balin (b. 1942), Paul Kantner (b. 1941), Jack Casady (b. 1944) and Jorma Kaukonen (b. 1940) had been folk and bluegrass musicians, and Balin had opened a folk-rock nightclub called the Matrix in 1965, where many of the local bands played. Employing the name of a fictitious bluesman (Blind Thomas Jefferson

Airplane); a former fashion model and singer, Grace Slick (nicked from a competing band called the Great Society); and two of that band's songs ("Somebody to Love" and "White Rabbit," which were fast becoming psychedelic anthems), the band was among the first from the new San Francisco scene to score a record contract, signing with RCA for $25,000 in 1966. The next June, Kantner's band played songs from their second album, *Surrealistic Pillow*, at the Monterey Pop Festival, where they were filmed by Victoria Leacock's father. Monterey became the ideal for every rock festival that followed. Driven by the two Top 40 hits, *Pillow*, recorded for $8,000, grossed $8 million.[27]

"We spent the next year dropping LSD every other day and sitting across the street from the Airplane mansion, waiting for them to come out," Bowman remembers. "I would just sit there and stare at the big house, as high as I could get, watching them come and go. The only reason I didn't do it every day was because acid only works every other day." Meanwhile, the seventeen-year-old became involved in her first love affair, with one of her fellow communards, the boy Lexy had followed to San Francisco. "She lasted about a week and then I moved in and we were together for several years," Bowman says. "I would cook the same thing every night. Tuna fish, noodles, and cream of mushroom soup."

One afternoon, Bowman was tripping down Haight Street in her hippie jeans when a man began menacing her in front of the Haight Theater, where the San Francisco Hell's Angels parked their motorcycles. "One of the Angels saw this guy jump on me and he jumped on the guy and threw him onto the roof of a car," she says. "And within three minutes there had to be fifty Hell's Angels there, all knocking the shit out of this guy. And I was just horrified, crying, terrified—more of the Hell's Angels than the guy." But she was about to see their angelic side. "I started trying to get away, walking back to my house, and these Hell's Angels escorted me, pushing their motorcycles to my house, and I remember walking up the steps and all the hippies ran out the back door, thinking the Angels were going to kill us," Bowman says, laughing.

That fall she got a job wrapping Christmas gifts at a San Francisco department store. After work her first night, she walked out into the unfamiliar city, and promptly fell into an excavation for the new Bay Area Rapid Transit subway system. A steel beam almost severed her foot. She began a series of repair operations. Released from the hospital, she'd go out, walk on the foot, "screw it up again," and end up back in the hospital.

Like so many who rode the second hippie wave following the Summer of Love, Bowman didn't think the Haight scene had soured at all. "I guess if you'd been here a year before you might have thought of it as a death of an era, but for me it was all new," she says. "Everybody was smoking pot and taking acid, and there was free music on the street."

In 1968 she, her boyfriend and another of their roommates established a commune near Stanford University in Palo Alto. Bowman took classes there in exchange for work as a guinea pig in its psychic research lab. For the next few years, she shared an essentially irresponsible existence with her boyfriend. "But graduate students were not nearly as crazy as the people in San Francisco," she says. "It was a nice house. We all had our own rooms and we ate real food and made money one way or another." In pursuit of nirvana, they smoked pot all the time and took psychedelic drugs regularly. "My boyfriend and I would set the clock for four A.M., then pop acid, go back to bed, and wake up high as kites. We would go to the Zen center, looking for spirituality. Actually, he was searching for it; I just wanted to get high, to tell you the truth."

AT THE END of 1967, Owsley Stanley (who, no longer junior to anyone, had legally dropped the "Augustus" and accompanying roman numerals,) liberated his remaining lysergic acid from its safe deposit box and telephoned Tim Scully.

"Now is the right time," he said.

They promptly headed to Denver to whip up more acid. For weeks, they "worked in shifts," Scully says. "I worked while Bear slept." The first batch was called Monterey Purple in honor of the Monterey Pop Festival. The profits, earmarked for more raw material purchases, went into offshore accounts set up by Billy Hitchcock, who'd moved to Sausalito with a new girlfriend, formed a partnership with a Swiss bank, and gotten a job at a new brokerage house happy to collect commissions and not look at his transactions too closely.[28]

Police were still following Scully everywhere. He'd even photographed one drug agent and published the picture in the *Berkeley Barb*. He remained determined to turn on the world—even after federal agents raided Owsley's tableting operation in Orinda, California, in December and Owsley decided the time had come to quit for good.[29] Scully had to get himself a backer, a new source for lysergic acid, and a large-scale distribution network. Owsley had briefly used the Hell's Angels, but Scully preferred not to deal with them.

He approached Hitchcock, whom he'd met through Owsley, suggesting that the Eastern heir finance his grand plan for a mass acid giveaway. Hitchcock wouldn't go that far, but according to Scully, agreed to bankroll him with loans and provided the name of a chemical broker in London. Hitchcock denies bankrolling the purchases of raw materials. "He did get repaid, and of course, he got lots of free acid," Scully insists.[30]

With the new source of supply in place, Scully got back to work. He and Sand each went off to set up labs—Sand's in St. Louis, Scully's back in suburban Denver. Before the year was out, they'd both been shut down. Scully's landlord had gotten a whiff of the lab while its occupants were out of town, thought it was a body, and called the cops. When Scully's assistants returned two days later, they were arrested. Scully called shortly afterward, and when an unknown voice answered, "Scully residence," he hitched a ride to Eureka, Oregon. "I tried it for a few days and decided not to be a fugitive. I just went back to living my life. So later, when I was *really* indicted, I didn't try to dodge it, because I'd decided already I'd rather pay the dues and have it over with."

Scully headed to Billy Hitchcock's place in Sausalito to hunker down and figure out what to do. While there, he met John Griggs, founder of the Brotherhood of Eternal Love, a band of drug-dealing hippies, born when a motorcycle gang of petty thieves first encountered LSD and retired their bikes and guns to run Mystic Arts World, an elaborate head shop in Laguna Beach, and a marijuana-smuggling operation. Griggs was another quasi-mystic who'd seen the truth on acid and wanted to make a new world. He'd incorporated the Brotherhood ten days after LSD was banned.[31] By mid–1968, the Brotherhood had spread its operation around the world, smuggling hashish from Afghanistan in Volkswagen buses and surfboards.

Griggs had bought a ranch near Palm Springs on Tim Leary's advice and invited his mentor to stay. Leary introduced him to Hitchcock. Hitchcock, Sand, Scully and Griggs tripped together and decided to go into business. The Brotherhood would take over the distribution of Scully's and Sand's LSD. Scully felt he didn't have to fear the righteous brotherhood. "I was looking for psychedelic, visionary people to distribute the acid, and the Brotherhood seemed gentle and honest," he says. "They weren't college graduates; they were diamonds in the rough. I could front them half a million dollars' worth of acid, and they'd come back with the money later."

Unlike the street-smart Owsley and Sand, Scully had never banked any money—that's not why he was making acid. So Sand and Hitchcock had to provide the funds to pay for his new lab in Windsor, California, near Santa Rosa.[32] Hitchcock opened an offshore account for Sand, and the Windsor property was put in the name of a Liechtenstein corporation

Sand established as a blind for cash transactions. When raw materials arrived from England, Hitchcock stashed them in his local safe deposit boxes, helped Scully cart lab equipment to Windsor, and stuck around to help tablet the final product.[33] "That was the last lab I had, the one I ended up doing twenty years for," Scully says ruefully.

In Windsor, Scully made the best and most famous acid of the late 1960s, Orange Sunshine. The Brotherhood's marketing campaign began when 100,000 doses were given away free at rock concerts. They gave Scully a trip to their ranch as his reward. He wasn't rich, but he was thinking bigger. While there, he sketched out his Leary-esque fantasy of an offshore lab—a state with its own laws devoted to LSD.[34] The more practical Sand got a ranch of his own outside Cloverdale, California.

BARBARA LEDEEN ENTERED Beloit College in 1967 as a political science major, still the moderate Democrat she was raised to be. "Lyndon Johnson, he's my guy," she says. "Except there's this war in Vietnam which is not okay. I didn't know anybody who was for it except for my father. I was doing political science and reading about communism, and it didn't sound all terrible." Communists had been for civil rights, and that was Ledeen's political touchstone. Her library was full of books by Richard Wright and Langston Hughes.

A year later, she was given a list of work-study job options for poli-sci majors. Copy girl at *The Washington Post* sounded good. Armed with the name of a contact and a list of Beloit students in Washington, she packed her bags. "I thought I was pretty cosmopolitan," she says. "I wasn't a virgin, anyway—already very radical." But she wasn't ready for her hazing: a conversation with her male boss in a strip club. "I didn't know where to look," she says. "We didn't have concepts like hostile work environment, so it was cope, girl, just cope."

She rented a basement apartment. "I was looking for trouble, and it was easy to find. I had gazillions of boyfriends, married, unmarried, this and that." She wore short skirts and little boots. (*Post* owner Kay Graham's one comment to her was, "Get longer skirts.") Ledeen tried pot but didn't get high. She did mescaline once and "was messed up for a long time," she says, "so I knew if I did acid I would really be in trouble." Drugs were not her thing. Neither was Washington. "How can you go to their cocktail parties if you're a journalist?" she posits. "If you're part of that, how do you critique it? I'm thinking, 'This is beyond corrupt. This is an outrage, this is terrible.'" It wasn't all bad. "It's 1968, a crystallizing, catalytic year for everybody," she says. She remembers peace marches and protests; the last HUAC hearings; how Martin Luther King's successor at the Southern Christian Leadership Conference, the Rev. Ralph Abernathy, led a Poor People's March on Washington, in which 3,000 protesters lived in tents for fifteen days on the Mall. And she remembers getting the phone call telling the *Post* that Robert Kennedy had been shot. "It was me on the phone. And I was at the foreign desk the night the Russians invaded Czechoslovakia; all the bells started ringing on the wire service machines and I had to call [editor] Ben Bradlee at home—*stop the presses!*"

In the nation's capital, Ledeen saw—up close and personal—how politics affected everyday life. She was so bemused that she stayed a second trimester, and tacked on the vacation time she had coming, too, "just licking it up," she says, from "the hypocrisy and the dishonesty and the palsy-walsy Washington scene" to "people dying and putting themselves on the line to change an inherently corrupt system." Finally, at the end of the year, Bradlee called Ledeen into his office. "You are like a little mouse eating a big cheese," he said. "Time to go back to college."

IN JANUARY 1968, the SDS National Office started organizing a trip to Cuba—the first by Americans in four years. Mark Rudd cut five weeks of classes and went; he was on the rebel island when the Vietnamese launched the Tet Offensive. He toured a hospital and a collective farm, visited university students and intellectuals, ate tomato ice cream, and did "a lot of partying," Rudd says. "I come back and I'm ready. I'd been won over to the cult of Che Guevara. 'The duty of every revolutionary is to make the revolution.'" He didn't care that Eugene McCarthy was astonishing the country. "We mocked those 'clean for Gene' people," he says. But Lyndon Johnson's abdication made him sit up and notice. "That was the moment the government decided it couldn't win the war."

Between classes, the Columbia junior's involvement in political conflicts escalated. In October 1967, he'd been part of a polite SDS march on Grayson Kirk's office. The following February, SDS confronted napalm maker Dow Chemical Company's campus recruiters. Then in March, Rudd became chairman of SDS. When Colonel Paul Akst, who ran the draft in New York City, came to the campus a few days later to answer questions about the draft, a member of the action faction pushed a lemon meringue pie in his face.[35]

Rudd led another protest against Columbia's role in an IDA research project for the CIA. Demonstrators invaded the administrative office in the elegant, domed Low Memorial Library and angrily demanded a meeting with Kirk, a sixty-eight-year-old whose imperious attitude infuriated the students. A few days later, when Kirk refused to link arms with students for the singing of "We Shall Overcome" at a memorial service for Martin Luther King Jr., Rudd stood up and grabbed a mike—echoes of Mario Savio—called Columbia's hypocrisy "a moral outrage," and led a walkout. Kirk gave a speech calling America's young "nihilists." "I know of no time in our history when the gap between the generations has been wider or more potentially dangerous," he said.

"We *will* have to destroy at times, even violently," Rudd responded. "But that is a far cry from nihilism. . . . We the young people, whom you so rightly fear . . . use the words of [poet] LeRoi Jones, whom I'm sure you don't like a whole lot: 'Up against the wall, motherfucker, this is a stick-up.'"[36]

"So," Rudd adds now, "anybody could see there was a confrontation building."

In its first foray on the racial front, SDS decided to co-sponsor a rally against a gym Columbia was constructing on the site of a public park that separated the elite school from the black neighborhood it abutted. The demonstration was set to begin at midday at a large sundial in the middle of Columbia's campus.[37] The SDS organizers hoped the crowd would invade Low Library with a petition supporting six students, Rudd among them, put on disciplinary probation for their role in the IDA protest— while committing the same infraction in the process.

At noon on April 23, the Battle of Morningside Heights was joined. Cicero Wilson, the new head of the Students' Afro-American Society, till then a quiet, moderate group, spoke stirringly, inspiring the crowd to action. The mob roared off to the gym site, where it tore down a fence before police made an arrest. Rudd demanded the student's release. When an administrator ignored him, the crowd headed back to campus, where whites and blacks started arguing over who was in charge.[38]

"When somebody gets arrested, you're supposed to react," Rudd says. "So we thought, 'Let's take a building hostage for the guy who got arrested.' So everybody rushes into Hamilton Hall and we find the Dean of the College. So we decided to keep him hostage, and the whole thing escalated from there."

Demands were issued: that the gym project be halted, and that the university end its support of war research, lift the ban on demonstrations, settle disciplinary questions like Rudd's in open hearings, and dismiss charges against student demonstrators. Although the dean, Henry Coleman, was released the next day, students seized more buildings in his stead, "liberating" five altogether.

A Strike Coordinating Committee entreated students to support the occupation. Rudd's negotiating position only hardened when a dean told him that no matter what else happened, he would be expelled.[39] Though some students were annoyed that their education had been put on hold—a group calling itself Majority Coalition blockaded the protestors Low Library and vowed to cut off food supplies—the occupiers succeeded in halting work on the gymnasium on the second day of their revolt.

The Columbia takeover made national headlines. A now-famous photo of one student, sitting at Kirk's mahogany desk, puffing on one of his cigars, outraged as many Americans as it amused. For radicals, Columbia was the best show in town. Tom Hayden, Jim Fouratt, Stokely Carmichael, H. Rap Brown and Abbie Hoffman were among the spectators. Brown made the *New York Times* with his suggestion that if the gym got built, the people of Harlem should blow it up.

"Then, at a certain point, they call in the cops," Rudd says. In the wee hours of April 30, 1,000 police cleared the buildings. Final box score: 524 students removed, 692 people arrested, 103 injured (including a professor, a reporter and 20 police). And Kirk's office was totally trashed. The next day the Columbia undergraduate community went on strike and effectively shut down the school. Faculty, students and administrators met to try to end the impasse. Structures were created to let students finish the semester, although many simply left for the summer. A student strike committee created a "liberation school" with courses on Buddhism, Blake and the student movement in Spain. The Grateful Dead played a victory concert. Police were posted campus-wide. The question of disciplinary action against the students remained unresolved.[40] "This is where I learned a lot about the battlefield," says Rudd. "Basically, all the radical faculty sat on the wall."

Early one May evening, the strikers held another on-campus rally, at which a speaker announced a new front in the battle against Columbia. Local residents had occupied a nearby university-owned tenement. Students sat in the street outside the building. Again, in the middle of the night, the police moved in. Rudd was among the sixty-eight arrested for disorderly conduct. At the local precinct, cops congregated to stare at him.

The next day, Rudd and three other participants in the IDA protest were called before a dean to discuss the situation. Later on that day, another sundial rally declared the dean's authority illegitimate before moving en masse to seize Hamilton Hall. The administration gave the students an ultimatum—leave or be suspended—and called the police.

Their first two actions were to rip down a poster of Chairman Mao and to arrest Rudd, charging him with riot, trespassing and encouraging others to commit crimes.

Rudd—along with five dozen others—was immediately suspended, but Columbia's punishment didn't end there. The registrar informed his local draft board, so by December, he could expect to be drafted.[41] But, in many ways SDS had won: the gym wasn't built, the blanket ban on indoor demonstrations was rescinded, Columbia split from IDA, new disciplinary procedures were instituted, Grayson Kirk resigned after students walked out of his last commencement address, and all over the country, students were radicalized by watching their counterparts being beaten on TV, proving Regis Debray's *foco* theory—at least in the minds of Rudd and his Debray-esque band of revolutionary exemplars.

WHEN THE YOUTHQUAKE hit Boston in the middle 1960s, it missed Tommy Vallely. One of his younger brothers wanted to be a Beatle, but not Tommy, whose sense of solitude had evolved into an air of independence. He worked in a gas station and at a drugstore to make money, which he spent on clothes and having fun. "Friends, girlfriends, beer, football games—I was a very straight kid," he says.

Vallely's older sister was a leftist in college, and his mother, who had a EUGENE MCCARTHY FOR PRESIDENT bumper sticker on her car, went to antiwar demonstrations in Boston. He thought they were "wrong, but not to the point where I want to get in an argument," he says. "There was a debate in my high school, too, and I stayed on the sidelines and watched." He was already thinking about enlisting.

In spring 1968, as Vallely's high school graduation neared, he felt his options were few: "Go to Newton Junior College or get a job," he says. "I was certainly not going to Harvard." Yet he was ambitious. He stumbles for long minutes over his reasons for enlisting in the Marines. It wasn't as if he had a great desire to defeat communism, but for him, "America always did good, and I wanted to do good." He wanted to be as proud of himself as he was of his country, "like the people that went to World War Two," he says. "I would get to wear the uniform, do something other people would respect." He pauses. "I certainly changed my mind fairly quickly about a lot of those things."

Vallely spent the summer partying and planning his going-away party. Only as September approached, when he would enter boot camp at Parris Island, did he start to get scared, "a reflection of how little I knew," he says now. He took infantry training at Camp Lejeune in North

Carolina, then headed to Camp Pendelton in California, the jumping-off point for Vietnam.

"In fall 1968, the Marine Corps is not a place you want to be," Vallely says. "We were ten percent of the fighting force and were taking about sixty percent of the casualties. You go to Vietnam in the Marine Corps, you're crazy. So I do, at this point, get scared shitless. I begin to be aware I might get killed, and I regret it. I'm a middle-class kid from Newton; my father's a judge, I shouldn't have done this. I'd overstepped my desire to be different. But I've committed to it, I've taken an oath, and I want to keep my honor."

Suddenly, he saw thoughtfulness as a virtue, and what he was thinking about was getting home alive. His company, India Company, 3rd Battalion, 5th Marines, "had discipline, it had good people, it had good officers," he says. "And it gave you a certain amount of confidence that if you understood the rules, you'd do pretty well."

Rule Number 1 was to make friends who would watch your back. Looking around his base camp outside Da Nang, a region the Marines called the Arizona Territory, he fell in with a group from Massachusetts who'd been "in country" for some time. One of them was Tim "Salty" Vallely (no relation), a veteran of more than a few firefights. Salty's fatigues were clean, his backpack worked, and he had an air of confidence.

"I'm going to show you how to get out of here," Salty told him.

"I'm your best student," replied Vallely, who instantly became the scholar he'd never been in school. No one talked about "the fucking war," Vallely adds. "There's no 'war,' okay? We're talking survival."

Vallely's unit saw a lot of combat. "The first time I thought the world had ended," he says. "It was at night, a small ambush, not a big deal. All of a sudden, from over a hill you see bullets, tracer rounds, we're receiving. I have a shitty pack; I don't have one of the nice packs. I can't get it off to shoot. By the time I get my pack off, the thing is over with. Someone got wounded but nobody got killed. And that's my baptism of fire. I couldn't get my pack off. But I watched these other guys and they were firing back, seemingly not scared. A few of those and your fear starts to go away."

The next hurdle was walking point—being the first member of his company to enter new terrain. "Big honor, big problem," Vallely says. "You have to react quickly, you have to have confidence, you have to shoot first and think later because if you don't, you're dead. You've got to scare them as much as you're scared. Not everyone's good at it. And I, unfortunately, was good enough at it that if I'd kept doing it, my name would be on that fucking [Vietnam Memorial] wall."

He decided he wanted to be a radio operator. Despite his stutter, he knew how to talk, how to describe what was happening around him, even under fire. Radio operators "knew a ton," he says, because they had to write and dictate reports. They were aware of the big picture. They were vital links in the chain of command. The better he did it, the less the chance he'd have to walk point again. "That concentrated my mind," Vallely says. He soon became the number-two radio operator in India Company.

"That's the basic story of what happened to me in Vietnam," he says. "I went, I survived, I became quite skilled." Of course, that wasn't the whole story, because the longer he stayed in Vietnam, the more aware he became of the war's foolishness. "Having been in dozens of villages, I got a very clear sense that the villagers were with the other side," he says. "And what we were trying to do was not going to work."

Neither, he realized, were America's air power and artillery as effective as claimed. As a radio operator, Vallely could make the night day. He could light up the sky with illumination canisters, call in artillery strikes, Huey helicopter gunships, spotter planes, and B52s, and adjust the fire from off-shore naval battleships. "But I couldn't call anybody to tell them what we were doing wrong," he says.

"One time we bombed the shit out of this village and all the kids played soccer afterward," he says. He remembers thinking, "That's exactly what *we* want, we're not here to burn villages. We're here to survive."

The troops were disciplined, not gung-ho. They did what they had to do. They had their doubts, but Vallely believes those doubts did not affect performance. "When the Marines were engaged, they did a good job," he says. But evil abounded amid the camaraderie and valor, "war crimes that affected me deeply," says Vallely. When a Marine in his company set off a flare in a pregnant woman's vagina, he would have killed the guy had he not been stopped. "We had that type of a person," he allows. "But the good guys outnumbered the bad guys by a lot."

At home, politicians were claiming there was light at the end of the tunnel, and the tide of the war was turning in America's favor. In-country, Vallely and Co. didn't think so. "The Marine Corps never bought that bullshit," he says. Then, once Richard Nixon became president—a few months into Vallely's tour—American strategy shifted to disengagement. "We were just trying to get out of there," Vallely says. "But the Vietnamese weren't disengaging, they were trying to throw us out, trying to win the war. And if you get ambushed, you fight."

* * *

IMMEDIATELY AFTER LYNDON Johnson's near-loss in New Hampshire, the vaunted Kennedy campaign operation sprang into action and John Gage was among those called. Would he run as one of about a dozen students vying to be delegates for newly-annonced presidential candidate Robert F. Kennedy at the upcoming Chicago Democratic Convention? Gage flew to Los Angeles; met Jesse Unruh, speaker of California's assembly and head of the state's Kennedy campaign, in a smoke-filled room at an airport motel; and agreed not only to be a candidate but to help run the California primary campaign.

Working through the spring with Berkeley law students and political pros from Massachusetts, Gage won a vote at the convention. Kennedy beat McCarthy and was suddenly a strong contender to replace Johnson. But moments after he declared victory in Los Angeles, Robert Kennedy was shot dead. "There we are in Berkeley at my campaign headquarters," Gage says. "Everybody is in tears. No one can understand how this happened. The entire thing has absolutely ripped our hearts out. And we go on to Chicago."

MARIANNE WILLIAMSON WAS fifteen in April 1968, when Martin Luther King Jr. was killed in Memphis, Tennessee. Her father got home from work as the bulletin came over the television. "I saw a look on his face I had never seen before. His eyes seemed to focus on something impossibly far away and with an intensely pained expression, he spat out the words, 'Those bastards.' In that instant, I lost my innocence. That day changed history, and it certainly changed me. My father was signaling to me, This is the way things are. I took another road than my father—love for what could be is a much stronger dynamic than anger at what is—but I am looking for the same perfect world."

That is now. Then, the stunning succession of events in her last two years in high school pulled Williamson away from God and love and impelled her toward protests and picket lines. That June, the day after Bobby Kennedy was shot, she and her friends went to a nearby park to commemorate the event. Though she didn't realize it at the time, she preached her first sermon. "I stood up and gave this extemporaneous eulogy and we all sat there like 'Whoa!'—including me. I mean, clearly I was fired up."

It wasn't long until she and her friends were scared off public life. "The bullets that dropped the Kennedys and King struck all of us," she says. "We received a very loud unspoken message: You will now stop arguing with the prevailing authority or we just might kill you, too."

For any individual, any generation, maturing is a two-step process. The first is severance, the second, the forging of a unique role. "We went through phase one," says Williamson, "we took to the streets, we made it very clear that we were disconnecting from the way our parents had done it, but our politics were ultimately not as profound as we thought they were. Because when it came to establishing how we were going to do it, the heroes who articulated that vision were killed in front of our eyes and our whole generation became like the son of Bobby Kennedy who saw his father shot and never recovered. He basically just got stoned and died. At that very, very critical age, we were frozen."

Not only that, Williamson, like many of her peers, had unprecedented access to three numbing agents that "had never before been so accessible to so many so young: Sex, drugs, and rock 'n' roll," she says. "I was never *that* wild. I was never a drug addict. But I was very much a child of my age."

THE NEWLYWEDS, RICHARD and Marilyn Leacock, moved into a duplex apartment in Chelsea, upstairs from the art critic Lawrence Halloway, who'd just coined the term Pop Art. Briefly, they lived a charmed 1960s life, summering on Fire Island, partying with actors, artists and intellectuals. Leacock and Pennebaker formed a company, and in 1964, Pennebaker traveled to England with Bob Dylan to make a documentary called *Don't Look Back*, while Leacock pursued his own quite opposite interests and made films about Igor Stravinsky and Leonard Bernstein. In 1967, they collaborated on a film about the Monterey Pop Festival. Marilyn, meanwhile, worked as a fund-raiser for the NAACP.

It all seemed colorful to Victoria, who dressed as a flower child for a costume parade on Fire Island, accidentally ate a hashish brownie ("The babysitter was very upset"), and giggled when her mother took down their poster of Janis Joplin in the nude because other parents were coming to visit. Leacock's travels, and the temptations that came with them, took a toll on the marriage. By the time Victoria began school, the marriage was over. Leacock-Pennebaker went bankrupt after an abortive attempt to make a movie with the French director Jean-Luc Godard, and Leacock took a job several hundred miles away as the head of the film department at MIT. Victoria remembers visiting neighbors one Christmas because her mother didn't want to be alone. Instead, Marilyn smoked hashish while her daughter slept on the couch.

"It was very much the caftans, Valium, *Valley of the Dolls* sixties," Victoria says. "And my mom got in with a set of chi-chi women who were all getting divorced, and they got her a fancy lawyer, so instead of just being hurt and sorting things out, it became nasty." For weeks on end, her mother sat at home in the dark. "Mom wanted a family, you know?" Divorce papers were filed naming three women Leacock had had affairs with—a writer, a pianist and an Andy Warhol superstar. "I always joked that if my mom was going down, she was going down with a good crowd."

The next Christmas, her mother slipped, tore ligaments in her knee, underwent an unsuccessful operation, began taking cortisone and painkillers and, when taken off the medication, went into a coma for three days and ended up with rheumatoid arthritis for the rest of her life. She started abusing what the Rolling Stones called "Mother's Little Helpers"—"Librium and Demerol and Valiums and Percodans—an array of capsules," Victoria says. Though some were for pain, "that wasn't the only reason she was taking them,' she adds. "My dad was in a real struggle to get her to stop taking so many happy drugs. He went to see her in a hospital and she was high as a kite and they said she had hidden all her drugs in her Tampax box."

Victoria was with her mother the following June on the day Robert Kennedy was killed. "My mom went into a deep, deep, deep depression," she says. "We tried to go to the memorial at St. Patrick's Cathedral. It was very hot and people were passing out. And finally, Mom couldn't take it anymore."

That summer, on crutches, back on Fire Island, Marilyn Leacock sat down wrong one evening and crushed four vertebrae in her back. "I was supposed to go and see *101 Dalmations* that evening and my mom had been carted off to the hospital, and my grandmother wouldn't let me go and I was having a tantrum, and finally she said I could go and she sent me alone," Leacock remembers. "I went to the movie theater and there were all these hippies on line. And I got to the front of the line and I didn't see any kids. And they said you had to go in with a grown-up. And the hippies went, 'Yeah, man, we'll take her in.'" Onscreen was *M*A*S*H*, Robert Altman's antiwar film. "My mother had just been taken away by paramedics, and the opening scene is very graphic; it's all this blood in the hospital." She ran from the theater. "It was just one of those awful, traumatic things where you know everything's starting to go wrong," she says.

A FEW DAYS before the 1968 Democratic convention, Jim Fouratt ran into Allen Ginsberg in San Francisco. "Allen said he'd had this dream the night before—a sea of red blood in Chicago, and he came and parted the seas and shepherded the sheep through. Very Allen. He had to go to Chicago. Allen was always on the scene."

TO DELEGATES, CHICAGO was a Potemkin village, with a façade of normality imposed over chaos, just as the nomination of Hubert Humphrey had been imposed upon a party seething with dissension. Every morning John Gage and the California delegation were picked up at their hotel by bus and driven down corridors of chain-link fence to the heavily secured Chicago Amphitheater. At day's end, they were bused back to their hotel and then went out on the streets to try to find out more.

Only a handful of protesters had actually showed up, but with the unwitting cooperation of the Chicago police and the Democratic party, they mounted one of the most hypnotic pieces of street theater in history. "The McCarthy kids were the target of vilification by the Yippies, because they bought into the system," says Fouratt. But when the police entered McCarthy headquarters and beat his volunteers as the convention anointed Humphrey, it split the country in two. Seeing its children clubbed in the streets radicalized a great swath of Americans and polarized the rest from them. The second American Revolution had begun. It would not be as successful as the first.

In Berkeley after the convention, Gage joined a protest called Stop the Draft Week, a series of marches attempting to shut down the huge Oakland Induction Center—the hungry mouth of the draft. In a few days it morphed from protest to resistance to disruption. At a rally before the march, Ken Kesey gave an essentially apolitical yet prophetic speech. "Look at the war, and turn your backs and say Fuck it!" he announced.

"Like nitwits, we did nothing to help Humphrey get elected," Gage says. "This is the sad story about purity. Sometimes you lose track of what it is you want, and of what is effective. What matters, and why politics matters, is that decisions are made about who lives and dies, whether there will be an inoculation program for kids."

Like many, Gage dropped out of conventional politics after Chicago. A recruiter from Harvard Business School had convinced him to give it a try, and though he still hadn't graduated from Berkeley, that fall he entered the elite B-school, where he studied while America—and the world—continued to boil and burn.

Soviet tanks had crushed Prague Spring a few days before the Chicago convention. In September, Mexican troops moved on student demonstrators in that nation's capital. In America, white radicals began building up the Black Panthers. By 1968, the Panthers were pop stars who played to the media and were played up in return; they even had their own fan magazine—the radical journal *Ramparts*. Two days after Martin Luther King was killed, Panther leader Eldridge Cleaver (b. 1935) was wounded and another Panther was killed in another shootout with police. "Let there be war," Cleaver said. He got his wish, and the rout of the Panthers began. Huey Newton was soon convicted of killing a policeman, and Cleaver fled the country for Algeria.

On October 31, Johnson stopped bombing North Vietnam, five days before Richard Nixon, who claimed to have a secret plan to end the war, was elected president. During this brief honeymoon that spring, Nixon began secretly bombing Cambodia. Then, on March 20, his Justice Department indicted eight alleged organizers of the Chicago convention disturbances, including Tom Hayden, Abbie Hoffman and Jerry Rubin.[42] The whole counter-culture was going on trial.

WHILE TIM SCULLY was tabbing Orange Sunshine, Tim Leary was back in court. He'd been arrested again, along with his third wife and son, for possession of two marijuana cigarettes, in Laguna Beach on December 26, 1968. The following May he got some good news, winning an appeal on his 1965 Texas conviction. Reporters converged on the Brotherhood's ranch, and a jubilant Leary announced that he was going to run for governor of California against Ronald Reagan and Jesse Unruh.[43] His euphoria was premature. The government promptly filed new charges atop those pending in Laguna and Millbrook. Then, in July, a friend of seventeen-year-old Susan Leary was found dead on the Brotherhood ranch with traces of LSD in her blood, just before one of the brothers was busted with a hash-filled surfboard. A month later, John Griggs died from suffocation when he vomited while stoned on psilocybin. Then Leary was retried in Laredo, found guilty, and sent back to Laguna for his next trial, where he was found guilty again and promptly incarcerated. Then, on Christmas Day 1969, the Brotherhood's head shop mysteriously burned down.[44] It had become a vestigial organ of their empire—they were selling cocaine and hash oil now, buying Porsches and a yacht, and setting up shell companies.

THROUGH THE SUMMER of 1968, Mark Rudd, the newly minted radical celebrity, worked out of a rented fraternity house across the street from the Columbia campus, planning demonstrations at the Chicago convention and a renewed student strike in the fall. He attended the annual SDS convention that June, where Maoists who believed in organizing workers for "class struggle" and the cautious original SDS leaders were confronted by younger action types. The Motherfuckers, a politicized band of poets-turned-SDS street toughs, nominated a garbage can for one of the three SDS leadership positions, National Secretary, but it lost to Bernadine Dohrn (b. 1942).[45]

That fall and winter Rudd traveled the country, raising money, giving speeches to students about what had happened at Columbia, and recruiting for SDS. Between times, he stayed in Chicago at a house called the National Collective, shared by his ideological guru J.J. and J.J.'s new girlfriend, Dohrn. As the assistant executive secretary of the National Lawyer's Guild (which represented radicals and the Communist party) she'd advised Rudd when he was doing draft counseling. Dohrn's beauty, leather miniskirts, unbuttoned blouses and sexual adventurism made her an SDS face on a par with the mediagenic Rudd, who had just made the cover of *Newsweek*. "Bernadine is the most attractive person you will ever meet," says Rudd, who also slept with her. "She embodied the independent and strong woman, which was part of the revolutionary idea. Not all our ideas were bad."

Campuses were exploding all over the country in early 1969: at San Fernando State and San Francisco State and San Jose; at Berkeley, where Ronald Reagan declared a state of emergency; at Howard and the University of Massachusetts and Rice; at Penn State, and the universities of Wisconsin and Chicago. At Harvard, SDS seized a building and, after injuries, arrests and a student strike, won a black studies department. At Kent State, SDS was so militant, most of its members got kicked out of school. At Brown, graduating seniors turned their backs on commencement speaker Henry Kissinger. Rudd was right; revolution *was* in the air—at least among priviledged youth.

The National Collective included the head of the New York SDS office, Jeff Jones; Dave Gilbert, the son of a Republican mayor; Swarthmore grad Cathy Wilkerson, whose father owned radio stations; Terry Robbins, SDS's Midwest organizer; and a group from the University of Michigan that included Billy Ayers (son of the chairman of Chicago's power company), his girlfriend, Diana Oughton (great-granddaughter of the founder of the Boy Scouts), and her college roommate Kathy Boudin, whose father, Leonard, was a leading leftist lawyer.[46] In the course of several months, J.J. put their violent thoughts on paper.

The document aimed to out-Marx the Maoists; the oppressed were

leading the way to world revolution, it said. "We took ourselves very seriously," notes Rudd dryly. Instead of recruiting bourgeois students with
talk of the workers' struggle, or battering their heads against a working
class they considered hopelessly reactionary, they proposed recruiting
youth to a world revolution led by the international oppressed.

In a riff on the Bob Dylan lyric "You don't need a weatherman to know
which way the wind blows," the group re-named themselves the Weather
Bureau. The Weathermen, as they were generally known, became the
most exciting thing in an overstimulated time: rock star revolutionaries.
At the June SDS convention, when a Black Panther, invited to speak by
the Weather Bureau, attacked the Maoist faction and then extolled feminism as "pussy power," the resulting fracas split—and then killed—SDS.[47]
The Weathermen and their allies sided with the Panthers, expelled the
Maoists, then walked out themselves, taking their star power (and the
records and assets of SDS) with them.

The Weather Bureau's first action was called to coincide with the
opening of the Chicago 8 trial that October.[48] "We did not call it the Days
of Rage," says Rudd, whose influence in the organization peaked that season. "The media called it that. We called it the October National Action."
They wanted to bring the war home, but the psychological corollary was
a desire to shed their white-skin privilege and middle-class upbringings
and, in essence, become the Panthers they worshipped—street-fighting
men and women.

Rudd continued building the organization, working with local collectives and "occasionally running around in the street at local demonstrations," he says. Groups of Weathermen and -women (some with their
breasts bared) would invade high schools and run through the halls
screaming "Jailbreak!"[49] They leafleted rock concerts and gave speeches at
movie theaters playing *Easy Rider*. Sometimes, though, the actions turned
violent. There were clashes with Maoists and staged confrontations with
police, planned to impress the street toughs they were trying to recruit.[50]
Professors were beaten at Harvard, teachers bound and gagged in a
Brooklyn high school. Cumulatively, these actions impressed no one but
the Weatherrevolutionaries themselves.

IN 1967, MICHAEL Fuchs had decided that law school would be a good
way to kill three more years. "I had no idea, really, what I wanted to do,"
he says, "and I had pretty good law boards," which got him into
Georgetown Law. But show business nagged him. "When I was younger, I
was always going to the movies, and as I got older I began to watch televi-

sion in a kind of systematic way," he says. At Union, when a roommate asked him why he watched so much, he'd answered, "I'm doing my homework."

The summer before his first year in law school, Fuchs worked in the office of Senator Birch Bayh, a job he won through an uncle who supported many Democrats. Back at school, he marched on the Pentagon. The next summer, he decided he was going to work for Bobby Kennedy's presidential campaign, impressed by how the pugnacious former prosecutor had evolved into a champion of the oppressed. "I had seen Bobby on Capitol Hill when I worked there. I thought Bobby really felt for the disadvantaged. And I don't care how late it came to him. The fact that he changed as much as he did was a sign of terrific growth." But instead of joining the campaign in June, he attended Kennedy's funeral. "It just took a lot of wind out of my sails."

Fuchs had lost his draft deferment, so he joined the Army Reserves. "Almost all my friends got out; I don't know how," he says. "I didn't do any of that. Though I didn't want to go to Vietnam."

Just as his second year of law school was starting, Fuchs was activated and sent to boot camp at Fort Jackson, South Carolina. "I'd been going to school straight and I'd never taken a break. It was good to put your mind to sleep. I found it an enjoyable experience, although I had some very rough times because I stood up to the drill sergeant. I was like a barracks lawyer. I stood in their way. Because some of these guys are fucking sadists. And there were enough of us who were older, who were law students, who knew that they just couldn't do that."

He saw two men die in training—one in a hand grenade accident, the other while cleaning his gun. "And I saw young kids go to 'Nam, like volleyballs being kicked over to the side, they had absolutely no control over their lives," he says. Once, on the rifle range, he was "coupled with a guy who had been recycled several times, which meant he was a moron—he couldn't get through basic training," Fuchs says. "This kid kept pointing his weapon at me. And I remember saying to myself, 'I'm going to die on this fucking rifle range with this moron.' It was further forged in me that I would try to have control over my destiny."

When he could, he talked to returning combat veterans, who told him Vietnam was a "poor man's war," he says. "There was an unbelievably high percentage of blacks over there. And I could see who went in from my own company, young kids, seventeen, eighteen, who weren't educated; the kids who had more wherewithal and more resources were able to avoid it." Like Fuchs. He was never called to serve. "Reservists got called up. But it would turn out not to be us. We did get called up once, for about a day, in a postal strike."

SIDELINED IN THE Yippies, but determined not to be erased by Abbie Hoffman, Jim Fouratt joined the White Panther Party, founded by John Sinclair (b. 1941), a poet, jazz critic and proselytizer of the virtues of marijuana and LSD, with several drug arrests to his credit. Sinclair ran a performance space in Detroit called the Artist's Workshop and a commune called Trans-Love Energies and managed bands, including the MC5 and (with a partner) the Psychedelic Stooges, both of which played at the Chicago convention.

Fresh from the Yippies, Fouratt was sympathetic to the White Panther agenda, expressed in its slogan: "Rock 'n' roll, dope and fucking in the streets." "I really felt popular culture was a revolutionary tool, and that rock did have political meaning in that it mobilized kids and gave them something to do."

The cultural alliance between rock music and the youth revolution had its roots in Dylan's and other folk singers' involvement in the civil rights movement. By 1966, the relationship had been formalized, as record companies began seeking out street bands by means of a new kind of executive, the "house freak," who related better than the then-typical record man, often as not a besuited Sinatra fan. The first house freaks were older than the audience they were hired to connect with, but the industry's need for credibility in the new culture led to the hiring of younger folk. Danny Fields, born just weeks before the bombing of Pearl Harbor, was one of the first. A Harvard Law dropout, former teen magazine editor, and rock PR man who knew Fouratt from the Warhol scene at Max's Kansas City, he'd been hired by Elektra Records, a folk and blues music label expanding into rock. After receiving copious propaganda from the MC5, Fields went to Michigan and signed them to a record deal. On their advice, he also saw the Stooges and signed them to his roster.

Almost immediately, Columbia Records came calling on Fouratt, in the person of Al Kooper, pianist on Bob Dylan's "Like a Rolling Stone." Kooper, an in-house producer for Columbia, introduced Fouratt to its president, Clive Davis, who'd just boldly announced the label's ambitions in progressive rock by signing Big Brother and the Holding Company, a San Francisco blues band fronted by a powerful singer named Janis Joplin, for an unprecedented $250,000. Davis offered Fouratt a job as his house freak.

Columbia had lots of rules. You could have nothing on your walls in your office, and there was a suit-and-tie dress code. Fouratt began to decorate his office walls and every night the cleaning crew would take down the posters he'd put up. Human Resources threatened to fire him for not disclosing his draft status on his employment application. Human Resources was fighting a losing battle. When Joplin and Co. came to visit Davis, he brought Fouratt, who'd met the band previously in San Francisco, into the room to make them more comfortable. They all promptly stripped.

That fall, Columbia had stumbled badly in an attempt to position itself as hip when it began running ads with copy like, "If you won't listen to your parents, the Man or the Establishment, why should you listen to us?" and "The Man Can't Bust Our Music." "There was a lot of flack in the counterculture about Columbia and that campaign," Fouratt recalls. Davis asked him to lend a hand to the advertising effort.

Fouratt was trying to serve two masters—Columbia and the "revolution"—with one advertising budget. He convinced Davis to run ads in thirty underground newspapers, as well as music magazines, thereby subsidizing the alternative press, which had grown since its beginnings in the mid-1960s to a national force that was as anarchic (the Liberation News Service, founded in 1967, had just splintered into bitter factions; the Underground Press Service was being run by a secretive drug dealer named Tom Forcade) as it was influential. The campaign (toned down with the headline "Know who your friends are") continued into spring 1969. A few months earlier, an FBI memo accused Columbia of "giving active aid and comfort to enemies of the United States," and suggested that pressure be applied to stop it. Backlash against the counterculture was building now that it had burst out of the cities and spread across the country. Soon, conservative stockholders of the parent company, CBS, heard the FBI message, says Fouratt, "and all the ads were pulled."

IN SPRING 1968, prosecutor Leslie Crocker Snyder was in the courtroom when Mark Rudd was arraigned after the Columbia University takeover. "I come into court, and these kids are approximately my age," she says. They talked to her like she was one of them, asked her how she could possibly prosecute them. "And I'm feeling sympathy for them, I'm feeling very ambivalent," she says. "But not ambivalent enough not to do it." After all, they were mostly released with disorderly conduct violations—the equivalent of parking tickets.

Snyder kept a diary those first few months she was a baby DA, and was later shocked when she reread it. She'd never known a cop, and she'd bought into her generation's distrust of them. "All cops lie," she wrote. But as she worked with them—doing things she felt were worthwhile— and learned that they could be trusted and didn't always lie, her beliefs began to change. "I was getting to see what cops had to face," she says. "And they were good to me. I was a novelty, a sweet young thing, and they liked women. And when they see that you will take care of them and you're a hard worker and you will do a good job, then they become very protective of you. And then, I was seduced."

A few months later, Snyder attended various hearings and trials in what became known as the Panther 21 case—an alleged conspiracy to bomb department stores and police stations and kill police officers. "The prosecutor was horrible," she recalls. "They all got acquitted, and it was the biggest travesty, and it was the prosecution's fault. And in my view, they were criminals, and I think they should have been convicted. Peaceful revolution, that's okay. Once the violence started, any sympathy I had dissipated, because cops started getting killed. It was partly political, but it was largely criminal. I was totally turned off."

On May 4, 1970 (two days after students burned down the ROTC building there), National Guardsmen fired sixty-one shots, four fatal, into a group of Kent State University demonstrators protesting the April 30 American invasion of Cambodia. That invasion and the dramatic shooting that followed reenergized the dispirited peace movement and kicked off another spring of student strikes, ROTC burnings and bombings, and campus closings, leading Congress to grant eighteen-year-olds the vote. But Nixon's troop withdrawals, which had begun in 1969 and accelerated under cover of massive U.S. bombing, and the introduction of a draft lottery—coupled with factionalism and rising violence on the antiwar movement's fringe— compromised the protesters' resolve. Demonstrations would continue into 1972, but for many, the killings at Kent State put the lie to the idea of peaceful protest.

Though she was horrified by the repression of political dissent at Kent State, Leslie Snyder just couldn't accept people killing cops and burning buildings. Her transformation was complete. Finally, she'd escaped the eighteenth century. This was real life, real crime. And she knew whose side she was on.

IN SPRING 1969, Doug Marlette spotted a book called *LBJ Lampooned*, with a cover illustration by the *New York Review of Books* artist David Levine (satirizing Johnson's famous display of his surgical scar—replaced by a map of Vietnam), and an introduction about cartooning by Jules

Feiffer. Political cartoons were enjoying a renaissance. "Lyndon Johnson's lying legitimized questioning," Marlette says. "Establishment newspapers were starting to do cartoons that were really subversive and outrageous. Jules, in that essay, gave me an intellectual framework. I suddenly could see what my job was."

That fall, having earned an associate's degree at community college, Marlette joined the junior class at Florida State University in Tallahassee. He declared a philosophy major, and presented himself at the offices of the campus daily, where he promptly won a job drawing cartoons. Immediately, a war began for the nineteen-year-old's soul, pitting the good boy, who looked like a Southern Rotarian and was so overpowered by what was expected of him that he now married his churchgoing girlfriend, against another Doug who drew like a northern intellectual and couldn't help but note the disconnect between the way he'd been raised and what was happening in his world. "I was trying to salvage the values I'd been taught in civics classes and in Sunday school," he says. "But the things I'd been taught did not square with killing people and denying rights."

Two months after enrolling, Marlette joined a group of students he hardly knew in a Volkswagen bus painted camouflage green for the overnight trip to the Mobilization march in Washington, D.C. Outside Atlanta, a gas station attendant told them they should go home and study. Instead, they turned up the music and offered Marlette his first puff of marijuana. He didn't like it. "I had a natural ability to enter that stoned, free-associative state," he realized. "I do it in my work. I saw that, so dope didn't hold much allure for me. I never took acid and I'm glad I didn't, because I think I might not have wanted to come back. Something in me knew." In homage to his natural state of buzz and beatitude, his friends took to calling him "Drug" Marlette.

Though he grew his hair long and kept pumping out antiwar cartoons for the newspaper, Marlette didn't much like the radicals he met on that trip—or later. "It was the most activist school in the region," he says, "but I didn't feel like one of them. I marched on the draft board, I demonstrated, but I was never a joiner. I'm not quite there, but my cartoons are. When I think back, I had a sophisticated vision for someone that young. I saw through the bullshit, recognized the Stalinist stuff. I was drawing cartoons that were questioning the war, but also the Nazi tactics of SDS, the anti-free-speech stuff. I did not identify with groups; still don't. I do not link up with causes. SDS sounded like Baptists to me. It seemed like the same thing I had grown up with, those crazy dogmatists who would send you off to a gulag."

That summer, the first draft lottery was held and Marlette drew number 10—an almost certain ticket to Vietnam. Though he held a student deferment, it would only last another year. "I was already thinking about applying to be a conscientious objector, so I did," he says. It wasn't an easy choice by any means. "I took it seriously. I was reading Tolstoy, Bertrand Russell, conscientious objectors from the past. But there are other ways of looking at it. My father was a military man. It was a way of expressing resentment toward the military for all the uprooting and dislocations. I had already served my country."

Marlette rejects the notion that rejecting the war was an act of cowardice. "It was too painful to me to feel that I was getting out of something," he explains. "It would have been easier to go into the army; I would have probably been on *Stars and Stripes.* I thought the Selective Service system was wrong. I thought I was compromising by being a CO. To do the CO thing was going along with the system and with the draft. Canada was not an option. I believed that the 'correct' thing for me would have been to go to jail. I thought I was being a wuss by being a CO So it was torture. My mother was ill, and my dad's coming home from Vietnam, and we're arguing about it. He felt he was being rejected. It was not a good time in my family." But in the end, when Marlette submitted his CO application, his father wrote a letter supporting it, offering to go back to Vietnam in his son's place.

STEVE CAPPS ENTERED junior high school in 1967. But he didn't take much notice of the new youth culture barreling its way across the country, though he'd finally been introduced to rock music by his older brother, who would induce Capps to spend the money he earned mowing lawns on records that would immediately disappear into his brother's room.

They weren't all Capps missed, living in the sanctum of suburban Schenectady. "I remember drinking in eighth grade, but I did not smell a whiff of marijuana until I went to college," he says. "My best friend and his older brother were kind of literary types. They would hang around this chicken coop at the back of their property, with Oriental rugs from the Salvation Army. I remember it being weird in there. I'm sure they smoked dope all day. But I didn't know! I was such a nerd."

He was more interested in photography. "I was taking buses downtown by myself, walking around with my camera in neighborhoods I probably shouldn't have gone into, just completely naive but in that completely self-confident way." And that year, he found another interest. His new school had programmable calculators and a Moog synthesizer, which made computerized music, "so in seventh grade I was doing logic programming, and that had a very profound impact," Capps says. "But I never thought I was going to become a programmer. It was just fun."

In 1968, his older sister came home from college for Christmas vacation with a book about a computer language called FORTRAN. "I taught myself FORTRAN, even though I didn't have anything to run it on," he says.

The next summer, Capps's brother heard about the Woodstock music festival being held not far away, coaxed Steve to come along and take pictures, and "made a halfhearted, lame attempt" to talk their mother into letting them go. "I think he got two milliseconds worth of consideration before she said no," Capps recalls.

Capps didn't really care. He wasn't part of that culture and wasn't even sure it existed. Kids in his school were wannabe hippies, "because we were too young," he says. "When I look back at pictures, everybody is dressed absolutely identically. So we thought we were doing our own thing, but we were really being conformists. And the whole hippie thing was about privilege. So you'd talk about peace and love. You'd say, 'We love people of all colors,' but there didn't happen to be any in your school. And in my naiveté, I assumed I would never see prejudice."

DONALD TRUMP WENT to work for his father in fall 1968. He bought and built properties around the country, refinanced some of his father's properties, co-oped, and made tax-free swaps with others, learning the real estate ropes.[51] The Trump business was worth a respectable $40 million—minuscule compared to the real estate dynasties of Manhattan. Fred Trump had hidden strengths, though, and his son would exploit them—as he exploited tax shelters to build a nest egg in his first years in business. The elder Trump knew key figures in the Brooklyn Democratic machine, a feisty anachronism and the last vestige of the political powerhouse called Tammany Hall that once ruled all of New York City. As those politicians moved up in their careers and into Manhattan, Donald would continue to support them, leveraging his father's relationships into real money.

But Trump was still wet behind the ears. He wore maroon suits and matching shoes—a sure sign of an outer-borough boy. His father's business was headquartered in a six-story red brick building in Brooklyn. Donald had business cards made up with the address of his East Side Manhattan apartment. "It was embarrassing," he says. "I couldn't say I had a Brooklyn office and go out with a model. So I put a desk in my studio apartment." It looked out on a water tower.

Trump joined Le Club, a decades-old private club on Manhattan's East Side, where the last of the 1950s playboys held court, and New York's *ancien regime* waited out the cultural revolution that had usurped them. "It was hard to get in," Trump says. But not many young people wanted to; at the time, the children of New York's aristocracy preferred to downplay their privilege. Not Trump. He applied for and won a membership, "and I was far and away the youngest guy."

Manhattan became Trump's graduate school. He majored in making money. He minored in sex, though, taking full advantage of the times and the extraordinary opportunities they offered to indulge in consequence-free promiscuity, "my second business," Trump recalls. It wasn't the counterculture by any means. "Le Club was totally oblivious to it. You understand that? They didn't give a fuck." Yet recognizing that the elusive quality of "cool" meant almost as much as money, Trump studied men like Le Club founder and fashion designer Oleg Cassini, thirty-three years his senior and "a great playboy," Trump says, a little awed. "He was Establishment. He wasn't idealistic. He would flow with the tide."

Behind Le Club's locked doors, the tide was running as high and wild as in the streets outside. "I once saw the most beautiful woman in the world swinging nude from a chandelier at four o'clock in the morning!" Trump marvels. People also took drugs at Le Club, but not Trump. "I never had a drug in my life," he says. "Somehow, somewhere in my life, I was persuaded not to do the drugs and alcohol. It was available to me. But something told me not to do it."

THE WOMEN'S LIBERATION movement had roots deep in American history, but since the suffragettes, its visibility had waned until Betty Freidan published *The Feminine Mystique* in 1963. Simultaneously, women in SDS, who'd been considered no more than adjuncts to its men, began acting up. In December 1965, following its first big antiwar action, SDS held a conference at the University of Illinois, where Tom Hayden's wife, Casey, and another member, SNCC veteran Mary King, argued in a paper that women were an oppressed group, just like Negroes, even inside the radical movement. A discussion of their work turned into the first women's consciousness-raising session, after participants moved to a separate room away from the men.[52]

By 1966, women's issues were on the movement's front burner. The National Organization for Women was formed that year by women who realized they were not being protected by the Civil Rights Act. The next year, a women's liberation amendment was brought to the floor at the SDS convention. A few months later, the first women's liberation protest was held when a group called New York Radical Women led by Jim Fouratt's sometime colleague, Robin Morgan, picketed the Miss America pageant on the Atlantic City boardwalk and tossed bras, girdles and copies of *Cosmopolitan* and *Family Circle* into a "freedom trash can." They were denounced as "bra-burners" and the pageant proceeded regardless. Judith Ann Ford, a bleached-blond baby boomer from Illinois, won, but the protest would be remembered long after she was forgotten.

The Women's International Terrorist Conspiracy from Hell (WITCH), an organization Morgan then formed inspired by the Yippies, soon spearheaded another scandal when it plastered New York with stickers inviting women to "Confront the Whore-Makers at a Bridal Fair at New York's Madison Square Garden in 1969." WITCH invaded the event and called the attendees "whores" and "slaves," expecting them to jump up on chairs in response to five white mice released onto the show floor. They didn't, and the action floundered but the movement moved forward as radical women's groups continued to form. In January 1970, a band of feminists took over the bimonthly underground newspaper *Rat* and turned it into a militant feminist publication. In its first all-women's issue, *Rat* published "Goodbye to All That," a diatribe by Morgan (reprinted later that year in *Sisterhood Is Powerful*, her seminal feminist anthology), which trashed male movement leaders by name. Identity politics had crossed the gender line.

NINA HARTLEY, REMEMBERS being at a peace march while still in a stroller, her brother being arrested in a Berkeley demonstration, and dinner parties with radical friends of her lesbian aunt's husband, who was a member of the National Lawyers Guild. But she says her parents, "beaten and bruised by the political system, had retreated from politics by the time I came along." A return to political involvement would have disturbed the thick scar tissue that covered their wounded lives. "There was a great deal wrong, and they weren't talking about it," she says. "If they did anything 'wrong' in raising me, they did not give me an adequate sense of pride in their history. I see now that through my entire childhood, my mother was angry at my father for destroying himself, and for disrupting her life in the process."

In 1969, Mitzi's parents sent her to Scotland for the summer. The older kids were out of the house, too. When Mitzi returned in September, her mother's latent feminism had come to the fore, and she'd begun to explore her unhappiness and anger. Desperate to save their marriage, the couple began therapy-hopping. "It was, in no particular order, Zen, primal scream therapy, group therapy, biofeedback, guided mescaline trips, and Reichian therapy," Hartley says. None of it worked. By 1971, when Mitzi was twelve and women's liberation was gathering steam, things had deteriorated to the point that she believes her parents each fell in love with the same woman simultaneously.

"The abandonment of my needs for my parents' is a motif in my life," she says. "I protected them from my problems and tried to help them with theirs. And I realize now that really oppressed me. They never called me names; they never hit me; if I asked for something I got it. But I didn't think to ask for anything. I felt very responsible for their misery."

Things didn't improve for them until 1972, when Mitzi's mother took early retirement from her latest job and devoted herself to Buddhism full-time. She briefly became more accessible, but by then it was too late to alter the course of her youngest's life. A year earlier, Mitzi's only friend, a tomboy who lived across the street, had moved away. Devastated, she'd fallen into a deep depression her parents were too self-involved to notice. "Or if they did, they felt guilty and didn't know what to do," she says. The next year, they took off for a Zen monastery and placed Mitzi, thirteen, with a guardian.

DAVE McINTOSH'S WORLD got larger in 1968. "I remember watching Robert Kennedy's funeral and Martin Luther King's funeral," he says. It made an impression when his grandmother, riveted to the television, muttered, "Enough is enough."

The day Bobby Kennedy died, McIntosh was stunned when one of his classmates said he was glad, because it meant a Republican would be elected president. "I was very conscious that year that there was a change going on in the country," he says. Yet the culture of Kendallville sheltered him from it. Race riots and antiwar protests were roiling the country and the nearby cities, Detroit and Chicago, but those disturbances seemed remote alongside the presidential campaign.

McIntosh considered himself a Democrat like his mother, who'd remarried a man who ran a roofing company and spent the late 1960s having two more children. In fifth grade, when his teacher proposed that her students hold a mock election with students managing in-class campaigns for Hubert Humphrey and Richard Nixon, McIntosh was on the Humphrey team, and was outraged when students found a Nixon button in the teacher's desk. They decided she was secretly—*yuck!*—a Republican.

His mother got into politics in 1971. The local city judge was a Republican good old boy who didn't think women should be allowed to play golf and would hit balls at female foursomes on the links. "He did that one time to my mom and she got so mad," McIntosh recalls. She said, "He doesn't deserve to be judge." She had to run in a primary before she got to take on the mad golfer, but she won election by a two-to-one margin and was reelected unopposed in 1975. Whenever there was a parade in town, she would bring the kids to ride on the Democratic party's float.

JIM FOURATT WAS coming home late from work at Columbia Records on June 27, 1969—the day of homosexual icon Judy Garland's funeral—when he noticed a bunch of cops in front of the Stonewall, a gay bar on Sheridan Square in Greenwich Village. They were raiding the place, hauling the mourner-revelers within off to jail. Some of the arrested—drag queens and kings—kicked up a fuss, and suddenly a routine roust became a full-scale disturbance. Fouratt began calling his radical friends, a gay Paul Revere announcing "There's a riot going on"—but none responded.

Candlelight marches alternated with rioting for five nights. Then, on July 4, at a public meeting of the gay community, Fouratt, dressed in leather pants and cowboy boots, grew infuriated as he listened to "a heterosexual psychologist talk about how gay people were not assimilated and had to project a nice image." Leaping to his feet, he yelled "Bullshit!" and inveighed against the stereotype of soft, sweet homosexuals and the "pigs" who oppressed them.[53]

"We marched over to Alternate University, on Fourteenth Street and Sixth Avenue, where Living Theater used to be." Fouratt says. They were given a room by a rock critic who was teaching a course on Rock and Revolution. The suddenly self-aware gays discovered identity politics and formed the Gay Liberation Front (GLF). Like the women who kicked off the modern feminist movement in a closed-door session at an SDS conference, "We realized we had to deal with our own issues," Fouratt says. "We weren't going to be peaceful any more."

Later that year, Fouratt moved into one of several GLF-sponsored men's communes. GLF practiced coalition politics—it built bridges to the Black Panthers and to a new Hispanic group, the Young Lords—and Fouratt began attending radical conferences and meetings nationwide. "We formed consciousness-raising groups," he says. "We asked questions. What does it mean to be gay? Where does identity come from? Where does this behavior come from? How much of it is a reaction to oppression? How much is survival? How much is pathology because of oppression? We organized about fifty chapters on college campuses." The GLF later spawned Lavender Menace, a group of lesbians who demanded their right to be gay and proud within the women's movement. "It was about the inclusion of straight people in the gay community and the inclusion of gay and lesbian people in the revolutionary community," Fouratt says. "It was going to change everybody."

AS GLF WAS being born, so was the Woodstock Festival. The night before Stonewall, Fouratt had moderated a public meeting on behalf of the concert's promoters and publicists, who wanted to head off any "community" opposition to it. The idea was to discuss what Woodstock should symbolize. Rumor had it the concert was a profit-making venture backed, at least in part, by drug profits, which Fouratt believes. "Pot—that's where their money came from," he insists. Hundreds of members of the underground press, the rock industry and the local movement filled the Village Gate nightclub as street leaders hectored the festival promoters, demanding the event be politicized. Ultimately, the radicals agreed to take some tables in the concessions area, but have no other role at the festival. Later, though, Abbie Hoffman would attempt to extort $50,000 from the organizers—and finally got $10,000.[54] "Abbie invades Woodstock Ventures and says, 'There ain't gonna be a fuckin' festival unless . . . ,'" Fouratt recalls. "He never knew when to stop. Abbie was correct in his read of the bourgeois entrepreneurialism going on. Except Abbie was a part of that, too."

Fouratt attended Woodstock in August 1969, in his official capacity as house freak at Columbia Records, but he left after a single day on the site. The Motherfuckers had burned twelve of the festival's sixteen concession stands to the ground as a political protest.[55] Hoffman was there, too, furious that he'd been denied the chance to play master of ceremonies. Fouratt avoided him. Later, high on LSD, Hoffman would take to the stage in the middle of The Who's set to lecture the crowd for having fun while White Panther leader John Sinclair was serving nine years in jail for possession of two joints.

Fouratt was appalled. "It was a nightmare," he says. "It was raining, it was muddy, everybody was on fucking drugs. Grapes were being served backstage [despite Cesar Chavez's strike on behalf of California grape pickers], and Joan Baez was eating them. Janis was all fucked up. Jimi Hendrix was all fucked up. Everything was being played out against the contradiction between what they're pretending to be and what their real goal is. We got out of there and flew to a little island off of Italy. I'll never forget. We got on that plane, hating Woodstock, got off the plane and saw the Italian newspaper headlines, and immediately worked it, that we had come directly from Woodstock."

Back in New York that fall, Fouratt quit his job at Columbia after losing several arguments with executives. A new band called Chicago Transit Authority changed its name to Chicago over Fouratt's furious objection, and another lame ad campaign—"The Revolution Is on Columbia"—was about to begin. "I said, 'That's wrong,'" Fouratt recalls. "I would have joined them if I had stayed."

ON AUGUST 13, 1969, two days before Woodstock, India Company of the U.S. Marines was part of a massive regimental search-and-destroy mission five miles north of its camp at An Hoa in Quang Nam province when a large force of North Vietnamese Army regulars, hiding in trees, ambushed Tommy Vallely's unit. They opened fire on the point with small arms, automatics, a machine gun and a rocket-propelled grenade. "We were in the open," says Vallely. "You never want to be in the open. And they were kicking the shit out of us." It was a situation American commanders strived to avoid—one in which technological superiority was neutered—and he watched as several men, including his company commander, fell wounded. Realizing that his unit had been separated from the company, he radioed for reinforcements.

Instead of sitting tight, though, he worked his way to a wounded man, took his rifle, and charged the machine gun emplacement, single-handedly keeping the NVA soldiers occupied as more Americans took up positions near him. He then marked the machine gun with a smoke grenade and ran back and forth across an open field as bullets flew all around him, shuttling between the wounded commander and the other soldiers in his unit, relaying instructions and pinpointing the NVA troop locations.

"But we have so many casualties we got to get the hell out of there, and it's nighttime, and we don't know where we are," Vallely explains. Grabbing a map, he led the survivors out of harm's way to a place called China Beach—"not like the TV show," he notes. "It's where survivors, not the wounded, went for rest." Not only did he win the Silver Star, one of the highest military honors, but he was promoted to chief radio operator. He downplays his heroism. "You're going to react or you're going to be dead," he says. "Lots of people who should get Silver Stars don't; the company commander just liked me."

At nineteen, Vallely made the most of the opportunity. He encouraged positions of responsibility for a couple of black Marines, lessening racial tension in his unit. And he barred those under his command from harming prisoners, and made it clear to the South Vietnamese—or ARVN— soldiers they sometimes reluctantly fought alongside that he wouldn't let them act up, either. "I would not let them beat up prisoners or villagers for information. They were bullies."

Vallely never saw a Vietnamese city. He was at base camp for his entire thirteen-month tour of duty in Vietnam, aside from the rare rest-and-relaxation break in nearby Da Nang. Excluding the abuse of Vietnamese, he saw few of the other excesses later portrayed in Hollywood's version of the war. "We had a little marijuana, some alcohol in the rear," he says, "but in the field it was considered a violation if you had any dope. You would be in big trouble. You would endanger other people. You'd fall asleep, someone would cut your throat."

Mail call provided some amusement and comfort. His mother and leftist sister reported to him on the antiwar movement. "My sister didn't know what she was talking about, but it didn't bother me," he says. "I liked the demonstrators. I don't remember anybody in Vietnam hating demonstrators. I only knew a few people who took great pleasure in the war. Some of my company might have a different view, because part of my interpretation is what I've come to think."

Offered an officer's uniform, Vallely almost signed up for a second tour in Vietnam. He wanted to go home and get into politics, but he had to think about it because he'd "gotten to be attached to some of the people in the company and if I stayed things would go better for them."

But he'd turned against the war by then. He thought it was insanity. "I wanted to stop it but didn't know how; I certainly wasn't going to be a Trotskyite," he says. He spent his last few months of service back at Camp Pendleton in California, teaching radio operations to raw recruits, partying, and getting into barroom brawls. "We would go fight to have fun," he says. "We would drink and punch people and wake up in the morning and go back to work."

LIKE MANY LATE boomers, Kathryn Bond Stockton feels she missed the 1960s. In January 1965, her entire family attended Lyndon Johnson's inauguration. Aside from listening to songs from the "love rock" musical *Hair* and wearing bell bottoms, she recalls "see[ing] it off in the distance, but it's never happening to me."

Drugs were not an issue. After her parents let her smoke a cigarette at age eight, she decided smoking was dumb. "That was my parents' style, instead of trying to create forbidden domains." Two years later, in 1968, her fifth-grade class took mandatory drug education. "They would pound into your brain how terrible drugs are, and how marijuana is incredibly evil, right up there with heroin," she remembers. "So you had no ability to distinguish among these things, but I have to say, they had no appeal to me." In the rare instances when she heard about drugs at all, it was when someone her brother's age or older who'd left town died of an overdose.

She entered sixth grade in 1969. Two months later, her father was elected mayor of Bloomfield, Connecticut. As one of his first actions, he started school busing to achieve integration. "I remember when I saw black children for the first time," Stockton says. "They seemed more important than the rest of us, and I idolized them, and I thought, These are just amazing people, that they could come into this white school. I kept imagining what it would be like if it were reversed. And a lot of these kids were great athletes, and I admired athletic prowess."

Despite her political consciousness, Stockton didn't pay much attention to the Vietnam War. "And I don't remember my classmates giving a shit, either," she says. Her brother, who was more radical than she, worried about the draft and grew his hair long, "sort of an issue in the household," she says.

Stockton had more pressing concerns. As she neared puberty, sex became a threatening subject. She took sex education classes that year, and upon learning how her English teacher's wife had gotten pregnant, decided he had to be profoundly evil. "I refused to think of my parents that way," she adds. She became a devoted fan of Barnabas Collins, the vampire in the TV soap opera *Dark Shadows*. "He was this darkly tragic figure and he would have relationships with women and everything would be going perfectly fine, and then he couldn't help himself, he would have to bite them on the neck," she says. "I felt I was a vampire figure. I was basically admired and liked and could be attracted to people and have them attracted to me, but there would always come a point when my secret would come out, and then I would not be able to have the people I'd want to have. So I was determined no one will ever know. I used to think about how much torture I could stand before I would admit it. And I don't even know what words I had in my head. I'm not sure I knew the word *homosexual*."

The neighborhood girls surely didn't. They invited Stockton for a talk one day and gave her an ultimatum: give up her friendship with the local boys and they'd let her in their group. "It was like a tribunal," she recalls.

"I know they felt they were doing this pathetic creature a wonderful favor. I went home and cried and told my mother, and she said, 'You don't have to do anything you don't want to do.'" Yet she did: she had to wear dresses, so her mother bought her one that became her favorite. It had a sword dangling from its belt. "She said Robin Hood had worn something quite like it," says Stockton, who decided that made up for the humiliation of dressing like a girl.

That summer, preparing for her move to middle school, Stockton was stunned and fascinated by photographs of the Woodstock rock festival. "People were running around naked, and that was kind of interesting. I remember seeing this world explode and thinking, *What's that about?* But you're just slightly on the border of it. It's not quite your world."

AT THEIR NATIONAL Collective in Chicago, the Weathermen were trying to live by principles set down by the Soviet leader Lenin. In classic totalitarian double-talk, he'd called it Democratic Centralism. "The reason we lead this organization is that we're right more often than anyone else," Rudd said at the time.[56] Now he thinks it was something else. "People joined these things the way people join religious cults—the surrender. The idea was to build revolutionaries. There was also a weeding-out process called criticism and self-criticism, which was a kind of psychological group terror in which people had to criticize each other and criticize themselves for their lack of revolutionary will or zeal or whatever." Many dropped out. "The earlier you left, the saner you were," says Rudd, who came to believe that the war in Vietnam drove the Weather Bureaucrats insane. "It would be interesting if we could ever get together again to talk about who was sane and who was not," he adds, laughing.

Rudd didn't take many drugs—yet. "We were high on revolution," he says. And on violence. "I've got myself a gun—has anyone here got a gun?"[57] he asked during a recruiting speech at Columbia that fall. The antiwar movement, distanced itself from the Weather Bureau, condemning its adventurism. Chicago Panther leader Fred Hampton called Rudd "a motherfucking masochist" and knocked him to the ground.[58]

Just before the Weather Bureau's public debut—three days of violent demonstrations—a bomb went off in Chicago's Haymarket Square, destroying a statue of a policeman. Did the Weather Bureau do it? No one knew, but its members had begun discussing violence and stockpiling guns.[59] On October 8, 1969 the second anniversary of the death of Che Guevara, the action known as the Days of Rage opened with a rally in Lincoln Park, site of bloody clashes during the Democratic Convention the year before. All signs pointed to a debacle. Barely one thousand people showed up—armed with clubs, cans of oven cleaner, heavy boots, football helmets, gas masks, brass knuckles and Viet Cong flags—and they were surrounded by battle-ready police. After a brief rally, the crowd swarmed into the streets surrounding the park, committing random acts of violence, not only charging the police arrayed against them but also wrecking the automobiles of innocents. Many were arrested. Some were shot by police.

Two days later, demonstrators fought another brief but bloody battle in the heart of the city's shopping district. This time, a city lawyer was paralyzed, scores more were injured, and 103 were arrested, Rudd among them. He'd arrived at the base of the blown-up statue, where a march was to start, and was immediately "jumped by a gang of ten Red Squad cops," who hit him, maced him and stuck him in jail, he says. "That was the extent of my action: busted the second I arrive."

Though the Weather Bureau claimed victory ("that we are willing to fight the police is a victory," J.J. said), their idols, the Panthers, denounced them for "Custerism." Rudd was daunted by the experience, and by the low turnout. "It really undermined my confidence," he says.

If they'd been true believers before, now they were angry, frightened ones forming a vision of American apocalypse. "A new leadership within the leadership gets formed," Rudd says. "The issue is: Who wants the Revolution the most? It's an issue of will. I tended to be a doubting person. I would get my will buttressed by being slapped around in the Weather Bureau.

Will became even more important after Dohrn announced that the group had to go underground and engage in covert armed struggle against the state. She wasn't the only one to have the thought. In November, Jane Alpert and Sam Melville, a couple who lived in New York's East Village and had spent the preceding months with a collective that set off bombs in places like New York's military induction center, a United Fruit Company warehouse, and the headquarters of IBM, GTE, Chase Manhattan, General Motors, and Standard Oil, were arrested when Melville was caught placing time bombs on Army trucks at a Manhattan armory. Shortly thereafter, out on bail, Alpert took LSD and had sex with Rudd, whom she considered a movement celebrity.[60]

Weather held a War Council in December 1969. A cardboard machine gun, posters of Fidel Castro, Che Guevara, Eldridge Cleaver, Ho Chi Minh, Lenin, Mao and Malcolm X, and another featuring bullets etched with names of enemies of the people like Richard Nixon, Ronald Reagan and, curiously, the actress Sharon Tate (just murdered, along with several friends, by a band of hippie cultists led by a long-haired ex-convict, Charles Manson) decorated the hall in Flint, Michigan, during this revolutionary Woodstock for 400 hard-core radicals.[61] It was highlighted by evening *wargasm* sessions, speeches, singalongs (to rewritten classics like "Maria" from West Side Story, which now went, "The most beautiful sound I ever heard/Kim Il Sung, Kim Il Sung, Kim Il Sung"[62]), group exercise and group sex, Rudd enthusing about killing pigs and blowing up buildings, and Dohrn in a miniskirt, rhapsodizing about the Manson murders (". . . they even shoved a fork into pig Tate's stomach . . .") and holding up a four-finger salute to the fork. Manson was America's nightmare. Now the acid-taking revolutionaries aspired to be like the acid-taking murderer. One participant recalled it as "group psychosis."[63]

After the War Council, Rudd was demoted. The consensus was that he'd lost his nerve. The National Collective split into cells of the most trusted, directed by four Weather leaders Dohrn, J.J., Jones, and Robbins; the rest of the organization was simply cut loose. They destroyed the records of SDS as they left. "We were going to start armed struggle against the state, offensive armed struggle," Rudd says. "I could have affected the events. I could have blown the whistle. I could have stopped it."

In New York, Weather's Cathy Wilkerson, Kathy Boudin, former Columbia honor student Ted Gold, Diana Oughton, Terry Robbins and others began making bombs. On their first outing, in late February 1970, they ignited three gasoline bombs in front of the home of the judge in the Panther 21 case, causing minor damage. "Free the Panther 21" was scrawled in red on the sidewalk. About a week later, they bought a hundred pounds of dynamite and argued for days about how to use it. Four days after that, at noon, there was an explosion on West 11th Street in Greenwich Village, and the home of the vacationing Wilkerson family collapsed. Gold, Oughton, and Robbins were beneath it. Emerging halfnaked from the wreckage, Wilkerson and Boudin borrowed clothes from a neighbor, and ran off. In the rubble was proof of a sharp change in the Weathermen's direction. The explosion occurred because they'd made a mistake while wiring an antipersonnel bomb, designed to kill people.

Mark Rudd went to the movies that night to establish an alibi and saw Michaelangelo Antonioni's *Zabriskie Point*, a pretentious film glamorizing radical violence, in which a house explodes—quite beautifully—at the climax, taking the gorgeous protagonists with it. When he got back to his collective house, his roommates shoved the next day's newspaper under his nose. "Isn't it an interesting irony, that instead of it being effective terror, we only killed ourselves?" Rudd asks today.

THREE DAYS AFTER the Days of Rage ended, John Gage helped organize the October 15, 1969, Moratorium demonstration that brought out two million people nationwide[64]—including the unprecedented 100,000 people who came to Gage's event on the Boston Commons, the day's biggest crowd.[65] That success earned him the job of running the Mobilization's Washington rally a month later.

Richard Nixon threw the movement a curve on November 3, when he announced his plan for Vietnamization—turning the war over to the Vietnamese—and launched an attack on the peace movement as an un-American vocal minority up against the silent majority. The peace movement was having problems of its own. Factionalism necessitated dividing the action in Washington, with separate entities in charge of separate events, beginning with a Death March from Arlington Memorial Bridge, concluding with the reading of the names of Americans killed in Vietnam at the White House, and including a march up Pennsylvania Avenue, a rally on the Mall, an ultraviolent Weatherman spree, and a Chicago 8 protest at the Justice Department.

Half a million people came to the rally. With its performances by Arlo Guthrie, Peter, Paul and Mary and the cast of *Hair*, and the calming presence of Hugh Romney, a/k/a Wavy Gravy, it reminded many of Woodstock. Many on the sound and lighting crew had previously done duty there. But it proved a logistical nightmare even before tear gas drifted over from a demonstration at the Vietnamese Embassy.

That didn't stop Gage. He moved a bus in front of the stage as a shield, in case some loony tried to shoot one of the speakers. By the end of the day, the backstage area was full of children who'd been separated from their parents. Exhausted, Gage was about to deal with them when he spied a wall of riot police moving slowly down the Mall toward him. A splinter group from the rally had unexpectedly marched on the Justice Department, and the police were clearing out all the lingering protesters.

"Wavy has one of these little boxes, when you pull a string, it starts to laugh," Gage recalls. "He'd walk up to some policeman and pull the string and the thing would start to laugh. It's really very funny." Only the police didn't get the joke. Bill Hanley, a ponytailed sound technician and son of a Boston policeman, went out next. He'd built the world's biggest sound system for Woodstock. He was sure he could get the cops to stop. Instead,

Gage watched as Hanley was maced and arrested. Finally Gage gathered all the lost children in the bus and planted himself in the door. When the police demanded entry, he refused. Miraculously, the cops backed off. "Then I had to get Hanley out of jail!" says Gage. "He had to get on the road down to the next event."

That was the last official show of the 1969 Rolling Stones tour, a two-day rock festival at a drag strip in West Palm Beach, Florida, that also featured Janis Joplin and Sly and the Family Stone. Fresh from jail, Hanley arrived and, faced with disorganization and chaos, called for the cavalry, in the form of John Gage.

The line between protest culture and counterculture was growing thinner. "I've got the governor of Florida showing up with state troopers, and troops stationed across the highway, and a tank with a water cannon on it coming to break in and arrest all the drug-crazed hippies, and two hundred thousand people, and canals and alligators—and mud, lots of good mud," Gage recalls. "Then the state policemen grab the first stoned kid they see and arrest him. Unfortunately for the governor, he turns out to be the son of the most prominent Protestant minister in Miami, who has some medical condition and is certifiably a non-druggie. Big publicity in the following weeks about this arbitrary exercise of police power."

Meanwhile, Gage was juggling phone calls from San Francisco. "The Stones are supposed to fly there next and do another concert, but nobody knows where. I'm supposed to airlift the entire operation: the world's biggest sound system plus six Super-Trooper lights on ninety-foot-tall stands from West Palm Beach out to California," Gage says. "And I'm tired." Luckily, he didn't follow the equipment. The concert was finally held in December in Altamont, California, where Hell's Angels hired to guard the stage jumped an apparently stoned man and stabbed him to death.

Extended Adolescence

CAMERON SEARS WAS eight years old when the Rev. Martin Luther King Jr. was killed. "That night is vividly etched in my mind," he says. His family lived in northwest Washington, and looking out the windows of his newborn sister's bedroom, he was awestruck by the orange glow of a city in flames. "We had National Guard driving around—it's martial law, basically—and my dad had commuted into the city that morning," Sears recalls. He was petrified—and not just for his father. Sears was attending public school at the time. "It was in a diplomatic area, so a lot of the students were affiliated with various embassies, some were even the sons and daughters of ambassadors, but a lot of the kids came from the ghetto, a very eclectic mix. And it really freaked me out, because a lot of my friends were black and lived in the part of town that was burning. I'd gone to birthday parties there, so that had a much bigger impression on me than Bobby Kennedy's assassination. Everybody was drawn to Martin Luther King in a very spiritual way, even if you were only eight years old."

The shocks kept on coming. Sears, whose parents had friends in the government, had a front-row seat, but only some of that summer's events made an impression on his preteen psyche. He does remember that a counselor at his day camp gave him a batch of blue-and-white McCarthy buttons and that he briefly became a supporter. "I gave them out," he says. "I thought it was a hoot. I was wearing tie-dye clothes; we made them at camp. I was totally into it."

Like many late boomers, though, Sears only got to live his generation's defining experiences secondhand. He never protested, but did dress up as a radical one Halloween. His third-grade teacher "had a fit," he says, and called his mother in for a chat. Sears was shocked; if radicals weren't acceptable, why were they always on TV? "I had a strong sense of Woodstock," he adds, even though he was only nine. "I knew it was a phenomenal happening. When my dad went out to San Francisco for work in the early seventies, I went with him, and I felt, 'Wow, San Francisco; this is it.'" Never mind that it wasn't anymore.

In 1970, the Sears family moved back to Massachusetts, to the Boston suburb of Lexington. Sears doesn't remember Earth Day, that spring's kickoff of what would become the environmental movement, but summers spent on Cape Cod placed him ahead of that curve. "We talked about conservation issues around the dinner table, because on Cape Cod, there was a lot of developmental pressure," he says. "The dredging of the harbor was an issue: Why was that good and why was that bad? What did that mean? So I had a very clear grasp of ecological concerns." The next year, he came upon his father's copy of *The Whole Earth Catalogue*.

First published in 1968, the oversize book purveyed tools aimed at communes, what *Whole Earth* author Stewart Brand describes as "intentional communities . . . bands of adventurous malcontents who were setting out to reinvent civilization, trying to get it right this time."[1] Most of its buyers were like Sears, who read it cover to cover, enjoying the running commentaries and cartoons in its margins that made the book much more than a mere catalogue. "I'm looking at solar energy and where to go get the hip backpack and how to go live an alternative lifestyle," he says.

Music played a big part in the Sears household. Since his grandfather had been the folksinging activist Pete Seeger's faculty adviser in high school, Sears would go backstage whenever Seeger played concerts in the Washington area. His mother transferred her love of classical music and the piano to her son—a soloist in his church choir—and his father loved jazz. Sears's own taste was diverse.

The lure of the waning counterculture was still strong. Both its attractions and dangers reached Sears through the media. He first smoked pot in seventh grade in 1971. He'd been curious ever since he saw a picture of a hippie smoking a joint on the cover of *Life* magazine, but he was scared off stronger drugs by *Go Ask Alice*, a 1972 made-for-television movie that portrayed a high school student's freakout. "At the same time, a friend's older brother committed suicide because he was having a bad trip," Sears says. "I had a cousin who became a speed freak. And because some of my friends' parents were teachers at Harvard and MIT, every once in a while we'd hear about a kid who went flying out a window, tripping his brains out. But that didn't prevent me from tripping a bunch."

Sears took his first LSD—Orange Sunshine—as a junior at boarding school. "And I remember doing a fair amount of windowpane," a later "brand" of acid. After experimentation and some proselytizing to friends, Sears "didn't trip so much anymore," he says. "It really wasn't my thing."

He'd turned into a teenage rebel, though. "I played soccer and hockey and I was a tennis player. But because I had long hair and I would smoke dope, the coach at this boarding school would fuck with me. I was the number-one singles player, but he would make me play number-two doubles. I got so fed up I quit." Instead, he'd go out backpacking. "I guess I didn't have a team consciousness," he says.

THE BARBARA LEDEEN who came back to Beloit College from the *Washington Post* was not the girl who'd left a year before. Her exposure to the power elite and the protesting masses had turned her into a Marxist. But the movement was moving faster than she was; back in the Midwest, she decided the new radicals didn't want her kind around. When her political theory class took a trip to the South Side of Chicago to hear Rev. Jesse Jackson (b. 1941) preach his doctrine of black self-empowerment, all Ledeen could hear was the civil rights movement rejecting whites, Jews, her. She was scared, too, by the Blackstone Rangers, a street gang from Chicago's South Side that briefly became the darlings of Midwest leftists.

"They're calling Jews honkies, so I'm out of there; I'm off the train, man." Within a year of finding her "team," she says, "you had no more team." Then came Nixon. "Poison gas," Ledeen says. "It reached the point where it was, pick up a gun or get out. All I could think about was getting out of this horrible country, because there was no corner of it that was not corrupt. Idealism had failed. The norm was the storm."

Her only refuge was literature. She'd saved two courses for her senior year: twentieth-century European literature—Hesse, Camus, Kafka and Brecht—and one on James Joyce. The existentialists gave her comfort. Not so the Joyce teacher, a married Irishman with whom Ledeen fell madly in love. "I was obsessed and he took advantage of my obsession," she says. At the end of that year, her parents expected her to go to law school, and in exchange for her reluctant agreement, her father gave her a round-trip ticket to Luxembourg, a Eurailpass, and $400. She had no intention of returning. Armed with a duffel bag and her nest egg, knowing no one and no languages other than English and Latin, Ledeen landed in Luxembourg in summer 1970, and hitchhiked through Paris to Barcelona, where she and a girl from San Francisco checked into a youth hostel in a little fishing village, on the Mediterranean coast. When they ran out of money, they hired out to work on fishing boats. "And not a single bad thing happened to us. We would leave around three A.M., come back in around seven at night. We'd throw out the nets, pull them in with the guys, have coffee with brandy in it in the morning, a big pot of fish stew for lunch. We did that for weeks. I was so stupid, it didn't occur to me what bad things could happen."

She hated America so much, she'd begun telling people she was Canadian. "Any anti-American demonstration in Europe I would go to," she says. From Spain, she moved on to Italy and Yugoslavia, where she came to rest again, selling paintings and explaining Bob Dylan lyrics to students in a Zagreb piazza. She finally called her parents and told them she wasn't coming home; they'd asked the State Department to find her, but she didn't want them to know where she was. Anyway, she was on the move again. "It was time to go, because I was not going to learn Serbo-Croatian."

There was another reason to leave Yugoslavia; her lover, the Joyce professor, was returning to Europe. They'd corresponded through the year, and now planned to meet, in spring 1971, on Elba, an island off Italy. But Ledeen had problems; her professor still had a wife. When she'd told her father she wasn't coming home for law school, he cut her off. She called him a corrupt capitalist and headed to Edinburgh. Why? The Scots were victims of British imperialism, and she'd heard students could rent dormitory rooms cheap at the University of Edinburgh.

"Then winter comes," she laughs, "and I have never been so cold in my entire life." So when she saw a want ad for an English tutor in Milan, she jumped. "Milan was close to Elba." She wrote her lover, met him at a hotel in southern Italy, and confirmed that he had no intention of leaving his wife. She lasted two more weeks in Milan, then begged her parents to take her back. "I had to admit defeat," she says. "It was awful." She moved home to Rochester, but soon returned to Washington, worked two jobs for several months, and socked away cash. "I buy another ticket," she sighs, "straight to Elba. But he was gone."

Forlorn, she was also resourceful and got a job organizing excursions for English visitors to a local resort. It paid well enough that she could rent a villa on a white sand beach, facing the Mediterranean. "All the fishermen, the housewives, the storekeepers know me. I can hitchhike around and nobody will bother me. My neighbors teach me Italian. It's idyllic. And then I get sick. And you don't want to be sick on Elba."

Ledeen ended up in a hospital in Rome, where she lost her appendix and made a friend, a fellow patient, the wife of the financial attaché to the Embassy of Sierra Leone, who rented her a room and helped her get a job at the Zambian embassy. "And we do black Africa," she laughs. "Fish heads and spicy bananas. And they have brought a niece of somebody in their family to be their household slave. She's not sent to school; they feed her the scraps; this is their culture; this is how they are. And I never even once say to them, 'Don't you think she should be in school?' "

The Zambian embassy made American corruption look benign. "Back home, they're starving to death, but these diplomats are living top of the line," Ledeen says. "They get shipments of caviar, champagne, the most incredible foie gras, they order suits from the finest tailors. And they never pay. Nobody speaks any known language, they speak what they think is English but really isn't, so I'm their communicator with the outside world. My job is to tell the grocers, the tailors, 'Sorry, he's not in today. And he won't be in tomorrow or next week, either.' "

THERE WERE CONTINGENCY plans in case the Weather Bureau's bombing at Fort Dix went awry, and Mark Rudd followed them in the hours after the West 11th Street townhouse exploded, helping the survivors regroup. As is the case with much of what followed, Rudd will still not go into detail. Briefly, he was listed among the presumed dead. He had an intermediary call his parents and assure them he was all right. They thought he was nuts and had told him as much, but they hadn't tried to stop him. The Weathermen had a vague plan to go underground, but the details hadn't been worked out. Now that was done on the fly. During the next two months, the Weather Bureau passed through a scrim of friends and supporters, communes and collectives, from Vermont to Oregon, and disappeared.

Still taking themselves seriously, they hunkered down and tied themselves in ideological knots trying to figure out what they'd done wrong, but they also had to deal with the logistics of being federal fugitives. A month after the townhouse bombing, the Nixon administration began planning a secret interagency crackdown on domestic terror—specifically targeting groups like the Weathermen and the Panthers. Rudd, Dohrn, Jones, Robbins, Boudin, J.J., Ayers and others were indicted in April for crossing state lines and inciting riots in Chicago. The case was assigned to Julius Hoffman, the infamous Chicago 8 judge. Four days later, a warrant was issued for Rudd's arrest when he failed to show up for trial on a riot charge stemming from the Columbia takeover.

Rudd was already underground, en route to San Francisco, where he was sent to an emergency meeting of the Weather Underground. He walked into a fierce argument.[2] J.J. was being blamed for what was termed the "military error" at the townhouse. "The problem with the organization was J.J.," Rudd recalls. "The error was armed struggle and going underground." Expelled, J.J. left the meeting and dropped out of sight.

Rudd was linked to J.J., so he fell farther down Weather's food chain. "I was already out of the Weathermen," he says. "The only reason I was at the meeting was because of who I used to be." He blamed himself. He was weak; he couldn't *do it*. And he couldn't go home. He was facing heavy felony charges and, he feared, the possibility of murder charges as well. Rudd was sent to San Francisco to join a collective and redeem himself. Dohrn, Ayers and Jones were nearby, living on a Sausalito houseboat. In May, Dohrn's voice was on a tape delivered to the underground press, declaring a state of war between the Weather Underground and "Amerika-with-a-K." A few days later the Associated Press and the *New York Times* got a note, signed Weathermen, threatening an attack against a "symbol or institution of American injustice." Two weeks later, a bomb exploded in New York's police headquarters, injuring seven people.

Beginning in summer 1970, and for months thereafter, Weather Underground bombings continued across the country. Early in 1971, Dohrn and Boudin blew up a women's bathroom in the U.S. Capitol building in response to the bombing of Laos. Following the shooting of black activist George Jackson in the yard at San Quentin Prison in August 1971, Weather blew up three offices of the California prison system.[3] After an uprising at New York's Attica Penitentiary, which resulted in the deaths of nine guards and thirty inmates, including Jane Alpert's lover Sam Melville, a bomb went off in the office of New York's corrections commissioner. The next year, shortly after America began bombing North Vietnam, Weather even hit the Pentagon—on Ho Chi Minh's birthday, no less.[4]

Rudd was blowing up buildings, too. He was working odd jobs, "trying to make a semblance of life, but more important, continuing with a political strategy which involved still more bombings," he admits. "But it was with a lot of caution, so nobody was hurt." Not all bombers were so scrupulous, but usually Weather approved of freelance copycats. "Part of the concept was exemplary actions that could be emulated," Rudd says. Even now, almost thirty years later, his is loathe to admit that he was engaged in terrorism. "We tended to differentiate between terror, or killing civilian people, and legitimate targets," he says. "You can blow up a bathroom in the Pentagon."

Rudd was told to make contact with the Youth Culture. This was Weather's new line—communicated in December 1970, in a manifesto named for Bob Dylan's song "New Morning." Rudd later said his comrades were a day late and a dollar short in discovering what they called Weather Nation, but he did his bit.[5] He grew his hair long, wore a disguise, lived in various apartments in San Francisco, hung out at Fisherman's Wharf, and hitchhiked up and down the California coast, making the hippie scene.

Weather Underground had an aboveground support network that helped with money, identification documents, and the difficult logistics of staying a step ahead of law enforcement. It also helped reconnect Rudd with a girl named Sue, his pre-strike Columbia girlfriend, in summer 1970; she stayed underground with him for the next seven years.

By that time, though, Rudd was suffering from depression. He'd gotten another woman pregnant. He and a dozen other Weathermen had been indicted again, in July in Detroit, for a conspiracy to bomb and kill. "There were moments of feeling suicidal," he says. "Was the rest of my life going to be this or prison? There was a lot of loneliness and fear and anxiety. A very tough time." But strangely, it all settled him down. Sue became his best friend and began to help him clarify what was happening and why. The next New Year's Eve, she and Rudd agreed they might strike out on their own. They bought a truck and began taking trips to Death Valley. They had to start a new life somewhere.

Early in 1971, Rudd told his comrades he was striking out on his own. No one argued. They thought him a shooting star, a creature of ego and publicity. "I was no longer functional as a true believer, as a soldier in that militant guerrilla organization," he says. "The logic of my leaving was obvious." Sue made arrangements to leave her job and disappear with him. They ended up in Santa Fe, New Mexico.

Rudd had many identities over the years. He was sometimes a greaser, sometimes a hippie, sometimes Tony Schwartz or Tony Goodman. His driver's license was in a different name, his car registered to a fourth. He was still trying to shed his white-skin privilege; now he understood the anxiety poor people live with every day. "Am I going to pay the rent, and will the FBI get me this week?" he says, laughing. Yet Santa Fe gave him peace. He settled on one identity, created a fictitious past, and worked construction. "We worked and we had friends, and we weren't obsessed with making the Revolution," Rudd says. "Well, Sue never was."

Things were fine until Rudd accidentally bumped into Jane Alpert, the New York bomber. Alpert had pleaded guilty on May 4, 1970, the day of the Kent State killings. Then, free on bail, she got on a train for the spring 1970 march on Washington and disappeared into the Underground. Still on the run in 1971, Alpert had a chance encounter with her ex-lover Rudd in Santa Fe. "Immediately after, Santa Fe was flooded with FBI agents looking for us," says Rudd. He packed and moved to Pennsylvania, where he and Sue lived for two years and had a son. They moved again in summer 1974, to a working-class neighborhood in New Rochelle, near New York City. Sue worked in stores and took care of children, while he kept doing construction work. The war in Vietnam ended when the Paris Peace Accords were signed in January 1973. Then the Nixon administration collapsed in the Watergate scandal.

Early in the Watergate investigation, it emerged that, galvanized by the 1970 townhouse explosion, the government had engaged in an illegal war against the New Left, accelerating a counterintelligence process begun after the Columbia uprising. An interdivisional intelligence unit was set up to cross-reference information gathered by the FBI, the military, the Secret Service, the Bureau of Narcotics and Dangerous Drugs, and other local and national police agencies, and a special litigation section was set up to pursue SDS, the Weathermen, the White Panther Party, and others.[6]

In June 1973, a federal judge ordered the government to disclose any evidence of burglary, sabotage, illegal surveillance, the use of agents provocateurs, or other espionage techniques used in the Weather investigation. Even though the Weather Underground was still bombing—in September 1973 it planted a bomb at ITT headquarters in New York to protest the coup that deposed Chile's elected Marxist leader, Salvadore Allende Gossens—the next month, the government dropped its case in Detroit; the following January, the Chicago charges were dropped as well. If they'd gone to trial, Rudd's lawyer Gerald Lefcourt claimed, he would have introduced evidence that, despite denials, the Nixon administration had drafted an illegal plan for centralized domestic counterespionage shortly after the Kent State killings, and put it into effect through a secret executive committee run by a Justice Department lawyer.

With charges dropped, Lefcourt called Rudd and told him he could come home. But he and Sue decided to stay underground. "I was in an ambivalent place," Rudd says. "I was detached from the organization, but I also was no less in opposition to U.S. imperialism." It took two more years of doing no more than not getting caught to finally change Rudd's mind.

By then, the Weather Underground was in disarray, having "evolved from terrorism to armed attacks that didn't hurt anybody, to becoming a publishing house," Rudd scoffs. They put out books and magazines (and even appeared in a documentary film) that reflected their latest ideology; under the influence of old-style communists, they were spouting "a standard, doctrinaire labor-workers line," and finally, Rudd says, had been seized by their own followers and "held hostage for their crimes." In a bizarre replay of the Stalinist show trials of 1930s Communists, they were purged from their own organization.

By 1976, Rudd was ready to surface. But after John Jacobs suddenly appeared, disrupting their plans, Rudd and Sue moved again and waited a year before finally emerging in September 1977.[7] "He's thirty years old," his father told *The New York Times*. "You get too old to be a revolutionary." Rudd unwittingly chose to surface on Rosh Hashanah, the Jewish New Year, a slow news day in New York; he made page one of the *Times* and swept past about 100 reporters as he entered the Manhattan district attorney's office. "I walked up from the subway a few blocks away, and there was this roar, and the cameras and everything," he recalls. "I thought there must be some event happening. So I walk into it, and it's me! I'm the event."

FIFTEEN DAYS AFTER the 1969 Moratorium, Jim Fouratt attended a regional conference of homosexual organizations, where a radical caucus called for support of the Panthers, the Chicago 8, the California grape pickers, and women's liberation—all of which outraged older gays, who wanted to live their lives in peace, and younger ones, who wanted to lead their sex lives in peace. Both disdained Goldilocks, as they called Fouratt, and his crowd of crazy revolutionaries.[8] In December 1969, the Gay Liberation Front splintered. Members of the new Gay Activist's Alliance rejected Fouratt's politics. Their attitude, he says, was: "Fuck the liberation and let's just deal with Gay."

Their rejection drove Fouratt even more firmly into the camp of the oppressed. He organized a group of gays and lesbians to go to Cuba to cut sugar cane with the Venceremos Brigade, which sent Americans to the communist island every year. "Two days before we were to leave, I was notified that I was not welcome, because I was openly gay." Homophobic Cuban officials feared he'd try to organize gay Cubans.

So Fouratt poured all his belongings into a VW van and drove to Austin, Texas, where there was going to be a gay liberation conference; he'd been invited to stay with a friend, the actor and screenwriter L. M. Kit Carson (b. 1947). But Fouratt was pulled over by police near Carson's house and charged with driving with an expired license. The police also found gay liberation and Black Panther literature, and copies of Mao Tse-Tung's famous little red book. "The next thing I knew, I was arrested for possession of heroin and guns, neither of which I had," he says.

Carson arranged for a wealthy friend to bail Fouratt out of jail. He was then confined to the man's property for a month, which wasn't bad; the man had an art collection and parties that attracted celebrities. Fouratt wasn't above singing for his supper. "I was the hippie," Fouratt says. "I hadn't really been around this kind of society."

Finally, Fouratt was allowed to plead guilty to possession of marijuana and leave Texas. When he went to a big antiwar demonstration in Boston in April 1970, he learned that in his absence, a rumor had started that he was an FBI informer. It could have been started by anyone, from his gay opponents to people jealous of his job at Columbia. He was also attracting government attention. He spoke at a May rally protesting the arrest of Bobby Seale for murder in New Haven and earned a statement in support of homosexuals from Black Panther leader Huey Newton in return. He attended a People's Revolutionary Constitutional Convention in Philadelphia that September. Having gotten to know Weatherman leaders before they went underground, he was helping them, too. The FBI, which had long ignored the New Left, now instituted the counterintelligence program that became known as COINTELPRO. Among its tactics were harassment and disinformation campaigns against radical leaders. Cops had even come to Fouratt's mother's door, saying he'd been involved in a bank robbery and asking for his picture.

Fouratt's parole officer in New York, who told him he couldn't associate with homosexuals, probably didn't like him gallivanting all over the country meeting fellow revolutionaries, either. But he took off for Seattle, for a meeting of the Weathermen support network, "something about moving people around the country," he says vaguely. Fouratt hadn't liked it when he heard that the Weathermen had been building anti-personnel bombs in that basement on West 11th Street, but that didn't stop him. "My allegiance was to struggle within that community tactically, but not to abandon them," he says. "And there's something very romantic about an underground. I knew where the safe houses were. All these groups had links to each other."

He was near the gay bars of Seattle's Triangle Square when he was nabbed for jaywalking by the police. That's when he found out his parole had been revoked. The marshals who flew him back to Dallas kept asking about Bernardine Dohrn. Finally, Fouratt got tired of it. "I'm Bernardine Dohrn," he said.

Again, friends in Texas set him up with a swell place to stay. His new hostess was five times married, with multiple Cadillac convertibles in a crayon box of colors. Through her, he met a gay minister and got involved in a group called the Purple Star Tribe, which took over a local alternative newspaper. Journalism was the bridge to his next stop, Washington, D.C., where he joined the Unicorn News Collective, which had started an alternative network by giving five-minute news summaries to college and noncommercial radio stations.

In 1972, Fouratt covered the Republican convention in Miami for Unicorn as Richard Nixon was nominated for a second term in office. Fouratt had an epiphany when he went to a rally in Flamingo Park, which had been given to the protesters in an attempt to obviate repeats of the Chicago riots. The event was sponsored by a breakaway faction of the Yippies, who considered Abbie Hoffman and Jerry Rubin sellouts. Led by Tom Forcade and Dana Beal, they called themselves Zippies. "I watched a mind-washing experiment," Fouratt says. Zippies were "giving acid to young people, and then taking them through classic brainwashing steps. They wanted to politicize these kids, who already were political because they were there, but for their own agenda, which was disruptive and nihilistic. Abbie was sort of stumbling around lost, because he was a leader but there was no movement anymore." Zippies tossed a pie in Rubin's face that week to remind him he was well over thirty.

All around them were the lost, the damaged, the chastened. The North Vietnamese were winning their war overseas, but the movement that helped them, drowning in its own narcissistic maximalism, was losing its war at home. Nixon won again. Politics no longer provided direction, and drugs rushed in to fill the void. Quaaludes had suddenly flooded the drug scene in 1972, numbing all who took them and inspiring a conspiracy theory that they were being distributed by the CIA to end the peace movement. For the committed, everything was falling apart.

"The middle seventies were dark times," Fouratt says. "I was trying to figure out what to do and how to be. You really had to decide what was important." He often stopped to reflect on his friends who'd died or gone underground, and he couldn't help feeling a profound sense of loss. "What doesn't ever get said is that these were smart, on-the-right-track kids who threw away everything," he notes. "These people no longer had any resources, any access, no longer could easily go back to careers. There's an incredible psychological price when you are a no-man or no-woman. When your dream is over, what do you fall back on?"

The Paris Peace Accords, signed January 27, 1973—the same day

Defense Secretary Melvin Laird announced the end of the draft—took whatever wind was left out of the antiwar movement's sails. Although the conviction of the Chicago 7 would shortly be overturned by a federal appeals court, the lives of several of the defendants had already spiraled out of control. Abbie Hoffman threw himself into drugs and promiscuity, and by mid-1973 was dealing cocaine. Arrested that August 28, he disappeared into the Underground. Rennie Davis renounced activism and swore allegiance to the guru Mahara Ji. Jerry Rubin spent 1971 to 1975 trying, as he wrote in a memoir, an even more extensive "smorgasbord course in New Consciousness" than that undergone just a year earlier by Nina Hartley's parents. Rubin's quest included est, gestalt therapy, bioenergetics, rolfing, massage, jogging, health food, tai chi, Esalen, hypnotism, modern dance, meditation, Silva Mind Control, Arica, acupuncture, sex therapy and Reichian therapy.[9] Hoffman and Rubin's friends, too, were in trouble. Tom Forcade, who'd continued to smuggle drugs after founding *High Times* magazine in 1974, fell prey to Quaaludes and committed suicide in 1979. John Lennon and Yoko Ono found a more old-fashioned way to deaden their pain: They took up heroin.

LESLIE CROCKER SNYDER wanted to prosecute felonies. Though her boss, New York's DA Frank Hogan, let her prosecute men caught masturbating in public toilets, he wouldn't let her near major crimes, let alone what she really wanted—murderers. "I was totally devastated," she recalls. Weenie-wagger detail just didn't cut it. "I'm not a moralist," she says. "If you want to live with someone, you should live with someone. If you want to be gay, be gay. If you want to smoke pot, smoke pot, as long as it's not going to affect your performance. I do believe in personal freedoms. I don't think anything is really aberrant as long as it doesn't affect others."

She'd decided to be a career prosecutor. "I wanted to go to the Homicide Bureau, which is considered the elite bureau," she says. It was also the ultimate bastion of testosterone. So she displayed some of her own, threatening to quit, and enlisting superiors in her cause. Finally, Hogan offered her a job prosecuting the least serious felony offenders, juvenile cases, which "a woman could only fuck up so much."

Snyder's sex was actually an asset; before the 1972 Supreme Court decision that made it far harder for women to avoid jury service, she typically argued in front of all-male juries. "I love men, they like me, and it was a great chemistry," she says. Not so with Hogan. After he finally let her try felonies, she asked for more—a place in the Homicide Bureau—as he tried to talk her into heading Consumer Frauds. "I've always seen you as a Betty Furness," he said, referring to the famous consumer advocate then considered a woman of the highest accomplishment. Finally, he came up with a foolproof plan to shut her up. "Bring me a letter of permission from your husband, and I'll consider allowing you in the Homicide Bureau," he told her with a gleam in his eye.

Homicide prosecutors were on call at all hours and often had to work in the city's worst neighborhoods, where there were few women police, no women detectives, and no women in the station houses where she'd have to take statements. "It was a very different time," Snyder says. "And Hogan's time was fifty years before that." Hogan was sure that Snyder, who'd recently married a pediatrician, would never get permission. He was wrong. Her husband acquiesced, several mentors went to bat for her, and she soon became the first woman to try homicides in New York City. Indeed, she was the only woman to make the bureau, which disbanded shortly thereafter. By then, Snyder had moved on.

In 1970, shortly before moving to Homicide, she'd tried a double rape-robbery, and learned how rape laws were skewed against women. Two women had been dragged at knifepoint into a Lower East Side tenement, where they were raped, sodomized and robbed. Sex crimes were typically tried before Hogan-esque male judges, who found the cases as confusing as they were distasteful. New York law then required corroboration of three separate elements of a rape: identification of the attacker, proof that force was used, and proof of penetration. The judge in this case insisted that although semen had been found in the women's underwear, that was insufficient proof of penetration—and set the rapist free. "I just thought it was outrageous, hypertechnical and unfair," Snyder says. "Women were just not worthy of belief."

Though she hadn't been involved with protests or the women's movement, the judge's remarks raised Snyder's consciousness—and snapped her experiences at Harvard, at Case Western, at the U.S. Attorney's Office, and in Hogan's office into sharp focus. "I had been able to do everything I wanted to do in my life. But all that stuff percolates, and suddenly you see it in its totally outrageous context," she says. The fact that more women were coming out of law schools, joining lonely pioneers like Snyder, made it seem ever more urgent that things change, and more possible that they might. "As women felt more free to do whatever they want in many ways, including sexually, they felt freer to speak out, to get laws changed, and to become more involved," Snyder says.

Snyder made contact with Hogan's Appeals Bureau, where prosecutors agreed that the rape laws were unfair and encouraged her to try to change them. In 1972, they did; henceforth, a rape victim's uncorroborated identification of an attacker was deemed sufficient evidence. Her victory did not go unnoticed.

Though other political movements had faltered, feminists were feeling their oats. Journalist Gloria Steinem had launched *Ms.* magazine in 1971. The Equal Rights Amendment passed the Senate the next year and was sent to the states for ratification. In 1973, the Supreme Court decision in *Roe* v. *Wade* legalized abortion, but Snyder, like many baby boom women, kept her distance from women's liberation, even as she worked with the Manhattan Women's Political Caucus, NOW, and New York Women Against Rape to revise rape laws further. The suspicion was mutual (she was a prosecutor, after all), but "clearly we all met on fervent common ground in these limited areas," Snyder says, "and it trumped the distrust. At that point, it kind of coalesced for me. What mattered was that women should be treated equally and have the same opportunities and legal rights."

The fight to change the rape laws went on for several years. Finally, in November 1973, a united front of women from all ends of the political spectrum testified at a New York legislative hearing, urging that *all* corroboration requirements be repealed. A year later, they were.

By then, Snyder was pregnant. The DA's office had no maternity leave policy, but she was granted one. When she returned to work six weeks later, she had a new boss. The aging Hogan had retired. The new DA pushed her to come back and take over the Consumer Frauds Bureau. She would do it part-time for a while, she agreed, but felt no passion for the work, and soon asked and was given permission to continue her rape work and form a Sex Crimes Bureau—the first in the country.

To prosecute rapists successfully, Snyder knew she needed more tools than the law gave her. "I'd witnessed any number of trials in which the defendant was forgotten," she says. "Most sex crimes offenders are recidivists, but you couldn't ask anything about the defendant's priors. But the victims had to take the witness stand, the cross-examination would go on for hours about every sex act they'd ever committed—nothing to do with the case, nothing to do with the defendant. Their morality, their prior sexual history became the focus of the trial. They became the defendant, basically. Women were utterly discouraged from testifying because of these antiquated laws."

In 1974, after a Women's Bar group asked Snyder to head its Criminal Law Section, she and another member researched and wrote a Rape Shield Law, a piece of legislation designed to ensure that rape victims not be put on trial themselves for their prior sexual history. Its passage in 1975 was the most exciting moment of her life.

Simultaneously, Snyder and three other assistant district attorneys were setting up their sex crimes bureau, concentrating on the most legally difficult cases from the moment they were reported, guiding, reassuring and shielding the victims. "So you had people who were interested in and knew about this crime, people who hand-held the victim, sent them to support groups, sent children to psychologists if needed," she says. "It was very exciting. Because you really felt you were helping."

Snyder continued to score legal firsts. She was named the first female bureau chief in the history of the New York DA's office. Then came Marvin Teicher, a New York dentist who was repeatedly accused of molesting his patients—rubbing them, exposing himself, even penetrating them—while they were under anesthesia. Because they were sedated when assaulted, their testimony was worthless in court. Teicher also chose his victims carefully—picking on disaffected hippie-ish girls less likely to be believed. For a year, Snyder tried to get him by conventional means, sending patients who thought they'd been molested back to see him again, wired for sound, but he was too cagey to get caught—even when faced with experienced undercover cops.

Finally, Snyder got a court order to plant a camera in his ceiling—video surveillance had never been requested before. Policemen posing as power company workers installed a camera focused on the dental chair, and set up a monitoring post in his basement. Then she sent in an undercover agent who looked like a hippie. The videotape was running as he knocked her out and felt her breasts. He would finally be convicted in 1977.

DOUG MARLETTE LEFT school in June 1971. He hadn't graduated because he'd failed to fulfill his six-hour foreign language requirement. But that didn't matter. He'd been accepted as a conscientious objector and to fulfill the requirements, he had to do two years of public service. He took a post with the nonprofit College Press Service. As the job didn't pay much and he had a wife to support, he also took a night job as a paste-up man in the art department of Florida's *St. Petersburg Times* and almost immediately got a promotion to a day job, replacing an artist who'd been busted for drug dealing. Six weeks later, he was fired as overqualified.

Through a friend back home in North Carolina he heard there were openings for editorial cartoonists at both the *Raleigh News and Observer* and the *Charlotte Observer*. He immediately flew north and applied. In the interim, the Supreme Court had declared that anyone who'd been drafted when Marlette was—a brief period when the Selective Service Act had expired and its future was being debated in Congress—had to be released. "So I took the job in Charlotte," Marlette says. "And the career begins."

His first cartoon for the *Charlotte Observer*, in January 1972, lampooned Richard Nixon's bombing of Cambodia. His first big local issue was school busing. He sided with the moderates who were for it and against "the concerned parents, who were really Segs"—or segregationists—he says. Their allies were doing things like burning crosses on the lawn of the federal judge presiding over the case. Archconservative Jesse Helms began serving as North Carolina's junior senator that year and became another target. "Within a few weeks I had petitions being sent in, demanding I be fired," Marlette says. After a year of Marlette, the publisher of the *Observer*—a member of the Knight family that owned the Knight-Ridder newspaper chain and "a racist and a reactionary of the extreme kind," according to Marlette—joined the chorus of detractors, complaining that their new pacifist cartoonist had come to town "both guns blazing." Knowing he was attracting national attention to their local paper, Marlette's superiors backed him up, but they moved his cartoons from the editorial page to the Op-Ed page just opposite, putting some distance between his work and the paper's masthead.

"The nation was polarized," Marlette says. "I got to learn my craft with these larger-than-life figures. I was drawing cartoons that were anti-segregation, antiwar, anti-Nixon, and anti-Helms in a place that was in favor of all those things. And doing it in a way that drove people crazy."

In 1974, he and his wife separated and divorced. That summer, Gerald Ford's ascension to the presidency marked the end of an ugly era. "It had been nasty, and that's one of the reasons my cartoons were so upsetting to people," Marlette says. "There was a certain gratitude for some kind of civility coming back. It got duller, though, professionally."

IT SUDDENLY SEEMED to Tim Scully as if there were cops everywhere. When Sand finished his Orange Sunshine production, Scully shut down the Windsor lab and spent his time learning to fly a plane, a Mooney M20E, which Billy Hitchcock had given him. Scully was en route out of

Napa County Airport when federal agents carrying a warrant from Denver converged on him. Accepting the inevitable, he waived extradition and spent the next year commuting to Denver, where his lawyers beat the charges by proving that the police should have had a search warrant before entering his lab. Legal ingenuity also overturned the convictions of Scully's accomplices.

Still, Scully decided to retire from the LSD trade. He'd done his time in the Underground Army, and it wasn't as if the world would be without acid. Scully had met a new backer/chemist who had access to raw lysergic acid, and brought him to Sand. Sand would still work at a lab in St. Louis and at a new one in Belgium.

Early in 1969, one of Hitchcock's associates had been caught at U.S. Customs with $100,000 in cash. Though the money belonged in large part to Sand and Owsley, the courier said it was Hitchcock's. In order to explain why no taxes had been paid, Hitchcock got his Swiss banker partner to say it was a loan.

Hitchcock, divorcing and afraid his wife might reveal his drug dealing, moved back to New York.[10] Scully headed to Albion, a little town in northern California. He'd grown scared of the consequences of his chemistry, and that played into a growing disenchantment with drugs, or at least with those who used them irresponsibly. He began building biofeedback instruments for use in drug rehabilitation programs—electronic measuring tools that help users alter consciousness without drugs. He'd been the subject of a biofeedback experiment in 1966, when he was in Los Angeles with the Dead, and a fascination with the idea of voluntary control of consciousness without drugs had lingered. Biofeedback helped Scully come down from the high "of doing something that we thought would save the world" and replaced it with "something considerably less dangerous while still making the world a better place," he says. He had dues to pay, and rehab programs were a good place to pay them. Most acidheads he met told him he'd changed their lives for the better, but "a small percentage had bad things happen," he says, and others went on to more dangerous drugs because they figured a government that lied about one must be lying about them all.

"I felt really bad about that," Scully says. "I still do. Knowing what I know, I would not have pushed so strongly to scatter acid to the four corners of the earth without any thought of channeling it to try to increase the likelihood that people who took it would use it responsibly. Producing tools to help people with drug problems was a step toward restitution." Ironically, the product of that mission—the $100 machines he made to help teach addicts and alcoholics to produce calming, meditative alpha brain waves—earned him more than LSD had. Which was lucky. Owsley's hidden drug profits had evaporated.[11]

In January 1970, with the stock market plunging from its 1960s highs, Billy Hitchcock's wife filed for divorce and included charges that she had seen him take Owsley's money, substantiated with documents from her husband's safe deposit boxes. Hitchcock flew to Switzerland, where he discovered that not only was all his money gone, he also owed the bank $1 million.[12] When negotiations broke down, the bank sued him and apparently sent its lawyers documents about his Swiss accounts—*and* those belonging to Owsley and Sand. The repercussions of these financial dealings would soon effect the entire counterculture.

In March 1970, Timothy Leary hired Michael Kennedy, the San Francisco radical lawyer, to handle a Supreme Court appeal of his Laguna Beach conviction. Kennedy had expanded his practice beyond radicals to include dealers and pornographers. Now he became the link between the drug underground and other clients in the Weather Underground. In September 1970, the Brotherhood paid the Weathermen $25,000 to break Leary out of prison. Leary later claimed that the middleman and mastermind of the plan was his lawyer, Michael Kennedy.[13] The Weather Underground picked Leary up outside the walls of a California prison. Mark Rudd helped set up an apartment for him. Others provided him with a disguise and false passport, and spirited him out of the country. "We are outlaws, we are free," the radicals boasted in a communiqué announcing the dramatic breakout.

Leary issued a letter a few days later saying he should be considered armed and dangerous, and eventually made his way to Algeria, where the exiled Black Panther Eldridge Cleaver double-crossed him by placing him under revolutionary house arrest. Finally freed from Cleaver's caress after an additional cash infusion from the Brotherhood, Leary abandoned his revolutionary pose and ended up in posh exile in Switzerland.

Just after Tim Scully beat his lab rap in Denver, he'd heard that a grand jury was investigating him again, this time for the Orange Sunshine lab in Windsor. Declaring that drug arrests of juveniles had risen 800 percent between 1960 and 1967, Richard Nixon's White House was cracking down even more. The problem was international and hardly limited to LSD. Marijuana smoking was epidemic, and by 1971, opiates were flooding America from Southeast Asia, where tribal warlords allied with the CIA's counterinsurgency efforts in Vietnam had launched a massive expansion of the heroin trade. That June, Nixon declared drug abuse "a national emergency."[14]

Gordon Liddy, Millbrook, New York's drug-busting DA, was now in the White House, coordinating the anti-drug effort. In May 1971, Laguna Beach police had busted a small-time dealer who'd given up the Brotherhood in return for leniency. Within a year, an intergovernmental task force uncovered what they called a major drug organization, a chain descending from the fugitive Tim Leary through Billy Hitchcock down to street dealers. In July 1972, a grand jury began considering conspiracy charges against the Brotherhood of Eternal Love. Fifty-seven people were arrested that August, huge stashes of hashish, LSD, cocaine, mescaline, and marijuana were confiscated, and two hashish oil labs were closed, but more important, the organization's unity was shattered. "Brothers" started ratting on one another.

Timothy Leary was indicted as the Brotherhood's godfather. Sand was arrested soon after, when someone left a sink running in the St. Louis mansion he was using as a lab and a concerned mail carrier saw the streaming water. The quality of LSD soon began to decline. Psilocybin and synthetic mescaline all but disappeared around the same time.[15] Drugs weren't over—marijuana would never go away and new kicks were just around the corner—but it was the end of the first acid era.

Sand was in jail for almost a year, fighting the St. Louis search. By the time his lawyers quashed it, he'd been indicted again, in April 1973—one of several indictments known collectively as the Brotherhood cases. The government's big break had come in March, when Billy Hitchcock turned state's evidence against his former friends. As part of its investigation of Nick Sand, the government had stumbled upon a lawyer named Peter Buchanan. Buchanan, Scully's lawyer, had aided in the laundering of the funds that purchased the Windsor lab property and Sand's Cloverdale ranch. When investigators contacted Buchanan, he volunteered to cooperate in exchange for immunity for himself, Scully and Hitchcock. Buchanan then called his clients and warned them that the government had obtained the bank records indicating Hitchcock's involvement.

In summer 1972, after grand jury subpoenas were issued to compel their testimony, Hitchcock and Scully went to Europe (separately, but at Hitchcock's expense) in order to avoid being compelled to testify. Just as the statute of limitations was about to expire, Hitchcock was indicted in federal court for tax evasion and securities violations. In February 1973, as he was turning himself in, he learned from a reporter that his wife had revealed details of his dealings with Owsley and his Swiss accounts. He decided he had no choice but to cut a deal. Scully thinks Hitchcock was also threatened by his family with the loss of his substantial inheritance.

As those cases moved inexorably toward the courtroom, Timothy Leary was arrested trying to enter Afghanistan from Switzerland and was sent back to California. Though he would long deny it, saying he only gave circumstantial evidence on the Weather Underground's foreign ties, it was widely thought that Leary made a deal with authorities and testi-fied before a number grand juries in various cases and jurisdictions against groups like the Brotherhood and the Weather Underground.[16] Michael Kennedy, representing Nick Sand, dropped Leary as a client and branded him a rat. Leary was finally paroled in 1976 after thirty-two months in forty prisons. In 1978, he married a boomer born in 1947 and moved to Laurel Canyon, where he took drugs, wrote books on outer space and futurology, toured the country doing a standup philosophy/comedy act, debated Gordon Liddy, lived the celebrity life, and became an early advo-cate of cyberspace. Leary's daughter, Susan, hanged herself in prison in 1990, after being accused of shooting her boyfriend. Her father died at seventy-five in 1996. In April 1997, some of his ashes were shot into space aboard a satellite (along with those of Gene Roddenberry, the cre-ator of the *Star Trek* TV series)—a fitting end for the Pied Piper of the Baby Boom.

HIS BRIEF SPELL of active duty in the reserves interrupted Michael Fuchs's education in the law. With a few months to kill before he could return to school at Georgetown, he spent the end of 1968 and the begin-ning of 1969 working odd jobs in Manhattan and traveling. He didn't demonstrate, go to Woodstock, or get lost in drugs. "I wasn't a hippie," he says. "Marching and stuff, I don't know what any of that accomplished. I stayed involved politically. I considered myself a liberal when it wasn't a dirty word. But I was marking time to get through school."

Inspired by his politically connected uncle, who in June 1967 flew to Washington to lobby for Lyndon Johnson's support for Israel's Six Day War, Fuchs was already looking beyond school. "You can do more good from a powerful position than you can as a social worker," he told a cousin entering that profession. Already, though, Fuchs was distancing himself from the power centers of Washington. "Washington at that time was a terrible fucking town, a desert," he says. "No Kennedy Center, there wasn't a restaurant open after nine o'clock at night." After six months in New York, he decided to stay and applied for a transfer to New York University. It wasn't what he hoped it would be, either.

"When I went to Georgetown, law school was very formal and disciplined, tie-and-jacket, *yes, sir,* stand up," he says. But things had changed"—students had run roughshod—"and at the end of that year, classes were suspended after the American invasion of Laos and Cambodia. "All grades and formalities went away. So those two years of law school became almost gradeless. I saw student power and attitude."

One positive manifestation of student power was the way law firms began to pander to promising law graduates. "The biggest issue in those days was pro bono," Fuchs recalls. "How much pro bono would your law firm allow you to do?" Using his pro bono allowance at the entertainment law firm that hired him when he graduated, Fuchs, who'd been a volunteer in Arthur J. Goldberg's failed campaign for governor of New York in 1970, went to New Hampshire in the early days of 1972 to work for Edmund Muskie "and became a part of history," he says. The Maine senator had run for vice-president in 1968 and become the front-runner for the 1972 Democratic presidential nomination, the moderate who would end the war.

As an advance man, Fuchs was part of the team that discussed what to do about a series of vicious editorials in the rabidly conservative *Manchester Union-Leader*. Its publisher, William Loeb, made great sport of liberals, and had not only pinioned "Moscow Muskie" for supposedly uttering a racial slur against French-Americans (who made up 40 percent of the state's Democratic vote) but also repeated gossip impugning Muskie's wife. Unaware that the purported racial slur was a Nixon dirty trick operation—a White House staffer had forged a letter containing the allegation—Fuchs advised Muskie to respond to Loeb in a speech outside the newspaper's offices.

Having moved on to the day's next stop, Fuchs wasn't there to witness the fruits of his labors, but as it turned out, his suggestion led inexorably to Muskie's Waterloo. Muskie stood hatless in a snowstorm defending his wife. "By attacking me, by attacking my wife," he thundered, Loeb had "proved himself to be a gutless coward." But then, he paused several times, his shoulders heaving, having seemingly lost his composure. The next day, the front page of *The Washington Post* and stories in other newspapers reported that he'd cried. Those reports—and their implication of instability—have long been blamed for his poor showing in the primary nine days later and for his eventual withdrawal from the race. Muskie would spend the rest of his life denying he'd cried, saying snow had melted on his face.

"My idea worked too well; it got too much publicity," Fuchs says. Like the press, Fuchs thought Muskie's melting snow story was "a very lame excuse," he says. "Reagan cried, Clinton cries every day, but in those days you couldn't cry."

Although Fuchs attended the Miami convention that summer, his days in politics were numbered. "I guess I got a little busier with my career," he says. He'd begun specializing in television law; his firm represented clients like sit-com star Dick van Dyke and talk show host Merv Griffin. Then, in 1974, Fuchs moved to a much smaller firm that worked in rock music and movies, and represented clients like Carly Simon and the producer Dino di Laurentiis.

Fuchs lasted nine months. "I was trying to find a career and some happiness," he says. "I didn't like being a lawyer. Law turned out to be not something fitting my personality. I mean, lawyers render a certain service, and I was probably not the best guy to be a service guy. I began to get restless and look around."

In 1975, he moved to the William Morris Agency as director of business affairs; in essence, he was the talent agency's in-house lawyer, but spent most of his time in the file room, studying contracts. "I lived in that file room," he says. "Because I was still of an age where I thought information was the key to everything. I even steamed open the Sonny and Cher divorce settlement."

KATHRYN BOND STOCKTON joined the girls' group in her neighborhood, only to see it split up as members headed off to parochial and private schools. Stockton stayed in public school. Her progressive parents wouldn't hear otherwise. Just after starting junior high school in fall 1970, she briefly decided she might be a feminist. "I remember a little period where I was arguing that girls should be able to play hockey," she says, but real feminism wouldn't enter her life for years. "I'd never met a feminist, never had a feminist class, never heard a feminist word in a classroom." Politics—feminist or not—didn't seem like a viable option; it required declaring who you were.

Religion became her safe escape. She sang in a Catholic church choir and went to mass in a Baptist church. She disdained Judaism because Jewish boys were no good at sports. "It's a weird form of homophobia," she observes. "You call people sissies because they can't do sports, and yet you've got this problem: you're gay." Finally, she settled on becoming an evangelical Christian. It was the time of Jesus freaks, blissed out instead of freaked out. Evangelicalism was a safe haven, thanks to its insistence on sex separation "because they're always so worried that anything sexual is going to take place," Stockton says. "*Perfect* for a gay child."

She became her group's resident intellectual, reading C. S. Lewis while they pored over their Bibles. "I was definitely cerebral. I had a lot of questions about the goofy stuff written by evangelicals." Because of her questioning nature, she stayed friends with a more secular crowd, too— "neighborhood friends, much more of their period. Definitely experimenting with sex, definitely doing drug stuff. And I'm in the swim with them, watching, but never participating." Though the drugs and sex part "didn't interest me so much," she says, "I wanted to be part of that cool scene."

Her parents were accepting, but she's sure that behind closed doors they were tearing their hair out. "I was, of course, constantly trying to convert them and all the Jews in the neighborhood, which was not cool at all." There was also a part of her troubled by the idea of telling anyone he'd go to hell if he didn't believe.

Always, in the background, was Stockton's secret. She was constantly falling in love with her girlfriends, connecting through their spiritual commitment. "But I was very anti-homosexual because of the religious stuff, and yet I knew that there was some disturbance here. I was some other kind of problem; I wasn't that problem," she told herself. Although her parents urged her to be tolerant of gays then coming out of the closet, she worried that if her mom and dad thought she was gay, it would kill them. "And I am dating boys at this time," she adds.

As a freshman in high school, Stockton started working in an outreach program at an Episcopal church in nearby Hartford, where she met her first boyfriend, a twenty-one-year-old working in a housing project her program targeted. He was from Texas, part Chicano, part Indian, dedicated to helping his neighbors. "I think he may have been gay, looking back on it," she says. "We had a very strong connection."

She liked him, but she was in love with a woman, a former wild-child hippie her little group had converted to Jesus. "I know my fascination with her had everything to do with the fact that she had had hippie experiences. I, in a sense, was her Christian mentor, and then we were mentoring each other. I felt like I had a girlfriend, even though she absolutely was not. She was very interested in boys."

Stockton's family were rabid Nixon-haters. Her father bought his first color TV just to watch the Watergate hearings. Her brother, who'd come down with mononucleosis, watched every moment of them "and I would sort of run in and out," she says. "I just loved the intrigue and piecing it all together, how Magruder fit in and what Haldeman was doing, and wanting him to be fried." She was a rare bird, left-wing evangelical. "I've never met another one," she says, laughing.

DAVID MCINTOSH WAS sixteen when Nixon was forced from office. He, too, followed the Watergate hearings intently, "fascinated," he says, by the drama. But if at the time he thought Nixon was evil "and got what he deserved," McIntosh was hardly a radical. He played tuba, had a job running a computer at a local plant that made sump pumps, and joined the speech and debate team, the Spanish club, the golf team, and the Eagle Scouts, which "reinforced those small-town values I didn't realize I was learning at the time," he says. He liked mainstream rock music: Three Dog Night, Stevie Wonder and Aerosmith were favorites. "Stairway to Heaven" was the theme at his prom, but rock was just music to him and his friends, not a soundtrack for rebellion. "There weren't a lot of problem kids in our school," he says, and there were no gangs or cliques or dropouts in Kendallville, Indiana.

McIntosh was typical, a good kid, an academic achiever, although not much of an athlete, which was unfortunate in a town where the year's biggest event is the high school basketball tournament. But he signed up as statistician for the basketball team, traveled to all the games, and got to "hang out with the team."

Drugs weren't an issue. "The drug at the time would have been alcohol," he says. "They'd drive to Michigan to get it and have drinking parties—if you were rebelling. I was one of those good kids that didn't."

THE SHOOTING OF students at Kent State University took place the day Steve Capps turned fifteen. Though protest "was in the air," Capps says ("We actually abolished our Student Council"), Kent State didn't have the meaning for him that it did for older boomers. "We cared about it. I'm sure we wore black armbands to school on Kent State Day. If you were a kid at that point, you were against the war. But it was a checkoff item, like asking a teenybopper today if she likes the Spice Girls."

Capps didn't indulge in typical teenage pursuits like television or drugs. "There was too much to do," he says, "and I already knew I had more ideas than I'd have time to pursue in a lifetime. I never wanted to check out mentally by watching TV or dropping acid because it was just too much fun to make things. Sorry to sound so Mr. Spock, but it's just illogical." So he spent his time with his best friend, making tapes imitating the comedy troupe Firesign Theater's Golden Days of Radio on LSD routines, or programming his school's computer.

An atypical ninth grader, Capps had quit the school's one computer class—reserved for seniors—because he already knew more than it covered. Then the school librarian asked him to automate the library, using a "donated 1959 computer that in its heyday was a million-dollar computer, but at that point was probably worth $5,000," Capps says. "I considered myself very lucky." And he was. He had a mainframe personal computer and got paid to program it. And no one dared pick on him because he was also co-captain of the school's football team. "So I was like King Nerd," he jokes.

TOMMY VALLELY RETURNED home to Newton, Massachusetts, in May 1970. Though Vietnam would linger long in his psyche, he adjusted fairly quickly, unlike fellow veterans unable to reintegrate in a society that wasn't exactly welcoming or interested in what had happened in combat. One friend who'd lost a leg in Vietnam and was still in the hospital would beg Vallely to smuggle drugs to him. Vallely did it once or twice, but finally refused, afraid of getting arrested. To his great regret, the friend later died of an overdose. "I'm not sure I would have survived if I lost a leg, but I never lost my bearings," says Vallely, who took a job as an asphalt inspector on the Massachusetts Turnpike.

Driving the highway every day, he'd listen to news of the war, trying to decide what, if anything, he could do about what he'd learned in Vietnam. "I was conflicted," he says. "I invested too much in this thing—I'm a fuckin' war hero—but I quit because I wanted to do something about the war." Finally, he found a way.

Father Robert F. Drinan, a Jesuit priest and official of Boston University Law School, had announced his antiwar candidacy in Vallely's congressional district that February. After winning a primary, he faced a longtime congressman who was a friend of President Nixon and head of the House Armed Services Committee in the general election. When the handsome Vietnam veteran volunteered to help the campaign, he was immediately sent out to accompany the candidate, so "wherever he went—fire stations, police stations, VFW halls—there would be a Marine with the peacenik," Vallely says. While working with Drinan, he met another, Vietnam veteran, John F. Kerry (b. 1943), another Silver Star hero who'd almost run in the same primary but dropped out of the race when Drinan won a local caucus vote. He and Vallely became fast friends.

After Drinan won election in November, Vallely got involved in the Vietnam Veterans movement. In late January 1971, his new friend Kerry was among a group of vets who met at a motel in Detroit for an ad hoc war crimes hearing, the Winter Soldier Investigation, named after the American revolutionary Thomas Paine's attack on "summer soldiers," sponsored by the four-year-old Vietnam Veterans Against the War and promoted by Jane Fonda. Attempting to show that the My Lai massacre—in which American soldiers killed hundreds of unarmed Vietnamese civilians in a South Vietnamese hamlet—was no aberration but a direct result of U.S. policy, they exposed everything from the murder of prisoners and civilians to illegal incursions into Laos. Although the testimony was read into the congressional record by Senators Mark Hatfield and George McGovern, the hearings attracted little attention, and much of that skeptical. So VVAW began planning a demonstration in Washington for April, as part of the peace movement's spring offensive.

Vallely was among the thousand veterans who kicked off the five-day demonstration the VVAW called Operation Dewey Canyon III (after the code names for the U.S. incursions into Laos) by marching to Arlington National Cemetery, many of them in fatigues and long hair, some in wheelchairs. The Nixon administration was ready for them; the cemetery gates were locked. Barred, too, from setting up tents on the mall or sleeping there as planned, the veterans vowed to stand up all night.[17] When a helicopter roared overhead as they returned to the Capitol for a rally, some vets raised their middle fingers, unaware that President Nixon was on board.

Later that day, the injunction against camping on the Mall was lifted by a federal court, but the next day, after they were allowed into the cemetery, the Justice Department won an appeal to force them off the Mall again. They stayed, without knowing that Nixon had decided arresting veterans would be bad image politics, but having heard from police and soldiers that orders to remove them would be disobeyed. The next day, the VVAW's spokesman, Kerry, gave eloquent testimony before the Senate Foreign Relations Committee. "How do you ask a man to be the last to die for a mistake?" the fatigue-clad Kerry said.

By the penultimate day of the demonstration, the vets were edgy and frustrated. Though they'd made an impact, they felt they were merely being tolerated. Their encampment had been infiltrated by Nixon spies, disinformation was being spread that many of them weren't veterans at all, and they assumed a fence that was being erected around the Capitol was meant to thwart their plans for a dramatic finale, a mass giveback of the medals they'd won, which they planned to leave on the building's steps. Despite the fence, this last piece of guerrilla theater proved a show-stopper. After the father of a boy killed in Vietnam played "Taps," his son's fatigue jacket over his shoulders, the vets stepped to the fence around the Capitol one by one and threw their medals, ribbons, canteens, discharge papers, citations and battle caps over. For hours afterward, tough, hard men stood there and cried.

Among the medals on the day's trash heap of history was Tommy Vallely's. "I was proud to get the Silver Star, and I was proud to throw it away," he says. "It was theater, good, big-time theater. I marched up, made some stupid statement, I don't know what I said; I'm embarrassed about how little I knew about the Vietnam War then. But my instincts knew something."

Back in Massachusetts that fall, he began college on the G.I. Bill, and, worked for Kerry in his 1972 race for Congress in Lowell, Massachusetts. Already a target of Nixonian dirty tricks for his work with VVAW—a Silver and Bronze Star-winner, he was painted as unpatriotic—Kerry's campaign was dramatic, and even had a mini-Watergate all its own. After hearing rumors that the candidate's phones would be sabotaged on election eve, Kerry's brother and Vallely overreacted, broke into the basement of his rival's campaign office, and got arrested. (Charges were later dropped.) Unfortunately, despite his matinee idol looks, auspicious initials (JFK), and the help of various Kennedys, Kerry lost the election.

Vallely, on the other hand, won a job. During the race, he'd hooked up with two political operatives-for-hire, John Marttila and Thomas Kiley, who incorporated in 1972. Based in Boston, Marttila, Payne, Kiley & Thorne helped write the rules for the modern political consulting business, offering a package of polling, strategy, advertising and operatives for then-young Democrats like Joseph Biden, Paul Sarbanes, Michael Dukakis and Thomas Eagleton. Vallely was one of a small team of political gunslingers who ran campaigns in the field. For the next four years, he alternated between studying and working races around the country, "writing papers on the road, trying to do my homework," he says. He really wanted to run for office himself, and hated "giving advice to people that didn't know shit," he says flatly.

Politics was more fun than school. In February 1974, for instance, Vallely worked as campaign coordinator for Richard VanderVeen, an obscure lawyer who ran for Gerald Ford's vacant congressional seat in Grand Rapids, Michigan, after the embattled Nixon named the genial

Ford his vice president. Though the district was solidly Republican, VanderVeen won by linking his opponent to Nixon. The victory was one in a series of upsets of Republicans that paved the way for Nixon's resignation that summer. Vallely went on to work for Morris Udall in his unsuccessful run against Georgia governor Jimmy Carter for the Democratic presidential nomination in 1976. But his life was on hold. "I'm just playing the game I'm in," he says.

JOHN GAGE, TOO, kept bouncing between education and activism. He still wasn't getting paid, but he had some money. He was in Harvard on scholarship, and his father had given him a few thousand dollars. That was all he needed. In 1970, he produced a benefit concert for peace candidates at Shea Stadium in New York, presenting twenty-two groups in eleven hours. In 1971, he co-produced several Washington demonstrations, including the May Day rally that followed the Vietnam Veterans march. Then he headed back to Harvard. Instead of finishing B-school, he switched to the Kennedy Public Policy School and started all over.

After a year, the siren song of politics drew Gage back when an organizer named Gary Hart came to Harvard to recruit for George McGovern's ill-fated 1972 peace campaign against Nixon. Gage had been on the East Coast since 1968. He was having girlfriend difficulties. So he agreed to pack his van, ship out, and work on the Arizona and California primaries for McGovern. He then shifted to McGovern's national campaign, where he was made a deputy press secretary.

Gage's job was logistical, neither political nor very glamorous. He was the engineer, the can-do guy—"We're going to land at two A.M. in Maine, and the vehicles have to be there, and ABC needs an extra truck, and on and on and on," he says. Meanwhile, events whizzed past at their usual pace. Nixon began to pull military units out of Vietnam. Third-party candidate George Wallace was shot and wounded by an assassin. National Security Adviser Henry Kissinger pulled his October Surprise on October 26, claiming that the Vietnam War would end within weeks. And a few days later, Nixon wiped the floor with McGovern.

Although Gage felt as if he'd headed an army that, wielding no more weapons than rustling branches, had managed to make the king open his fortress door and fight, he was still devastated. "You don't find out until later that public opposition actually caused people to change plans," he says. "I went back to school to try to pick up the pieces of my life."

Gage spent another half-dozen years at Berkeley in graduate limbo, teaching and working toward a doctorate in economics. "The beauty of mathematics was my primal therapeutic pathway," he says. After Nixon's resignation in 1974, Gage, married and about to become a father, learned he'd been on Nixon's famous enemies list. "And I'm studying math and econ," he says with a hearty laugh.

He still dabbled in politics, producing several rallies for Jimmy Carter's presidential campaign, but his community organizer days were over. "I wasn't doing very much," he admits. "I can't remember what I did."

WHILE LESLIE CROCKER Snyder was revolutionizing rape laws, zealous attempts were under way to root out police corruption in New York. From 1967 to 1970 Frank Serpico (b. 1936), an undercover detective who looked like a hippie, and several colleagues had collected evidence of corruption and payoffs in the city's police department. When he got no response from the city, he went to the *New York Times* and spurred the formation of the Knapp Commission, which held two years of hearings and alleged that half the police force was in some way corrupt. Though he was a cop, the ponytailed Serpico became a counterculture hero, especially after he was shot in the face during a drug bust and retired in 1972, later becoming the subject of a book and a hit movie. He moved to Europe for years, studied Eastern philosophy, treated the lingering pain and depression he suffered with alternative medicine, lived in a solar-powered cabin in the country, and neither voted nor read newspapers.

Though Serpico left the country, the mood he represented remained. At Richard Nixon's second inaugural, 100,000 people demonstrated, but the counterculture had mostly gone to ground. Patricia Hearst's kidnapping in February 1974, and her subsequent apparent transformation into Tanya, a bank-robbing revolutionary, was symbolic of the downright weird state of radical politics after a half-decade of Nixon. Jerry Brown's election as governor of California said much the same in the mainstream. Hemlines dropped along with the nation's birth rate. Perennial culture vulture Allen Ginsberg dropped out of politics altogether to co-found the Kerouac School of Disembodied Poetics in Colorado. And prophetically, streaking—a new form of self-exposure—and *People* magazine, a harbinger of the coming obsession with celebrity, both made their debut in 1974.

The 1973 Arab-Israeli war led to an Arab oil embargo and an energy crunch that kicked a hole in an economy defined by affluence and growth since 1945. Nixon imposed oil and price controls. For the rest of the decade, gasoline prices rose geometrically as supplies dwindled, the dollar was devalued, the stock market went into a long slow slide, jobs dried up, and inflation and unemployment multiplied dangerously.

In response, America read Alex Comfort's *The Joy of Sex* and Erica Jong's *Fear of Flying*, watched *American Graffiti* and *The Exorcist*, and gave up consciousness-enhancing drugs in favor of numbing Quaaludes and cocaine.

For those who didn't drop out but continued to engage in a public life, the new spirit of the times was either cleansing, vengeful or both. The minor robbery that turned into Watergate had repercussions that rippled throughout society. The Senate Select Committee on Intelligence and Rockefeller Commission hearings of 1975 opened new Pandora's boxes of illegal government plots, including assassinations and domestic spying.

In New York, Abraham Beame, a tiny, uncharismatic municipal accountant, succeeded the glamorous, patrician John Lindsay as mayor and immediately stumbled into a fiscal crisis of historic proportions as his city ran out of money and teetered on the brink of default on $8 billion in short-term municipal debt. At the end of 1977, Beame would lose his post after a single term to an insurgent Democrat, Ed Koch, running on a conservative platform of fiscal discipline, support of the death penalty, and opposition to unions. It was a political sea-change in a city that had long prided itself on a liberalism it could no longer afford—and a symbol of the national mood.

In 1976, John Keenan, Leslie Snyder's former boss in the Homicide Bureau, was appointed to oversee the criminal justice system and made Snyder his Chief of Trials, the number-three prosecutor in an office dedicated to prosecuting the sort of abuses the Knapp Commission had revealed. But for the next three years, every major case she was set to try was thrown out of court and she spent her time "prosecuting a lot of cops" for minor offenses Snyder says. She'd gone into her new job filled with optimism and excited by the challenge of weeding out corruption, but what she found was that the anti-corruption forces were corrupt themselves, that they'd distorted the law, browbeaten witnesses, and presented illegal evidence in their zeal to win indictments.

"My beloved cops were on the pad," she says. "I don't think I ever suspected the level of corruption that existed. Everyone hated us. But it was a great learning experience."

THOUGH HE CONTINUED managing properties in Brooklyn and Queens, in 1973—just around the time Abe Beame, of Brooklyn, was elected mayor—Donald Trump's father, Fred, gave his son a free hand in Manhattan. The twenty-seven-year-old went looking to buy. It was a propitious moment. With New York City in terrible financial trouble, the bottom had fallen out of the city's commercial real estate market.

Trump hired a Brooklyn PR man with a Manhattan real estate specialty, and made large donations to politicians in both parties. In 1973, when the government charged the Trumps with racial discrimination at its rental properties, Donald also hired Roy Cohn, the notorious, politically wired former counsel for Joseph McCarthy's Senate subcommittee, as his new lawyer. (He eventually signed a consent decree in that case, but kept Cohn on regardless.) And he hired Louise Sunshine, a fundraiser for New York's Governor Hugh L. Carey, as his political lobbyist.

In 1974 and 1975, Trump made the prescient deals that marked his emergence as a major figure in American business. In July 1974, the bankrupt Penn Central Transportation Company agreed to give Trump the option to develop two of its freight yards—vast tracts of land on the Hudson River.[18] Then, in 1975, Penn Central sold Trump the bankrupt Commodore Hotel on East 42nd Street, next to Grand Central Terminal, for $10 million.

New York was desperate in those years, and Trump knew it. Even so, his moves presaged the bravado baby boomers would bring to the financial markets in the next decade. Deal in hand, he convinced the Hyatt Hotel chain—then without a New York location—to join him in a partnership; he would renovate the Commodore, they would manage it. He then approached the Equitable Life Assurance Society and won seventy million dollars in mortgages. These deals were predicated on his ability to get a tax abatement on the property—something that had never been done for a private commercial developer. So Trump sold the hotel for one dollar to the Urban Development Corporation, and leased it back for ninety-nine years for a small fee in lieu of $56 million in taxes.[19]

Late in 1975, the city announced plans to build a new convention center at the southernmost tip of Manhattan. Trump called a press conference and unveiled a proposal to build it on one of the Penn Central yards, instead. Though it would take years to make it happen, the convention center was eventually built there, and Trump walked away with a hefty commission on the sale of the property to New York State.

Trump's next move proved crucial. From friends of Louise Sunshine, he learned in 1975 that a financially shaky conglomerate might be willing to sell the building that housed Bonwit Teller, a department store on the prestigious corner of 56th Street and 5th Avenue, as well as the lease for the land beneath it, which had twenty-nine years left to run. The deal, which included the $5 million purchase of air rights from Tiffany & Co. next door, allowing him to build a skyscraper on the lot, took years, but was completed in 1979. His timing was impeccable; transactions begun while the city was distressed were completed as the New York real estate business turned around, and zoning and tax concessions soon let him erect his name in brass letters over one of the best locations in the city.

"Every developer in the world was after this site, and I ended up getting it and it was a huge fuckin' coup," Trump crows. "And nobody really knew who I was. You have to understand, there was no Trump per se."

WHEN THE BROTHERHOOD of Eternal Love trial finally opened in November 1973, it focused on Nick Sand and Tim Scully. Both were charged with tax evasion and masterminding a worldwide scheme to sell LSD. Finally, Hitchcock, who'd agreed to pay tax liabilities and fraud penalties totaling nearly $850,000 and plead guilty to tax evasion and violating margin regulations, got immunity.[20] Before the trial, he loaned Scully $10,000 for legal fees and tried to get him to plead guilty, Scully thinks, so he would feel better about testifying himself. Scully was led to believe the government was really after Sand, but the prosecutors' best offer was four years in prison in exchange for Scully's testimony. "There was no way I was going to be a rat *and* go to prison," he says, laughing. "Going to prison was scary, but going to prison as a rat was even scarier. So I was able to maintain my high ethical standards."

Hitchcock, who'd moved to a Tucson cattle ranch, claimed Sand had been the financial backer of the scheme and portrayed himself as an errand boy. The defense said it was not Sand but Hitchcock, and claimed he'd invested hundreds of thousands of dollars in the scheme. Sand's lawyer, Kennedy, convinced Scully he should be the one to throw a Hail Mary pass for the defense. So Scully testified, that he'd had no profit motive but wanted to turn on the world, and argued, that Orange Sunshine wasn't LSD–25 at all but another of Albert Hofmann's discoveries, ALD–52, a slightly different, and therefore technically legal, chemical. "We wanted to stay one step ahead of the law," Scully testified. He says he'd found the new formula in his constant quest for purity, and had kept ALD's existence a secret until then because of the drug market's bad reaction to STP. Unfortunately, the ALD–52 Scully was foolish enough to introduce into evidence had decomposed—and turned into LSD!

Scully and Sand were found guilty, but Kennedy's tactic deflected the judge's wrath away from silent Sand onto the loquacious, dangerously idealistic loophole artist Scully. The judge accused him of "smirking" and "intellectual arrogance," and he ended up sentenced to twenty years, five more than Sand.[21] When Scully's lawyers then won an appeal of his $500,000 bail and he was released from the McNeil Island Federal Penitentiary on an island in Washington's Puget Sound where they'd briefly been jailed, Sand got out, too.

On September 11, 1976, their appeals were denied. Scully flew back to McNeil Island at his own expense, and presented himself at the gates. Sand snuck out the back of his houseboat in Sausalito and disappeared while his girlfriend held federal agents at bay, and continued making LSD and other drugs in Mexico and Canada until he was arrested in Vancouver an astonishing twenty years later. In January 1999, the same judge who'd first found him guilty sent Sand back to prison to serve his original fifteen-year sentence plus five more years for jumping bail.

BY THE TIME she left home for Pomona College in Claremont, California, in fall 1970, Marianne Williamson had begun her transition from good girl to, as she describes it, "a weird juxtaposition." In high school, she'd been attracted to drama. Once she got to college, though, she fell under the spell of philosophy, cast by an equally theatrical fellow student, Lynda Rosen Obst (b. 1950), who later became a Hollywood producer. Two of the few Jewish girls in school, they roomed together, discussed Kant, Kierkegaard and Sartre, and double-dated two philosophy professors during the next year and a half. "I looked up to her," Williamson says. "She taught me the *I Ching*."

Obst graduated from Pomona in 1972, and Williamson promptly dropped out. "I just couldn't find my niche, and I started unraveling," she says. In 1993, on the television show *20/20*, Williamson said her parents were alcoholics and she "was stoned for twenty, twenty-five years." Now she tempers both statements, saying, "We all come from dysfunctional families," and that while she was troubled—"Who in their mid–twenties isn't?—"she got high "no more, no less than anyone else I knew."

Williamson took to the domestic hippie trail, spending time in Berkeley, New Mexico and Austin, Texas. During those years, she revved up her metaphysical quest. "In the sixties, politics and spirituality and philosophy were married, however tenuously, and bound together by the music," she says. "But as we move into the seventies, spirituality and politics divorce. And many people said, Until we change our consciousness, nothing is really going to change anyway, so forget politics. I believed, as I still do, that an angry generation can't bring peace to the world, and I began to understand Gandhi's precept that we must be the change we want to see. The genuine mystical path is a search for the most real, not the least real."

Like her peers, Williamson was spoiled by the sense that high as she might fly, close as she might come to danger, she could always bail out and go home. Her mother never stopped asking what she was doing with her life, and she sometimes wondered, too. "I never stopped being a middle-class Jewish girl. I knew if things got too bad I could call Daddy. We were protected by our parents. In another generation I would not have been indulged." In time, her friend Lynda Obst began to worry about her, warning her to "stop bringing stray mystics home." But Williamson didn't see her men that way. "I always loved brilliant men," she says. "Still do."

In New Mexico, she lived with a designer of geodesic domes. Spherical dwellings made up of a network of triangular elements, domes were the homes of choice for the delightfully contradictory back-to-earth futurists who inhabited the communes of the early 1970s. Patented in 1951 by the visionary inventor and futurist R. Buckminster Fuller (b. 1895), who famously coined the expression Spaceship Earth, they became the physical expression of the New Age movement thanks to their "free," almost mystical design, said to impart a feeling of wholeness to those inhabiting them. Though Williamson practiced serial monogamy, not promiscuity, her parents still worried about her. "I think they were very concerned, frustrated, exasperated," she says. "I should have been in law school." Instead, she was waiting tables and temping.

Williamson sought what she believed was her birthright: happiness. For ten years, she hopped, skipped and jumped through fields of esoterica, ever more miserable at her inability to find what she was looking for. She cast the I Ching, read books by Carlos Castaneda, the mysterious author who wrote of Mexican shamans and their explorations of the frontiers of psychology and pharmacology, sat in on courses in Chinese philosophy at the University of New Mexico and on medieval philosophy at The University of Texas. "Religion and philosophy and spirituality were my all-consuming passion, but there was no way that I could get a Ph.D.; I was always in and out of places," she says.

Watching from a distance, her parents grew increasingly frustrated. "My mother would say, 'What are you going to do with that? What is that going to turn into?'" She knew couldn't "find the door," she says. "How could I have? The niche didn't exist then. What was anybody going to say? She's going to be a what I am now? What's the word for it, y'know? It didn't exist."

* * *

NINA HARTLEY'S SEXUAL education began with feminist literature her mother brought home that led Mitzi to examine her cervix when she was twelve. Around that time, her brother was the first to show her a copy of *Playboy*. On her thirteenth birthday, right about the time she began to menstruate, a male cousin gave her a copy of *Our Bodies, Our Selves*, the 1971 feminist classic about women's sexuality. "I had access to all sorts of tremendous information without it being awkward," she says, "and it was earth-shattering, it changed my life." She found she was fascinated with babies and bodies, and read anything she could get her hands on that described the mechanics of sexual behavior—"about menstruation, and ovulation and testicles and vas deferens and things like that," she says. She loved to look at classical art, particularly when breasts or penises were involved. "I was literally a voyeur."

At fourteen, she discovered pornography, which had been liberated from the strictures of American Puritan tradition in the mid-1960s by a handful of pioneer publishers and was openly available in liberal Berkeley. "Oooh, I would sit in a used bookstore for hours and read in my bib overalls and braids," she says. "My sex life was all in my head and in books, but I found out I had an immediate positive response to pornography. Then, around the corner was a swinging 1970s kind of couple I babysat for. I was looking in their closet and I found high heels and an Afro wig and Louis Comfort's book *The Joy of Sex*."

She read the breezy sex manual over and over, half a dozen times, and did the same with the famous madam Xaviera Hollander's memoir, *The Happy Hooker*, Betty Dodson's *Liberating Masturbation*, and David Reuben's *Everything You Always Wanted to Know About Sex (But Were Afraid to Ask)*. "Neglect allowed my mind to go where it wanted to, and sex was where it wanted to go," she says. "But I'm doing it with the tools my mother gave me. She brought those books in the house."

Though some of her neighbors were convinced she was already a sex fiend—"my girlfriends were sisters whose parents did not want them to play with me because they were afraid I was going to turn them into lesbians"—she'd still never even masturbated. "I remember being in the bedroom with them and getting naked and feeling breasts, and inserting things into vaginas, but it wasn't sensual," she says. "It was mechanical."

Her only heterosexual experience came when, at a Renaissance Fair in 1973, she allowed herself to be pulled into the kissing booth, untied her hair, pulled her blouse down below her shoulders and sold French kisses for a dollar. "I loved it," she says. "A public place with people around? Cool. Nothing bad gonna happen to me. But I didn't feel safe in private. I didn't know how to handle that energy. I didn't have sex for another four years. I didn't date at all. I hardly necked."

In 1974, when Mitzi and her parents moved to a Zen community near Carmel, her isolation grew. She has no memory of Watergate. She would sit in the town library poring through forty-year-old *Life* magazines or sit home listening to Broadway musicals. "I had no one to pull me out of myself," she says. "And I had no example. My parents were closing inward." When they moved again, to a Zen farm in Marin County, Mitzi asked if she could return to Berkeley, where the high school had a college-level theater department. She never lived with her parents again. In 1977 they both became ordained Zen priests. "If they'd insisted I live with them, everything would have been completely different."

In tenth grade, Mitzi finally found a social life. She joined the drama department as a costumer, and worked on several plays. She saw herself as terminally shy and unable to focus; others saw her as bright, sarcastic and sexy. Sex was all around her—it was Berkeley in the mid-1970s. Although she'd identified herself as bisexual by fourteen, she wasn't having any. She adopted the look of lesbian separatists. "Birkenstocks, overalls and flannel shirts, absolutely no glamour, no makeup at all, didn't start shaving my legs until I was twenty-one," she says. "Not because I hated men, but because I had such low self-esteem I didn't want anyone to notice me."

It was the same with drugs. "My friends did them," she says. "I didn't try pot till I was eighteen. And then they had to force me. I was a good girl, I think, still trying to get Mom's attention." Her only outlet was folk dancing, which allowed her the physical expression she craved without an accompanying emotional burden.

Mitzi—now living in her parents' house with an older brother, his wife, their infant child, and a succession of roommates—finished high school in 1977, got a job as a short-order cook in a hamburger joint, and promptly lost her virginity. Right before graduation, she'd had a near-sex experience with a boy from the drama department. "He was petting me all over and I was absolutely tingling and alive, and I knew that if he'd just do this to my clit I'd come, but I stopped myself," she recalls. "That summer, I thought, What was I scared of? I'd never been that turned on before. He'd been with a lot of girls, had a lot of sex, he was good at it." She smiles. "But I was that repressed, I could not let go." Finally, one afternoon, she did let go, and the result was "extremely not unpleasant," she says, "just not pleasurable" because, though she knew about birth control, she let him have sex with her without it. "And I'm worrying the whole time, 'How could I be so stupid as to allow this to happen?'"

Shortly afterward, Mitzi began dating her dance teacher—a man twice her age. "He had a savior complex, and I needed saving," she says. "I was desperately lonely, desperately confused, so I basically ended up going to high school for another four and a half years. I would help him teach folk dances. I really liked that dancing." He introduced her to jazz, theater, movies and LSD. They didn't have intercourse for months, and when they did, after she took him to see a film of the S&M novel *The Story of O*, he tied her up and blindfolded her, and she let him think it was her first time.

Her teacher boyfriend was a devotee of *est*, the movement driven by Jack Rosenberg, a car salesman in Philadelphia, who abandoned his wife and family in the 1960s to create a new identity, Werner Hans Erhard, and join the New Age craze in California. In 1971, melding aspects of Zen Buddhism, Scientology, the philosophies of Jacques Derrida and Martin Heidegger, and techniques he'd used in a previous job training door-to-door encyclopedia salesmen, he started Erhard Seminars Training (or *est*), promising followers he would increase their self-awareness and help their potential blossom through what was essentially instant therapy. Though thousands swore by it, and claimed it was better than therapy for helping them break habitual behavior patterns, detractors thought the training was fast food psychology and referred to devotees as *est*-holes.[22]

Mitzi's boyfriend used *est* to avoid emotional communication. He told her he wouldn't take responsibility for anything not directly communicated to him. "What an older woman would have known was, that was just an excuse not to have to pay attention and intuit his partner's emotional needs," Hartley says. After a while, the always tenuous relationship went sour, but Mitzi hung in. "I had to learn a lot of things, which is why I was there."

Throughout those years, San Francisco was a mecca for the business of pornography. The city's reputation as a modern sexual frontier state began with Gold Rush prostitutes who lent their names to some of the city's streets and continued in the famous topless bars of bohemian North Beach. In 1957, Beats were in the vanguard of sexual openness when Allen Ginsberg and Lawrence Ferlinghetti were acquitted on obscenity charges for publishing Ginsberg's poem "Howl." That same year, the Supreme Court redefined obscenity as material "utterly without redeeming social value."

The approval of a birth control pill by the Federal Drug Administration in May 1960 pushed the sexual vanguard toward the American norm. By the mid-1960s, millions of women around the world were taking the Pill. Its impact was best summed up by the writer, ambassador and LSD user Clare Booth Luce: "Modern woman is at last free as a man is free, to dispose of her own body, to earn her living, to pursue the improvement of her mind, to try a successful career."[23]

In 1969, sexual outlaws were in. *Oh, Calcutta!*, a sexually explicit revue, debuted on Broadway; swingers swapped spouses at California's Sandstone Ranch and Sexual Freedom League; Bob Guccione challenged the avatar of the early sexual revolution, *Playboy* magazine's Hugh Hefner, with *Penthouse*, which dared to show female pubic hair; Philip Roth published *Portnoy's Complaint*, his paean to masturbation; John Lennon and Yoko Ono appeared nude on the cover of a record called *Two Virgins*; and Jim Morrison of the Doors (b. 1943) was arrested for flashing his penis onstage in Miami. In 1970 a national Commission on Obscenity and Pornography declared that pornography had no significant effect on crime or delinquency. Rapidly, the porn film form evolved through displays of masturbation and physical contact between men and women to finally break the last taboo and show explicit sex.[24]

Among those pushing the envelope were several San Franciscans: Alex deRenzy, whose 1969 documentary, *Pornography in Denmark* (the Scandinavian country where depiction of sexual penetration was decriminalized that year), was the first widely seen porn movie; Jim and Artie Mitchell, better known as the Mitchell Brothers, who made films for their own theater, The O'Farrell,[25] and Gerald Damiano, whose 1972 film, *Deep Throat*, brought porn into the mainstream, selling fifty million dollars' worth of tickets.[26] By 1973, when Erica Jong extolled the "zipless fuck" in her novel *Fear of Flying*, hard-core was everyday and brothels were everywhere in the sexual supermarket of New York's Times Square. Soon, miniature equivalents sprang up across America.

That year, Mitzi's introduction to their world came when, still in high school, she'd snuck into her first hard-core movie, *Autobiography of a Flea*. A costume drama directed by a woman, it was based on an erotic classic she'd read. "I was astounded and transformed," she says, her voice going all gooey. "I wanna *do* that. I knew I was hung up about sex, and I hated it. I didn't like how uncomfortable and unsure of myself I felt. I didn't like not being good at it. I hated it that the culture said you couldn't get sexual skills without emotions. I had no emotional skill. I was scared to be alone with a guy. I did not know how to steer." Not long afterward, she induced her new boyfriend to take her to a strip club. "I was getting all juicy and wet," she says, and he fell asleep."

As the relationship stumbled along, Mitzi began to flirt with bisexuality. The same girlfriend from high school who'd made her smoke marijuana, an artistic bisexual, "basically seduced me," Hartley says. It wasn't hard. At twelve, she'd wondered what other girls' breasts felt like, and years later, the curiosity had only grown. "So, we end up in bed together and for me it was the most amazing—it was like, *Wow, smooooth!* No hair." Her boyfriend had a beard. "And I was going down on her, and didn't know what I was doing, didn't know if she came or not and that was the first time I realized, girls are complicated." But also appealing. "And I wanted to do more." So they tried three-way sex with her boyfriend, while taking LSD. "And that was as close as I ever came to a bad trip," Hartley says, "seeing him be tender and exploratory with her when he had not been that way with me. Freaked me out. He ended up having to take her home and he was very angry about that. He thought, I'd had her, why couldn't he?"

AS VICTORIA LEACOCK'S ailing mother's condition worsened and she was in and out of hospitals and rehabilitation clinics, Victoria was often alone. "I don't know where my brothers and sisters were when I was a kid," she says. Sometime in 1970, Victoria began to be sent to live with other families for months at a time. One had a son Victoria's age, Gordon Rogers, and they became close friends. "He'd bite me and we'd fight, and he'd copy my homework," she says. "So I got to have a sibling."

Victoria's father, who was teaching film at MIT, was a flitting presence. He would take her to the Caribbean once a year. Or show up in New York and take her to gloomy dinner parties and crazy restaurants, where they ate with her uncles, the other documentarians, "and I loved it when I saw him," she says. But mostly, she took care of her mother, who was completely bedridden by the time Victoria turned twelve. She could talk, though. "My friends loved staying over because we'd stay up and talk about adult things and she treated us as equals. We'd go grocery shopping and make dinner. I started signing her checks when I was around ten."

Leacock was at her grandmother's in Illinois during the Watergate hearings, when she was eleven. "My grandmother became obsessed with the hearings. I would beg to go over to other kids' houses and watch *Kung Fu.* Or *The Waltons.* Or anything. I hated Nixon because he was so fucking boring." Back home, she went to school about two days a week, and spent the rest playing nurse. She resented being responsible for an invalid, but she knew she had no choice.

* * *

THROUGH A SPANISH girlfriend, Barbara Ledeen met her first terrorist in 1972. He was an aboveground supporter of one of the dozen liberation groups then operating in Europe with Soviet assistance, Spain's ETA-Militar, a Basque nationalist group seeking independence from Spain. "He was a real Communist," she says. "This was not make-believe. And educated, articulate, multilingual and culturally sophisticated. I'm waiting for somebody like that." His name was Vincente. She moved into his apartment in Rome, a fifth-floor walkup, coldwater flat across the street from a prison.

They shoplifted food, bathed in freezing water, and attempted to live up to an abstract revolutionary ideal. But when Vincente told her she'd soon have to "lose" her Judaism and pick up a gun, she began to have her doubts about his business. Then Vincente came down with a kidney infection and returned to Madrid for treatment. While he was gone, Ledeen got distracted. She sometimes modeled for another friend, an Egyptian dress designer whom she'd met when she'd first arrived from Elba. One day, early in 1973, the designer called her at work and said, "There's an American I want you to meet."

"I don't talk to Americans," Ledeen replied. She hadn't spoken English in months; she was even dreaming in Italian. "He's got money," her friend said, and his wife had run off with his best friend a few weeks before. What the hell, Ledeen thought, she could rip off the ruling class for a meal at a good restaurant. So she and Michael Ledeen (b. 1941) went out to dinner. "I didn't weigh 100 pounds," she recalls. "I look at the menu and start ordering everything from beginning to end. And the bread that was left on the table and the sugar, I put in my pocketbook."

Michael Ledeen, a historian and author, was in Rome on a grant to write a book about the flamboyant Italian warrior-poet Gabrielle d'Annunzio. A student of Italian history, he'd arrived the year before from Washington University, where he was a professor of history and had campaigned for George McGovern. His allegiance was not to party, though, but to whoever stood against evil and mass movements.[27] He equated the totalitarianism of the fascists with that of the communists. To his dinner date, his passionate anti-fascism made up for the fact that he was anti-communist, American, Jewish, and altogether the sort of man her father might like.

After dinner, they walked back to his apartment—a glorious sublet compared to her hovel. "He offered me an Armagnac," she remembers. "And I'd never heard of Armagnac, but an American who lived in a great apartment, who knew from Armagnac, who spoke perfect Italian, who used the subjunctive? *Hmmm*." Then she asked to use the bathroom, "and there's a bathtub," she continues. "I hadn't seen a bathtub in I don't know how long. There's only so much you can suppress for the revolution. A long, hot soak in this bathtub was all of a sudden a very important thing." After he agreed that she could use it sometime, he took her home in a taxi, shook her hand, and asked if he could call the next day. "I hadn't been treated like that by a man in I can't tell you how long."

The two began an affair that was still going on a couple months later when Vincente returned from Madrid to collect his girlfriend for a jaunt to Cuba. He planned to hook up with the Palestine Liberation Organization, "which I could not do," Ledeen says. She wasn't even sure he'd been in Madrid. "He could have been at some terrorist training camp." She told him they'd reached the end of the road, "and off he went to do his revolutionary thing," she says. As his parting shot, he told her that if she gave up the cause, she'd end up a piece of Chippendale furniture.

Five months later, in July 1973, when Michael Ledeen's grant ran out and he had to return to Washington University, she agreed to accompany him. There was only one problem. "Michael had a ticket back to the United States that said Mrs. Ledeen, so I needed to be Mrs. Ledeen." They called their parents on a Friday and married that Monday in the Spanish chapel beneath the synagogue in Rome.

After Rome, St. Louis paled. Ledeen's former wife lived down the street. He had little reason to be there; he'd been denied tenure before leaving for Rome. That's when Barbara, who'd been told she couldn't conceive, got pregnant. At the end of the term, it was an easy decision. Back to Rome, where the Ledeens became part of a coterie of anti-fascist, anti-communist intellectuals. "They ratcheted up my intellectual curiosity," she says. One, Renzo De Felice, was a former communist who'd abandoned the party after it crushed a popular uprising in Hungary in 1956 and gone on to author a multivolume biography of Italy's fascist World War II leader, Benito Mussolini. Despite voluminous archival research, it outraged Italian communists by arguing that Mussolini was not only a popular leader but that his fascist philosophy grew out of the same dirt as communism. That became the subject of a book, *Interview on Fascism*, in which De Felice answered questions posed by Michael Ledeen.

As in America, these former leftists were finding their way toward the next political trend, a neoconservatism that rejected social engineering in favor of individual freedom. They weren't there yet. In summer 1974, the Ledeens cheered the fall of Richard Nixon. "We go out of our way to get a front page of the *New York Times* in Rome and frame it and put it on the wall," Barbara says. "My husband still has it in his office." Michael was changing, and Barbara was following, if a bit reluctantly. "We had knock-down dragouts about it," she says. "He'd say, 'Can you not understand that [leftists] are not who you believe them to be? Look at how many innocent people have suffered.'"

Their circumstances changed along with their politics. Michael won an appointment to teach at the University of Rome, which made Barbara, as she puts it, "the *signora* of the *professore*." Using the proceeds of the De Felice book, the Ledeens abandoned their bohemian lifestyle and moved to an apartment near the Vatican. Barbara returned to America for the birth of her daughter in December 1974, then hurried back to Rome.

In 1975, Michael Ledeen was named Rome correspondent for *The New Republic*. After its purchase the year before by Martin Peretz (b. 1939), a former radical and Harvard social theory lecturer, and his wife, an heiress to the Singer sewing machine fortune, the formerly liberal opinion magazine began a slow drift to the pragmatic center. The next year, Michael Ledeen hooked up with Claire Sterling, another ex-communist who'd been a Rome-based journalist for many years, to pen an article for the magazine tracing the connections between Italian leftists and the Soviet Union.

"They upset the entire apple cart," Barbara says. "It was a huge deal." Ledeen had become quite controversial. His pariah status on the left was cemented when he was consulted by the Italian justice ministry on terrorism.

Terrorism was spreading, Americans were being targeted, and Ledeen was the only American teaching at a school where professors were being shot at on campus. Worried for their safety, Ledeen sent his documentary evidence on terrorist financing back to the States for safekeeping, and he and Barbara followed. In 1976, Walter Lacqueur, an author, historian and member of Georgetown University's foreign policy think tank, the Center for Strategic and International Studies (CSIS), hired Michael to join his staff and found a magazine, *The Washington Quarterly*. They returned to America just as Gerald Ford left the presidency, early in 1977. Michael moved into an office at CSIS, just down the hall from Richard Nixon's National Security Advisor, Henry Kissinger, who laughed at his framed *New York Times* page. Barbara promptly plunged into a deep depression.

IN THE EARLY 1970s, after years of goofing off and taking drugs in Palo Alto, Cynthia Bowman broke up with her boyfriend, moved out of her commune, went back to San Francisco, and got a job assisting one of the many orthopedic surgeons who'd operated on her over the years. Though still a beauty, she could no longer model, thanks to the scars on her leg. But she could party, especially after winning a $100,000 settlement in a lawsuit she'd filed over her accident. She bought a fur coat, moved into an apartment in one of San Francisco's best neighborhoods, and found a new boyfriend—a drug dealer associated with the Brotherhood of Eternal Love. He took her to Europe, where business mixed well with pleasure.

By 1974, her money and boyfriend gone, Bowman went looking for a job. Once again, she fell into a pot of honey, at *Rolling Stone*, the nation's leading rock magazine. Thanks to its founder Jann Wenner's riches and the Falstaffian excesses they paid for, Wenner's accomplishment has sometimes been overshadowed in the many accounts of his life and high times. A quintessential boomer, born in January 1946, he inspired his father to open a baby formula company the next year, and grew up in prosperous San Rafael, California.[28] Wenner attended Berkeley but avoided the Free Speech Movement, preferring to spend his time laying the groundwork for a media career, working as a gofer for NBC during the 1964 Republican Convention.[29] After taking his first LSD trip, Wenner sought out the *San Francisco Chronicle*'s music critic, Ralph J. Gleason, befriending the influential columnist and becoming something of a protégé. Wenner launched a column, "Something's Happening" (bylined "Mr. Jones"), in the Berkeley campus newspaper, then went to work for *Sunday Ramparts*, an offshoot of the radical magazine. When it went out of business in May 1967, Wenner took a civil service exam, hoping to win a job as a mailman.[30]

He got the idea to start a magazine from Chet Helms of the Family Dog, a concert-promoting commune, who wanted to do the same. There was already a magazine for new rock fans, *Crawdaddy*, founded in 1966, but it was full of serious essays. When he proposed to do something livelier to Gleason, the critic signed on, giving the venture ballast and the funds to pay for a prototype. His girlfriend's family kicked in more. To save money, he used the defunct *Sunday Ramparts* printer, paper and typeface, and to find readers, he spirited away a radio station's mailing list Helms had hoped to use for *his* magazine.[31] In late October, just a few days after the Death of Hippie rites, *Rolling Stone* hit the newsstands.

It was quickly established as the voice of the baby boom, and Wenner as its Henry Luce, its Hugh Hefner, the man who'd bottled an era's cultural lightning. Gleason was long gone, but had been replaced by a talented group that included Owsley Stanley's roommate Charles Perry,

Greil Marcus, Jerry Hopkins, who'd managed a drug paraphernalia store, and Ben Fong-Torres. When Bob Dylan, who'd been in hiding since a motorcycle accident in 1966, emerged from seclusion three years later, he gave his first interview to Wenner. When John Lennon did the same a year later—ripping into the Beatles and other sacred cows of the 1960s—*Stone*'s role was sanctified.

For years afterward, *Rolling Stone* ruled—despite the fact that it had no black writers and no more than knee-jerk coverage of black music, was less than innovative, and was hagiographic toward its editor's friends. It was also as inconsistent as its peripatetic readership. *Stone* vacillated between being a music magazine and something more ambitious. Briefly, in 1969 and 1970, it ran exposés of the Rolling Stones concert at Altamont and the Manson murders, and biting political articles, before retreating to the safety of music. Wenner, a rock groupie just like his readers, ping-ponged between his magazine labors and enjoying their fruits. Then, in the 1970s, *Rolling Stone* reengaged and became the last red-hot center of the New Journalism. Big bands like Grand Funk Railroad were drowned out by literary noisemakers like Hunter Thompson, Joe Eszterhas, Timothy Ferris and Howard Kohn. Their *Stone* was controversial, but it made money; between 1973 and 1975, when Bowman arrived as Fong-Torres's secretary, ad revenues doubled.

She still can't say how she got the job. "I didn't know how to type. I knew nothing about writing or grammar. I was highly unqualified. But I must have been endearing or something." Bowman soon graduated to a job she could do—music librarian.

About a year later, Bowman and a band of *Stone* staffers went to see Steve Martin (b. 1945), a comedian just gaining national stardom, in a San Francisco nightclub. When she ran into Bill Thompson, the manager of the Jefferson Airplane shared some of his cocaine and she won a job as the in-house publicist for the very band that had inspired her runaway scheme and filled her acid dreams. "He took me to meet the band the next night and I quit my job at *Rolling Stone*." Just in time, in fact, for the next year, Wenner moved the magazine to New York. The change of venue proved symbolic; Wenner was now a multimillionaire and his publication the very first pillar of what's now called the New Establishment. The punk rock revolt that began that year did as much to discredit the magazine as the Sex Pistols did to slime Queen Elizabeth and corporate rock. Though *Rolling Stone* put the Pistols on its cover, it downplayed punk and New Wave music, because Wenner, whose tastes ran to Loggins & Messina and Jackson Browne—and who was then running around New

York with the Kennedys, and Hollywood-on-the-Hudson types like Richard Gere—didn't quite get the art of punk noise.[32]

Bowman thinks she was running on looks and personality. "'Cause I certainly didn't have any skills," she says. But then, she wasn't exactly working at IBM. The Airplane was still fueled by sex and drugs and the revolutionary politics of its hit 1969 album, *Volunteers*. It had supported the Weather Underground. In April 1970, Grace Slick, a graduate of the New York finishing school Finch, had brought Abbie Hoffman as her "bodyguard" when she was invited to a White House tea for Finch alumnae with Nixon's daughter Tricia. Slick, who had powdered LSD in her pocket, planned to try and dose Nixon with it. White House guards wouldn't let Hoffman enter, and the pair gave up their plan, but the story got out and furthered both their legends.

In subsequent years, a dealer was in residence at the Airplane mansion, and jumbo nitrous oxide tanks were stored in the basement. Backstage, their road manager carried a clear plastic tray with divided sections for vitamins, methedrine, cocaine, LSD and aspirin.[33] "I'd walk in every day and there was a gram of cocaine on everybody's desk," Bowman says. "By lunchtime we would have identified somebody in the universe that was having a birthday, and [a secretary] would go out and buy four or five bottles of Dom Perignon and we'd be smashed by two in the afternoon. And then we'd take cocaine all afternoon to stay awake. Then Bill Thompson and I would go back to his house and play backgammon all night. And then we'd start all over again." Band members were constantly getting busted for drugs, obscenity, resisting arrest, drinking, driving under the influence—in short, for being themselves.

Grace Slick had been married when she joined the Airplane, but her husband was soon past history. In the meantime, Slick became part of the sexual roundelay of rock 'n' roll, sleeping with Airplane drummer Spencer Dryden (b. 1938) and Doors leader Jim Morrison, among others, before getting pregnant by Paul Kantner in 1970. That fall, with Slick sidelined by her pregnancy, the band splintered into several offshoots, including Hot Tuna and Kantner's Jefferson Starship, which was nominated for a Hugo Award for the science fiction of its first album (credited only to Kantner), *Blows Against the Empire*. With each such success, the cracks in the Airplane's fuselage widened. Born with the counterculture, the band was splintering along with its audience.

In January 1971, Slick gave birth to a daughter who was briefly named god—Slick was having a goof with a nurse—and then China. In February, Marty Balin quit the group, the first of a series of departures. In May, Slick was hospitalized after crashing her Mercedes into a wall while racing with Jorma Kaukonen, with whom she'd just had a one-night fling. Though the group would make several more records before formally breaking up in 1978, they played their last live show as Jefferson Airplane in September 1972.

By 1975, when Bowman arrived on the scene, the band she'd loved as a girl effectively no longer existed. Slick, Kantner and a constantly changing cast of others were still touring, but as Jefferson Starship, and the comings and goings were often more interesting than the music they made. Balin, who'd sworn he'd never play with them again, would parachute in, record a love ballad, and then leave as suddenly as he'd come.

Hedonism remained their watchword. Slick, alternating between alcohol and cocaine, fell in love with the Starship's twenty-four-year-old lighting director. By the end of 1975, Slick and Kantner had split, and he and Bowman hooked up. "Everybody was hoping Paul would find somebody to love," Bowman says, "because he was making Grace's life a nightmare."

Bowman moved into Kantner's house and into the fast lane with Jefferson Starship. In November 1976, Grace Slick married her lighting designer in Hawaii. Bowman was her maid of honor. Then in June 1978, Slick's drinking, combined with a stomach flu, disrupted a tour of Germany. When the band failed to take the stage at a rock festival there, local fans and American soldiers based nearby "burned a million dollars' worth of our equipment," Bowman says. "They burned our Mercedes. The cars were just melted. Our band was underneath the stage locked in a cage. Our Jewish band members were terrified. We had to be smuggled out in the dark in a bus." At their next show, in Frankfurt, Slick stuck her fingers up the nose of a fan in the front row. She left the band the next day, returned to America, and after several drink-related arrests, entered a rehabilitation program.

Slick wasn't the only problem. Back at home, Bowman and Kantner's relationship began to sour. At first, "it was flowers all the time and Dom Perignon," she says. "We were very attracted to each other. But after that, it was one long series of arguments and disagreements. We just didn't get along. He lives like Howard Hughes—stacks of newspapers and stuff everywhere. So as interesting as we thought each other was, we couldn't be in the same house, even if it was a thirty-room mansion."

GANGS RULED HOLLIS, Queens, when Russell Simmons was in junior high. "I was a warlord of the seventeenth division of the Seven Immortals when I was fourteen years old," he says. "But gangs back then was more hitting you with a pipe than shooting you with a gun. They were gangs like you read about, sometimes fighting each other, but mostly it was about wearing your colors on your back—a family thing, extra family."

As in white communities, drugs were all around as Simmons grew up. "My eighth-grade friends were shooting heroin," Simmons says. "Everybody was a heroin addict, my brother included. The number-one heroin corner was two blocks from me, and everybody would stand on the corner and sell heroin. A hundred people would be out there, so I was always aware of the drugs and the rest. I somehow got away from the shit, I don't really know how. You saw everybody else do it. Everybody was fucked up."

One force that stood against drugs was Islam, and its upright representatives, a constant presence in the neighborhood. "I remember Black Muslims on my corner," Simmons says. "On every black corner. And if you'd go to Steak-and-Take"—Philly cheese steak restaurants owned by the Muslims—"you'd straighten up. The effect of the Black Muslim movement in my community was unbelievable. Suddenly everybody's walking around with a suit and tie and they're selling magazines and they don't look like hell. You ain't gonna be a heroin addict in front of that."

Islam notwithstanding, Simmons started taking soft drugs in tenth grade. "All through high school I smoked a lot of pot. Most black kids were not into LSD, but we used to like LSD a lot." He bought it from his Jewish friends in Queens Village.

Simmons also sold pot. "Niggers had nothing but, 'Go to school and be a teacher.' That's why my father was a teacher. Own a store? No. Be a numbers runner, be a drug dealer, or be a teacher. That's what the black community teaches, still. No one is going to say, 'Start a business.' That's not part of the culture."

Dealing pot was part of the culture, and it was safer than selling heroin. "You'd still stand on a corner and everyone's selling heroin next to you," Simmons says. "But you go out and buy two pounds of weed, and a nickel bag costs you eighty-five cents and you sell it for five dollars, and you sell twenty nickel bags standing on Hollis Avenue in four hours, you know, you're a fuckin' hero! I had one thousand dollars on me one time, and I didn't have a job. I was a kid. And the idea of being fly and cold and fashion and all that was a big deal."

Simmons knew all about black separatism and identity politics, but didn't go that route. "I didn't feel any pressure," he says. "I was hanging out with my white friends, I was hanging out with my black friends."

Things were changing. The races were mixing, a little, at least among younger baby boomers. "Everybody was getting ready to change. There was a whole group of people who had that idea. Sometimes they'd come together, through me."

IN 1975, DAVE McIntosh left Kendallville, Indiana, to spend his senior year in Switzerland. He'd wanted to be a congressional page, but the local congressman, a Democrat, put his mother off with vague mutters that it was a bad idea. Years later, when a cocaine and sodomy scandal involving pages and congressmen broke open, McIntosh finally understood.

Having known several exchange students in his school, McIntosh hopped at the chance of a year abroad. He was placed with a stolid Swiss family in a town on the German border. "They were interested in America culture, but it was like Indiana—a few years behind the cutting edge." He spoke German and learned that in middle Europe, as in mid-America, American power was valued as the first line of defense for freedom. "That took me aback and opened my eyes," he says. "That sense of America's role in the world came through an older generation in Europe."

Back in Kendallville, a young congressional candidate named Dan Quayle, the grandson of a powerful Indiana publisher, came to speak at East Noble High School. "He was a young guy, longish hair, enthusiastic, talking to us about how, as a young person, he wanted to get involved in government and change things so we'd have more freedom." Quayle had been working for his father as an associate publisher when polls showed a fresh face could oust the Democratic congressman in his and McIntosh's district in 1976. Used to gray-haired local pols, the high-schooler found him "really exciting to listen to," despite the fact that Quayle was a Republican. "I didn't have my thoughts in order, so I'm sure it was his style and youth and energy that was attractive to me," McIntosh says. Not long afterward, he graduated second in his class and headed to Yale University to study politics and economics.

DOUG MARLETTE HAD only been drawing professionally for three years, but in 1975 he got his first syndication deal. Now his cartoons appeared all over the country and his earnings increased substantially. "I didn't really know what to do with it," he says. "I suddenly had more money than I ever expected to make." At the urging of a woman he was dating, he bought a blue Porsche 914.

Marlette disdained the quasi-religious movements ubiquitous in the mid-1970s. "It's like those old truths of Sunday school," he says. "When you drive one demon out of the Gadarene swine, ten thousand come in to replace it. If God is dead we find some other way in which we can feel special and elite and chosen. None of which are as time-tested or true as, say, Judaism or the Catholic faith. I've always had radar for phony, flaky stuff."

Marlette developed other obsessions. At twenty-seven, he threw himself full-time into learning to play the banjo, and within a year was playing in a band in clubs. The next year, disco hit Charlotte. He was one of the few single men in the paper's newsroom, and women started asking him to join them, taking dance lessons in clubs. "I learned how to dance and I spent a couple of years going out every night. I never knew how much women love to dance. But I became a snob. It didn't matter how great-looking a woman was if she couldn't dance." Years later, his friend Pat Conroy, the novelist, would kid him about that time. Whenever Conroy went on a book tour, he'd meet women who were disco "friends" of Marlette's.

"My twenties were an extended adolescence," he allows.

It was a good time to be funny; the children of *Mad* were everywhere. They'd been bred on the Jewish humor of Lenny Bruce and Bob Newhart; the black sass of Dick Gregory, Bill Cosby and Richard Pryor; the ensemble energies of Chicago's Second City comedy troupe and The Committee of San Francisco, which gave the world Woodstock's Wavy Gravy; the Smothers Brothers, those formerly All-American folkies whose prime-time comedy and music show was canceled by CBS in the early days of the Nixon administration because of their overt antiwar attitude; the surrealistic Firesign Theater; and George Carlin, arrested in 1972 for his routine about "seven words you can't say on television."

The *Mad* boomers who'd have the most impact of all were at a magazine called *National Lampoon*. The *Lampoon* was a descendent of the *Harvard Lampoon*, a preppy, upper-class product until the early 1960s, when it was taken over by a gang of mavericks who began producing biting parodies of national magazines. After a 1966 parody of *Playboy* and a 1968 take on *Life*, the *Lampoon*'s editors caught the attention of the publisher of *Cheetah*, an unsuccessful mass market psychedelic magazine. Henry Beard (b. 1947), Doug Kenney (b. 1947) and Rob Hoffman (b. 1947), and the team that gathered around them put together a comedy record, *National Lampoon's Radio Hour*, and a 1973 stage show, *Lemmings*, which parodied Woodstock as a symbol of a generation hurling itself off a cliff. The show opened that January at The Village Gate starring John Belushi (b. 1949) and Chevy Chase (b. 1943). A year later, those two became the heart and soul of the ultimate expression of generational self-satire.

On August 11, 1975, the last American soldiers left Vietnam. Two months later to the day, *Saturday Night Live* debuted on NBC, bringing impudent, cynical, often corrosively mocking comedy into the mainstream. The show's writers had a lot to work with. Reality had just offered up Charles Manson follower Lynette "Squeaky" Fromme taking a shot at Nixon's successor, the genial, undistinguished Gerald Ford, seventeen days before Sara Jane Moore, a political activist, shot at him again. In between, Patricia Hearst had been captured and put in jail.

Marlette listened to *National Lampoon's Radio Hour* once a week. "I still remember the first *Saturday Night Live*, when Michael O'Donoghue stuck long needles in the eyes of Tony Orlando and Dawn," he says, chuckling. In the depths of the Me Decade, this handful of comedians kept their generation's maverick spirit alive through laughter. "I feel a great affinity with and gratitude for what was going on there," Marlette says. "They were like a commune, being paid huge sums of money and getting famous by being subversive."

EIGHTEEN MONTHS AFTER arriving at William Morris, in 1976, Michael Fuchs was asked to join the fledgling pay cable network Home Box Office, known for broadcasting full-length theatrical movies uncut, uncensored, and commercial-free. When Fuchs learned that the job involved programming, making creative decisions and putting shows on the air, he jumped. "I thought I had good instincts," he said.

Four-year-old HBO had only 600,000 subscribers and was losing a fortune when Fuchs arrived. Launched in November 1972, its first broadcast, seen in 365 homes in Wilkes Barre, Pennsylvania, was a hockey game. The first movie it aired had an auspicious title, *Sometimes a Great Notion*. HBO aired its first original show a few months later: the Pennsylvania Polka Festival from the fairgrounds in Allentown. It also offered well-produced coverage of boxing matches and the Wimbledom tennis tournament.

HBO's owner, Time Inc., had long been a bastion of print journalism. After television was blamed for the demise of *Life*, Time Inc. had started investing in broadcasting. It bought and built cable TV franchises, including Manhattan Cable Television, and started HBO as a subscription programming service, transmitting its signal from microwave dishes strategically placed on rooftops. Cable systems were then isolated, local concerns offering no economies of scale, and these investments were losing millions. "Little did the print masters know," Richard M. Clurman wrote in his study of the company, *To the End of Time*, "that their wires in the ground and their dishes on stilts, which were draining so much capital and causing such executive anguish, would one day be half the company."[34] And little did they know that a "wired" world was a mere two decades away.

Not to say that the company was entirely clueless. In 1975 HBO's president, Gerald Levin (b. 1939), leased access to satellites allowing its signal to be beamed nationwide. Its first satellite broadcast that September was a heavyweight championship fight, "The Thrilla from Manila," pitting Muhammad Ali against Joe Frazier. The move to satellite caused worry at the broadcast networks and a bounce in Time's stock price, yet the division kept losing money. Nick Nicholas (b. 1939), a financial analyst who'd become president of Manhattan Cable, was moved to HBO in 1976 as president as Levin became chairman. Fuchs was one of several new executives who joined HBO that September; he was director of special programming, adding sports to his portfolio within a year.

The networks still ruled television, with 92 percent of the market. "HBO wasn't network television," Fuchs says. "It was countertelevision. Our job was to attack the Establishment. I wasn't joining any club, I was cutting against the grain. If there was ever a place that fit my personality, it was this. I would say to myself, 'Aren't you lucky that you found a place where you can succeed by being different?'" Cable had only two things going for it: good reception and HBO. "And HBO had an unbelievable inferiority complex," Fuchs says. "I coined a phrase we all laughed at, but it turned out to be true: 'We will change the face of broadcast television.' It was like a little kid with a slingshot saying, 'We will turn back the Nazis.'"

At first, HBO's original programming was limited to standup comedians like Robert Klein, broadcast live in concert. But Fuchs's superiors decided that in order to improve its negotiating position with the studios that licensed movies to HBO, the cable channel needed to produce more independent programming. "Network programming was so homogenized," Fuchs says, "so I bought in and helped create the philosophy that no one would buy this product if it wasn't different."

His first programming decision set the tone of the next eighteen years. In October 1976, Fuchs had to produce a comedy show, and the available talent boiled down to a choice between the Las Vegas comic Pat Henry and the boomer comic Steve Martin. Fuchs didn't know who Martin was and had to ask around. Then, the weekend before HBO's show was taped, Martin made his debut on the new *Saturday Night Live*. Not only was his one-man show a sensation, but all across the country, people started using his catchphrase, "Well, *excuuuuse* me!" Martin then went out on a tour pegged to HBO markets. "And by the time he came to New York," Fuchs boasts, "kids were doing his act with him."

As one-man shows starring Andy Kaufman (b. 1949), Richard Pryor (b. 1940) and Robin Williams (b. 1951) followed, HBO began to be seen as an experimental, permissive oasis in the television wasteland, and local cable operators made it their chief sales tool and their premium offering. "Network was homogenized," says Fuchs. "Everything was rehearsed, on a set, on video. It looked like shit. I was going to do a different style, a standup comedian in his natural habitat." HBO grew rich—it turned its first profit in fall 1977—because it started out too poor to buy established stars and lavish, empty network productions. And the comedians kept alive the spark of Fuchs's social conscience. "In those sleepy years, the comedians we specialized in were more socially relevant than the fucking politicians," he says.

Young Adulthood

STEVE CAPPS ENROLLED in the Rochester Institute of Technology in 1973. He could have gone anywhere. MIT tried to recruit him. "But I had thick glasses and zits on top of zits, and I was afraid if I went to MIT I would just be a nerd for the rest of my life, even though it turns out I have been."

Rochester had one of the best photography schools in the country. Its admissions officers promised he could study there and take a double major in computer science. But on arrival, he was forced to choose a single major, and since a favorite teacher had told him photography was a great hobby but a lousy profession, he chose computers. Only then did he discover that in those days before personal computers, he had to share the school's mainframe with others, who constantly crashed the big machine.

Though he hadn't lived with his parents since twelfth grade, staying in Schenectady to finish school while they moved to Connecticut ("I was squarer than a T-square and trustworthy enough to live alone," he says), he'd begun fighting with his father. "I didn't say fuck you, but I thought that. And we'd get into fifty-mile arguments about the right to wear no shoes." So when Capps returned for his second year at Rochester, a friend's new motorcycle suggested a solution to his dilemma. "I was a lost soul, definitely," he says. "I didn't know why I was in college. It was not challenging. Within a week, I'd dropped out."

He'd worked for General Electric Credit that summer ("if you're a son of GE, you get a great job at GE") and had made "a ton of money." So he went back, made some more, bought a motorcycle of his own, and within a month had taken off with his buddy to ride cross-country. He got as far as New Orleans, where his friend had an accident and "lost his gusto for traveling," Capps says. "It was just bad enough to deflate his Easy-Riderness."

His buddy crated his 350CC Honda and hitched home, but Capps decided to keep going. Though his father was furious and had vowed not to help him, he'd left a cache of funds with his mother, who sent money orders to post offices along the way. A hitchhiker they'd picked up was heading to Key West, and Capps decided to go, too. "I had discovered the *Whole Earth Catalogue*," he says. "Some kids became Jesus Freaks, I was definitely a Whole Earth Freak. So I lived in a landfill dump in Key West, great view. I scrounged a mattress—a vinyl one, so it wasn't too stinky. And I rigged up a desk because I like to draw and write. I had a whole little Hooverville setup."

Though he was the only permanent resident of his dump, other travelers would come and go. During spring break 1975, a whole pack of kids from Georgia moved in and soon discovered that flowers growing at Ernest Hemingway's house, a local attraction, contained the hallucinogen atropine. "They go eat these flowers, they're all hallucinating, and that's the night the cops do a sweep. Somehow, I round them all up and get them out of there." But he'd lost his home. "So I changed dumps," Capps says. "There was another landfill, next to a campground that you could sneak on to get a hot shower. I just kind of sat—and wrote nothing. It seemed profound at the time. My motorcycle wasn't working right. I finally said, 'Forget it. Going home.'"

The Rochester Institute of Technology had a work-study program, so when Capps got home from his aborted cross-country jaunt, he simply returned to his job and awaited a new semester. "I had a huge war chest at that point," he says. He also had his first girlfriend. When she suggested they build a log cabin on her family's land in the Adirondack Mountains, he dropped out again. "I still had aimless urges," Capps says of the bicentennial summer of '76.

Back at school that fall, he heard about a work-study job opening at Xerox, automating the technical library in one of its labs. Having already automated his high school library, he "walked in and blew away every other candidate," Capps says. Soon he was "making more money than you can imagine and learning ten thousand times more than I could in school." Here, not in the Whole Earth fantasy of his Key West Hooverville, was the real social revolution.

Capps met his first personal computer, the Alto, at Xerox. The Alto was conceived in the imagination of Alan C. Kay (b. 1940), a doctoral student at the University of Utah, where the Advanced Research and Projects Agency (ARPA) had established a tiny computer science department in 1966, run by a pioneer of computer graphics. In 1969, in a doctoral dissertation spiced with an epigraph from the hippies' favorite poet, Kahlil Gibran, Kay proposed the Dynabook, a personal computer small enough to tuck under your arm, complete with keyboard, screen, and enough memory to store a novel.

A few months later, New York-based Xerox opened the Palo Alto Research Center (a/k/a Xerox PARC); the copying company had seen the future—the paperless office—and decided to plan for it. PARC's engineers included several trained by the researcher who first proposed windows-based computing and the point-and-click device that came to be known as the mouse. In the next few years, PARC developed many of the innovations that would drive the PC industry, including laser printers; high-speed communication between devices (PARC's ETHERNET was essentially a traffic cop that kept data moving without collision); bit-mapped screens; and WYSIWYG (what-you-see-is-what-you-get) software that produced screen images identical to printed output.[1]

In September 1972, Alan Kay joined a PARC team working to build a PC. Completed the following spring, the Alto was the first fast, compact computer with a full-resolution screen. Xerox immediately ordered up several thousand and set to work making it consumer-friendly.

By 1974, PARC researchers had created the first word-processing software. A year later, its engineers demonstrated easy-to-understand graphic user interfaces (GUIs) with icons and pop-up and drop-down menus obviating hard-to-learn commands. But inexplicably, Xerox never capitalized on its collection of computing innovations, choosing instead to put its marketing muscle behind a dedicated word processor—in essence a typewriter with enough memory to store a page or two. The Alto effectively died.

Just a few months afterward, Capps found one of the discarded machines stuck away in a closet at Xerox's lab in Rochester. For the next year, Capps worked on the library automation project by day and played with the Alto at night. Then, just as he decided to cast his lot with the University of Utah's pioneering computer graphics department, Xerox offered him a full-time job at its nearby Webster Research Center if he'd agree to finish his degree at Rochester, tuition paid—a lucky thing, because most of the pioneers had long since left Utah. With the money he'd saved, he bought a house near his office and became a full-time hacker, writing programs for a combination laser printer/copier.

"What better life could you have?" he asks. "If you wake up at two in the morning with an idea for a program, you walk to work and code it all night! As long as you did your job, which was pretty ill-defined anyway, you could use a computer all you wanted. And you were given one day a week to do anything." He was having so much fun, he doesn't even remember when he graduated from college. "I have a degree," he says, vaguely. "Somewhere."

As part of his job, Capps would regularly visit Xerox PARC in California. "In typical twenty-one-year-old style, I assumed I was an equal to all these demigods who had created the whole thing at PARC," he says. At Rochester, engineers spent their entire careers developing copier toner, and one mathematician's lifework was to stop paper from curling when it passed through Xerox machines. The atmosphere at PARC was infinitely preferable. But how to get there?

JIM FOURATT RETURNED to a New York City reveling in decadence in 1974. It was in many ways the swan song of the 1960s—drugs were everywhere, sex was as free as it would ever be. In the straight community, glam rock and androgyny were the new styles. The gay world had turned to single-issue politics—putting sex above all, "sex for sex's sake," sprinkled with drugs, Fouratt says. In the wake of Stonewall, gay discos, run by the Mob, flourished, providing havens for all sorts of sexual and pharmaceutical excess. "Everybody is taking drugs," says Fouratt. "Quaaludes, speed, some cocaine, a lot of pot." He smirks. "A vibrant underground culture."

Fouratt thinks that in the wake of Stonewall, the powers of the city decided to decriminalize gay sex by unwittingly adapting Wilhelm Reich's dictum that a population kept in an orgasmic state will not be political and creating a "hands-off zone where every sort of oppressed desire got manifested: anonymous sex, compulsive sex." The new license didn't just apply to gays; throughout the mid-1970s, massage parlors, brothels and sex clubs for all sorts burgeoned. But after a decade spent in the closet while straight people had frolicked and enjoyed *their* sexual revolution, the city's gay population embraced their new freedom with special fervor.

Open trucks parked overnight along the Manhattan waterfront became "the trucks," a destination for anonymous male sex. Backroom bars, designed for furtive sexual encounters, were the latest thing. At the Anvil and other bars, performers and patrons practiced "fist-fucking," the insertion of forearms into lubricated anuses for sexual gratification, while trend-hounds from the fashion and entertainment industries clamored to get inside and watch. Clone culture—a new super-butch style among gays featuring short haircuts, buff bodies, jeans, flannel shirts and heavy boots—even included a set of handkerchief codes that advertised one's sexual preferences.

Everything was defined by sex. "As much sex as you could have—not my vision of gay liberation," Fouratt says. "Which probably saved my life." Seeking distance Fouratt decided the time had come to reinvent his career. He moved to Hollywood with his latest boyfriend and started looking for acting work again. He kept his radical ties, which both diverted him and held him back. He became an outspoken member of the Actor's Guild, attempting to organize its members for various causes, got involved in a strike at the local Gay and Lesbian Community Center, and joined the Socialist Media Group, which adopted the slogan "Everybody Is a Star" and attracted a handful of Hollywood leftists.

Like Fouratt, many political people had decided to infiltrate the culture industry. "And the Socialist Media Group was set up to be a conscience, so people didn't get bought out," Fouratt says. "Of course, they all did." Fouratt, on the other hand, believes his activities landed him on an informal blacklist. "It's a town where you don't make trouble," he observes. "You don't make trouble if you're a fuckin' star; you certainly don't make trouble if you're a nobody."

Fouratt lasted three years in Los Angeles, most of it on a downward slide, drinking and surrounded by what he calls Organic Junkies, who exercised and drank carrot juice by their pools all day and, like their East Coast disco brethren, drugged and danced all night. He woke up one afternoon surrounded by empty pints of vodka. "I walked out of that house with thirty dollars in my pocket, got on a plane, and came back to New York."

There a new music called disco had become the pulsing beat of gay culture. Fouratt never much liked disco. For all the behavioral liberty it brought about, its machine-like beat and hedonistic culture struck him as retrograde. The 1970s phenomenon was quickly embraced by many Boomers, though, among them those who hadn't succumbed to the lures of the 1960s and, having gone to work and made names for themselves instead in businesses like fashion, entertainment and the media, could suddenly buy the adolescent pleasures they'd missed.

The king of disco was Steve Rubell, born in Canarsie, New York, in 1943, the son of a postman and a teacher. During college at Syracuse

University, he enlisted in the National Guard to avoid going to Vietnam. When his unit was rumored to be heading there anyway, he transferred into military intelligence. From there, it was on to a brokerage house, where Rubell made some money in penny stocks. Then he opened a chain of steak restaurants. In 1974, Rubell hired Ian Schrager (b. 1946), a friend from college, as his lawyer. Together, the two bounced around New York, landing one night in a disco called Le Jardin, and decided they wanted one of their own. On the day after Christmas 1975, they opened the Enchanted Garden in unfashionable Douglaston, Queens. In 1977 the pair crossed the river, connected with Manhattan's gay-fashion-entertainment axis, and found themselves the center of things.

Rubell, a nebbish with a nasal voice and ingratiating manner, turned their new club, Studio 54, into fame's temple and the apotheosis of disco society. He coddled celebrities. Beginning with a birthday party for Bianca Jagger a few weeks after the club opened in 1977, Schrager and Rubell would finance regular fêtes for the bold-faced set. Those parties were the bait that lured lesser-knowns to line up outside Studio's doors. At a red, white, and black party for Paloma Picasso, they served $40,000 worth of salmon, caviar and champagne. For Valentino, they imported a circus, and for Giorgio Armani they hired twenty violinists in white tails to play in the lobby and the Ballet Trocadero de Monte Carlo to perform onstage.

Cocaine—pharmacology's analogue to the era's narcissism—was Studio 54's holy sacrament. Rubell even created private places where his precious celebrity set could indulge. It was the Roaring Twenties all over again. A strict entry policy permitted the rich, the powerful and the young and beautiful to indulge in every mode of sexual and pharmaceutical experimentation. Even reigning progressives were drawn to Studio's brief, bright flame. Carter administration aides and Kennedy family progeny were sometimes among those dancing or drugging the night away.

In summer 1978, Fouratt had set his sights on the music business. He'd begun managing a rock band, one of the groups creating an underground alternative to disco and corporate rock in the era of *Saturday Night Fever* and *Frampton Comes Alive*, and was steeping himself in the post-punk music then emerging from England, when a friend took him to a once-successful disco called Hurrah. Hurrah's decline had been driven by the raging popularity of Studio 54. Fouratt went to Studio 54 too, and was simultaneously fascinated and appalled. "Their value system was to get ahead and to use whatever and whoever they could to do it," he says. "It wasn't about young people, except as props and lures. You could be bought and sold and cocktailed and fucked. That's the truth."

Fouratt knew just how Hurrah could compete.

YOU REALLY DIDN'T need a weatherman to know which way the wind had blown. *Saturday Night Live* ruled television, Steven Spielberg (b. 1947) and George Lucas (b. 1944) were beginning to make waves in Hollywood, and cartoonists like Doug Marlette and Garry Trudeau were doing the same in the nation's newspapers. The former fringe had begun its move to the American center, when a presidential candidate who quoted Bob Dylan came roaring out of the South like a fresh wind.

Jimmy Carter, a born-again Christian, nuclear engineer and peanut farmer from Georgia, took office promising "a world order more responsive to human aspiration." Immediately he granted unconditional amnesty to all Vietnam-era draft resisters, inviting those who'd left the country or gone underground to come home. He followed that with more startling, progressive actions that seemed inspired by 1960s activism: announcing that American foreign aid would be cut to countries that violated human rights, opening talks with Vietnam to normalize relations, signing a treaty to return the Panama Canal to local control, postponing production of the neutron bomb, and mediating secret talks between Arabs and Israelis that ended in peace between Egypt and Israel.

The rise of Carter allowed Southerners to indulge in identity politics and group pride—to find the good in their redneck version of *Roots*. For Marlette, who'd looked north for education and enlightenment only to find more narrow-minded bigotry and provincialism, the late 1970s were a time of rediscovery. "The narcissism of the Me Decade wasn't only manifested in a shallow jogging-disco-do-your-own-thing-whatever, but also a healthy delving into tradition, history and self," he says.

Marlette began studying the Civil War as the source of his own rebel streak, reading William Faulkner and traveling to Nashville's Grand Old Opry and to the music clubs of Austin, Texas, where he immersed himself in the outlaw music of Willie Nelson and Waylon Jennings, "finding resonances and beginning to appreciate the authenticity," he says. Again, he saw himself reflected in the music of Bob Dylan, who by 1978 had declared himself a born-again Christian and recorded an album of religious songs. "That did not bother me a whit," Marlette says. "What was interesting was his instinct for the truth of the Jewish tradition. It's radical, rooted. That was the beginning of this generation rediscovering what we had rejected."

It was also the moment when Marlette was "discovered," singled out in a *Time* magazine article on Jimmy Carter's New South. "It was kind of hip to be a Southerner," he says. "Carter legitimized that." Unfortunately, the new president also had what Marlette calls the Southern Disease. "It's a love affair with defeat, a kind of self-destructiveness masked by a virtuous, arrogant, pious knowing what's best," Marlette says. "You think you can snap your fingers and have things be the way you want them. The Clintons have some of that, too. Hillary thinks she knows better. There's a kind of self-righteousness Hillary has that Carter had. But it's not enough to be right. You've got to be able to work with other human beings. That takes another kind of a genius."

Carter's years in office did offer ripe targets for a political cartoonist: the energy crisis (Marlette's cartoon showed a driver trading his firstborn for a fill-up), nuclear power (a plant shaped like a pair of dice), the Equal Rights Amendment (as pigs are led to a slaughterhouse, sows demand equal rights), abortion (a Supreme Court justice in the door of a clinic telling a poor woman, "If you have to ask how much, you can't afford one"), and the rise of fundamentalism in Iran (Carter slamming his head against a stone wall shaped like the Ayatollah Khomeini) and in America (Christ crucified on a TV antenna).

Jimmy Carter's cleansing of American society was overshadowed by the nation's continuing economic distress and by an event that happened in California in the summer of 1978, at least partly in response to those troubles. The passage there, by a vote of almost two to one, of a ballot item known as Proposition 13, which cut property taxes and the social programs they paid for in half, spelled the end of New Deal-era optimism, symbolized by an active, paternal government, and the beginning of what some called a new realism and others a new mean-spiritedness. Although it took the seizure of hostages by fundamentalists in Iran and Carter's failure to free them to finally kick the legs out from under his presidency, there was already a sense that Carter wasn't the answer.

AFTER HIS FAMILY moved to Sacramento, California, Cameron Sears's last year of high school was quite different from what it might have been at his tiny boarding school in Maine. "I'd had long hair and ridden a bike to school, but that just wasn't done," he says. "Kids were driving fancy cars, and the people were really flaky, in my opinion."

A year later, Sears was ready to escape. "I didn't go to college right away," he says. "I needed some time to sort it out." He enrolled in a three-month mountaineering course in Wyoming with the National Outdoor Leadership School, and spent weeks at a time in the American outback.

On his return, Sears enrolled in the University of California at Santa Cruz and spent the next five years earning an undergraduate degree. "Nobody was doing it in four years any more," he says. With the job market clogged with earlier boomers, it was just as well to extend your adolescence.

Santa Cruz was a highly progressive university. Many of his friends worked on the school's organic farm. There were no grades, although concern about the viability of that policy set in while Sears was there. Sears was well aware that there was a recession going on. Gasoline prices were skyrocketing, and Ph.D.s were driving taxis. He felt sure it wouldn't affect him. "Somewhat naively, I thought I was always going to be a soldier in the environmental movement," he says. "Not necessarily as an activist chaining myself to trees—although I was certainly willing to do that. But I wanted to operate on a higher level. I wanted to affect policy. That was my goal."

JOHN GAGE MADE his last foray into politics in 1980, when Ted Kennedy made an abortive run for the presidency. "I thought it was time to push for a change that would emphasize people who really were suffering, and so I said, 'I'll do it.'" Then he watched a videotaped interview with Kennedy. "They asked him, 'Why are you running?' Essentially he didn't have an answer. My heart sank." But he did his job—"get the plane into the air and into a five-media-stops-per-day campaign"—straight through the convention, where Kennedy lost to Carter, who then lost to Ronald Reagan. "So I went back to academic life," Gage says.

But he wasn't content. The abstractions of math and statistical physics couldn't explain human behavior. That's when he discovered something infinitely more satisfying: computing. A few years before, Gage had come upon Berkeley's mini-computers when a university computer system administrator and fellow grad student named Bill Joy (b. 1954) introduced him to software that did mathematical typesetting. "I discovered the populism of a system that allows anyone to create beautiful mathematics on a page," Gage says.

The computer revolution had begun in the late 1950s. At that time, there was only one paradigm for computer use. Manufacturers like IBM, Digital Equipment Corporation, Wang and Data General sold black boxes—huge mainframe computers with magic inside. "We're the priests with the keys to the temple; you've got to come to the priests," Gage says, satirizing the prevailing proprietary attitude. At MIT, computer aficionados (for there was no computer science department yet) began attempting to improve the software that ran the school's multimillion-dollar IBM mainframe computer. They called themselves "hackers,"[2] and though they seemed worlds away from the dope-smoking, anti-logic radicals then coming of age on less technocratic campuses, they had the equally radical idea that the keys to the temple of computing should be freely available to anyone, not only those approved by the priests. Indeed, they felt that all information should be free, so it might be shared and bettered.

In the early 1960s, the hackers got their hands on the tool that would wrest computing from the priests forever—the minicomputer. Though they were as big as refrigerators at first, these machines were revolutionary: unlike huge room-size mainframes, they were accessible, nimble and inspiring to those who didn't want to put on white shirts and ties and join IBM's army of bureaucrats.[3] By the 1970s, computer science and the hacker ethic had spread across the country. Computers offered a safe haven of logic in an increasingly illogical world. For students on the run from the collapsing 1960s youth culture, computer culture was a godsend. Here was something they could control.[4]

In the Bay Area, schools like Stanford and Berkeley formed the vanguard of the cyberrevolution. Beginning in 1969, they were all hooked up to a Defense Department-funded network called ARPAnet. ARPA, the Advanced Research Projects Agency, had been funding computer research since the end of World War II, investing about a billion dollars on advanced projects to make a better military. To kill people efficiently, you need to find them, so ARPA put money into radar and acoustic detection systems that would listen for the propeller beat of Russian submarines, and into computers to analyze those signals. It put money into materials, chip technology and university computer departments that could help airplanes fly faster and higher. But ARPA also funded pure computer research, allowing hackers to take its money without the slightest guilt.[5] At MIT and Stanford, some ARPA money was even spent developing early computer games like Spacewar and Adventure.

The ARPAnet was developed to make the most of scarce computing resources by connecting users and resources, even at a great distance, but it soon turned into a communications medium as academics, technical types and an avant-garde of ex-hippies, science fiction aficionados and anarchists began connecting through a new technology called electronic mail.[6] ARPAnet was based in "the belief that systems should be decentralized, encourage exploration, and urge a free flow of information," Steven Levy wrote in *Hackers*, a history of the computer revolution.[7] Similar values had driven the now-waning youth movement.

Key computer research was also taking place at Bell Labs, the phone company's scientific arm, which developed a computer operating system called Bell UNIX. Bell Labs was part of AT&T, which, as a government-sanctioned monopoly, was not allowed to market its creation commercially. Instead, it licensed the system to universities, the military and corporate researchers for a small fee, along with the right to alter the source code, its programming foundation and the hacker-esque obligation to share improvements with other users.

Bill Joy was one of the student programmers who dug into the program, creating a version known as Berkeley UNIX. In 1980, Joy rewrote a set of standards (computer instructions written in code) known as TCP/IP networking protocols, which systematized communication between computers on the ARPAnet. Without TCP/IP, "you could be getting it all but not understanding a word I'm saying," explains Gage, who by 1982 was working with Joy on Berkeley's computing strategy. "Bill put the new protocols out free on the Internet—very Berkeley—and everybody took his code and made their computers work. He became the God of Internet-distributed computing. Anybody in the world could now be in the conversation." A year later, the Domain Name Service came into being, a sort of cyberspace city planning agency, and the word *Internet* started being used in place of ARPAnet.[8]

As the Internet was being born, a separate group of computer boomers was creating the computer revolution's other essential component: cheap hardware. While Gage was working on the McGovern campaign, a group called Community Memory was installing a public computer terminal, open to anyone, near a record store in Berkeley. In 1971 a science fiction fan named Lee Felsenstein (b. 1945), who'd been arrested at Sproul Hall on December 2, 1964, and then joined the staff of the underground newspaper *Berkeley Barb*, gained access to his first computer.

Felsenstein was one of the pioneers—many of them former activists—of what would soon coalesce into a populist movement to bring computing power to the people. All over the Bay Area, others were having the same idea, and by 1975, the first commercially available PC, a bare-bones affair called Altair 8800, based on a new microprocessor chip made by a Santa Clara company, Intel, was made available in hobby kit form (although without any programs or input devices like keyboards or mice). On March 5, 1975, two computer kit enthusiasts held the first meeting of the Homebrew Computer Club at one of their homes in Menlo Park. Within four months, the meetings had grown so large, they had to be held in an auditorium at Stanford. In June, Felsenstein started chairing those meetings.[9]

Among those frequenting Homebrew—sharing information, advances, and even code, as required by the tenets of hackerism—were engineers from Hewlett-Packard, including shaggy-haired Steve Wozniak (b. 1940), often accompanied by a high school friend just back from a hippie trek to India and a spell in an Oregon commune, Steve Jobs (b. 1945). Jobs was working for Atari, which was then developing a computerized game called Pong. In college, Jobs and Woz, as he was known, had built and sold blue boxes, illegal devices that let users make free long distance calls. Now, inspired by Homebrew, Wozniak set out to build his own computer. By that winter, it was done, and Jobs, dazzled by his friend's invention, insisted they build and sell them. Financed by the sale of Jobs's Volkswagen bus, they incorporated in spring 1976. Jobs, who was proud of his hippie roots and often went barefoot, named the company Apple after the Beatles' record label.[10] Meanwhile, Wozniak created a new machine, the Apple II, which would include a color terminal. It wasn't as advanced as the Xerox Alto, but at least you could buy an Apple.

TIM SCULLY HAD a plan to use his time in prison to earn a doctoral degree and continue the psycho-electronic explorations he'd started while out on bail. In 1974, just after his release on appeal bond, Intel had introduced its 8008 chip, the key component in microcomputers. Scully built a physiological monitoring system around one for use in drug and alcohol rehabilitation programs. Then, when Intel's 8080 chip followed in 1975, he built a computer to detect and record changes in consciousness in biofeedback sessions.

He'd introduced himself to the prison's psychological services staff at McNeil Island during his first sojourn there and corresponded with them while he was out on bail, in the hope they'd allow him to set up a biofeedback program when he returned. He was afraid prison would be full of the sort of guys who'd beaten him up in high school. Instead, he arrived with a rep as a drug czar who didn't rat, and his worst problem was convincing inmates he couldn't sell them acid. But after he got an inmate job as an assistant to one of the resident psychologists, he *could* get them high, help them relax, and combat stress—with biofeedback.

While out on bail, Scully had met a woman suffering from cerebral palsy who could only communicate by laboriously pointing out letters one at a time to her parents with a telegraph key attached to her knee. After he'd been at McNeil a year, Scully got permission to build her a microcomputer and program it using principles of cryptography, allowing the young woman to communicate up to thirty times faster, and later, to write and print out notes and essays. It was so successful, he began building them for other disabled people, adding extensions that controlled devices from page-turners to light switches. When inexpensive speech synthesizers came on the market, he added those, too, so users could have their messages read out loud. Federal Prison Industries took note and began a program to build the machines and offer them to speech-impaired veterans. Though the costs of customizing the device and gaining necessary approvals made the project unfeasible, years later, Scully rewrote the program for PCs and distributed it free on the Internet. The project won him an award as 1979's Outstanding Young Man of the Year from the Washington Jaycees, which had a chapter inside the prison.

Scully was indeed an outstanding prisoner. "My first priority was to stay out of trouble with the inmate population, because the penalty could be death," he says. "Second was to stay out of trouble with the staff. After that, I just wanted not to rot away." He taught classes in computer design, programming and tai chi to fellow inmates, and wrote a dissertation on his biofeedback experiments, earning a Ph.D. He also won a sentence reduction. In August 1979, he was released to a halfway house in San Francisco.

JUST AS NEW YORK began to rise from ruin, Donald Trump got married. Ivana Zelnickova was one of a group of models who came to New York to promote the 1976 Olympic Games in Montreal. Trump spotted her across the room at the singles bar Maxwell's Plum and used his pull to get her a table. She proved to have more character than the Le Club cuties he was used to. In 1977, they were married by Norman Vincent Peale, the high priest of positive thinking.

"Which is probably a good thing, because it kept me out of trouble" during the hedonistic glory days of the disco era, Trump says. "If I hadn't got married, who knows what would have happened? You had drugs, women and booze all over the fuckin' place."

That summer, the couple rented a guest house in Long Island's exclusive Georgica Association; the beachfront property belonged to radical lawyer Michael Kennedy. After being lauded in a *High Times* survey of top drug lawyers, he had begun to represent its publisher, the former Yippie and Zippie Tom Forcade. When Forcade committed suicide in

1978, Kennedy—who'd been named a head of the charitable trust in which Forcade put his assets—took over the drug magazine. His path would keep crossing his clients' and tenants' as he followed the evolving Baby Boom in search of fresh legal fees.

AFTER HE CAME home in 1977, Mark Rudd decided to say nothing about his years underground, "because what could I have said?" he asks. "The Revolution is still strong? I'm sorry for what I'd done? It was a no-win situation. So I just shut up." Though all federal felony charges against him had been dropped, Rudd still worried that he would be hauled before a grand jury on the Weather Underground, even that he might face murder charges from the townhouse explosion. "But there was nothing from the townhouse, nothing stemming from subsequent bombings, nothing from the bombing of the Pentagon, breaking Tim Leary out," he marvels. "Nothing."

Instead, he was arraigned for several misdemeanors and released on modest bail. The next day, he flew to Chicago, surrendered again, and was given permission to return to New York. "*WSP*," he whispered to lawyer Gerald Lefcourt after the proceedings. "White-skin privilege prevailed," he explains. "I felt somewhat ashamed of the tremendous ease with which I reentered society." Ultimately, he would plead guilty to criminal trespass in New York and receive an unconditional discharge. A second guilty plea in Chicago cost him a $2,000 fine and two years' probation.

While he awaited the disposition of those cases, Rudd and Sue married and moved into an apartment in Brooklyn. Sue was pregnant and gave birth to their second child, a daughter, the following May. During the pregnancy, Rudd reestablished contacts in the pacifist community, but discovered he was a pariah to some former radicals. When he ran into two members of the faction that had taken over Weather, they were openly hostile. But for every bad experience, there was a good one. When he attended a celebration of Vietnam's admittance to the United Nations in 1977, an official of the government thanked him for helping liberate his country.

When he moved back to New Mexico in 1978, Rudd discovered that most people were willing to live and let live. He's glad he goes unrecognized. "I had more than fifteen minutes of fame and don't even want thirty seconds anymore," Rudd says. "I prefer to be a real person in a real community."

As Rudd settled into his new life, others came up from the underground. Cathy Wilkerson surfaced in 1980, was sentenced to three years, and served less than one. Billy Ayers and Bernadine Dohrn emerged, too; remarkably, Dohrn had been in New York, waitressing in an Upper East Side restaurant called Jim McMullen, a favored haunt of the city's ruling class. Charges against Ayers had been dropped. Dohrn was fined and sentenced to probation.

The saga of the Weathermen finally came to an ignominious close in October 1981, when Kathy Boudin, Dave Gilbert and Judy Clark were arrested following the botched holdup of a Brinks armored truck in Nyack, New York. After the purge of 1976, the trio had formed the May 19 Organization, named in honor of Ho Chi Minh and Malcolm X's birthday. It functioned as a support group for the Black Liberation Army, a gang of terrorists or gangsters (depending on your point of view), itself an offshoot of the Black Panther Party.

After Nyack, Jeff Jones and several lesser Weatherevolutionaries were busted, too. Jones was let off with a fine and probation. The May 19 group wasn't so lucky; Boudin was sentenced to twenty years in jail and Gilbert and Clark seventy-five for their part in the robbery and murder of two policemen. "They're still there, and they're still writing," says Rudd. "If you look on the Internet, you will probably find shit of theirs." He dismisses the tract he found there by a May 19 survivor as "long, unreadable." But then, when Rudd gave a speech at a rally on the anniversary of the shootings at Kent State University in 1989, Bernadine Dohrn got up and walked out. Though he's in touch with some of his former comrades-in-arms, "few of them figure into my life intimately," he says. Yet Rudd still admires Dohrn, who spent seven months in prison for refusing to testify to a Brinks-case grand jury.

WITH HER SEMI-FAMOUS father off in Boston and her model mother bedridden, celebrity culture became Victoria Leacock's touchstone. Her fascination with fame was fed by the television, which was always on. "Mom would have it on from 7:00 A.M. to 3:00 A.M. I was watching a *lot* of TV." Leacock's other cultural reference point was Judy Garland, a favorite of her mother's and the tragic heroine of so many gay men in the Village. "I was a gay man," she jokes. She and her friend Gordon—soon to realize he was gay—would put on dresses and tease their hair. Her mother recognized the need for escape. Her eighth-grade graduation gift to Victoria was a single ticket to the 1976 Lincoln Center premiere of Martin Scorsese's *New York, New York*, starring Garland's daughter, Liza Minnelli.

Leacock became obsessed with Minnelli and tried to emulate her. She sold Avon cosmetics to her friends to earn money to take acting and dance lessons. When her idol opened in a one-woman Broadway musical, *The Act*, in fall 1977, she waited backstage every Saturday with home-made presents and cards. Soon enough, she became Minnelli's pet fan, with full backstage access. She met the first boy she ever kissed there: Blake, director Gower Champion's son. She also met Diana Barrows, who played Annie in the eponymous musical, who was equally obsessed with celebrities. The girls' moms enjoyed each other as well, so they all became the best of friends, lightening young Leacock's burden.

The girls started sneaking into concerts, benefits, premiere parties and the second acts of Broadway shows together. They also went to Studio 54. Old enough to be baby celebrities, but too young for much else, they just watched. Victoria's mother always wanted a full report. "I'd come home and tell my mom we danced with the guy from *Murder by Death*, because that's who Truman Capote was to me. Who knew? We'd come home at midnight or one in the morning, stay up talking until three, then skip school the next day because we were tired." Her grades suffered, but she didn't care.

Victoria was on line to get into Tavern on the Green for a tribute to director George Cukor in spring 1978 when she met Andy Warhol. A reporter asked if she was Bianca Jagger, Warhol's date. Leacock was four-teen, wearing a ten-year-old dress of her mother's, hair in a ponytail. Warhol laughed and told the reporter that Jagger was in the lady's room. Leacock told Warhol that she'd gotten an A in art class by emulating his famous Campbell's Soup paintings, done the year before Victoria was born. "And I'm gonna be an actress and I want to be a filmmaker and I love *Interview* magazine and by the time we got through the buffet line, he looked at me and said, 'Why don't you come visit me at The Factory on Friday after school?'" She did so, and the visits continued every Friday until she graduated from high school.

"I just thought celebrities and artists and writers were the most amaz-ing, God-sent creatures, because my father was one," she says. Since her father was absent, Warhol became a surrogate. He was so nice, she refused to believe people who told her he could be a social vampire.

"How was your science test?" he'd ask. "Did the boy you like in math class look at you?"

DESPITE A FEW "little iffy periods" involving gangs and drugs, Russell Simmons was a fairly good student in high school. Graduating in 1976 and thinking to become a sociology teacher, he enrolled in City College of New York and moved near its campus in Harlem, the uptown Manhattan neighborhood long the center of black urban culture. After he was fired from an Orange Julius hot dog stand for throwing rinds in the street outside, he began selling ersatz cocaine—it was actually a commercial incense called Coco Leaf, made from the same plant. Though its pharmaceutical properties had been deactivated, it still caused a telltale "freeze" or numbing, just like cocaine, when it touched mucus membranes.

Decimated by heroin, black culture wasn't what it had been. Sports and music were still outs for black youth, but the music had changed. "Fucking disco was being forced on the black community," Simmons says. "Somebody decided that the music industry should invent a pop music out of black music," just like the spineless, preening, corporate rock that had formularized rock 'n' roll. Record companies "were competing for crossover," sales of black music to whites, "and disco was their vehicle. It was corporate black music." Simmons thought of it as music that made it easy for white folks to dance.

Not unlike the white rockers creating "new wave" in answer to corporate rock, Simmons and several like-minded young men began ferreting out a new music. Together with Curtis Walker (b. 1959), who sold so much Coco Leaf incense he was nicknamed Kurtis Blow,[11] Simmons went to cavernous gay clubs like the Loft and the Gallery, "because that was the hip thing to do in Harlem," he says. "We used to take tons of hallucinogenic drugs and go there, straight guys standing with their arms crossed. That was the hip place for music and we all wanted to be in the music business."

Just after his sophomore year at CCNY, Simmons got arrested carrying "six bags of weed," he says. "My parents were furious. I got in a lot of trouble. I had a whole year's worth of reporting to a parole officer. I'm two steps away from living in jail. But that gave me the energy to start my own shit; it made me become a club promoter."

He and his friends formed The Force, promoting rap parties for collegians like themselves in clubs like Harlem's venerable Small's Paradise. Rap, the music that would make him famous, was springing up all over uptown New York in the mid-1970s. It grew out of black American preaching; the mid-1960s rhymes of Cassius Clay; the black power poetry of 1960s artists like The Last Poets (who'd been introduced to the Baby Boom via the soundtrack of Mick Jagger's movie debut in the decadent film *Performance*); jazz fusion pioneers like Gil Scott-Heron (b. 1949), who recorded the proto-rap "The Revolution Will Not Be

Televised" in 1969; boastful black radio deejays like Frankie Crocker and Pete "DJ" Jones; and "toasting," a marriage of West African praise singing with Jamaican reggae. In the early 1970s, toasters like Big Youth and U-Roy would rhyme over "dub"—instrumental—reggae recordings played on massive sound systems at outdoor dances in Jamaica; by 1973, recordings of their toasts made it to America.

Jamaican-born Clive Campbell (b. 1954), who'd come to the Bronx in 1967, began playing deejay at dance parties in a housing project's rec room. One night, he noticed he could isolate sections where the funk records he played broke into percussion. Experimenting, he discovered that by using two turntables, he could continuously hip-hop between those percussion tracks—which he'd name "the breaks"—driving dancers to distraction. He'd also "toast" his friends over the sound system, chanting rhymes about them. When he began playing regularly at a club called Twilight Zone, proving that his raps could fill a club more cheaply than bands could, his solo experiment turned into a social scene.[12]

Other deejays like Joseph "Grandmaster Flash" Saddler (b. 1958) and Afrika Bambaata (b. Kevin Donovan, 1960), a former street gang member dedicated to ending gang violence, were attracting crowds of their own, at parties on basketball courts and in parks, schools and clubs all over the Bronx and Queens. The deejays were constantly trying to top each other. Grand Wizard Theodore accidentally invented scratching in 1975, moving a record back and forth in syncopated rhythm beneath a turntable's needle. Renamed Kool DJ Herc, Campbell added dancers, the Nigger Twins, who inspired a new dance style called breaking, a series of lighting-fast moves and acrobatics performed during the breaks by competitive dancers Herc called b-boys.[13] Bambaata formed a troupe called Zulu Nation; Grandmaster Flash had the Furious Five.

Dancers flocked to their parties. As rap spread, the art evolved through rapping battles between the musical gangs. Graffiti artists were fellow outsiders, so these new ghetto prophets, inspired by a messenger named Taki who wrote his name, or "tag," on every surface he passed, painted ever more elaborate pieces of art on tenement and subway walls. Some of them allied with the rappers and began papering black neighborhoods with leaflets for shows. Bootleg tapes started circulating. And the cultural collision of art, movement, and music soon had a name: hip-hop. Simmons and his friends, relatively new to the scene, were determined to be part of it. Wearing a big gold medallion spelling out his nickname, Rush, Simmons promoted his first hip-hop party in 1977. Worried about debuting in the hothouse of Harlem, he started in Queens with his school friend Kurtis Blow as the entertainment. Under the slogan "Rush: The Force in College Parties," they promoted dances starring Blow, Eddie Cheba, DJ Hollywood and Grandmaster Flash, and their business grew so fast that within months, they were filling the ballroom at the Hotel Diplomat in Manhattan with up to 4,000 paying customers.

Rappers "were bigger than music stars, and they didn't have records!" Simmons exults. But they didn't draw quite the same crowd as the one pressed against the velvet ropes of Xenon, the Studio 54-like disco just up the block. Street kids and, very soon, suburban wannabes, they could get rowdy. Simmons admitted to *Village Voice* journalist Nelson George that there were often security problems; he and Blow would sometimes take refuge in the Diplomat's bulletproof box office.[14]

Rap was "totally from the streets," Simmons says. "A rebellion."

STEVE WOZNIAK WAS a believer in the hacker ideal. While he was working on the Apple, a competing idea entered the PC Garden of Eden and was quickly condemned as an unmitigated evil. Initially, the first small computer, the Altair, was shipped without an operating system. Then two computer-savvy friends from Seattle, Paul Allen (b. 1953) and Bill Gates (b. 1955), co-founders of what would become the software behemoth Microsoft, heard about the Altair and offered to create a basic program to run it. It was called Altair BASIC, modeled on the clunky but easy-to-use BASIC programming language developed at Dartmouth in the 1960s, and subsequently championed by the People's Computer Company in Berkeley and its founder, Bob Albrecht. Albrecht, a *Whole Earth Catalog*-type character, was the Johnny Appleseed of West Coast computing, and BASIC was his seed.

After Allen successfully sold the program to Altair, Gates dropped out of Harvard and began to debug—or perfect—it. Unfortunately, Altair's manufacturer had already started shipping machines without BASIC, so members of Homebrew, who'd gotten hold of an earlier version, started copying it and giving it away for free, as hackers had done since the 1960s. Gates, already working on versions for other microcomputer brands, was furious. His dream was "a computer on every desk and in every home, (all) running Microsoft software." This copying was a bad start. In an act that would reverberate for decades to come, Gates, then nineteen, wrote a widely circulated "Open Letter to Hobbyists," pleading with them to stop stealing his software. "Who can afford to do professional work for nothing?" Gates wrote. The Homebrew hackers dismissed him as a whiner.

From then on, the computing world broke down into two competing (if sometimes overlapping) camps, a war between two Baby Boom paradigms. On one side were post-hippies like Wozniak, Gage, Felsenstein and Joy, still openly idealistic. On the other were the new vanguard, folks like the software tycoon Gates, who believed in profit-making, proprietary, closed-model computing. Somewhere in the middle were the Apple crew, who played both ends against the middle, acting tastefully hip while they sold a proprietary hardware system (Jobs won out over Wozniak on that score).

At first, the big computer companies couldn't have cared less. Hewlett-Packard, for instance, had turned down Wozniak when he brought his Apple design to them. In 1977, major corporations like Commodore and Radio Shack began marketing microcomputers. It wasn't until fall 1979, though, that the still-quixotic microcomputer met its Sancho Panza, when VisiCalc, a spreadsheet or accounting program written for the Apple II by a Harvard Business School student named Dan Bricklin (b. 1951), went on the market. It was the so-called "killer app" that introduced first thousands, then millions of people to computing. The spreadsheet was followed by word processors. "With that combination," Gage says, "the little ugly box on your desk became useful."

By 1980, Apple was earning more than $100 million a year and poised to go public.

The next year, the giant IBM finally admitted it had been humbled by microcomputers and introduced its PC, but it, too, needed an operating system. Every consumer computer had one. Operating systems were necessary buffers between normal folk and the arcane language of machines. Apple had its own. Most others microcomputers used CP/M, for "Control Program/Monitor." IBM wanted CP/M, but a series of mishaps kept its executives from buying it before they met with Bill Gates about his BASIC program. When Gates learned IBM had no operating system, he sprang into action. A nearby company had one called QDOS ("quick and dirty operating system).[15] As John Gage tells the story: "Gates went out the back door, bought QDOS for some tiny amount of money, ran back to the IBM guys and said, 'I've got it for you! When do you want it? And by the way, we need an exclusive contract because you have to get to a volume that will make it worth my time. I just want a little part, but I want that little part.'"

Gates named the program MS-DOS. "He got a monopoly contract with IBM," Gage relates, "and off he goes."

* * *

Barbara Ledeen at
Beloit College, 1968.

Barbara Ledeen outside her Maryland
home, 1998.

Marianne Williamson performing her cabaret show, 1978.

Marianne Williamson in 1999.

David McIntosh, high school freshman, 1973.

David McIntosh on *Meet The Press* following Newt Gingrich's resignation, 1998.

Tim Scully (right) building a linear accellerator, 1960.

Tim Scully in Albion, California, 1998.

Cameron Sears, sixth grader, 1971.

Cameron Sears on the Tuolomne River near Yosemite National Park, 1996.

Cynthia Bowman at her desk in the Airplane Mansion, 1976.

(Courtesy of CORBIS/Roger Ressmeyer)

(Courtesy of Katy Raddatz)

Cynthia Bowman in San Francisco, 1999.

Leslie Crocker Snyder graduates law school, 1966.

HON.
LESLIE CROCKER SNYDER

Leslie Crocker Snyder at work in New York State Supreme Court, 1996.

Steve Capps graduates
high school, 1973.

Steve Capps with his daughter,
Emma, 1998.

Michael Fuchs, Al Gore and Christopher Reeve
at the White House, 1995.

Michael Fuchs at his first public
performance, 1950.

Mark Rudd addressing students cut off from occupied Columbia University, April, 1968.

(Courtesy of AP/World Wide Photos)

Mark Rudd at home in Albuquerque, 1995.

(Courtesy of Cary Herz)

Kathryn Bond Stockton and date at a friend's wedding, 1974.

Kathryn Bond Stockton in 1994.

Doug Marlette in Charlotte,
North Carolina, 1974.

Doug Marlette in his office
at *Newsday*, 1998.

John Gage and farm workers organizer Cesar Chavez at the University of California at Berkeley's Sproul Hall, 1965.

John Gage at a software developer's conference, 1999.

"Mitzi" (a/k/a Nina Hartley), age 15, 1974.

(Both photos courtesy of Nina Hartley)

Nina Hartley, sex star, 1998.

Thomas Vallely at his base camp in Vietnam, 1969.

(Courtesy of Tom Vallely)

(Courtesy of Bill Crawford)

Thomas Vallely and two North Vietnamese Army officers near Danang, 1985.

Donald Trump (with pointer) unveils his convention center, 1975.

Donald Trump on his helicopter, 1988.

Russell Simmons in Hollis,
Queens, 1965.

Russell Simmons and
wife Kimora, 1999.

Jim Fouratt, house hippie at
Columbia Records, 1969.

(Courtesy of Jim Fouratt)

Jim Fouratt, in his Danceteria II office, 1982.

Victoria Leacock and her father Ricky in New York's Central Park, 1965.

(Courtesy of Victoria Leacock)

(Courtesy of John Dolan)

Victoria Leacock and Rent composer Jonathan Larson in New York, 1994.

(Chuck Pulin)

Michael Gross at Max's Kansas City, New York, 1974.

(© by David Bailey/Camera Eye Ltd.)

Michael Gross in London, 1999.

UNDER JIM FOURATT'S direction, Hurrah was an instant success—a rock disco, an artistic anti-Studio, and an early cauldron of what would later become known as alternative culture—the Caucasian analogue to hip-hop's revolt against disco. What Hurrah's clientele lacked in money and power was more than made up for in independent creativity. "They all came to New York to be downtown artists," Fouratt says. "I wanted to bring the downtown culture uptown." Roy Cohn, the right-wing icon, a closet homosexual and lawyer for and constant presence at Studio 54, "would never have gotten into Hurrah," says Fouratt.

In place of disco, Hurrah hosted bands like Gang of Four, the Contortions, the Dead Kennedys, and the Feelies—and paid them a large portion of the door receipts. After nine months of his socialism, capitalism reared its ugly head when the club's owners demanded Fouratt pay *them* more and the bands less, and he walked out in a huff. Fouratt's next collaboration, with a German émigré named Rudolf Pieper (b. 1946), started badly. In October 1979, their first club, Pravda, opened the day American hostages were seized in Iran and folded after only two nights. Their next venture, which opened in spring 1980, was a raging success.

In part, that was because Studio 54's Steve Rubell and Ian Schrager had gone to jail that February. Rubell's brazenness ("The profits are astronomical," he would boast. "Only the Mafia does better") and his and Schrager's visibility had brought the law down on the duo. It turned out they'd stuffed bags of cash in the ceiling and tucked cocaine into one of their two sets of books. Their conviction for income tax evasion was a sign of the times. The 1980s were definitely going to be different.

MARIANNE WILLIAMSON'S WANDERINGS brought her to New York City, still intensely unhappy, drugging, drinking and overeating. Linda Obst, who'd moved to New York, introduced Williamson to Albert Goldman, a one-time Columbia University English professor who'd just completed a biography of Lenny Bruce. She became his Girl Friday. When she went through a painful break up with a boyfriend, he fired her, later recalling her as "profoundly confused" and constantly crying. "He certainly did not have eyes to see the likes of me," says Williamson, who nonetheless considered him a mentor.

Soon she was on the road again, ending up with a musician boyfriend in San Francisco, where she practiced Zen Buddhism, read the existentialists, and lingered over a Ouija board. "Most people are afraid of change," she says. "I'm afraid of not changing. I think that's what God does with people in their twenties. I wasn't on the straight path that my mother would have wanted me to be on, but hello, it turned out okay. I write books now based on what I learned then.

After she and her boyfriend returned to New York, she started appearing as a cabaret singer in small Manhattan clubs. Between songs she talked about the history of the music she was performing. "I would do long monologues about Gershwin, Kern and Harold Arlen and how so many of them were children of Jewish immigrants, the children of cantors, and how fascinating it was that they became lyricists because their parents couldn't speak the language very well. And how American popular music, torch songs and rock 'n' roll, grew out of gospel and Jewish music, out of a yearning for God." Williamson's patter often went over better than her singing.

Williamson first saw the 1,200-page, three-volume book called *A Course in Miracles* on a table in the apartment she and her boyfriend had borrowed. Later disavowed by its author, an emotionally disturbed, Jewish-born Columbia University psychology teacher named Helen Schucman, *A Course in Miracles* was supposedly dictated over a span of seven years by "a voice" the author decided was Jesus Christ. Billed as a correction to Christianity, stressing love and forgiveness, the course posits that poverty and illness, pain and suffering, materialism and negativity are all unreal, that only God is real, and that surrendering to God and doing good works will engender "miracles": good health and epiphanies of self-knowledge and self-worth. "God has established miracles as my right," the course proclaims, a gospel of divine entitlement likely to appeal to baby boomers. The course's lack of organization (its publishers encourage independent study) was another selling point to a generation turned off by the Judeo-Christian establishment. "Offering religion without rules, salvation without sacrifice," as one critic put it,[16] a cult sprang up around the book, which has sold about a million copies since it was published in 1975.

Williamson read the introduction and was intrigued. When she delved deeper, she was put off by the book's overt Christianity. The following winter, Williamson found herself reinspired to seek out a copy, but before she could—*miracle!*—her boyfriend brought one home.

"We had not talked about the book that whole year," she says. "I looked at him in surprise and he said, 'I thought it was time.'" Now she saw its use of Christian terminology as a metaphor for unconditional love and acceptance, and began to accept its message herself. A few weeks later, when she returned to the Foundation for Inner Peace, a non-profit organization that began as a group supporting parapsychological research, but eventually became best known as the publishers of the book, to buy a copy for a friend, she met a woman who was flying to Williamson's hometown of Houston that very day to give a talk about the book. Williamson, who'd decided the course was "spiritual psychotherapy,"[17] was intrigued to learn you could make a living doing such things. For the next year, she studied the course and worked at the foundation. Then, in 1979, she broke up with her boyfriend and abruptly went home to Houston. She's never said why.

"Did something horrible happen to you?" I ask her.

"Yes."

"Want to talk about it?"

"No. I can't comfortably do that. But it humbled me, and if you speak from a place of having been through something, people subconsciously know it."

Which may be why, at this point, when I ask if she feels the sexual behaviors of the 1970s would be possible today, her answer, referring to a novel and film about a woman who goes to bars looking for men and finds deadly trouble instead, seems portentous, even if it is also a bit of a non sequitur.

"If my daughter did what I did I'd be scared to death," she says. "Even before *Looking for Mr. Goodbar* came out."

The horrible thing, whatever it was, was followed by "what I think would today be termed a nervous breakdown—a highly underrated method of spiritual transformation," Williamson says. She lived with her mother in Houston for a few months before she took an apartment, worked more odd jobs, sang in more cabarets, turned thirty, and married a businessman in a big, traditional wedding.[18] The marriage lasted "a minute and a half," according to Williamson.[19] It's another moment in her life—"a wake-up call," she says—that she prefers to not discuss in anything but general terms. "In astrology, there's something called a Saturn return: the first significant trial period in a person's life," she says. "You become who you are between twenty-eight and thirty. Rarely does a person's life not take some radical turn."

Entering five-day-a-week therapy with a psychiatrist who coincidentally turned out to be another devotee of *A Course in Miracles*, Williamson slowly started getting better and had the notion that she could help herself by helping others. She opened the Heights Book Store, a homey place where she sold New Age books, ran a lecture series and arts club, sang torch songs on Sundays, and started a *Course in Miracles* study group.[20] She began remodeling the bookstore in 1983, but one night, after the carpenters left, she had the sudden premonition that she wouldn't be staying put.

A few weeks later, a girlfriend announced she was moving to Los Angeles, and suggested to Williamson that with her knowledge of books and metaphysics, she could get work there with the Philosophical Research Society. Founded in 1934, the PRS was led by an occultist and thirty-third-degree Freemason named Manley P. Hall (b. 1901), who authored books and pamphlets on what he called "esoteric teachings." His grand opus, *The Secret Teachings of All Ages*, encompassed Eastern religion, Masons, Druids, the Kabbala, Rosicrucianism, Gnosticism, Atlantis, the riddle of the Sphinx, parapsychology, astrology, the occult, mysticism, the controversy over who wrote William Shakespeare's plays, mystic Christianity and the Knights of the Round Table.

Though he came out of the tradition of American Transcendentalists, Williamson says, Hall's interests overlapped those of boomers on a quest for enlightenment and spiritual guidance. That phenomenon was reaching its peak of influence at the end of 1970s, just as Williamson hunkered down back in Houston. "The esoteric tradition says that in the last twenty-five years of every century there's a yearning for deeper understanding," she says.

Promising the dawn of a utopian Age of Aquarius, speaking of karma, auras, channeling, meditation and reincarnation, carrying crystals and Tarot cards and giving off a whiff of divine mystery, pantheistic New Age religionists were in synch with the counterculture's lingering distrust of science, logic and materialism. "Most of us came to see that a drug takes you to the top of the mountain but can't keep you there," says Williamson. "As a matter of fact, you will be hauled violently back to the bottom. Because ultimately everybody must do the climb themselves."

Williamson disagrees with those who say the human potential movements of the 1970s were a rejection of Judeo-Christian beliefs. "It was definitely an opening to the mystical elements of Christianity," she says. "And for Judaism, it wasn't so much escaping the confines of dogma. Rather, we were a generation that hadn't been taught our own religion. The great tradition of Eastern European Judaism was killed off by Hitler. So we were not taught the mystical roots of our own religion. The Eastern religions never lost their mystical roots. In twentieth-century America Judaism and Christianity played footsies under the table with the materialistic order. So the children said, If I can't get my mystical food here, I'll go wherever I can find it."

DAVID MCINTOSH VOTED for Jimmy Carter in the 1976 election, or rather, voted *against* Richard Nixon's appointee, Gerald Ford. He was, he says, "involved in the remnants of the left" at Yale, at least until he joined the Political Union, a campus group that brought speakers like George McGovern and William F. Buckley to campus. It was divided into factions ranging the political spectrum. "The progressive party on the far left was basically dead, defeated," he recalls. The liberals were "the big monolithic party," he says, "mouthing nostrums but not really that thoughtful. That's where I thought I was coming from."

But his politics had begun to evolve. While he was at Yale, the Political Union returned to its original role as a debating society, and he took part. One conservative got under his skin his junior year when she scolded him and told him his Christianity and belief in individual freedoms were anathema to liberalism. "She challenged me as a friend, as a philosophical adversary within the union. And I realized you don't want to guarantee equal results, you want to give people equal opportunity and let them make the most of it. And that was more a conservative than a liberal notion. The label I'd given myself wasn't in accord with the things I believed."

By 1980, the year he graduated from Yale, his conversion was complete. He'd begun to feel that Jimmy Carter couldn't do anything right, and the Democrats running against him—Jerry Brown and Ted Kennedy—weren't much better. Ronald Reagan, the former governor of California, who was running for the Republican nomination for President, was more appealing.

"At the beginning of the year, I was still clinging to the notion that I was some sort of progressive Democrat," he says. "But I remember watching Carter's malaise speech, and then watching Reagan harken back to the things Dan Quayle had expressed that I didn't really pick up on in high school, that you can change things from a conservative perspective." He announced he'd voted for Reagan at the family Thanksgiving a few weeks after the election. "Traitor," they called him.

"I've worked at gradually winning some of them over," he says.

CYNTHIA BOWMAN AND Paul Kantner's love affair was over, but their professional relationship continued. She was with the rock star when he had a cerebral hemorrhage in his room at the Chateau Marmont hotel that October, as the Jefferson Starship was recording an album in Los Angeles.

"We called an ambulance, and because he was Paul Kantner, everybody assumed it was a drug overdose," Bowman says. "I tried to explain it wasn't." When the city ambulance insisted on taking them to a city hospital, Bowman forced them to stop on the street as they passed Cedars Sinai, one of the city's best hospitals, and carried Kantner in through the emergency room door herself.

It looked as if he wasn't going to make it. "We were on the phone working out the details of his will, he was saying goodbye to his daughter; it was horrible," Bowman says. "They were just about to crack his head open when there was a miraculous recovery, the bleeding stopped; the doctors said the chances of that happening were one in a million." Two weeks later, Kantner was released from the hospital and returned to San Francisco to complete the record there. Then Grace Slick, who'd joined Alcoholics Anonymous in the interim, rejoined the band, and they all went back on the road together.

"I don't know how we managed to survive," Kantner told a reporter the following summer, backstage at a Starship show.[21] Bowman thinks she knows. The wife of a band member had just found religion, she says. "The whole band was in the chapel praying."

HAVING LOST HER professional momentum in the special anti-corruption office, Leslie Crocker Snyder decided to step off the career tread-mill in 1979 and spend more time with her family. "I can't conceive of a life without a career, but I can't conceive of a life without a family first." Snyder had always wanted to see criminal law from the defense side of the court-room. So she opened a midtown Manhattan office, and took private cases and court-appointed jobs for indigent defendants. There were so few women doing the latter in federal courts that she found herself much in demand. She handled sexual harassment lawsuits and defended a bank rob-ber and a vicious murderer. The latter was convicted, but Snyder took some pride in the fact that she kept the jury deliberating for three days and nights.

She enjoyed her three years as a part-time defense lawyer. "I realized that I really loved being in the courtroom," she says. And that she had a greater affinity for prosecution than for criminal defense. "But when you're in that courtroom, you are trying to win," she adds. "And it became absolutely clear to me that I am a total advocate. Yeah, I was viewed as aggressive and ballsy, but I think of myself that way."

So when her old boss John Keenan asked her to rejoin him as chief of New York's Arson Task Force in fall 1982, she jumped at the chance to supervise a staff of young lawyers and to write new arson legislation. She'd always planned to go back into public service, and her children were both in school. But years before, Keenan had also encouraged her to submit an application for a judgeship—and suddenly her name was in play.

Snyder didn't have a lot of respect for the judges in New York's criminal courts, a collection of barely competent political appointees and eccentrics. (One judge always wore sunglasses; another carried a gun.) Many got their jobs as so-called "midnight appointments" by departing officials, but Ed Koch, New York's new anti-machine mayor, had changed that, instituting a screening process and long-lasting judicial reforms.

After interviews with a number of screening committees, Snyder met Koch, who made the final appointments from a list of approved candidates. "I hear you're too aggressive; that's the only knock I've heard against you," Koch said. She bit her tongue and got the job. Years later, she reminded the famously aggressive Koch of his comment, and told him he'd had a lot of nerve to make it.

HER HIGH SCHOOL principal called Kathryn Bond Stockton to his office shortly before graduation to say that under no circumstances could she mention Christ in her valedictory speech, as a member of her evangelical group had before her. Her parents defended their daughter's rights, assuring him she would be tasteful and thoughtful. In her speech, she talked about transformation, "about how lives can take right-angle turns," she says. "The truth wasn't told why *my* right-angle turn was necessary, but I don't know if I was conscious of that."

Stockton enrolled at the University of Connecticut to study biochemistry in anticipation of becoming a medical missionary. "I'd basically been a math-science head all through high school, so I was very highly trained, I had won all the medals, but I started to get bored." Tired of calculus and chemistry, she tried classes in experimental psychology, philosophy and ancient languages her second year.

As time went by, her evangelical friends started getting boring, too. She'd joined a group called the Navigators that expected its members to "get up at this time of day and read your Bible in this way and I thought it all reeked of Republican militarism, which was striking me as bogus." So she joined a liberal Christian group, where at a meeting some gay Christians addressed the Bible's proscription against homosexuality and how they interpreted it. "I'd never met a person in college who said they were gay." At the time she was dating a boy, an older philosophy student who loved Gore Vidal and played piano.

Stockton wrote her senior thesis on the paradoxical nature of Christianity, how it puts together apparent opposites like God and man. "You have to embrace two things at once: Death is life," she says. "And that was enormously appealing to somebody who had been a contradiction throughout her life and needed to hold opposites together."

She thought about entering an evangelical seminary; her brother suggested Yale Divinity School. She snapped that Yale was godless, but then became intrigued. "Evangelicalism believes that you have God-ordained gender roles, and that men can be pastors and women can't," she says. "I really chafed against that." So she applied to Yale, won admission, and within a year discovered she preferred intellectual challenge to evangelical certainty. That year, she met her first feminists—"very powerful, interesting women"—in her dorm. Then she realized she was also surrounded by, "sexually experimental people trying to figure out what their gender is," she says. "And I'm beginning to think, 'You know what? God can love gay people.'"

By her second year at Yale, Stockton had been politicized. At a time when most protest was coming from the right—from anti-tax activists, right-to-life advocates and opponents of gay rights—the anti-nuclear movement, revived in the mid-1970s after "No Nukes" protests at the Seabrook nuclear power plant in New Hampshire, was ablaze following the March 1979 accident at the Three Mile Island power plant in Pennsylvania. A Washington demonstration that May felt like old times, thanks to the presence of comedian Dick Gregory, baby doctor Benjamin Spock, consumer advocate Ralph Nader, and Jane Fonda and her then-husband, Tom Hayden. Then, in September, a series of No Nukes concerts at New York's Madison Square Garden revived the rock-protest connection. President Carter's announcement the following February that he was reinstituting draft registration, followed hard by his abortive raid on Iran to free the U.S. hostages, gave the new "movement" a second front.

Stockton's political awakening followed a religious conversion. "I was no longer an evangelical; I was a political Christian," she says. "I'm writing papers on God as a person. To come down as this oppressed person and die destitute on a cross—what could be better than that?"

Election Night 1980 was meaningful in quite a different way. "I was just crushed," Stockton says. "I remember saying to my mother, 'It's so ironic. I go through all these years being an evangelical Christian when they have no political clout anywhere in the country, and just when I'm no longer an evangelical, here comes the right wing.'"

Stockton's Yale friends were intimately involved with the Plowshares movement, a loose group of about sixty religious activists that began on September 8, 1980, when the longtime antiwar Jesuit priests Daniel and Philip Berrigan and six others entered a General Electric plant in

Philadelphia, damaged missile nose cones and poured blood on documents. In Connecticut, their focus was the Electric Boat shipyard, maker
of Trident nuclear submarines and a leading beneficiary of the new
Reagan administration's massively increased defense spending. Stockton's
new friends demonstrated at Electric Boat often. "They were passionately
involved and I was extremely interested in their passion," she says.

Midway through her final year at Yale, Stockton befriended another
"straight" woman in her dorm who also had a tendency to date gay men, and
they became lovers. "I was thrilled," Stockton says. "Both of us having our
first sexual relationship; she's having like not a shred of guilt, wants to tell
everybody, I don't know what to do with that. I'm not in New York, not in
San Francisco. Nobody is talking about gays outside of those places. I did not
want to let my parents know, and I did not want to cease to be this person I
had worked so hard to be, excellent student, scholar, athlete—I was impris-
oned by that 'good' thing."

Stockton tried to quit the love affair. She left for graduate school at
Brown in the fall, but ended up back at Yale most weekends. When her
lover moved to nearby Providence to become a hospital chaplain, she
finally decided to let her parents "see this relationship unfold before their
eyes," hoping "they would just know what it was."

IN 1980, THE future Nina Hartley decided to go back to school. She
began taking classes at a junior college and realized she wanted to
become a nurse-midwife, "to help women, and also because I decided
that was the only way I was going to learn to surrender. To really let go is
to have to go through labor. You've got to let go; it's a natural force you
cannot resist. My feminism came straight through the natural birth
movement, out of the stirrups and the drugs and the strapping down. I'd
known about my alienation and repression since I was twelve years old. I
knew then how body-armored I was. I knew I needed to learn."

Her midwife was about to deliver her. He worked in the coffee shop
where she'd gotten a job. "Hi," he said, "my name's Dave, and I'm non-
monogamous." He was a thirty-one-year-old political activist from
Detroit, a former member of SDS who'd moved to Berkeley for its politics and was disillusioned to find they'd become elitist, divisive and were
on the wane. He lived—in a committed but nonexclusive relationship—
with a woman named Bobby Lilly, and had long since learned to warn any
woman he was attracted to right off the bat about his sexual preferences.

Dave became Mitzi's confidante. "He put words to what I was feeling," she says. "And he wasn't coming on to me sexually, because he had three other girlfriends." They'd hang out, give each other massages, and talk. She slept with a woman he was dating. Finally, she asked him to sleep with her.

Immediately, Mitzi found the sexual happiness that had eluded her. "He was the first competent lover I'd had," she says, "who could play and stop and go and give and take. He'd been dating asexually experienced, feminist co-eds who believed in their right to sexual pleasure. He took pride and delight in being good and passionate. The morning after our first time, we're in the shower together, and I reach up and take out my diaphragm and there was blood. My period had started, but the mess didn't faze him. I knew he was the guy for me."

Incredibly, Dave's lover Bobby Lilly approved. "She liked the way Dave acted when he saw me," Hartley says. "I remember thinking it was too good to be true that there was someone as cool as Bobby. But at first, I so wanted nonmonogamy to be possible that I didn't go meet her in case it was all a lie." Hartley grins ruefully.

Understandably, Mitzi's boyfriend, still on the scene, saw Dave as a rival. He'd found a new young girl to mentor, which had made Mitzi want to win him back; but once she did, she didn't want him anymore. About that point Dave, leaving town for six months, finally convinced Mitzi to meet Lilly, and though she was, as Hartley puts it, "ninety-five percent het," the two women became lovers during three-way sex with Dave. "She's my first regular pussy," Hartley says. "And she's so receptive, so femme, such a pillow queen, 'More, ooh, good, more, more.' It was like getting a Stradivarius your first time out."

Lilly started hanging out with Mitzi and ended up in bed with her and the soon-to-be-gone boyfriend. "She and I never fucked unless Dave was there," Hartley says, "because she needs dick. I mean girls are nice, but give her a penis, thank you. So we end up in bed together, and my boyfriend is transformed into a masterful lover. With me he never lasted more than five minutes, but Bobby's coming and coming, having one orgasm after another. After that, our sex problems were my fault. And that was the end." After a brief but futile spell of couples counseling, she and the boyfriend finally parted ways early in 1982. Mitzi was still living in the house in which she'd grown up. That September, Dave and Bobby moved in, and have been there ever since.

Dave was acquainted with the San Francisco adult entertainment scene, and would sometimes, take the bus across the bay to San Francisco, and visit the Mitchell brothers' O'Farrell Theater. At Mitzi's urging, he shared his favorite stops with her—she enjoyed peep shows where "loops," continuously cycling porno shorts, played in coin-operated booths—and they would often discuss her unrequited desire to be a stripper, to have that kind of confidence. For months they used it as a private fantasy. Mitzi would dance for him. He would teach her moves, tell her what he liked to see and what went on in an audience member's head.

Mitzi had begun to develop a sexual philosophy based on her decade-long pursuit of information in the Bay Area liberated zone. Exhibitionism, voyeurism and bisexuality were all normal, she'd decided, as long as they were consensual. It was all about "retaking, reclaiming, defining sexuality for yourself," she says. "I like looking at girls."

But should she—could she—become a sex worker herself? She, Dave and Bobby began a yearlong discussion of that question that resembled an SDS self-criticism session. Children (and beneficiaries) of the sexual revolution, they asked themselves whether it was possible to be in the sex industry without betraying their political beliefs. Could Mitzi fuck for money, even if she enjoyed it, and still be a feminist? Was it wrong to get pleasure from arousing men? Could she take money and not be an exploiter? Was her desire to exhibit herself defensible? What about her desire to bed other women? "Can this be done?" Hartley says. "Can we indulge this fantasy? Dave was a purist. It was important to him not to muddy his politics, but at the same time he was digging having a coed stripper girlfriend."

Once they decided she would try it, they invented a character, Nina Hartley, for her to play. "Now she's me," Hartley says. "Fifteen years ago, she was my idealized self—confident, sexy, comfortable with herself, all the things Mitzi wanted to be. We took my exhibitionist, bisexual, people-pleasing nature and gave it a backbone and a form as opposed to being strictly hedonist and narcissistic. We channeled Mitzi into a complete ideology. What would a feminist sex worker look like? What would she believe? How would she act? What would she do?" Later, when anyone charged that Dave was her Svengali, Nina would patiently explained that this was what she'd wanted long before she met him, and that acting that way was anathema to him.

Finally, one Tuesday night, they went together for her debut at the Sutter Street Cinema, a sex emporium. "He's in the audience and I'm in the dressing room with all the girls," Hartley says. "And I was the only amateur, the other girls were only there for the twenty-five dollars you get for showing up. And I'm terrified, they're all slapping on the bracelets, putting on the makeup. I was never cool, never hip, I disdained popularity contests and girls who would tilt their head over and brush their hair and toss it up. I'd had the lesbian hatred and distrust of women like that and men who liked them. Real superiority feelings. But then I'm doing a show, loving it, dancing, fucking myself with a vibrator on stage. It was so cool. The first time I was in a roomful of naked people I was immediately at home."

Mitzi, or rather Nina, had found her place in the world. "My first sex job after the kissing booth was exactly what I wanted—a live lesbian show in a peep booth," she says. "It was a round room, mirrored windows around it, chair, paper towels, wastebasket, revolving round bed, another girl. I loved it because I wasn't dancing for the guys, I was dancing for the mirrors, having sex with a girl, then we both went our separate ways. I got into the sex business because I was too chickenshit to be a whore, and I wanted easy, effortless access to pussy." She also got to indulge her own voyeurism. If they wanted to, the men in the booths around her could switch on a light so the performers could watch them masturbate. "That was the best," she says. "I got to look in a safe environment."

Six months later, she moved to the O'Farrell, the pinnacle of the live porn business, and added lap-dancing to her repertoire, gyrating on men's laps for a few dollars a minute. She did it every weekend for a year and a half while continuing nursing school. "I would take the bus over," she recalls. "Loved the lap dancing. Loved the actual contact with the guys, the casualness of it, the fact that there were rules and regulations and limits, but within that you were free to negotiate your own behavior. If I could have jerked them off, I would have. If I could have given blow jobs, I would have. And I was doing a dildo show, and every week I'd ask the girls, you want company onstage? So, sometimes once a week, sometimes twice a night, I got to be on the stage with the girl doing a hard-core sex show. It was sex without relationships, a supportive, safe context. None of that relationship shit. I didn't want to be in love with you to have sex with you."

She was an instant hit with audiences—and no wonder; her enthusiasm showed. "I love showing them my body and they'd look and they'd be enraptured," she recalls. "Absolutely attentive and respectful. And I realized that first year how much power there was in not hating them for looking at me. And I realized that talking dirty is not about giving the guy what you think he wants. Talking dirty is telling him what's real. My clit, my pussy, my breasts, what I like. And they never got tired of hearing it because it was sex talk by a half-naked girl sitting on their lap. And I realized how easy it was to make them profoundly happy. And I knew they weren't going to follow me home." That's because Dave would always show up at the end of her shift.

PRISON DIDN'T LESSEN Tim Scully's interest in consciousness expansion. While in a halfway house in 1979, he continued making biofeedback instruments. One institution interested in his work was the Stanford Research Institute, which was studying parapsychology—remote viewing, telepathy, precognition and telekinesis—funded by the military. "On odd-numbered days I believe that they're real, on even-numbered days I'm skeptical," Scully says. The researchers at SRI thought Scully's equipment—which allowed two test subjects to synchronize their brain waves—might increase parapsychological abilities.

"It's real stuff being done by real scientists," he says, "but when you get into parapsychology, the bar gets raised exponentially because the results are so hard to believe. You really-really-really have to prove it." In order to do so, Scully formed a company, Pacific Bionic Systems, to build non-vocal communication and biofeedback instruments (including electric trains that ran faster when burn victims learned to direct their blood flow to regions needing healing, and a Pong game that helped teach patients to control damaged muscles). He also manufactured a machine designed by a researcher to encourage extrasensory perception—and ended up teaching a course in designing equipment to measure ephemeral parapsychological phenomena.

In the worlds in which he operated, Scully found that his criminal record didn't hurt, and sometimes helped. "People in biofeedback or parapsychology or the computer industry all tended to have a pretty positive view of somebody who had been involved with psychedelics," he says. Still, denied a job at a Mendocino County community college because of his felony record, Scully became extra-cautious. "I didn't go to Grateful Dead concerts or hang out with people I had known before, because I didn't want to be in the wrong place at the wrong time and get in trouble again," he says.

He hadn't lost the business abilities that got him his own house in college. By the early 1980s, Scully's little biofeedback business had grown into a corporation selling and servicing microcomputer systems and running a psycho-physiological research lab. Scully also taught and lectured at a number of colleges, joined several professional organizations, and, after the FDA began regulating biofeedback instruments, adding expensive and complex approvals to the process, branched out into custom equipment design, making complete physiological monitoring systems and a microcomputer that monitored weather inside tornadoes.

He liked computers. "Programming gives you an opportunity to construct a world of your own where you're completely in control, and the outcome depends on how good a job you do," he says. "It's very attractive to introverts because it's less messy than dealing with real people, who are so much less predictable. On another level, as computers got less expensive and more powerful, there were tremendous possibilities for doing socially useful things with them. And on the more crass level the microcomputer era created really good opportunities for making a living. So it's been a wild ride."

Scully went to work for the Children's Television Workshop (albeit through a subcontractor) when it began planning an amusement park based on the PBS children's show *Sesame Street*. The park was originally going to feature biofeedback computer games. When budget cuts killed that project, Scully designed coin-box and keyboard interfaces, and then wrote educational games. Late in 1982, he wrote his first computer game, Honey Hunt, for Milton Bradley, the toy company. He went on to write more games for computers built by Atari, Apple, VIC, and Sony. Once again, he was changing the consciousness of children and through them, the world—only this time he was doing it completely legally.

BARBARA LEDEEN'S PERSONAL and political paralysis lasted through the Carter administration. To fight her way out of depression, she needed to "work out who has the truth," she says. "That was the only way that you could find something worth believing in." She was hardly alone.

Ledeen's conversion had begun even before she left Italy. Like many, she considered the revelations of Aleksandr Solzhenitsyn's *The Gulag Archipelago*, published in 1974, a turning point. Then came the communist takeover of Southeast Asia in 1976. Within a year, so-called "boat people" began to flee the new Marxist regimes in Vietnam, Laos, and Cambodia, as news came from those countries of killing, torture and mass suicides. Many gained a new perspective on the "liberation" movements they'd once supported without question. Ledeen was stunned, in 1979, when Joan Baez testified before Congress on the plight of the boat people and published an open letter—signed by eighty-five prominent activists—to the Socialist Republic of Vietnam charging that "the cruelty, violence and oppression practiced by foreign powers in your country for more than a century continue today under the present regime." Says Ledeen, "It took enormous devotion to the ideal of truth to look at the boat people and say, 'Omigod, I bear some responsibility.'"

In 1981, Michael Ledeen was hired as a special adviser to Alexander Haig, Ronald Reagan's Secretary of State, who'd spent several months at CSIS after leaving NATO. When Haig resigned in 1982, Ledeen became a consultant to National Security Advisor Robert McFarlane. Ever since, MIchael Ledeen has been shadowed by accusations of being, as the former journalist turned White House operative Sidney Blumenthal (b. 1948) once called him, "a mysterious ideological adventurer."

If that's true, this new career began when the Ledeens met a Russian dissident named Vladimir Bukovsky in 1976. Together he and Michael set up "a network of people in Europe, working to overthrow the Soviet Union by sending in computers and tapes and printers and fax machines," Barbara says. In 1981, they were part of the loose association of organizations that created Radio Free Kabul, broadcasting into Afghanistan, where Soviet troops were fighting anti-Communist *mujahadeen* guerrillas. In 1983, they formalized their operation, uniting groups from eleven totalitarian countries as Resistance International. It was funded, in part, by the National Endowment for Democracy, established by the U.S. Congress in 1983 to fight authoritarianism and promote democracy. Both Resistance International and a subsequent group begun by Bukovsky, the Center for Democracy, took a leading role in the ongoing—and eventually successful—effort to undermine the Soviets.

By 1982, Barbara Ledeen had given birth to a second child and was working as the assistant editor of *Biblical Archeology Review*, which ran an article on Jerusalem's Temple Mount, site of Solomon's ancient temple, where Abraham came to sacrifice his son Isaac; where Jesus taught and threw out the money-changers; and from which Mohammed ascended into the presence of Allah—an event commemorated by the Dome of the Rock, the Muslim mosque that now stands near the site. After fifteen years of research, an Israeli physicist had claimed to have found the foundation stone of the Temple, which held the Ark of the Covenant containing the tablets of the Ten Commandments—not under the mosque, as had long been assumed, but some 300 feet away. Ultranationalist Israelis demanded the Israeli government take over the Temple Mount, reserved for the Islamic faithful for fourteen centuries. Fundamentalist Christians, citing indications that the Second Coming was at hand, got into the fray.

Ledeen's teenage rejection of Judaism had wavered as the result of her marriage. She and her husband—who had strong pro-Israel sympathies and felt the Temple Mount had geopolitical implications—went to Israel to investigate. "I meet a bunch of Christians who are intelligent, erudite and articulate. I wouldn't call them a whole lot of fun, but these were not people to be contemptuous of. They're trying to live their life in accordance with what they believe to be true, trying to rise to a higher level of being." For Ledeen, this was a revelation on a par with meeting Bukovsky. "I was looking for something larger than myself to dedicate myself to," she says. "I now knew the world was not as narrow as I thought. I learned to look for the facts."

Ledeen's respect for facts continued to evolve, in large part, because of what she calls the disinformation campaign aimed at her husband. She says the smears were started by communists and repeated by American leftists to tarnish the Reagan regime and her husband, who has successfully pursued libel suits in Europe against some of them. [22] As the stories had it, he was supposedly in league with a secret lodge in Italy in the early 1980s. The lodge, the membership of which included leaders of Italy's intelligence service, to which Michael Ledeen had been a consultant, was said to have created a shadow regime within the Italian government. Ledeen had supposedly "set up" President Carter's brother, Billy, just before the 1980 election by revealing his business dealings with the Quadafi regime in Libya. In addition, he was supposed to have been responsible for fabricating the story of a "Bulgarian connection" in Mehmet Ali Agca's 1981 assassination attempt on Pope John Paul II, "framing the left for the crimes of the right," as leftist writer Alexander Cockburn put it. [23]

"The veil fell from my eyes as the attacks proceeded," Barbara says. She went to work for Reagan's Defense Department. She'd decided that "the [liberal] establishment had become completely anti-democratic, and we were the real revolutionaries."

BY MID-1978, MONEY had become a problem for the Leacock family. Victoria's parents were in an alimony fight. She left private school and entered New York's High School of Art and Design. Again, her attendance was sporadic. They had terrible luck with mother's helpers. One embezzled money, another quit by sticking a resignation note inside a sandwich she'd made for Victoria's lunch bag. "Glamour got me through," she says. "It was like my prize for being a nurse the other twenty-two hours a day."

Marilyn Leacock died on June 19, 1980. "I had a great mother until I was sixteen, and then I had my father," Victoria says. "He flew down that day." Coincidentally, the lease on the apartment where she'd lived was running out. He suggested she move to Tangiers and finish school at his alma mater, but she opted to live with the Rogers family, who'd offered her their spare room.

She still wanted to be an actress. She started a Xeroxed magazine called *Curtain Call*, and spent her spare time interviewing actors for it and then selling it in front of Broadway theaters. More important, she started dating. One of her first beaux was an artist who worked for the punk rock band The Ramones. He introduced her to a whole new world of nightclubs—the downtown equivalents to the uptown discos she'd frequented. "One night, five different people offered me cocaine," she says. "I said, 'No, no-no, no-no-no.' I went home. I was totally sober. It was midnight. And a woman's voice, perhaps it was my mother, said: 'Victoria, drugs will keep you sober, make you thin, you'll love them—and you'll die.' So that was why I've never tried drugs. It all made sense."

Though she didn't want drugs, she did want to lose her virginity. Unfortunately, many of the boys in her "theater-fashion-weirdo" clique in school were gay. She dated one for a year before realizing why he wasn't interested in having sex. "I was thrilled to find out," she exults. "It wasn't me!" She also learned that sex sometimes came with a high price. "I went to the abortion place many times with friends," she says.

She'd been apolitical most of her life. Nixon's resignation taught her that "everything was corrupt, you couldn't believe in anything," she says. She perceived Carter as a sincere failure. And Reagan scared the hell out of her. She'd visited Hiroshima when she was in Japan and had become obsessed with the idea of imminent nuclear obliteration. Reagan's militarism encouraged these fantasies, and his courting of the religious right "was really making us paranoid," she says. She found no solace in feminism, which suggests to her not Gloria Steinem or Simone de Beauvoir, but "feminist" commercials on TV, like the one featuring a woman singing, "I can bring home the bacon, fry it up in a pan, and never let you forget you're a man."

"Everything was media, I guess, in my neck of the woods," she says. The news the media carried in the 1980–81 school year was often scary. In December, Beatle John Lennon was shot and killed outside his home by a demented fan. Jodie Foster, child star of Martin Scorcese's *Taxi Driver*, was being stalked by another nut. Interest rates hovered at 16 percent. Children were being shot and killed in Atlanta. Blacks were rioting in England. Solidarity was striking in Gdansk, Poland. U.S. military advisers were heading to El Salvador, raising the specter of another Vietnam. And

then Reagan was shot by John Hinckley a few months after his inauguration. Her friends walked around in a state of shock. "A lot of us wanted to
escape, or we wanted to make things happen in theater or film to express
our discontent," she says.

In spring 1981, Leacock accompanied friends to Adelphi University, a
school in a nearby suburb, for auditions to enter its acting school. She
hadn't given college a thought, but when she walked in, she announced
that she wanted to try out, too. Though she hadn't even applied for
admittance, she auditioned and to her amazement, she was accepted.
That September, Leacock worked the lights in a school production of
Godspell. "Of course, I fall in love with the person playing Christ," she
says. His name was Jonathan Larson, and he was a senior and something
of a prodigy. "I said to someone right then, 'He's the one.' After the
rehearsal, I said something like, 'You're really talented and handsome,'
and he went, 'You're really beautiful,' and that was the beginning."

Larson was different from anyone she'd ever met. Raised by intellectual Jewish parents in the suburbs, he wrote original cabaret productions
for the drama department, many of them political. The first show
Leacock worked on was *Sacrimoralimmorality*, an attack on the Moral
Majority featuring Christian soldiers who gave Nazi salutes. Others were
about abortion, women's rights, being gay. "There was a group anxiety
that someone else's morals would take away our freedom," she says. But
there was no feeling of solidarity with early boomers. "They fucked up
and sold out everything they were fighting for," Leacock says. "They all
got jobs and got married and got fat. That's what it looked like to us, at
least. We grew up with people taking American hostages and hating our
guts. We felt there was nothing we could do. Though we all changed our
mind after we skipped our first vote and realized, we'd better get out
there, someone's got to!"

Larson and Leacock started dating, "and I finally lost my virginity,
which was a great triumph to me, because I was eighteen and desperately
trying not to be the last person in New York who hadn't." Within a week
they had a fight, broke up, and became best friends.

During Leacock's first year at Adelphi, Reagan began cutting spending,
taxes and the federal budget. "There's enough fat in the government that
if it was rendered and made into soap, it would wash the world," Reagan
once said, and he intended to reverse the strongly interventionist govern-
mental philosophy that had held sway since Franklin D. Roosevelt's New
Deal. Although prices and interest rates began to drop, his promised "sup-
ply-side" economic rejuvenation didn't happen as fast as he claimed. The

balanced budget would take years. "None of us really understands what's going on with all these numbers," said Reagan's budget director, David Stockman (b. 1946).

Some of the deepest cuts came in the budgets of the National Endowments for the Arts and Humanities, which funded museums, dance and theater companies, libraries and universities. After many of her favorite teachers lost their jobs, Leacock dropped out of Adelphi just before her third semester, at the end of 1982.

PAUL KANTNER OF the Jefferson Starship had begun to clean up his act after his daughter came along. "The day China was born, he stopped snorting cocaine," says Cynthia Bowman. "After his cerebral hemorrhage, he stopped drinking." Bowman still drank and smoked pot. "I was really pretty wrapped up in that whole road scene," she admits.

She was on the road with the band in spring 1981 when she discovered she was pregnant. Noticing that Bowman was out of sorts, Grace Slick, who was in an adjoining hotel room, administered a pregnancy test. Doing the math, Bowman figured out she'd probably conceived a few months before, on a night when she'd had a cocktail too many and gone home with Kantner. "Grace flew out the door and ran down the hall to tell their manager, he told Paul and then all of us were sitting around, trying to figure out what to do," Bowman recalls. "And there weren't really very many options because Paul was absolutely clear—he's a Catholic and abortion is just not an option. We'd broken up, the last thing on my mind was to have a baby with Paul Kantner. But after having a little pow-wow with Grace and Paul, we all decided I would go ahead and have the baby and we'd figure it out."

Though the pregnancy was unexpected, it was also serendipitous. "The day I found out I was pregnant I stopped smoking, drinking, everything," she says. "I'd been irresponsible for a long time and gotten away with it, but now I had a baby to take care of. That was my motivating factor. It had nothing to do with Reagan or politics or anything. I grew up when I got pregnant. That's what changed everything for me."

She and Kantner quickly decided they not only wanted the baby, but wanted to raise it together. Bowman moved back into Kantner's house, an assistant was hired to handle her Starship press work, and she went to exercise classes and "acted like a pregnant person," she says. Alexander Bowman Kantner was born on January 1, 1982, with Slick in attendance, and "turned out to be the best thing that ever happened to either one of us. He's an A student, an artist, a musician. He has no interest in drugs or alcohol. In fact, he came home last night from a party at which a bunch of adults were acting goofy because they'd had too much to drink, and he said it made him sick seeing people like that. And I thought to myself, 'Oh, thank God you weren't born twenty-five years ago.' He has no memories of his parents being like that."

Bowman and Kantner soon broke up again. "The reason we never got married was because we didn't get along and I'd moved in and out so many times I can't even count them," she says. "If we were going to raise a healthy kid, we couldn't fight constantly." She packed up and moved to Mill Valley. She was still the Jefferson Whatever's PR director, but her days there were numbered, too.

Paul Kantner was fed up with Jefferson Starship. He'd reorganized the band around a new singer (after Slick and Marty Balin left yet again), but commercial reality forced it to depend on outside writers, as 1980s bands needed middle-of-the-road hit songs to survive, and Kantner's songs, stuck in the 1960s, were no longer commercially viable. Even after Slick rejoined the group in 1984 they couldn't crack the Top Ten. The less well they did, the more Kantner resented the new reality. He couldn't adapt, couldn't tame his chaotic muse for life in the constricted universe of the three-minute pop song. And he hated himself for letting a pimple cream sponsor the Starship's tours, even though he understood that such arrangements were a necessary evil to cover the huge expenses of touring.

"He didn't want to play the songs," Bowman says. "He didn't need the money. He comes from a folk background and that was the antithesis of what he wanted to do. It got very unpleasant. Paul wanted to continue doing what he'd been doing, but Volunteers of America was not happening when Reagan was in office—absolutely not—and there were new people involved who really didn't appreciate the history of the band and just wanted to make money. Everybody had families to support and Grace decided to side with [the other band members]."

Increasingly associated with Kantner, Bowman was seen "as the enemy" and began to avoid the office. Finally, she and Slick had "what you might call an altercation," she says. "One version of the story is she fired me. The other version is I told her to kiss my ass. I can assure you that both things happened. And so I left and never went back and had to find other work. And that was the best thing they ever did for me, because forcing me out of that little spaceship got me onto my own."

IT WAS TIME for something new in clubland. A friend of Jim Fouratt's told him about a multilevel after-hours club on Manhattan's West 37th

Street that was about to go broke. He offered to fix it and they agreed. He called Rudolf Pieper, who signed on. The place was named Danceteria. With only a $25,000 budget to renovate it, they called on young artists like Keith Haring (b. 1958) and David Wojnarowicz (b. 1955) from the thriving downtown clubs that had filled the void left by Hurrah. Haring, who became a busboy, did one of his first installations in the club. "I walked in one day and Rudolf was tearing it down," Fouratt recalls. He started to protest and Rudolf replied, "It's the busboy, Jim; don't be so serious."[24]

The summer of Danceteria was the last moment of culturally sanctioned libertinism. Though uptowners clamored to get in, Fouratt only admitted a few of "the bodysuckers who would come in from jaded society to feed off our energy," he says. "It was a fabulous time, the last great pre-AIDS, pre-crack party. People still remember that summer, when they all got laid, they all got drugs." All but Fouratt, that is. He'd come down with hepatitis in the waning days of Hurrah, when he, too, went on a bit of a binge—drinking and doing cocaine—wound up in the hospital, and from there, a twelve-step program. He'd only been straight for a few months when Danceteria opened. "And everybody was on drugs!" he says. "It wasn't groovy, cool, hip. It was just nuts. All my friends were really fucked up."

Danceteria was closed after eight months for not having a liquor license. Rudolf and Fouratt moved to G.G. Barnum's—a drag queen bar with trapeze acts and gangsters"—not my idea of gay liberation," Fouratt says. But in the basement, he found the original decorations and candy-striped furniture from the Peppermint Lounge, where Fouratt had gone with the Beatles—and so they restored the name and revived the old club. Next, the duo went to work at the Underground, another cavernous disco. And an old friend turned up: Jerry Rubin, now married to Mimi Leonard, whose father co-founded the Esalen Institute and coined the term "Human Potential Movement." Leonard had gone to work on Wall Street in 1980, and Rubin followed, becoming marketing director for a brokerage house.[25] That July, he wrote a piece for the *New York Times* Op-Ed page about his conversion to capitalism. "I know that I can be more effective today wearing a suit and tie and working on Wall Street than I can be dancing outside the walls of power," he wrote. "I have learned that the individual who signs the check has the ultimate power. . . If I am going to have any effect on my society in the next forty years, I must develop the power that only control of money can bring."[26]

In April 1981, Rubin began giving parties in his apartment for stockbrokers to meet clients. The gatherings soon became quite successful among New York's young professionals—mostly boomers with a sudden need to get ahead in the world. When their brokerage house went out of business shortly thereafter, Rubin and Leonard accepted an invitation to move the parties to the Underground.[27]

Soon after that, Rudolf and Fouratt had moved on, as they were wont to do, working briefly for Steve Rubell and Ian Schrager, who were out of jail, then opening Danceteria 2 in February 1982, with art installations, a dance floor, a performance floor, a lounge floor and rooftop parties in summer. Once again, the deal descended into acrimony and litigation— only this time between Rudolf and Fouratt. Fouratt ended up broke and angry, but years later decided he'd been forced from club life at just the right moment. It was no longer the stage for artistic and cultural exploration it had once been. "MTV was starting," he says. "And it's what destroyed nightlife."

Of course, boomers were behind the new venture. Having grown up on rock and television, the cable station's president, Robert Pittman (b. 1954), boasted of having the attention span of a flea. A corporate comer ever since he became a teenage deejay in Jackson, Mississippi, in 1970, Pittman was named the program director of WNBC radio in New York in 1977. He was only twenty-three. Ten years later, the "Hippie from Mississippi" epitomized the late 1980s.

In 1979, Pittman married Sandy Hill (b. 1955), an editor at *Mademoiselle*. Bob had just moved from WNBC to the nascent Warner-Amex Satellite Entertainment Co., where he started out on The Movie Channel an HBO-like movie channel, then moved to MTV. On August 1, 1981, MTV, the all-music cable network, became a reality. But it wasn't a success yet. In 1982, MTV was reportedly losing $20 million a year. "All I worry about is winning," Pittman told the New York *Times* that year. By 1983, MTV was kicking out the boundaries of television. Ratings rose 20 percent, and by the fourth quarter the network was turning a profit. "MTV was a pet idea of mine," Pittman told the *Daily News* in 1986. But the true architect of MTV was John Lack (b. 1944), the man who'd hired him. Pittman was the general contractor who followed Lack's design. Still, he got the credit. In 1984, Pittman was runner-up to *Time* magazine's Man of the Year Pete Ubberoth. But it was the MTV mogul who was leading the culture.

Riding the zeitgeist became an obsession for both Pittmans. In 1986, Sandy would launch a daily fashion video show on cable TV and start running charity benefits in an attempt to enter New York's wealthy social set, and by the early 1990s, they became one of Manhattan's most promising young couples before they separated and divorced—a not atypical trajectory. After several overreaching attempts to go into business for himself, Bob went back to work for an old boss, Steve Ross of Warner Communications, eventually settling into a post running Six Flags Amusement Parks. For her part, Sandy got heavily into mountain climbing, trying some of the world's tallest mountains. Several people accompanying her on an expedition to Everest died in extreme conditions, inspiring books and articles that blamed their deaths on her insistence on reaching the top against all odds. That didn't stop her. Sandy Hill, as she's now called, still goes out with what passes for New York society. And after a brief exile at Century 21 real estate, Bob Pittman now rides the zeitgeist again as the president of America Online.

Pittman was hardly alone in turning the symbols of freedom and liberation into new sources of wealth and social position. Drug dealers had been doing it all along, as had purveyors of drug paraphernalia from pipes to posters; fashion designers like Yves Saint Laurent (b. 1936) and Calvin Klein (b. 1942), who made upscale versions of street styles; and the hip capitalists of the music business. "Their mentality said, 'I'm going to get as much as I can for me,'" a disapproving Fouratt says, "because that was the only thing that worked. The Nixon-Reagan years demonized social consciousness. The politics of greed replaced the politics of compassion."

WHILE STEVE RUBELL and Ian Schrager were still in jail, many former Studio 54 habitués, Victoria Leacock among them, stopped going to the club.[28] Following its brief renaissance when Rubell and Schrager reappeared, the club floundered again under the ownership of Mark Fleischmann. He quickly turned to a new breed of party promoters to fill the space and its till. A one-time booking agent for lecturers, Fleischmann called an old client, Jerry Rubin, after he'd held three of his "networking parties" at the Underground, and lured him to Studio 54 in March 1982.[29]

Rubin's events became so successful that a year later, they caught the eye of Bob Greene, the Chicago columnist who'd known him since the days of the Chicago 8. Greene had overheard someone joke that Rubin had gone from head of the Yippies to head of the Yuppies, Young Urban Professionals. When Greene wrote about the phenomenon in his nationally syndicated column, the word entered the vernacular, and became a self-definition for millions making the same transition as Rubin. The following January, Yuppies went mass market with the publication of *The Yuppie Handbook*.[30] And that October, Rubin and Abbie Hoffman—

who'd surfaced from the underground in 1980 and served time in jail on reduced charges—even went out on a lecture tour, billing themselves as Yippie versus Yuppie.[31]

In the mid-1980s, Rubin announced a plan to take his networking company public, but never managed to do it. He moved to Los Angeles in 1991. Still chasing the ever more health-conscious boomer market, he worked as a distributor for a company that sold powdered nutritional drink mixes until he died in 1994, hit by a car on Wilshire Boulevard.

THOUGH HE'S LOATHE to admit it, by 1981, HBO's Michael Fuchs had become a cocky, free-market Yuppie too, a major player in the entertainment business. HBO had just launched a second network, Cinemax. While less than a third of American homes were on cable, 300,000 new households were signing up a month. Studio attempts to horn in on HBO's action were being thwarted. When 20th Century-Fox, Columbia, Paramount, MCA and Getty Oil tried to launch a cable outlet, Premier, the Justice Department stopped them, but pay television and videocassettes were increasingly seen as Hollywood's salvation. For the first time, movie executives were calling their products "entertainment software."[32]

Fuchs, promoted to senior vice president the year before, was feeling feisty when a critical reporter from the *Christian Science Monitor* came calling that April, just after the announcement that HBO would become a twenty-four-hour-a-day service. Fuchs ticked off some of his achievements: a TV adaptation of Broadway's *Vanities;* one-man shows starring Diana Ross, George Carlin, Lily Tomlin, Bette Midler and Barry Manilow; and a *Consumer Reports* show that could only run on a network without advertising.

Fuchs says he was still a caring Kennedy Democrat, still committed to fulfilling his childhood vow to do good things, but Reagan's election that year had soured him on political activism. "I just felt like the world had ended," he says now, perhaps explaining why, not long after Reagan's inauguration, he waved off the *Monitor* reporter's suggestion that HBO wasn't doing enough public service programming. "There's no mandate here to do public service," he snapped.

Fuchs's goals clearly lay elsewhere. He predicted that cable would soon interact with computers and telephones. "The 1980s will be the period when all the amazing versatility of TV and cable is realized," he said. "To be part of this business is like holding on to the tail of a comet."[33] Convergence would remain a promise unfulfilled for twenty years, but that didn't stop Home Box Office.

"Great movies are just the beginning," was its new slogan. Its advertising budget had been increased 80 percent, and it was about to begin producing its own shows and films. "I found television getting more and more gutless and having less and less a point of view," Fuchs says. "I wanted to move in where they were vacating. I believed in reality-based programming. And to me, a comedian standing up, doing his thing uncensored, was real. The quickest way to get something on the air on HBO is say, 'The networks would never touch this.'"

HBO had turned the corner. Its competitors lagged far behind. Time's video group was producing almost half of all Time Inc. profits.[34] That year, Time Inc.'s CEO was replaced by the head of video, Dick Munro. "HBO looked like it was going to eat the universe, it was growing so fast," says Fuchs. Time's long-held devotion to the division between church, or the editorial side of the company, and state, the business side that sold advertising, was "one of the unsung reasons," Fuchs says. "They understood the First Amendment." When local governments attempted to stop him, legislating censorship of cable broadcasts in Utah and Miami, HBO fought and won crucial First Amendment court cases. Time even let him air George Carlin's "Seven Words You Can't Say on Television" *after* a court declared it obscene.

"We were for real," Fuchs says.

DOUG MARLETTE HAD begun six years of psychoanalysis in 1978. He'd spent years feeling guilty about his talent and the self-involvement it entailed. "If I thought of something quickly and easily, it could not be good," he explains. "I had to torment myself for hours. It took years to get spontaneous and direct and just do it. Therapy saved my life. I would have just blown apart otherwise. The self-destructive forces within me would have just had their way."

The next year, on the edge of the 1980s, he'd been the first cartoonist ever to win a Nieman Fellowship at Harvard, which allows journalists to take a year off and get paid to study. "I sat at B.B. King's feet and listened to him play the blues. I held the lamp for Robert Penn Warren as he read poetry. I heard John Updike, John Irving, William F. Buckley, Art Buchwald. I gave up my syndication, and then I started over, a risky thing to do, but it was worth it. I was ready for a change." He turned thirty and married again as well. "That was the beginning of learning about commitment and hard work and all that stuff," he says.

Marlette returned to Charlotte a full-fledged Yuppie with a Cutlass Ciera and a mortgage, "an emotional teabag—the zeitgeist just flows through me," he crows. "I don't see anything wrong with being young or upwardly mobile or professional. What are you supposed to be? Downwardly mobile? Amateurish? Old?" He started wearing a suit and tie even though nobody at the *Charlotte Observer* cared.

He gave up drinking and stopped being the "designated id" in his social set. He began getting up at 5:00 A.M. and going into the office early, before anyone was there, doing his daily cartoon and then working on a new comic strip he'd conceived. Double deadlines meant he'd never have time to torment himself again. "As Freud says, maturity is the ability to love and to work," Marlette says. "I was learning both those things. I needed to learn discipline. And it made me more creative."

Creating a comic strip wasn't easy. Eventually he gave birth to "Kudzu," set in Bypass, North Carolina, a sleepy Southern town (so named because the big state highway goes by without an exit), and its residents, Kudzu Dubose, a dreamy, awkward adolescent much like Marlette, who wants to go to the big city and be a writer; Maurice, his black best friend, a neo-gangsta wannabe; Kudzu's Uncle Dub at the filling station; his pet parakeet, Doris, and the preacher Will B. Dunn. The immediate success of the strip gave Marlette an instant six-figure income, but also taught him a lesson. "You look forward to seeing your comic strip on the Sunday pages; that's a big moment," he says. "The Sunday morning comes when my comic strip debuts and it's not in the *Charlotte Observer*. They 'forgot.'" His conclusion? "Not only was I taken for granted, but also punished for succeeding."

His experience at Harvard had invested his op-ed cartoons with new, mature shades of gray. His reactions were no longer knee-jerk. When John Belushi died of a drug overdose, Marlette drew a coke-snorting Blues Brother with a death's head, and his friends accused him of drawing a right-wing cartoon. "I think it's more important to feel than to feel good," he replied. "We live in a culture where the thing to do is gloss over symptoms, or take it to Jesus or blame whoever. From cocaine to Prozac, it's all the same, and I began seeing that as the deadening of the human spirit.

"Believe it or not, wearing a coat and tie was how I began understanding my role as an artist," he says. "The great novelists see the whole picture. Dostoyevsky, Tolstoy, Dickens, they empathize with the thief and with the saint. They feel the whole thing, and they show the whole thing. Ideologues don't." Even though he had a new appreciation of authority, he attacked Reagan relentlessly, because he saw no subtlety or empathy whatever in the president's conservative republicanism. "Have you ever been to a Republican convention?" Marlette hoots. "You can feel the assholes slamming shut! The answer is not imposing your thing on other people." Having grown up with fundamentalism, he was especially predisposed against it. "I know its wickedness," he says. "I know its arrogance. How it compromises and belies its own claims."

Since his beginnings in 1974, Marlette had been drawing Jim and Tammy Faye Bakker, the cheesy prom king and queen of televangelism and a local phenomenon in Charlotte long before they became a national embarrassment. In 1987, Bakker was exposed for committing adultery with a church secretary, Jessica Hahn, and in 1989 was sent to jail for defrauding thousands of contributors to his ministry.

Marlette's portrayals of Bakker's PTL television ministry lampooned its religious theme park, Heritage U.S.A., as a sort of Six Flags Over Jesus, a liquor-free, trailer-trash playground; and their ostentatious lifestyle as a perverted playing-out of the frustrated desires of the troubled souls in their flock. Bakker had built the five-acre water park for $8 million, calling it "pretty fancy bait" for a fisher of men.[35] "So I drew Jesus being baptized by John the Baptist with Jim Bakker coming down a huge water slide in a big rubber ducky," Marlette explains. Bakker held the cartoon up on his TV show and called Marlette a tool of Satan. He started getting complaints and crank calls from all over the country. He politely explained that the Charlotte *Observer* personnel department had a policy against hiring tools of Satan. "I understand those people," the cartoonist says. "I understand what they're doing. Turn over your autonomy to something else. But I can't do it."

IN 1980 IVANA Trump went to work as the Trump Organization's vice president for interior decoration. The Grand Hyatt—which opened that year—set the style for all followed it. One design critic described it as "overstated opulence."

Donald Trump admits that he strived to be the quintessential Yuppie, building glittering bronze, brass, glass and marble buildings full of luxury apartments and shops that offended architecture critics but had undeniable appeal to those reveling in Reagan-era wealth. Trump's cockiness was a piece of it. That year, when he began demolishing Bonwit Teller to make way for the glittering new edifice that would become Trump Tower, he ordered the demolition of two Art Deco bas-relief friezes and an intricate grillwork that had decorated the building, a piece of irreplaceable art he'd promised to the Metropolitan Museum of Art. He later claimed it would have cost $500,000 to fulfill that promise, and that the removal would have endangered passers-by. Those claims were mocked by preservationists and newspaper editorialists, but he brushed them off. The sculptures didn't really interest him; building did. "I really enjoyed what I was doing. I didn't do it to say, 'Fuck you' to the rest of the world," he says. "I didn't do it to say I'm better than this one or that one. I did it because I really liked it."

Trump Tower opened in 1982—and immediately became a business success and a tourist attraction. Everything about it was designed by Ivana in her inimitable style, from the doormen's Disney-ish uniforms to the eighty-foot-high atrium and waterfall lined in breccia pernice marble. She was pregnant with their second child during the Tower's construction. In October, Ivanka Trump was born. At age thirty-six, Donald Trump began telling reporters he'd already done everything he ever wanted to do. Now, there was nothing left but to become the glaring embodiment of his time.

RUSSELL SIMMONS ALMOST graduated from CCNY. "I went four years, I had one hundred and fourteen credits," he says. "And then I dropped out." He quit in winter 1979, when he had his first hit record after three years of promoting parties. All that time, he'd been circling the edges of the music business in dance clubs like Club 371 and Disco Fever in the South Bronx and the Harlem Renaissance, and, though he hated the music they featured, gay discos. "The gay disco deejays made the charts!" he says. "They made whatever the fuck chart they wanted. They decided. In New York, there was only gay disco radio."

Then Simmons heard his first near-rap record, "King Tim III," by the non-rap Fatback Band and thought, "We might really be in the record business one day." The same month, a black-owned label, Sugarhill Records, put a trio of non-rappers together in a studio and came up with "Rapper's Delight," by a group they dubbed the Sugar Hill Gang. Driven by the sampled bass line of Chic's disco hit "Good Times," the song sold two million copies and introduced America to rap.

"Rapper's Delight" was a novelty hit—and a watershed. Soon after hearing it, Simmons and Kurtis Blow wrote and recorded a rhyme about Santa Claus in Harlem. "The next thing you know, I had 'Christmas Rappin'' under my arms," Simmons says. "I was in the record business!" Some listeners weren't so sure.

Simmons would go to middle-class clubs for blacks, "begging them to play the records," he says. "But those niggers were never going to, because they're niggers in suits and ties and they don't want to hear that shit. They look at the world they live in. If they want to be rock-and-roll and take drugs, they're never going to get out of jail. They've got to have a strict attitude about life. That's why middle-class black people are so uppity and bourgie; it's to survive. Otherwise they'd be fuckin' crackheads."

They weren't alone in hating rap. So did Frankie Crocker, a local radio monument. "I don't care how many records you sold, to Frankie Crocker, that's ghetto music. Frankie Crocker thought 'YMCA' by the Village People was hip. He's one of them niggers who didn't like niggers, or didn't like that cultural thing."

Then Kurtis Blow's Christmas record got played by deejay Larry Levan (b. 1954) at New York's best gay disco Paradise Garage and in April 1980, Blow played there live. In May, his second single, "The Breaks," came out and went gold with 800,000 copies sold. "Christmas Rappin'" soon matched those sales. Simmons started managing Blow, and signed him with a major record label. Simmons had given the record a false order number in the record company's ordering system. "We put it out, and it made a lot of noise in the street, and they were getting a lot of orders," he says. "That's how the Kurtis Blow deal got done." Rap was still a tiny subculture; Simmons had to fight for the right to make a full-length record. "Kurtis Blow had two gold singles before they let him make an album," he says. "That's unheard of." But finally he did; Blow's eponymous album was the first full-length hip-hop release. Rap was inching its way from street hustle to mainstream music.

For the next six years Simmons ran on overdrive, going to clubs ("Bentley's started at six o'clock in the afternoon, Danceteria started getting hot at nine o'clock, at four in the morning you can stop in the Garage or the Fever"), taking drugs (cocaine, angel dust), and working. "But I was more having fun," he admits. "I loved the music, the whole thing. It was now starting to evolve, to become respected and understood."

He was too busy for politics. "I was getting too high to give a fuck," he says. But he did notice what budget cuts in education did to Harlem, where he lived. "I felt bad; no one was going to school. Those opportunities were going away. But I wasn't a political activist, or even aware. Unfortunately."

Rap quickly infiltrated the hippest white clubs: the Mudd Club, the Peppermint Lounge, Danceteria. Simmons was an ambassador "wherever alternative clubs were starting to develop," he says. "I knew lots of people in every group at every club. I'd have friends in every world." So did Fred "Fab 5 Freddy" Braithwaite (b. 1959), an artist Simmons calls "the all-purpose Art

Nigger." Braithwaite, an artist and rapper, introduced the second-generation Warholites at Mudd to rap, and was soon honored by the new wave band Blondie, which released "Rapture," an homage to hip-hop, featuring lead singer Debbie Harry (b. 1945) rapping about her new friend.

Simmons got grief for border-crossing. "What do you want to go there for?" people said to him. "Bunch of faggots there." "Them niggers is ghetto; they'd murder us." "They're a bunch of drugged-out punk rockers."

"All the people were cool; it's not about color," Simmons says. "It's who's got the same interests, who's interesting and fun to be around, and that's the end of it." It was also good business. Simmons knew that crossing over, reaching white kids, was what he wanted. He never referred to the music he produced as rap; he called it black teenage music. In 1982, Simmons put Kurtis Blow on tour with the punk rock band The Clash, opening up a whole new record-buying audience.

Rush Productions, Simmons's management company, grew through the early 1980s. In 1982, he encouraged his younger brother, Joseph Simmons (b. 1964), and his friend Darryl McDaniel (b. 1964) to form a band, adopting the nicknames Run and D.M.C. respectively. After graduating high school that spring, they added a friend, Jason "Jam Master Jay" Mizell (b. 1965), to scratch their turntables, and recorded their first single, which became a minor hit on the R&B charts in 1983. "Kurtis Blow, Fearless Four, Run-D.M.C., Whodini, Orange Crush—I managed all those bands, produced records, oversaw management, helped develop their careers," Simmons says. Simmons dressed Run-D.M.C. in black hats and leather suits, giving them an indelible image.

In 1983, Simmons met Rick Rubin (b. 1963), a suburban white boy who was going to New York University but spending much of his time programming a drum machine and hanging out in rap clubs. "Every beat he plays is a smash," Simmons says. He'd produced "It's Yours," a single by T-La Rock and Jazzy Jay that caught Simmons's ear on the radio with its pop music-like structure. When they started hanging out together, Simmons began to incorporate Rubin's rock 'n' roll-bred attitude, trading in his sport jackets and penny loafers for jeans and Adidas sneakers. When the duo heard a demonstration tape by a sixteen-year-old from Simmons's Hollis neighborhood, they decided to start their own record company, Def Jam. They changed James Todd Smith's name to L.L. Cool J (b. 1968), dressed him up in a memorable uniform of sharp-creased Lee jeans and a Kangol hat, invested $4,000 each and in 1984, recorded his first single, "I Need a Beat," in Rubin's dormitory room for $700. It sold 100,000 copies.

That same year, Simmons met the Beastie Boys, a trio of well-to-do Generation X punk rockers: Adam "MCA" Rauch (b. 1965), Mike "Mike D" Diamond (b. 1966) and Adam "Ad-Rock" Horovitz (b. 1967). Their first rap single, "Cookie Puss," which sampled a prank phone call the group made to Carvel Ice Cream, bridged the gap between punk and hip-hop, and caught Rubin's ear. They soon signed to Def Jam.

By 1985, Rush Productions was managing twenty-two streetwise acts, and at age twenty-six, Simmons was about to make his move into the big time. That year, he made his first movie, *Krush Groove*, a fictionalized version of his and Rubin's story that included songs by many Def Jam acts; a $600,000 distribution, marketing, and promotion deal with CBS/Sony; and L.L. Cool J's first full-length album, *Radio*, as well as Run-D.M.C.'s *King of Rock* and the Beasties's *Licensed to Ill*.

Those records helped chart the course of rap into the mainstream. Under Rubin's influence, the Beasties and Run-D.M.C. both incorporated sampled rock guitar riffs into their sound. The Beasties, who toured as an opening act for Madonna that year, made the invitation to rock fans explicit with their metal riffs, parodic B-Boy patter, and anthemic single, "Fight For Your Right (to Party)". In a first since the 1960s, Simmons had also succeeded in institutionalizing a new sound that would outrage adults (older baby boomers primary among them) in direct proportion to how much it appealed to the young—the first successful update of the boomer-era youth-marketing paradigm.

The best was yet to come. In 1986, Run-D.M.C. recorded a rap version of the rock band Aerosmith's first hit song, "Walk This Way," with that band's singer, Steven Tyler (b. 1948), and guitarist, Joe Perry (b. 1950). Not only was the song a monster hit, the first rap single to break into the Top 5, it also broke the anti-rap rule on MTV—winning priceless exposure among white teenagers. Rap had crossed the color barrier. "It was alternative music," Simmons says. "Cool people across the country knew."

With CBS money behind it, Def Jam immediately became the world's leading rap label. Run-D.M.C.'s second album sold 2.5 million copies, L.L. Cool J's first sold 3.5 million (he'd eventually make four consecutive platinum albums), and the Beastie Boys' debut, the first rap album to hit #1 on *Billboard*'s pop record charts, sold a staggering 4.8 million copies.

There was still resistance from record companies, but Simmons doesn't think it was racism. "It was just new music," he says. "They had a nigger department, but the niggers didn't like this either. Niggers especially didn't like it. I was playing nigger to the niggers. They're afraid of change. You don't want to see records coming out you don't understand all over the place in your world. A forty-five-year-old record executive is not listening to that shit. So they put us behind their R&B records for radio play. But we just completely shit on R&B, killed it." Even then, they told him rap was a fad. "You know," Simmons says, chuckling, "they've said, 'It's just a fad' every year for twenty years now."

As early as 1980, Simmons had known better. That's when Polygram flew him and Kurtis Blow to Europe, where "Christmas Rappin'" had made the charts. "I'd never been out of the country," Simmons says. "I had my passport. Polygram put me on a plane. We sniffed all the coke in Amsterdam, we hit all the weed spots, and we partied and they treated us like we were rock stars, and I was rich from that day on."

THE COMPUTING GOLD rush was in full swing by 1982, fueled by two groups—creators, looking for powerful but versatile machines, and consumers, looking for the cyber version of a can opener. There were millions of them. So, "almost everywhere you turned there were millionaires," wrote Steven Levy in *Hackers*. "That smell of success was driving people batty."[36] Personal computing had long since passed hippies like Steve Wozniak by. In Silicon Valley, people snickered over how Woz had blown his fortune from the Apple stock offering producing massive rock concerts.

The arrival of ever-cheaper screens, computer memory, and microprocessors, essentially entire computers on a single chip, meant that graphics-capable computers once costing $300,000 could now be built for $20,000. They'd recognized the potential for this in the early 1970s at Xerox PARC. Now a group of graduate students at Stanford University, also in Palo Alto, California, turned another of the copier company's missed opportunities into a multibillion-dollar company. As part of his electrical engineering studies at Stanford, German science prodigy Andy Bechtolscheim (b. 1955) combined inexpensive off-the-shelf memory and microprocessors to create Stanford University Network—or Sun— workstations, linked into a cross-campus network. Xerox had built similar devices, but when the Defense Department's Advanced Research Projects Agency, the same group that put together the Internet, investigated buying them, it decided they were overpriced and approached Bechtolscheim. After failing to find a manufacturer, he enlisted two business students to write a business plan and find financing, and Sun Microsystems was incorporated to make the machines in February 1982.

There were many markets for Bechtolscheim's computing product, including the computer graphics division at Lucasfilm, the movie company making director George Lucas's *Star Wars* trilogy. Lucas's special effects magicians had been using Bill Joy's hopped-up UNIX operating system on Digital Equipment's VAX, a huge, expensive computer. The Sun workstation was a major improvement—"a little box that went as fast at one-tenth the cost," as John Gage puts it—so Lucasfilm suggested Bechtolscheim approach Joy about using his software on it. Joy introduced Bechtolscheim to Gage.

He was an immediate convert, and joined up as Sun's evangelist, the guy who knew how to explain things and how to turn wish lists into reality. "These workstations are an incredibly powerful tool you could use to build other tools, they're for serious computer people who are trying to build telescopes, design chips, design bridges, run battlefields and drilling rig platforms," Gage says. "None of them were the same people that your average computer VP would know. We represented a new rebel alliance."

Joy and Gage brought with them something as important as Berkeley UNIX: the idea that giving away software and unveiling its secrets, its source code, would be good business—and sell lots of Sun workstations—in the long run. "Free speech, open exchange; that's the ethic of the scientific community," Gage says. "More conversation rather than less. And more light, more light, more light. Allow communities to develop. A side effect of that, of course, is that dangerous communities will develop. But the health of the body politic depends on everyone being able to converse."

A year after their introduction, IBM-PCs, which were even smaller than Sun's mini-computers, had become a stiff challenge to the Apple II in the still-young personal computer market. Though Apple was still making huge profits, its market share plunged that year because unlike Apple, IBM let others use its PC architecture, increasing its market share. Sun's cyber neo-hippies would also take on those who clung to the proprietary standard.

Sun's customers "are people who have already decided what they need: networking, source code, openness, quick, communication Gage says. "They don't want to talk to a sales guy. They want to talk to Bill Joy or to somebody close to Bill, who could take them through what needs to be done at two in the morning when the cable shorts out and they can no longer control the telescope."

His customers were boomers just like him. They demanded instant gratification. "This was a social phenomenon," Gage says. "Open-systems guys are the hot-rodders who have to add their own thing. Looking at source code is like opening up an engine compartment. Because they could see inside it, they could be inventive in ways you could not be in the normal commercial world. They could hot-rod."

For Gage, it was all a great reminder of how he'd felt a decade earlier, when George McGovern won his nomination for the presidency. Maybe things really did work the way he'd once thought—and, lately, was thinking again. "You could make a serious change with one person. One smart kid could fundamentally alter a business or a political structure."

"I DON'T CARE to be a hero, ever," says Tommy Vallely. Indeed, throughout the years he worked as a political consultant, Vallely avoided Vietnam vets, particularly those who hadn't readapted to civilian life as well as he had. At least a little guilty that he had a support system at home—parents, money, political alliances—and they didn't, he resolved not to look back.

"It's hard," he says. "A lot of these people were in tough shape. Fucked up. I didn't want to deal with them. I've never been a member of a VFW, I'm never going to be. It's not that I dislike them, I just don't want to deal with that." Instead, he worked to build a life for himself. "I'm just playing the game I'm in, trying to get people elected," he says, "I work very, very hard at it." He learned about national politics, met members of the media, and married and had a daughter in 1979.

Vallely finally got a shot at elective office himself in 1982, when fate and politics arranged a seat for him in the state legislature, where he wound up serving for six years. "I was an insider, never gave a speech, couldn't give a speech," he says. "I learned how to be a public person. It was a very hard thing for me. And I was clumsy at first, so scared it would keep me awake at night." He realized he still wanted to run for Congress. So while serving, he started studying for a master's degree in public policy on scholarship at Harvard's John F. Kennedy School of Government. "And this time, I'm a pretty good student," he says. "I'm not a great student, but I can do it."

His friend, fellow vet John Kerry, became the Lieutenant Governor of Massachusetts under Michael Dukakis in 1982. Earlier that year, Vallely had sponsored legislation to create a Special Commission on the Concerns of Vietnam Veterans, and then become its vice-chairman. Shortly after the election, the commission revealed that the federal government had turned down the chance to investigate a big concern of vets, Agent Orange.

In January 1979, a federal class action lawsuit had been filed on behalf of 4.2 million Vietnam veterans against three manufacturers of an herbicide containing dioxin called Agent Orange used to defoliate vast swaths of Vietnam.[37] They alleged that Agent Orange caused cancer and other health problems—and Vallely was interested. Someone quite close to him had suffered from what he was sure were Agent Orange side effects. In December 1982, the commission ordered a study of the problem.

By the following June, Vallely was fed up. He told a reporter that most of the people who'd testified were from activist groups representing a troubled minority of veterans. He was angry that the Agent Orange study had been pushed aside by more political concerns like the issue of prisoners of war. Finally, Chris Gregory, a VVAW member and close friend of Kerry and Vallely, was appointed to head a Massachusetts Agent Orange program.

In 1984, when the state's senior senator, Paul Tsongas, retired, Kerry decided to run for his seat. Vallely, whose wife was wealthy, says he was hiding out on their 160-acre farm, studying John Deere catalogs at the time, "hoping Kerry doesn't call me 'cause I want to buy a tractor and I don't want to deal with him." After running a TV commercial showing him speaking in front of the Vietnam veterans memorial, Kerry was criticized by the same veterans who'd tried to usurp Vallely's hearings. Kerry was tarred as Ho Chi Minh's candidate. So Vallely helped organize the Dog Hunters, a group of about 100 Vietnam veterans, to support him.

"The Vietnam War started again with me during the Kerry election," Vallely says. When Kerry was sworn in early to finish the ailing Tsongas's term in office, Vallely visited the Vietnam Veterans Memorial in Washington for the first time. Designed by Maya Lin (b. 1959) a student at Yale, the V-shaped polished granite wall, set into the earth like an outcropping of rock and carved with the names of 58,000 dead and missing soldiers, is a chastening, gut-wrenching place to visit for veteran and protester alike. "It had a fuckin' huge impact on me," says Vallely. He'd had a friend who died in Vietnam named James Coleman, a big strong Texan, and when he saw an elderly couple searching for their son's name on the wall, the father wearing cowboy boots, Vallely's internal dam broke and he sobbed.

Not long afterward, John Kerry, now a senator and just back from Nicaragua, where he'd been embarrassed by a misbegotten attempt at lone-wolf diplomacy, was invited to a performance of *Tracers*, a play about Vietnam written and performed by veterans. The Vietnamese ambassador to the United Nations was also invited, and Vallely joined them. As the senator and the ambassador chatted in French, a Vietnamese aide took Vallely aside and asked him if Kerry would visit Vietnam for the tenth anniversary of the fall of Saigon that April. "No, no, no, the senator's not going to Vietnam," Vallely thought. "He just got back from making a fool of himself in fuckin' Nicaragua." When he said he didn't think so, the Vietnamese diplomat asked if Vallely wanted to go instead—and something clicked.

Vallely did go to Vietnam, shortly after another party that included dozens of returning newsmen (among them Walter Cronkite, whose turn against the war following the 1968 Tet Offensive made broadcast—and American—history) and Arizona congressman John McCain (b. 1936) a former pilot who had been a POW and would later become a senator. Afterward, McCain would sum up the lesson of the war: "The American people and Congress now appreciate that we are neither omniscient nor omnipotent, and they are not prepared to commit U.S. troops to combat unless there is a clear U.S. national security interest involved," he said. "If we do become involved in combat, that involvement must be of relatively short duration and must be readily explained to the man in the street in one or two sentences."[38] The McCain Doctrine would be operative for years to come.

IN 1983, HIS last year at college, Cameron Sears joined Friends of the River, a decade-old environmental group in northern California. Since moving to the state, he'd been whitewater rafting for pleasure and business and first got involved in river-related protests in 1978 to protect the Stanislaus River, where the Army Corps of Engineers had commissioned the construction of a $100 million dam that would submerge the river under a reservoir. California fought for the state's right to limit the reservoir and keep the river open for rafting and fishing. After that right was granted, demonstrators converged on the state capitol to urge Governor Jerry Brown to request that the reservoir not be filled. He agreed, but despite the institutionalization of environmentalism in the Carter administration, which had even given Earth Day's founder an official job, the tide was running against "tree-huggers." After Ronald Reagan's election, environmental activism had grown more militant—at least on the fringes not co-opted by corporate America.

Continued threats to the river encouraged more overt activism among Sears and his friends, some of whom chained themselves to rocks in a vain attempt to stop the filling of the Stanislaus reservoir after Congress refused to add it to the National Wild & Scenic Rivers System in 1979. Four years later, the floodgates were opened and the river was drowned.[39] "It was a devastating blow to that community, and to date they still don't really use the water," Sears says. "It doesn't generate any power. And it just killed the river. It was one of those remarkable resources, up against one of the last really big dam projects in America."

That same year, Friends of the River sought to protect an even more pristine body of whitewater, the Tuolomne River, just outside Yosemite National Park, when it was threatened by a hydroelectric project. Though a bill had been drafted adding it to the wild rivers system, it hadn't been put into effect. "So in my senior year and a year after that, I was consumed with protecting this river," Sears says. He worked as an intern at Tuolomne River Preservation Trust, lobbying on Capitol Hill. And the following summer, he helped run a program of five dozen trips on the Tuolomne, taking "anybody who would go with us down that river to show them what was going on."

Sears was paid a pittance to run the program, recruit volunteers and guide trips, but he didn't mind. "I either lived at my parents' house or the river companies had little houses up in the foothills of California, and you'd just pull your sleeping bag out and that's where you stayed. My single vision was to work for the environment."

As part of that effort, Sears sought out rich folk willing to help, "all manner of people, from movie stars like Richard Chamberlain to congressmen—whoever we could get that had influence." Among them were his longtime heroes the Grateful Dead. In a letter to the band, he wrote: "Water politics are the issue of the day. Without water this state is no state." He'd just about given up on a response when, two months later, the Dead's manager called him. "I've got twenty people who want to go on this river with you," the man said.

"So I take them on a no-strings-attached kind of trip," Sears continues. "None of the band came. It was all the office workers and their kids, basically. And we all became fast friends. We do a few more trips, we're going gangbusters, getting along famously. And they give me a check for ten thousand dollars to give to Friends of the River."

Later that year, the battle for the Tuolomne was won, and Sears moved to San Francisco to start "groveling to find a job in an environmental community where everybody wants you to be an intern and work for free," he says. As in the wider world, all the good jobs were taken by people ten years older than Sears, "and they're entrenched, you know?" he says. "Because the people who got into the movement in 1970 were completely dedicated, and by 1985, they had only just achieved a level where they could eke out a living. Instead of making fifteen grand a year, maybe they were making thirty-five, big-banana wages at that time."

Finally, he accepted the idea that he'd have to get a real job. Luckily for Sears, the previous summer, he'd taken rock impresario Bill Graham on a river trip after one of his executives bought a business on the Tuolomne. "He was completely blown away," Sears remembers. "No phones, no nothing, just three days of bliss. We stayed up until seven in the morning. We took some Ecstasy, and we were just raving around the campfire. Now, granted, he was high, but he wanted me to be his personal guide. He wanted to buy a river company."

"This is just incredible; where else can we go?" Graham demanded. "You're my ticket."

Sears was boggled. "This guy is trying to set me up in business." It was a Yuppie's dream, but he didn't know how to play it. "Yuppies are anathema to me," he says. "So I'm like, 'Jesus Christ, what do I do?' I talk to my friends at Grateful Dead. They say, 'Be careful,' because they didn't really trust him. Wow. Bizarre." Sears trusted his Dead friends. He was by then dating the daughter of the woman to whom he'd handed his letter about the Tuolomne River. Instead of accepting Graham's backing, he proposed to create an adventure travel division inside Graham's company, to organize bimonthly, low-cost trips for his employees, based on a program Doug and Susie Tompkins (both b. 1943) had set up inside their fashion company, Esprit. "It was a way for people to connect and get real," Sears says. "We can go skiing in the winter, we can go biking up in Napa Valley, we can go sailing on the bay. I knew I could pull it off. And he bought it. So I start doing these trips. But it didn't really work as well as I'd hoped. It turns out people who work twelve hours a day don't really want to be with one another on the weekend."

IN 1980, ONE of Steve Capps's Xerox colleagues, a hardware hacker, had told him about the Apple II personal computer. Capps wasn't very interested, because his rescued Alto was far more sophisticated. But his friend's enthusiasm proved infectious. "He put in a requisition to buy an Apple II, and it shot up to VP level and we were told we couldn't buy it, it was against corporate policy because we were in the computer business." Xerox was only talking about computers, though; Apple was making them. So the frustrated hacker got a job at Apple through one of several former PARC-ites who'd moved there.

A year earlier, Apple chairman Steve Jobs and a team of his computer designers had toured Xerox PARC. Inspired by what they'd seen, Jobs had gone back to Apple and sketched out an idea for its next product, a computer called Lisa (named after a daughter he'd sired out of wedlock) that would incorporate most of PARC's best ideas. Capps's hacker friend was hired to join the Lisa hardware team.

Two months later, early in 1981, Capps paid him a visit. Within a few minutes, he knew he wanted to work at Apple. "When I'd dropped out my father said, 'You're not going to amount to nothin',' and I said, 'I'm going to be a millionaire before I'm thirty.' I had notebooks filled with ideas. I go out to Apple and there's a bunch of people who are like this, they're all just maniacs, trying to get something done."

They were trying to get rich, too, Apple's anti-Establishment image notwithstanding. Larry Tesler, the scientist who'd given Jobs the demonstration at PARC and joined Apple shortly thereafter, not only hired Capps to work on Lisa's laser printer, but convinced him to ask for a lot more money than he'd been making at Xerox. "There was a whole 'I'm gonna get mine' undercurrent," Capps says. Steve Wozniak, who'd represented Apple's altruistic side, was fading from the picture. Though he'd still stop by and play video games with his friends, he was no longer active.

Hired in September 1981, Capps moved to California with his girlfriend, another computer science student from Rochester. Briefly, he and several other ex-Xerox employees argued against borrowing the Alto's software. They soon realized that the Apple software designer who wrote the graphic interface (over a weekend, according to in-house legend) had actually done a better job than PARC had, perfecting aspects of the program that hadn't actually worked in Xerox's version. Now Capps was in the thick of it. Not only did he do his job, he also wrote several computer games for Lisa. It was the games that caught Steve Jobs's eye.

Though his selling skills were beyond question, the mercurial Jobs was somewhat less accomplished as a manager of people. After Apple went public, he'd given up day-to-day control of the company to a professional manager. Early in 1981, furious that that CEO had assigned Lisa's development to another executive and aware that Lisa was in trouble—during its gestation, Lisa's software had outgrown its hardware and it was effectively obsolete before it shipped—Jobs had looked for a way out. He found it in another executive's pet project; a team was trying to develop an easy-to-use, $600 personal computer called Macintosh. Jobs elbowed his underling out and converted Macintosh into a project to develop a smaller, cheaper, hacked version of Lisa, a Volkscomputer.[40] Just as he stole ideas from PARC and then Lisa, Jobs also stole people. He hand-picked a team of designers and engineers, and sequestered them in their own building, over which he sometimes flew a Jolly Roger flag; the Mac team were pirates, stealing whatever they needed.

They were on a mission. "Don't you want to make a dent in the world?" Jobs would demand. "This is going to be as revolutionary as the telephone." Convinced that they were doing something earth-shattering, they lived on soda and pizza, constantly pulled all-nighters, and worked like maniacs. "Steve would set unattainable goals, but he was a good enough salesman that he got people to believe in him, and he knew which strings to pull," Capps says. Sometimes the Mac team would compare Jobs to Jim Jones, the religious cult leader who'd induced some nine hundred of his followers to drink Kool-Aid laced with cyanide in a mass suicide in the jungles of Guyana in 1978. "You can't start asking questions, right?" says Capps. "You've just got to drink the purple Kool-Aid."

Capps joined the Mac effort late in the game—in 1983. The launch was set for a few months hence, but the burnt-out Mac team was at wits' end. Though the groundwork had been laid, they were unable to finish the software. Capps, already known as a demon code writer, was assigned to help another software designer, Bruce Horn, finish the Mac's most important piece of software. Finder was the first thing that appeared on the screen when a Mac was turned on. Before Windows, it was a window onto the little machine's many wonders. The philosophy behind Finder, like all Mac applications, was to make a computer fun, easy-to-use, intuitive, and above all, appealing to an artistic sensibility. Anyone who didn't find joy in its wonders could be dismissed as a Luddite or a cretin. It was meant to make the Mac the opposite of the clunky machines that used Microsoft's DOS operating system, like IBM's PC/XT, which had just been introduced.

While the rest of the Mac team gave prerelease promotional interviews, touting the Mac's wonders, Capps and Horn, hidden away in a conference room, spent eighteen-hour days trying to ensure the computer would live up to its hype. Sometimes Jobs would bring visitors around to show what the Mac team was up to. Once the visitor was the man whose software ran on PCs, Bill Gates. "You knew immediately who was the alpha male," Capps says, wryly. "Gates was just this software dink who didn't have a clue." Jobs, no dink, was dating Joan Baez. He'd bring her around, too, and the software designers would throw *Sesame Street* characters onto the screen so she could see that the Mac "didn't look like every other green-on-black computer."

Fact is, those demonstrations notwithstanding, the Mac didn't work.

"We were in trouble," says Capps. "It was pretty, but it was completely nonfunctional." Within a few months, though, Capps and Horn were able to build on the solid underpinnings written by another coder, Andy Hertzfeld, and make it function. Capps still had his doubts. The Alto he'd used at Xerox was far more sophisticated. "From a raw technical computing point of view, I was going way downhill," he says, but locked away under the Jolly Roger, even he became a believer. Even if Xerox *had* sold the Alto, it wouldn't have gone for $1,500, the price at which Jobs now said he planned to sell Macs. Even when Jobs and his latest CEO, John Sculley, formerly of Pepsi, suddenly raised its price to $2,495—rather expensive for a Volkscomputer—Capps didn't waver from his belief that they were after something special.

The Macintosh was formally announced in January 1984, with a $400,000 commercial shown only once, during that year's Super Bowl. Some forty-three million viewers watched as a woman dashed into a dingy room full of what Capps calls desk clones listening to an Orwellian Big Brother figure lecturing from a video screen. After she hurled a sledgehammer at the image, exploding the screen, a narrator intoned, "On January 24th, Apple Computer will introduce Macintosh. And you'll see why 1984 won't be like 1984."

The challenge to IBM was so startlingly direct that the commercial would be replayed over and over on news shows, implanting the Mac in the public's mind. A week later, at Apple's stockholder meeting, Jobs pulled the first Mac out of a bag. "Hello," said a synthesized voice. "I am Macintosh. It sure is great to get out of that bag." Jobs didn't mention that Capps and Horn had pulled three consecutive all-nighters, ending a mere two hours before Jobs took the stage, to get the machine to do that.

Though it could actually do very little, the Mac, *Time*'s Joshua Quittner would later write, "made mortals suddenly see the beauty and empowering potential of a desktop machine. . . . ordinary people could now make computers do extraordinary stuff."[41]

Unfortunately, the hype proved more extraordinary than the Mac's reality. "After the initial raft of Yuppies went out and plunked their twenty-five hundred dollars down, sales fell flat," says Capps. "And the reason was we didn't have spreadsheets, and corporate people would look at it and say, 'What can I do besides draw pictures of a shoe?' It was a toy. But that's why we worked so hard on it. Technology itself isn't all that interesting. How well we deliver that technology to humans is my focus."

Jobs was right. The Mac was "insanely great," and would soon find favor as the personal computer of choice for creative people, but it wasn't so great for Apple's business, which peaked the following year. Meantime, sales of the company's older Apple II computers, which sold to spreadsheet users—not artists—were slumping. Jobs began fighting boardroom battles with CEO Sculley. In 1985, the company reported its first quarterly loss and laid off 20 percent of its workforce. Plans for an improved Mac fizzled.

Capps, blissfully unaware of the political intrigues at Apple, paused long enough to marry his girlfriend and then busied himself improving Finder while waiting for his next assignment. "We were talking about a Mac phone, about a handwriting machine, we were all thinking revolutionary, but sales were in the toilet. The world was not exactly going along with our revolution."

That September, Jobs stormed out of the company. "It was surreal; we all go over to his house, and he's bemoaning his lot in life," Capps recalls. "I'm walking around going, 'This is a big house.'" Soon, Capps quit, too. "I was burnt out and all the cool people had left," he says. He wrote a little more software for Apple in exchange for a new computer, cashed out his stock—while the price was depressed; "a big mistake," he says now—and took off for Paris with his wife. He wanted to learn French. And he wanted to write software "for the good of the world," he says, laughing at himself. "I still had the extremely naïve idea that if you do something cool, the world will reward you."

Maturity

BORN AFTER THE draft expired and too old for it by 1980, when Jimmy Carter reinstituted Selective Service registration, David McIntosh regrets having missing out on military service, which he feels certain would have been a character-building experience. Law school at the University of Chicago was a philosophy-building experience, buttressing his new belief that government exists "to protect individuals and their rights, not to make decisions for them," he says.

Along with three friends he'd met at Yale, McIntosh founded the Federalist Society at the beginning of his second year in Chicago, inspired by the Reagan administration's proposal to decentralize what it considered the most pervasive, unmanageable, ineffective, costly and unaccountable government in American historya radical vision that sought to transfer federal power to states and localities. The policy, a return to those propounded in *The Federalist Papers of 1788*, not coincidentally provided a counterweight to the liberal orthodoxy that dominated law schools.

"Liberalism and the counterculture had taken root both in style and in a lot of the legal teaching," McIntosh says. "Most conservatives didn't know there were others on campus. So we'd have lunch together and twenty students would show up and be surprised to find people who had similar views." They were encouraged by conservative professors Antonin Scalia at Chicago (who became their chief adviser, and later a Supreme Court Justice), and Robert Bork and Ralph Winter at Yale, who would also soon be appointed to the federal judiciary. Requests to form chapters poured in from all over the country. The back end of the Baby Boom ('til then better known as a breeding ground for criminals, suicides, druggies and other malcontents) was also giving birth to a very new kind of activist.

The summer before his final year of law school, McIntosh worked in a Chicago law firm that offered him a job in its Los Angeles office after graduation. He accepted, practicing real estate law there and sharing an apartment with a friend who helped run a local church youth group. McIntosh began taking their charges on ski trips, weeklong jaunts to Mexico to build housing for squatters, and side trips to Disneyland. "It was the blessing of the circumstances," he says, that he found wholesome activities even in Sodom-by-the-Sea, where some of the young lawyers in the firm lived a party-all-night lifestyle. "I'll go out dancing, but I'm not going to stay out all night, and no thank you to the marijuana-and-cocaine-type thing," he says.

McINTOSH'S PARTYING PEERS weren't the only cocktail shakers in the new club scene, or the only manifestation of the burgeoning conservatism of the Reagan era. In 1980, the publication of *The Official Preppy Handbook* signaled the return of inherited wealth and station as social signifiers. Around the same time that Jerry Rubin brought his networking parties to Studio 54, Gwynne Rivers, the beautiful, well-connected daughter of the painter Larry Rivers, went to work there too, as a party promoter, responsible for luring young clubgoers from her prep school set. Back in New York in 1982, Victoria Leacock joined that crowd while helping her friend Jonathan Larson find theaters to mount his first musicals. When Leacock realized she needed a paying job and an apartment of her own, Rivers introduced her to Mark Fleischmann, Studio 54's new owner, who hired her as his personal assistant in January 1983.

Her workday began at 10:00 A.M. in Fleischmann's office in a hotel he also owned, and ended at 1:00 A.M., when the club owner's limousine would take her home to a room she rented in another hotel. Life in Fleischmann's milieuwas a roller coaster of promoters, refined druggies and lowdown aristocrats. Leacock quickly learned who was who on the club scene, how to pronounce their names and keep them happy, how to design special invitations, and how to hand-address envelopes—social skills largely forgotten since the sloppy 1960s. "I also discovered power, because I made the guest list," she says.

She was no longer starstruck. "Whatever magic happened at the club came at such a high cost," she says. "By the time you got to the fucking party you knew all the horror it took to get there, and barely wanted to be there. And the hangovers in the morning. And I was having my own hangovers for the first time in my life." She was also having a torrid affair with a psychiatrist more than twice her age.

"It became very ugly," she says of the nights she saw people stick their noses in the rugs and sniff, hoping the dust contained cocaine. She started pouring Kahlúa into her morning coffee, and graduated to vodka and tequila as the day wore on. "I knew I had a problem, but I waited six years to do anything about it." In July 1983, Fleischmann and his partners sold their hotel to Steve Rubell and Ian Schrager, who'd decided to go into the lodging business.

Leacock had the sense to leave the club scene when Rubell and Schrager took over Fleischmann's office (and turned the place into Morgan's Hotel, foundation of the empire that is now Ian Schrager Hotels). She moved to London to go to theater school. Her last act at Studio 54 was to throw a party that would start a trend that would soon snowball. She and D. A. Pennebaker's son gave a "Second Generation" party for the children of Melvin van Peebles, Rip Torn and Geraldine Page, Anthony Quinn, Dustin Hoffman, Jerry Stiller and Anne Meara, Sidney Lumet and Gower Champion.

"We had a lot of similar character traits," Leacock says. "A feeling of being very in but for all the wrong reasons. And we all came out of this jaded period of time, and were trying to make some good out of it."

The party was a success, but Leacock's sojourn in England was a failure. Acting school sucked the desire to act right out of her. She returned to New York determined to become a producer or director but first, briefly, went back to work for Fleischmann organizing parties at a restaurant he'd bought when Studio 54 finally closed. New clubs had replaced it, of course. The latest was Area, the last gasp of urban boomer hedonism.[1] Leacock started going there. Though she didn't partake in the coke-sniffing and furtive sex in the unisex bathroom stalls, she was no model of decorum. "Looking for love became a much more random thing," she says. "And I started drinking a lot more."

AFTER SETTLING IN Albuquerque, Mark Rudd earned an education degree and got a job teaching remedial math to junior college students. Throughout the preceding decade, even when living under the most adverse circumstances, the tall, handsome, articulate Rudd had been a girl magnet. Groupies came with the territory. When times were tough, he had a tendency to indulge—which had become an issue with his Weather comrades. For a time, his girlfriend Sue had anchored him. "I survived those rough years because I had a partner," he says. "But after we hit

Albuquerque, the external constraints were off for both of us." They separated—he says the decision was mutual—after he got his degree.

For the next eighteen years, Rudd had "lots of relationships, good and bad." He stayed true to his general beliefs, at least, even if he engaged in as much issue-hopping as bed-hopping. "I have a tendency to involve myself in what's hot," he says. "I put huge amounts of effort into a movement, and then it dies down and I put it into another."

Ronald Reagan reenergized him. Reagan's initiatives against what he deemed the Evil Empire of communism inspired several large anti-nuclear demonstrations in New Mexico. Rudd threw himself into planning them. "I was not a general," he points out. "I did the work as much as anybody else." When the *Albuquerque Tribune* discovered the presence of the radical in its region, he ducked their offer of an interview, explaining that publicity "could do a number on me."

Rudd was seeking to balance the personal and the political. In 1982, he and his children and friends began building the house he now lives in, a solar adobe in a semirural, predominately Chicano barrio. "It heats and cools itself, and we did it ourselves," he says. "I've been living in it since 1984." Shortly after he moved in, Reagan was reelected.

One of Reagan's great concerns was Nicaragua, the Central American country that had been controlled by the Marxist-Leninist Sandinistas since their overthrow of the forty-five-year-old Somoza family dictatorship in 1979. Their opponents, the Contras, had been denied military aid by Congress in October 1984. Oliver North (b. 1943), an official of the National Security Agency (NSA), saw a way to raise clandestine funds to continue the Contras' war. The money came from Iran. Five years after fundamentalists deposed Iran's Shah, the Reagan administration placed the Islamic Republic on a list of countries that, because of their support of terrorism, were deemed untrustworthy and subject to strict export controls. Then, over the next eighteen months, twenty Americans, including the CIA's station chief in Lebanon, were kidnapped in Beirut.

Early in 1985, advisers to Israel's President Shimon Peres met with arms dealers from Israel and Iran—Manucher Ghorbanifar, a former officer of the Shah's secret police, among them—to discuss the possibility of a trade of weapons for the American hostages in Lebanon. That May, Barbara Ledeen's husband Michael, a consultant at the NSA, went to Israel and met with Peres to discuss Iran. On his return, Ledeen told Robert McFarlane, the head of NSA, that Ghorbanifar had a secret agenda: a plan to overthrow the fundamentalist Islamic regime.[2] Secretary of State George Schultz tried to cast doubt on Ledeen's statement, implying he was putting Israel's interests above those of the United States, but the plan had engaged the imagination of the White House. By late summer, U.S.-made missiles were en route to Iran via Israel, and the profits from the sales were routed back to the Nicaraguan Contras.

As the war in Nicaragua heated up, it became Rudd's new issue. "I saw it as Vietnam again, what I'd started out fighting," Rudd says. "I don't think I ever felt that the Sandinistas were that heroic, but I thought that they were doing their best to build a more just society."

Americans had been backing the Sandinistas since 1979, when the Nicaragua Network was formed to support what was then still a guerrilla army. By the mid-1980s, it had more than 100 chapters. "We were a check," Rudd says. "We prevented the United States from becoming directly involved, so the military had to use surrogate troops and covert warfare." In February 1986, Rudd spent four weeks building houses in Nicaragua with the New Mexico Construction Brigade.

That year, after Reagan announced his Strategic Defense Initiative, the space-based missile defense system better known as Star Wars, Rudd quit his teaching job and got a contract to write a revisionist history of the Vietnam-era antiwar movement. His publisher urged him to make it autobiographical. "It took a long time to write it, and I was very dissatis-fied," he says. "There were many things I was ambivalent about. One is, why did I opt for violence? The second is my womanizing. The third is privilege and access to money. Even when I was underground and under a different name, I could easily get jobs, because I'm articulate." Unable to resolve these nagging issues, Rudd finally shelved the book.

HAVING SEX ONSTAGE snapped Nina Hartley's life into focus. She could have it all, career and family, even if both were a bit out of the ordi-nary. She could also embody the sex-positive message of *Our Bodies, Our Selves*. In 1984, she decided to dive in the deep end and start making porn movies. She answered a few ads for actresses, "but the people were just so icky," she says, definitely not the sort with which a feminist would associate. Then, one afternoon, her boyfriend Dave met a director, Juliet "Aunt Peg" Anderson (b. 1938), in the Berkeley Bowl supermarket.

Anderson, a Finnish feminist and former teacher, had been writing a master's thesis on porn when someone dared her to do a movie. By 1984, she was one of a small cadre of feminist sex workers beginning to make a mark, insisting that their lifestyle could be an acceptable choice for intel-ligent women, despite the claims of traditional feminists that pornogra-phy encouraged rape and was degrading to women.

Hartley's onscreen debut came in one of the first porn movies shot on video instead of film. As dramatized in the 1997 mainstream film *Boogie Nights*, within the world of X-rated movies, filmmakers had pretensions to art. Video was considered a lesser form, lacking even the modest production values and nods toward plot and character that supposedly elevated porn's golden age in the 1970s. Video producers were concerned with volume, not quality, and soon caused the bottom to drop out of the porn movie market. But by then Hartley was established as a star. After completing her nursing degree in 1985, she began cranking out movies. She's made four hundred and fifty in fifteen years. "It was almost impossible to get away from me," she boasts.

Hartley was savvy about marketing herself. "You could tell I was enjoying myself," she says. "It was important for me to showcase women enjoying sex, the role model of a happy, active, into-it female. I smiled at a penis, knowing people would notice. And I was consistent. I couldn't control the movie, but I could control my performance." Having married Dave, she insisted on his presence on sets, which kept things on an even keel. "Feminism told me I didn't have to do what I didn't want to do," she says. "I'm sure other girls who had VICTIM stamped on their forehead had more horrible experiences."

Until she began making films, Hartley managed to hide her work from her parents, telling them she was a cocktail waitress and a sportswear model. After "Nina" did an interview with the *San Francisco Chronicle*, though one of Mitzi's brothers called. "Do you know how upset Mom is?" he asked. It got worse when she learned about Nina's three-way marriage. "We're close, but estranged," Hartley says.

Politics had been anathema in the small world of pornography until the mid-1980s, when several separate groups of women in the industry began banding together, seeking a measure of control over their own destinies. In 1983, a group of late-1970s New York porn performers, all nearing the end of their onscreen careers, banded together in a consciousness-raising and support group.[3] Simultaneously, Nina Hartley and Bobby Lilly met Kat Sunlove (b. 1945), a former radical, at the premiere of Hartley's first movie. Sunlove, a Texan with a master's degree in political science, had been a union organizer, a wife and mother, and director of a Big Brothers program before moving to the Bay Area, where she changed her name and worked as a dominatrix, an adult performer, and a producer of workshops on sadism and masochism. She also wrote a sex advice column for *The Spectator*, a local sex newspaper descended from the 1960s underground newspaper *Berkeley Barb* (which had spun off its sex ads into the offshoot in an exercise in political correctness in 1978—and promptly died from loss of advertising income). Sunlove, who became *The Spectator's* publisher and president, brought Lilly and Hartley into the nascent pro-sex movement on the West Coast.

Sex-positive feminism was a reaction. It began in 1979 when, after *Roe v. Wade*, mainstream feminism veered into neo-Victorianism in search of its next issue. Inspired by the formation of Women Against Violence in Pornography and Media three years earlier, NOW began a campaign called Take Back the Night, tying sexual permissiveness to rape, and Andrea Dworkin (b. 1947), who'd begun reading porn in her first, abusive marriage to a Dutch radical, published *Pornography: Men Possessing Women*, an anti-porn polemic. Dworkin's extremism was such that she would later equate all sexual intercourse with rape, saying, "Sexual relations between a man and a woman are politically acceptable only when the man has a limp penis."[4] Along with Gloria Steinem, Susan Brownmiller and others, Dworkin was one of the founders of Women Against Pornography, which gave tours of New York's Times Square sex district.

Also in 1979, Catharine MacKinnon (b. 1946), a Yale-educated lawyer who'd opposed the Vietnam War and supported the Black Panthers and women's lib, published her landmark study, *Sexual Harassment of Working Women*. In it, the daughter of a Republican judge who'd once said sex in the workplace was only to be expected, argued that workplace sexual harassment was more than a private harm; it was discrimination. While that construct had merit, under MacKinnon's extreme interpretation, it led to situations such as the one in which a college teacher was forced to remove a photo of his wife in a bathing suit from his desk.[5]

In the early 1980s, sex permeated society. Public sex venues—gay bathhouses, movie theaters, and bookstores, S&M and fetish clubs like New York's Mine Shaft and Anvil, and swingers' spots like Plato's Retreat operated openly in major cities. Health clubs promised hard bodies, and we all knew what those were for. Even if you didn't have one, advertising promised that almost every product, whether a new car or a new pair of Jockey shorts, was a shortcut to whoopee. Sexual fruit was no longer forbidden, but a backlash was brewing.

Unlikely as it sounds, AIDS wasn't an issue in the porn world. Hartley says most performers who contracted HIV in the 1980s were known to have engaged in unprotected anal sex or to have used needles—and other porn people avoided them. They also felt safe because the conventions of porn limited the exchange of bodily fluids. They didn't discuss it; denial was a mental prophylactic. "Heterosexuals in the sex business were like heterosexuals everywhere'Can't happen to us!'" Hartley says.

Concurrently, people nationwide who'd felt disenfranchised during the political and social upheavals of the preceding decades were finding their voice through newly resurgent conservative and religious fundamentalist groups. Millions, including many boomers—some who were always silently conservative, some who were becoming more so as they settled down and placed new emphasis on families, careers, and economic concerns—were redefining themselves. In 1981, the *New York Times* reported a sudden shift in political affiliation among people born between 1946 and 1955. "A year ago that group was 56 percent Democratic and 30 percent Republican," the paper said. "Today it is 44 percent Democratic and 43 percent Republican."[6]

Encouraged by the Reagan Republicans and by evangelical preachers who were reaching millions via satellite and cable TV broadcasts, they were leading a charge toward—or retreat to—old-fashioned ideas like commitment, romance and even the restoration of chastity and virginity as virtues. America wanted its hymen back.

Leading the way were groups like the National Federation for Decency, which declared advertiser boycotts and letter-writing campaigns against television shows, movies and musicians, and the Moral Majority, a coalition of conservative Christians and anti-abortion right-to-life groups that declared war on "filth" in 1985. The Moral Majority was founded by a right-wing journalist, Paul Weyrich (b. 1942), fronted by the evangelist Jerry Falwell, and supported by politicians like North Carolina Senator Jesse Helms, who summed up the new attitude when he said, "Surely it is not just coincidental that, at a time in our history when pornography and obscene materials are rampant, we are also experiencing record levels of promiscuity, venereal disease, herpes, AIDS, abortion, divorce, family breakdown, and related problems."[7] As early as 1982 a *New York* magazine cover had asked, "Is Sex Dead?" *Esquire* answered: "The Sexual Revolution: R.I.P." *Time* put herpes, a new, incurable venereal disease, on its cover, and reported that twenty million Americans had it.[8] Jimmy Carter's lustful heart had given way to Nancy Reagan telling us to just say no.

The fundamentalists and conservatives forged an unlikely alliance with feminism. Dworkin and MacKinnon had met when Dworkin put MacKinnon together with Linda Lovelace, the star of *Deep Throat*, following the publication of her memoir, *Ordeal*, in which she revealed she'd been coerced to make the movie under threat of death.

In 1983, Dworkin and MacKinnon taught a class on pornography together at the University of Minnesota. After testifying at a zoning hearing on behalf of a local group trying to ban porn shops, the two were asked to write a city ordinance defining porn as a violation of women's civil rights. Lovelace testified at the hearings, and a law was signed in May 1984. Though immediately vetoed by the mayor of Minneapolis, it made MacKinnon and Dworkin feminist superstars. At that year's NOW convention, Dworkin led a march against porn.

Soon a coalition arose to oppose the Dworkin/MacKinnon position on First Amendment grounds, including the American Booksellers Association, the ACLU, and the Feminist Anti-Censorship Task Force (among the signatories were 50 prominent feminists, like Betty Friedan and Kate Millett). The anti-porn movement wouldn't be stopped. In 1984 the Reagan administration set up an investigating commission under Attorney General Meese, and the Justice Department launched a simultaneous attack. Reagan had found a domestic equivalent to the Soviet Evil Empire. Politicians clamored to bang the anti-porn drum. The Parents' Music Resource Center was formed in 1985 by a group that included the wives of Senators Gore, Packwood and Thurmond to promote hearings against salacious rock lyrics. In 1986, an official of the Meese Commission threatened to boycott chains like 7-Eleven, Rite-Aid, and KMart if they didn't stop selling *Playboy* and *Penthouse*.[9]

The underlying political assumption was that baby boomers, the great beneficiaries of the sexual revolution, were feeling guilty about past pleasures and their unplanned side effects and were ready to renounce the libidinous behaviors of their youth. But generalizing about the Baby Boom will get you in trouble every time. Though there were certainly boomers who felt that way—some in the forefront of the new fundamentalism—just as many treasured their sexual liberation despite the price paid for it, and were ready to go to the barricades again to protect it.

San Francisco lesbians were just then supplanting gay men, whose ranks were being decimated by AIDS and accompanying second thoughts, at the forefront of the pro-sex movement. "Lesbians were claiming the right to fuck without romance that gay men had claimed for years," says Hartley, who joined a like-minded group to form Californians Against Censorship Together in 1986, to defend the adult industry. The Meese Commission reminded Hartley of "the Red Scares that fucked up my father," she says. "It brought to mind people's attacks on [birth control advocate] Margaret Sanger. Even if I hadn't been in the business, it would have concerned me." The group lobbied for free speech in the state capital and against restrictions on pornography at the twentieth-anniversary meeting of NOW in Denver that year.

Hartley became their frontwoman "because no one else would speak out in public," she says. "It became imperative because the propaganda from the other side was so strong. Sexual control is the bedrock of social control. The 1960s were about discovering that. And the culture has been at war over that issue ever since. I agree with a lot of what feminists say about sex as commodity, but you don't get rid of that by getting rid of sex."

CORPORATE LIFE WAS good to the maverick Michael Fuchs. He was made chairman of the board and chief executive officer of Home Box Office in 1984, but he was also handed a huge problem. "Though the eighties were starting to boom, HBO's business was not," Fuchs says. The number of subscribers paying monthly fees had been growing by millions a year, and HBO had made plans based on that growth rate, despite Fuchs's warnings about the looming threat of videocassettes. When growth stopped dead thanks to increased competition from them and from new premium cable competitors, the company only stayed solvent because it had a deep-pocketed parent. HBO wasn't Time's only speed bump. A series of failures derailed the ambitions of several Time executives, leaving Gerry Levin and Nick Nicholas as heirs apparent to Time Inc.'s CEO Dick Munro—all cable guys.

Nothing was simple at Time, though, and executives constantly played musical chairs. Fuchs hired Frank Biondi in 1978, only to become his employee in 1983, when Biondi was named HBO's chairman. Within a year, Biondi was fired and Fuchs promoted to chairman in a shakeup that also saw Levin demoted and Nicholas positioned to take over the top spot at Time. Fuchs and Nicholas then teamed up to strengthen HBO. It was hardly a weakling; it had long made Hollywood dance to its tune. "The license deals were gigantic, and that created enormous tension," says Fuchs. When the studio tried to fight back, HBO started making end-runs around them to get rights to films, even financing them independently, becoming the largest backer of feature films in the world.[10] That infuriated the studios, and Fuchs didn't help matters by boasting, "I will bring Hollywood to its knees."[11]

"I've never had the respect for Hollywood so much of our society has because I know the emperor has no clothes," he explains. "And the movie studios felt angry and stupid, having missed this opportunity (to cash in on the new revenue stream of cable) being driven by their movies."

Though he was arrogant and on a roll, Fuchs didn't join in the money madness of nouvelle society. He says it disgusted him. "When I went to speak at colleges, they wanted to know how to get my job instead of hearing me talk about what they should believe in." Once, after a speech in Philadelphia, he and MTV's Robert Pittman was chased to the train station by students pushing their résumés on the pair. "I'd never seen anything like that. I'm not anti-capitalist. You participate, you try to earn money and invest. But I'm against the worship of the rich, of celebrity."

Still, he was in the entertainment and celebrity business. In 1986, Fuchs convinced Barbra Streisand to appear in her first full-length televised concert in two decades, and he cut a deal with boxing promoters Butch Lewis and Don King to present a heavyweight "world series" of boxing matches that produced the next world champion. And when a young boxer, Mike Tyson (b. 1966), won that title, he made a deal with Fuchs that would pay him more than $25 million dollars over the next two years and begin his transformation into a celebrity nightmare.

Many of the projects Fuchs greenlighted were about more than making money. "Good citizenship is good for business," he'd decided. A series of bio pics spotlit his personal heroes—Soviet dissident Andrei Sakharov in 1984, TV news pioneer Edward R. Murrow in 1986, South African anti-apartheid advocate Nelson Mandela in 1987, and Nazi hunter Simon Weisenthal in 1989. Only a tiny percentage of HBO viewers knew who any of them were, so Fuchs would educate them. "But this was not PBS," he says. "This was not an elite audience." Instead of making these movies with obscure English actors, he made them with stars and promoted them as events. "We were very good at spin," he says, better still at spinning product toward boomers with the money to buy both subscription cable services and the equipment to receive them.

Many boomers were belatedly starting families. "When you have kids and you can't go out as much, television becomes more important," Fuchs notes, and he knew how to reach them. "Although I'm single, I thought of myself as very much typical of the HBO audience," he says. He loved Robin Williams, Billy Crystal and Whoopi Goldberg. In 1986, he helped create Comic Relief, a four-hour live benefit comedy show starring the trio to finance health care for the homeless, a feel-good balm for boomers.

His issue-oriented programming decisions were carefully calibrated to be provocative yet beyond reproach. In 1987, HBO broadcast a special, *How to Raise a Street-Smart Child*, tied to a community outreach program to warn children about the dangers of victimization by adults. (The parents of boomers had called it talking to strangers.) Fuchs was also responsible for a documentary, *Down and Out in America*, that became the first pay-cable program to win an Academy Award. Then, in 1988, HBO won the cable industry's first primetime Emmy Awards.

Fuchs had long felt guilty that he'd served in the Reserves while poorer, less advantaged boomers went to Vietnam. One summer in the 1970s, he'd shared a beach house with a girl whose boyfriend was a veteran and "told stories of what it was like to come back to America, to veterans' hospitals where guys were paralyzed and rats would come in and chew on their toes and they wouldn't know it," Fuchs says. "They'd put him on Thorazine because he got so angry." Fuchs had joined the board of the Vietnam Veterans Ensemble Theater Company, or VetCo, the group that mounted the Vietnam play *Tracers*, and resolved to make a film that offered a positive portrayal of the once-maligned and too-often-ignored Vietnam vets. In the mid-1980s, a director brought him a book of eloquent letters written by soldiers in Vietnam called *Dear America: Letters Home from Vietnam*. Though some HBO officials were skeptical, Fuchs financed the project to the tune of more than a million dollars. Actors and veterans from VetCo provided the narration.

Fuchs couldn't have accomplished all he did alone; he not only had a major corporation behind him, but also the various wire-owners who'd financed the miles of coaxial cable carrying HBO across America. Still, he took pride in pointing out that competitors like Atlanta entrepreneur Ted Turner (b. 1938), who put his local station, TBS, onto satellite in 1976 and added CNN in 1980, Kay Koplovitz (b. 1945), who started USA Network in 1977, and John Lack, who'd conceived the flamboyant MTV, were relative latecomers compared to him. Fuchs is even prouder of having created a new template for entertainment marketing. Years later, Bob and Harvey Weinstein (b. 1954 and 1952 respectively), brothers who'd shown counterculture movies and produced rock concerts while in college, would pull off something similar at their Miramax Pictures—and be hailed for innovation. That brings out the combatant in Fuchs. "HBO had much more impact on America than Miramax has had," he says. "Miramax had a little impact on the motion picture business. It's a little oasis that occasionally makes a good movie. But HBO revolutionized television. And immodestly, I invented original programming on cable. And I started to pitch cable owners on promotion and public relations."

Slowly, HBO's business turned around, but just when Fuchs might have relaxed, in 1985, his father was diagnosed with cancer. "It had me totally discombobulated," he says. "It put me in a time of indecision and confusion." He dithered about buying an apartment and about marriage.

"I almost settled down," he says. "I felt that this shouldn't happen to you without a family, and really, the next woman who came along was the woman I decided to marry." That woman was the actress Brooke Adams. Fuchs ran into her one day, immediately cast her in an HBO movie, popped the question and announced their engagement. They broke up almost as abruptly. "Since then," the *New York Times* magazine reported in 1989, "his social life has included a range of companionship, from an heiress to an anchorwoman to a schoolteacher." (In the next few years he would add a celebrity activist, a world-class athlete, and at least one more actress to that list before proposing to a former actress in 1999. Though friends doubt he'll actually walk down the aisle, he insists, "It's about time.")

IN 1984, CYNTHIA Bowman became a single mother. "I had this infant," she says, "I'd left his father, we had no financial agreement, I was basically hoping he was going to do the right thing." Kantner did, and ever since, they've shared parental responsibility for their son. To pay her part, Bowman took freelance publicity work. One client, the singer/songwriter Boz Scaggs, had opened a restaurant, asked her to publicize it, and encouraged her to start her own business.

Bowman had a lot of catching up to do. The world had changed while she'd been ensconced in the narcotic cocoon of rock 'n' roll stardom. "My little world was pretty cool," she says. "I wasn't concerned about anything else." Now she had no choice.

In 1984 she opened Cynthia Bowman Public Relations. Soon, the San Francisco Symphony asked her to be their liaison to the local rock 'n' roll community, and recommended her to the San Francisco Opera as well. Rock stars had become accepted members of the mainstream community in the liberal Bay Area—and targets of opportunity for cultural fundraisers. Bowman, in the right place at the right time again, became the intermediary.

She couldn't entirely leave her past behind, though. In March 1985, Paul Kantner left Jefferson Starship, which promptly released three number one songs. Kantner descended into depression. "He was devastated," says Bowman. "People were worrying about him blowing his brains out." Just when she thought she'd gotten out, she moved back in to his house.

JUST AS KATHRYN Stockton arrived at Brown University in 1982, an academic trend from France took hold on American campuses, altering innumerable educational and political assumptions. Years later, its tenets would be derogated as political correctness. Stockton had already used the term at Yale Divinity School. "We used it to talk each other down," she says. "People would get so earnest, so self-serious. We even had T-shirts printed up: NUKE THE WHALES."

Stockton had given up her plans to study for a doctorate in either clinical psychology or philosophical theology, deciding that their generalizations were too easily challenged and that literature might be a better laboratory for applied philosophical and religious principles. When she heard about the new discipline, "Theory," which focused on historical and cultural context instead of just words, she didn't like the sound of it. Theory had its origins in the French philosophy of the 1960s called Structuralism, which argued that individuals were shaped by deep structures—social, psychological and linguistic—they don't control. It also said that Texts, sets of words and symbols, are not the product of an author but of the structures and the systems their authors inhabit. Structuralism was a profoundly different way of looking at human discourse and interaction—and proved to be tailor-made for a late-blooming lesbian.

Stockton explains it all with a metaphor. "Between you and your own skin, there is language," she says. "If I touch the back of my hand, one can say I'm touching the skin, but really it's language touching language. The direct contact we think we have with the world is massively mediated— by language and other things; we only communicate through this very complicated system of substitution. You have to understand the complex things that pass between people on the backs of words. There is something profound about that."

Structuralism was just a linguistic pit stop on the road to Theory. Poststructuralism added a new wrinkle: that language and society themselves can only be understood in their economic, political, and cultural context. Then came Deconstructionism, which held that all texts in Western culture were based on classic oppositions like light versus dark, good versus evil, and man versus woman, with the first always deemed superior. But since darkness, the absence of light, depends on light for its very existence, their opposition is open to interpretation—an attractive notion to someone on the wrong end of oppositions like male versus female and straight versus gay.

In Theory's world, certainty is impossible, identity is fluid, and there is no truth, no justice, only relationships of power. So when these ideas first crossed the Atlantic in translations in the late 1970s, they found a ready audience among academics who'd cut their teeth ten years earlier on opposition to systems and the not-so-absolute truths that propped those systems up. Having tasted victory—and subsequent defeats—in the era's various movements, these "tenured radicals," as the conservative writer Roger Kimball called them, banded together in self-promoting circles and sought to force change on campuses where nonwhites and non-males were now studying in unprecedented numbers.

In the Reagan era, ever more multicultural college campuses rediscovered their traditional role as bastions of opposition. Theory replaced Marxism and its homegrown offshoots as the basis of that opposition. The new academic activists wanted to make their theory manifest and, being typically impatient baby boomers, didn't want to wait for the process to play out. They began to question disciplines like literature, history, and in extreme cases, science, asking if supposed universals were not in fact bound to a set of liberal white male-driven assumptions about race, class, culture and gender. Though that humanist ethic had given them their voice, they still found it oppressive. Why not *our* tribal truths? they asked.

To a young gay woman who'd just realized where she fit in a society in which she'd never known a lesbian, Theory was a great gift. Stockton and a small group of feminist friends would study dense, jargon-laden books by French philosophers "to figure out what are they saying and then what do we think about what they're saying." They discovered that Poststructuralism was a window on "how the linguistic game has been fixed in ways that are obviously disadvantageous to women. Our linguistic system really puts Man and things Masculine at the center. So much of gender thinking in Western civilization is based on a notion that men and women are opposites, so that if man is rational, woman must be irrational, if man is human, woman must either be demonic or angelic." For suddenly deconstructive Stockton, here was proof that falsehoods propped up the patriarchy.

IN THE AFTERMATH of the Danceteria 2 debacle, people around Jim Fouratt began to get sick and die. An epidemic of pneumonia had started in the gay world, and was first made public by the Centers for Disease Control in June 1981.[12] A New York skin doctor named Alvin Friedman-Kien had found a cancer, Kaposi's sarcoma, in gay men who'd had frequent, multiple sexual encounters with as many as ten partners a night. Many of them were also drug users.[13]

By the end of that year, the demi-monde was buzzing with concern about something scientists called Gay-Related Immune Deficiency (GRID). Fouratt's oldest friend had fallen in love with a singer named

Michael Callen (b. 1955), who'd come down with it. Several Danceteria performers and a journalist who'd written about Fouratt had caught it, too. When Fouratt visited the journalist in the hospital, one of the performers, Klaus Nomi (b. 1945), was in a room down the hall. "That was the first time I faced this," Fouratt says with uncharacteristic brevity.

Looking for a way to help, Fouratt discovered an organization started in August 1981, Gay Men's Health Crisis (GMHC). A co-founder, a gay writer, Larry Kramer (b. 1935), had made himself a pariah in his community in 1977 by openly questioning the carnality of white, upper-middle-class, urban gay culture in a novel with the provocative title *Faggots*. "All we do is live in our ghetto and dance and drug and fuck," he wrote in his satiric plea for love and commitment. Late in 1981, Kramer again played Patrick Henry, with a series of articles on GRID in a gay newspaper the *New York Native*.

Few wanted to listen. The city's gay elite was closed to Kramer's warnings; it had institutionalized promiscuity as a cornerstone of gay identity and culture—and was now getting support in that view from academia. Just as Kathryn Bond Stockton found validation in Theory, gays claimed the same benefit from anonymous sex.[14] After attending a few of the initial GMHC dinners, Fouratt felt his fellow homosexuals would find it easier to accept the reality of their situation if GRID weren't seen as a *gay* disease. Others—including many gay doctors—were equally uncomfortable with the first word in GMHC's name. The disease had already crossed out of the gay population; hemophiliacs had begun to contract it through blood transfusions. That July, researchers coined a new name, AIDS, for Acquired Immune Deficiency Syndrome.

Fouratt quickly organized a new group, Wipe Out AIDS, in the hope that women and heterosexuals might join the fight. He put his hippie experience to work by sponsoring consciousness-raising sessions about how to avoid AIDS and whether it was possible to survive it. Others had also begun to raise the fine point that it was certain sexual practices, not homosexuality itself, that transmitted the disease. Late in 1982, Callen and a former gay prostitute and backroom bar habitué co-wrote an article decrying the notion that frank talk about responsible sexual behavior stigmatized the gay world. Though denounced as prudes and charged with encouraging homophobia, they collaborated the next year with Callen's doctor on the first safe sex instruction pamphlet, *How to Have Sex in an Epidemic*.

Though he kept a hand in the music business, managing several artists, Fouratt became a full-time AIDS activist. Wipe Out AIDS continued to sponsor informational meetings for the next two years. At one, as an expert discussed the health benefits of a macrobiotic diet, Fouratt found himself thinking, "What does macrobiotics really give to someone? A sense of discipline. What is the biggest problem gay men have with their lives? Lack of discipline, lack of self-control." He decided his group should advocate discipline, which meant championing an unpopular honesty. In 1984, Fouratt joined a Safer Sex Committee calling for doors to be taken off stalls in the gay bathhouses. That idea won him few friends.

Wipe Out AIDS was renamed HEAL (for Help Education AIDS Liaison) and began organizing 1960s-style agitprop actions to encourage sex education. HEAL members put out piles of safe sex literature in bathhouses and graffittied the walls of sex clubs with slogans like *AIDS Lives Here!* and *Sleaze Breeds Disease,* and were beaten by security men at one club in response. They researched who owned the gay establishments and discovered it was mostly gay people, not the Mafia, as in the sixties. "Gay entrepreneurs were worse," says Fouratt. "The only places willing to put up safe sex posters were the Mafia clubs."

Despite the insistence of the activists on their right to have sex, the public came to agree with Fouratt and his more careful fellows. By 1985, public sex of any kind—gay or straight—was no longer tolerated. Across the country, cities began to close down gay baths and straight sex clubs like New York's infamous Plato's Retreat, finally turning the page on 1960s-style promiscuity.

WHEN MARIANNE WILLIAMSON presented herself at the Philosophical Research Society in Los Angeles in 1983, her sketchy résumé proved a godsend. There was an opening for a lecturer on *A Course in Miracles.* Her first appearance, advertised with handbills, was enough of a success that the society offered her a yearlong lecture series, every Saturday morning.

Supporting herself with secretarial temp jobs, Williamson lived for those Saturdays. "When I started speaking in 1983, self-help yuppies were not my audience," she says. Addressing people in their fifties, the sort who might have come to hear Aimee Semple McPherson preach half a century before, Williamson combined her growing knowledge of the *Course* with her experiences as a seventh-grade debater and 1970s lounge singer and realized, "I am an orator; that's what I do."

After about a year, her audience began to change. "Gay people started trickling in," she says. "AIDS had hit Los Angeles. All of a sudden, you had a population in dire crisis and when they went to their churches, they were being told they were a bunch of sinners. Profound human crisis was the crucible out of which my career sprang."

Gay men could relate to Williamson. She was chic, charismatic and best of all, a former good-time girl who'd discovered being bad wasn't enough. She gave them hope and ginger ale and conducted heartfelt question-and-answer sessions after her talks, strolling through her audience like an afternoon TV talk show host. They called her a jazz philosopher and compared her to Janis Joplin, sharing her pain in order to succor others. "One night there were seventy-five people and I remember feeling scared," she says. "I shared that, and I got such a strong, strong feeling and message: Nobody here is thinking you're perfect, Miss Williamson. Your responsibility is to be honest." Soon she'd added Tuesday night lectures, then started renting out space in churches and halls so she could speak to even larger crowds. She professes not to know how word got out. "How does anybody find out anything?" she asks.

JUST BEFORE SHE'D gone to England in 1983, Victoria Leacock went to a fundraising dinner at the home of the head of the new American Foundation for AIDS Research. She didn't know anyone who had the disease then. Two years later, a half-dozen people she knew had gotten it, all gay. She continued to live dangerously. Her drinking escalated. She started blacking out and getting into romantic situations that were something less than romantic.

Change was indicated. But where to go? In the mid-1980s, New York rich and poor separated. On the club scene, yuppies stayed uptown and celebrated their money alongside Europeans who flooded the city looking to make some of their own, while those who would have once been in the counterculture went downtown and celebrated art and their artistic lifestyle.

Leacock got a job as the receptionist at *Details*, then a black-and-white journal of the downtown scene, published by a woman called Annie Flanders, who'd run a pop fashion boutique in the 1960's.[15] Downtown had replaced uptown as the source of the city's cultural heat, as surely as Area had replaced Studio 54. *Details* was the new bohemia's update on the underground newspaper, covering not revolution but fabulousness.

Leacock stayed two years, rising to advertising manager. She loved her new milieu, full of simultaneously entrepreneurial and artistic types fixated on a new paradigm of self-expression. "This was a group of talented people trying to be very individualistic," Leacock says. "It was, 'Let's celebrate us, let's celebrate our friends.' All of a sudden, fame was more accessible. I could be famous. You could be famous. We could all be famous."

* * *

IN MARCH 1983, Leslie Crocker Snyder became a judge in New York's criminal court, handling arraignments, bail and motion hearings, and a few misdemeanor trials. Her star rose quickly in troubled times. Crime in the city had exploded. By the 1980s, the municipal courts were overwhelmed. Snyder moved as many as 300 cases a day—offenses like low-level drug crime and shoplifting—through her courtroom.

The atmosphere worsened markedly in 1984 when a highly addictive, smokable form of cocaine called crack hit America's streets. Crack shattered the complacency of baby boomers, who'd long considered drugs a private matter, and only occasionally a problem. Despite years of negative reinforcement, even heroin had retained a certain glamour, perversely encouraged by the overdose deaths of troubled rock stars, comedians and actors. Into the early 1980s, many boomers were eager to try, or at least know about, the latest new drug. High prices gave them a strange exclusivity, even when the experience was downright seedy, but crack's price—as low as $1 a vial—allowed almost anyone to become a buyer or seller. Most of the defendants Snyder saw in court were black and Hispanic. "That doesn't mean I didn't see a few white Yuppie types come through," she says. "But yuppies were buying drugs inside, whereas the minorities were out on the street, much more subject to being arrested." Drug crime had left the relatively innocent days of the Brotherhood of Eternal Love behind.

Perhaps it was a coincidence, but post-crack, the latest drug fashion among boomers was rehab. Age and abuse had taken their toll, and the drug scene suddenly lost any lingering allure and turned downright scary. "No codes, no rules, because crack, as we all now know, was not only highly addictive, but also had a total aspect of violence," Snyder says. "Dealers were taking over streets, shooting people from rooftops. There were wanton killings. Crack just overwhelmed everything."

AFTER TWO YEARS arranging adventure travel for Bill Graham Presents, Cameron Sears was ready for a change when his friends at Grateful Dead Productions called in 1987. Although they hadn't been in a recording studio in seven years, the Dead were still one of American rock's premier live attractions, playing to audiences from aging hippies to teenage flower-child wannabes wanting an alternative to the "no future" nihilism of Generation X.

It was a turning point for the Dead. A year earlier, while on the road with Bob Dylan, its leader, Jerry Garcia, had gone into a near-fatal five-day diabetic coma, brought on by years of debilitating drug use. Ironically, the experience echoed the Dead's first Top Ten single, "Touch of Grey," which, as its title implies, dealt with issues of age, if not infirmity. Even so, the single, which got regular exposure on MTV, vastly increased the band's audience, and changed the nature of its concerts. Suddenly the Dead's traditionally mellow audience had to share arenas with rowdier, new-breed fans whose reaction to the peace and love set was, all too often, to kick it in the face.

That was the atmosphere when Sears joined Grateful Dead Productions as an assistant to the group's manager. "So now I'm in the music business, which I know nothing about," he says. His first meeting with the band was more like a hazing. When he tried to get the Dead onstage, the drummer snapped, "Don't talk to me or any of my friends ever again." Then, at 4:00 A.M., he was awakened by the news that the keyboard player had trashed his room. Sears found him half-naked, sprawled in a mess of broken furniture, plate glass, and ketchup. The drummer, who'd been sleeping in the next room, appeared, yelled, "Clean him up and make him shut up," and slammed the door in Sears's face.

By mid-1990, Sears was managing a band that was still controversial, three decades after the Acid Tests. Sears's predecessor had quit after a year in which two fans died, one breaking his neck outside a show in New Jersey, and the other while in police custody in Los Angeles, high on LSD. Just as he took over, the Dead's keyboard player died of a drug overdose.[16] Traveling with a twenty-three-ton sound system and a similarly weighty entourage of family and friends (still sometimes including the august Acid King, Owsley), Sears was in charge of a high-tech New Age caravan that sometimes killed.

Nonetheless, he was in heaven. "I *still* have to pinch myself sometimes," he says. Not only was he working for his adolescent idols, but it was a multimillion-dollar business. Unfortunately, municipalities around America had long since lost their innocence about the side effects of rock and roll concerts. "So we were constantly having to deal with police chiefs and city bureaucrats," Sears says. "The kids of people who turned on to the Grateful Dead in 1968 were now coming to our shows, and there were those who resented the persistence of geezer rock 'n' roll." Now that rock's latest fashion, the alternative ethic, had crashed into the world of Deadheads, "we started having difficulty with our audience," Sears says. "The rebellion against authority espoused in the sixties reinvented itself in a way that is anti-everything. So we would have these kids, maybe as many as five hundred to a thousand, literally homeless, following us around with a very aggressive attitude. Their attitude was, Jerry Garcia would want me to take drugs and break into the venue. So we'd write impassioned, well-crafted statements to these kids, asking them to chill out. Jerry signed them in his own hand. But these guys were such jerks, there was absolutely no conversation with them."

Rock's tradition of rebellion had evolved, in its third next generation, into "an anger that's unchannelable," Sears says. "There's no resolution to it. They'd say, 'The world's a shithole, there's no prospect for me.'" And the Grateful Dead, who'd espoused the freedom that had now mutated into anarchy, weren't alone in failing to come up with answers.

DAVID McINTOSH WAS enjoying real estate law, but when his Federalist Society friends, who'd gone to work for the Reagan Justice Department, called and invited him to Washington in 1986, he jumped at the chance. In the intervening years, their creation had become influential on and off campus. All twelve of the Reagan administration's assistant attorneys general were members or friends of the society.[17] Co-founder Lee Lieberman was working as a clerk for justice Antonin Scalia at the Supreme Court. McIntosh got a job alongside another co-founder, Steven Calabrese, as a policymaking special assistant to Attorney General Meese, who'd prosecuted Berkeley Free Speech Movement protesters in 1964 and been made the nation's top law enforcer in 1985 after serving as Reagan's chief of staff.

Their influence was quickly felt throughout Washington as they sought to limit what they termed "judicial activism" by overturning liberal court decisions and screening nominees for the federal bench. "America was somewhat divided," McIntosh says. "Americans wanted to have it both ways, wanted to have bits of the sixties revolution of freer lifestyle *and* a traditional moral standard." He felt challenged to chart a course between them.

His boss tended toward tradition. In speeches, Meese railed against judges taking the law into their own hands, ignoring the Constitution, and usurping the rights of localities to set their own judicial standards, and spoke out against several landmark Supreme Court decisions, including Miranda, which mandated that police tell arrestees their rights, and Cooper v. Aaron, the 1958 case that desegregated schools in Little Rock, Arkansas.[18]

As Meese's whip, or manager, McIntosh ensured that the attorney general's directives were carried out, "a tremendous opportunity for somebody interested in Constitutional law," he says. "There were real intellectual debates going on inside the Justice Department, and we were filing briefs on abortion, on property rights. A lot of the career attorneys in the Solicitor General's office were on the opposite side of these issues."

MEESE'S TEAM DID not prevail in their controversial attempt to overturn *Roe* v. *Wade*, the 1973 Supreme Court decision that legalized abortion. McIntosh, who believes life begins in the womb and should be protected, had often argued about abortion with friends. "My view was we were talking about an intellectual issue and then I found out it had a real impact in someone's life," he says. A friend told him, "I had an abortion; does that mean you think I'm a bad person?" Wanting to stay consistent and true to his conscience, but not condemn those who held different views, McIntosh found safe refuge in federalism. "With one national standard, you've got people on all sides feeling unhappy," he says. "You'd have a better chance of consensus if you let communities or states decide whether they wanted to allow abortions. So Indiana could have a consensus where abortions are rare, and in New York, they'd be more readily available."

At twenty-nine, McIntosh moved to the Reagan White House as a domestic affairs aide under the new chief of staff, Howard Baker, and helped draft legislation "on everything from tax cuts to welfare reform to missile defense systems," he says. Just as important were the lessons he learned about politicking. "There's a lot at stake and staff people are all fairly ambitious," he says. "You don't leave your backside unattended."

DONALD TRUMP'S RARE ability to erect buildings on time and on budget dazzled bankers, who gave him unlimited credit. Trump was selling skill, without question; but he was also selling his obsessive bravado. That, and the compulsive spending that went with it, made him one of the tycoons of *Women's Wear Daily*'s nouvelle society, the latest insurgency against the stolid institutions of American power.

This new generation of wealth was the first to include baby boomers, whose wishes were now being fulfilled by a variety of economic factors ranging from the ever-growing federal debt to its private equivalent, the high-yield securities known as junk bonds touted by Michael Milken (b. 1946) of the investment house Drexel Burnham Lambert. In the hands of hostile-takeover artists and mergers-and-acquisition experts engaged in leveraged (i.e., financed with borrowed money) buyouts, junk bonds played a key role in retooling old companies for a new millennium and financing a new generation of American businesses like MCI, CNN and

Steve Wynn's casino empire. Their credo was simple: "Greed is good," as Gordon Gekko so memorably put it in the movie *Wall Street*, written and directed by Oliver Stone (b. 1946).

Corporate debt increased from $774 billion in 1979 to $2.1 trillion in 1989, growing 2.5 times as fast as the economy. Junk bonds represented about 28 percent of that amount. Called junk because they are the last to be repaid in the event of bankruptcy, the bonds were highly risky to investors. They were risky for issuers, too. Some, like fashion designer Calvin Klein, who expanded his business with Drexel bonds, were quickly driven to the brink of bankruptcy by high interest payments. But the stock market kept rising, as did real estate prices, speculation and the celebrity heaped on perceived leaders of the new pack of financial wolves, many of whom swept through the corridors of Wall Street and past the tables of museum benefits buzzed on cocaine. Counterpoints to the crack dealers of the crumbling ghettoes, they, too, were hunters looking for a kill. Who would control Getty Oil? RJR Nabisco? Who would head the Forbes 400? Who'd mount whose head on the wall?

They bought and sold junk, took over some companies, gutted some with downsizing, built others with deregulation, fought politicians one day and supported them the next. They lived in trophy houses with trophy wives, were barbarians in business but turned into lambs when they stormed the social barricades. Though many were older, Henry Kravis (b. 1944), Ronald O. Perelman (b. 1943), and Trump proved that baby boomers could do it, too. They also helped nudge their generation rightward on economic issues: against organized labor and big government and toward free trade, deregulation and tax cuts.

Between 1985 and 1990, Donald and Ivana Trump lived large, trading in their Hamptons rental for a forty-five-room Georgian weekend estate on five acres in tony Greenwich, Connecticut, and combining two triplex penthouses in Trump Tower into a Versailles-in-the-Sky. Trump bought cereal heiress Marjorie Merriweather Post's ocean-to-bay 118-room Palm Beach estate Mar-a-Lago (complete with private golf course and 400-foot beach), Saudi arms broker Adnan Khashoggi's 282-foot yacht, with its gold-plated bathroom and waterfall, a football team, two Atlantic City casinos, the Plaza Hotel, a Boeing 727, several helicopters, a small airline, and full-page ads in major newspapers criticizing American foreign policy, sparking rumors that he would run for President.

If that wasn't enough of a display of hubris, the Yuppie Icarus alienated his political allies in New York by demanding a billion-dollar, twenty-year tax abatement to build something he called Trump City, with 7,600 luxury apartments, a mall, a 9,000-car garage, a nine-acre riverfront park and twelve skyscrapers, one of which would top out at 150 stories—giving New York (and Trump) bragging rights to the world's tallest building. Unimpressed, New York's Mayor Koch called Trump "piggy, piggy, piggy," and the developer responded by dubbing the three-term Mayor an incompetent moron.

Trump admits that, sitting atop a personal fortune variously estimated at $1 billion to $3 billion, he looked to see if others were as impressed with him as he was with himself, but never once looked inward at his motives or at what he'd become. He was the ultimate solipsist. "I don't know if that was the ethic of the age," he says. "But it was my ethic. Everything I touched turned to gold. The Grand Hyatt wasn't supposed to work. The convention center wasn't supposed to work. Nothing was supposed to work. And they all worked. So you don't listen to anybody, because they're all idiots."

CYNTHIA BOWMAN HAD cut her ties to her adolescent rock idols in 1985. Unlike many of her former fellow freaks, she didn't go yuppie, though. "I maybe bought a couple of suits, so that when I went to a meeting at the symphony people could relate to me better, but I did not look like one of them. And I did not think like them, either."

She redressed her life, however. "I realized that if anything ever happened to me, my kid wouldn't have a mother," she says. "I really wanted to be somebody my kid could be proud of."

Drug casualties had long been a part of the rock scene. An original member of the Jefferson Airplane, Skip Spence (b. 1946), had exacerbated his paranoid schizophrenia with repeated applications of Owsley LSD and ended up institutionalized for years before his death at age fifty-two. Other musicians had been felled by overdose, liver failure, heart attack. "If you don't figure it out, you die or you go to jail; if you do, you survive," Bowman notes summarily. She didn't suddenly go straight—she's stayed friends with pot smokers—but she banned both marijuana and cigarettes from her house when her son caught a cold after being exposed to secondhand smoke.

Then there was AIDS. Like most boomers, Bowman had friends among its the early victims in the mid-1980s—and couldn't help being affected. "Since 1984, there have only been a few men in my life," she says. "When Alex was born, I decided I was eliminating all the riffraff and emotional turmoil that comes along with it."

* * *

IN JANUARY 1986, a group of six criminal court judges were promoted to New York's Supreme Court, to handle the explosion of felonies related to crack. "No one wanted to do those violent drug gang cases," Snyder recalls, "because they were perceived to be extremely dangerous. But they're important, they sounded interesting, they had to be done." Snyder's forte became multiple-defendant A–1 narcotics felonies—complex cases involving the sale or possession of large quantities of drugs and the violence that often accompanies them.

Once crack dealers started getting arrested, Snyder heard her first wiretap evidence of Colombians from the Cali cocaine cartel talking about wholesale distribution, and was shocked. "We're not talking junkies and nickel bags," she says. "We're talking greed, violence, they don't care who gets in the way. And I start feeling this is very serious stuff." Even more serious than the typical midlevel heroin dealer raking in $500,000 a week.

One early case involved a defendant who'd turned down a plea bargain of four years to life—a tiny sentence for major drug dealing. "But the problem with going to trial is that the judge hears and sees the evidence," she says. What Snyder heard—that the dealer was a member of organized crime, used his wife to take phone messages about drug deals, and took her and their infant on drug runs—convinced her to give him the maximum sentence allowable by law. "That was my first twenty-five years to life sentence, and I thought about it a lot," she says. She decided that in her courtroom, at least, a line would be drawn against mayhem.

Snyder thus became anathema to criminal lawyers. "Clearly, the Constitution tends to protect defendants, not victims," she says. "We have a job protecting defendants' rights, and I do it. But I'm also always aware that victims have rights, too." Early on, defense attorneys argued when Snyder cut off abusive or humiliating cross-examinations of victims. They don't anymore. "People know me now," she says with a smile. "I don't put up with a lot of crap in my courtroom." Defense attempts to overturn her decisions didn't dent her determination. In her first five years on the Supreme Court bench, her decisions were affirmed on appeal seventy-one times and reversed only three.

THROUGHOUT HER YEARS at *Details*, Victoria Leacock continued producing plays for Jonathan Larson. Aside from that, her life was spinning out of control. She started calling Alcoholics Anonymous, asking about meetings, then ran away to Europe "and exiled myself," she says. When she returned, heavy, unhappy, blacking out instead of falling asleep and waking up with shaking hands, she finally went to a meeting.

A few days later, in August 1988, she had dinner with and a lecture from a girlfriend named Ali Gertz. Two years younger than Leacock, Gertz had been one of the underage preppies who'd frequented Studio 54. "I was going out on a lot of first dates that wouldn't amount to anything, falling into the arms of the person I was with because I was not in a position to extract myself from those situations," Leacock says. Gertz decried her carelessness, then called it an early night. She wasn't feeling well. Two weeks later, she was in the hospital. A few days after that, Leacock got a phone call from a mutual friend.

"Ali has been diagnosed," she said.

"Oh my God," said Leacock, "It's cancer."

"No, Vicki, it's AIDS."

Leacock sank to the floor, clutching the phone. "I really had this crystal-clear knowledge that my entire life had changed at that moment, and that if Ali Gertz could get AIDS, anybody could." It took months before Gertz figured out how she'd contracted the virus. Her boyfriend of three years tested negative. She'd slept with perhaps six other men, and she managed to find and eliminate all but two of them. Finally, someone reminded her of a one-night stand she'd forgotten.

"Why?" she asked. "Is he sick?"

Came the reply, "Well, no, he's dead."

It turned out Gertz had caught the disease from the second man she ever slept with. She'd lost her virginity at sixteen to a summer romance, then spent the next year and a half flirting with one of Studio 54's bare-chested bartenders. "They finally made a date while her parents were out of town for the weekend, and he came over to her Park Avenue apartment and brought roses and champagne, and they slept together, and it was very good, and they decided to stay friends," Leacock reports. She'd asked him if he was gay; he'd lied and said no. Five years later, she'd come down with pneumonia. No one in the hospital thought to run a test for HIV, the virus that causes AIDS, until she'd been there for two weeks without improving.

Gertz asked around about the bartender, and learned that his family had refused to pick up his body from the morgue after he'd died. "That is when Ali became a political activist," Leacock says. "She was really appalled." She realized that before it spread further, someone had to tell the world that AIDS wasn't a gay disease—or a punishment for immoral behavior. "It's funny," says Leacock. "I took care of my mom for six years. She died. I was an alcoholic within a year. I finally stopped drinking, and that's when Ali was diagnosed. I had my calling and I was ready for the job."

In spring 1989, Gertz's mother called a *New York Times* reporter to ask why the paper never wrote about AIDS in the heterosexual community. He replied that no women with AIDS would come forward. Ali would. Her story ran on a Saturday when Gertz was away. When she came home, her answering machine had broken down after fielding 216 messages. Gertz gave interviews to *People* and television's *20/20*. *Esquire* named her its Woman of the Year. She began traveling the country, speaking about AIDS in schools. Her message was, "It can happen to you," Leacock says. "It's not Them anymore. It's our sister, our daughter, my best friend."

Leacock meanwhile, got a new job at the New York Shakespeare Festival, and kept pursuing her dream of producing Larson's musicals— and his of reinventing the American musical. Since they couldn't get financing for a full production of his rock opera, *Superbia*, Larson turned his attention to a one-man show about turning thirty and the collision of his own doubts and insecurities with the cruel fact that his best friend from childhood had been diagnosed as HIV-positive.

Cruel facts were accumulating in Leacock's life. Her surrogate brother, Gordon Rogers, with whom she was sharing an apartment, started limping, then slowly lost control of his appendages—a result of Guillaime-Barr disease. For three months he was on a respirator. Just as he began to recover, he learned that he, too, was HIV-positive. Then their roommate, Pam Shaw, came down with a yeast infection that wouldn't go away. She wasn't promiscuous, she never did IV drugs, and her gynecologist told her there was no need to be tested, Leacock says. But there was—she had AIDS. "She had no immune system," Leacock says.

BARBARA LEDEEN'S RÉSUMÉ lists her occupation from 1984 to 1988 as director of communications for Ronald Reagan's deputy undersecretary of defense for trade security policy, Stephen Bryen (b. 1942). A friend of her husband's, Bryen was a former congressional aide and protégé of the assistant defense secretary, Richard Perle (b. 1941), who oversaw "secure technology transfer policy in what became the final battle against the Soviet Union," she says.

Bryen hired Ledeen to promote their work in the press, to help explain their mission to technology companies whose foreign sales might be affected, and to fight opposition from government agencies that sometimes put business interests ahead of national security. Extraordinarily, despite her Marxist background, Ledeen was able to win top-secret security clearances. "If you told the truth, it was okay," she says. "The issue was blackmail; you couldn't blackmail me. So I went to work in the belly of the beast, at the Pentagon, where I had demonstrated. And to say that I felt like a piece of shit is not even close. I would think, How do I expiate my stupidity? Sometimes I would say it and they would say, Fine, let's go fight communism."

After her third child was born in 1986, Ledeen was embroiled in the biggest scandal of the Reagan era, the Iran-Contra affair. Shortly after the arms-for-hostages deal was first proposed to her husband, he'd been sidelined—kept out of the loop by his NSA colleague (and until then, friend) Oliver North, and Oliver Poindexter, who'd replaced Robert McFarlane at NSA. Only later did Ledeen found out why. North had not only pursued the Iran arms deal, but, in an apparent attempt to obscure his own diversion of the profits to Nicaragua's Contras, wrote an e-mail to Poindexter claiming that Ledeen was taking fifty dollars per missile from the Iranians.[19]

North's secret triangle trade continued until fall 1986. When it was revealed, Reagan was forced to fire him, Poindexter resigned, and a special commission began investigating the NSC. That November, shortly after Attorney General Meese disclosed the Iran-Contra connection and the FBI began a criminal probe, Ledeen was let go as an NSC consultant and asked to leave his think tank. An independent counsel, Lawrence Walsh, was appointed to investigate the deal and the Ledeens, the beginning of a long nightmare for the couple.

"They went through our phone records for seven years, they went through my children's bank account funds, my little Pentagon lunch money account," Barbara says. "The head of my twelve-year-old daughter's middle school said to her, 'Is your daddy guilty?' My son couldn't get into another school because his dad was controversial." Murky stories were recycled. "Michael was a sitting duck for this," Barbara says. In 1989 the Reagan administration ended, and she left the Pentagon. "The Bush people are the other Republican party, the moderates, and they got rid of every Reagan appointee," she says. "The fight we'd fought on tech transfers was no longer viable. But we had done the job." Though the Berlin Wall fell on November 9, 1989,[20] during Bush's presidency, it was Reagan and his team who properly got the credit. Though proud of the small part she'd played in it, Ledeen felt there was still much left undone by the Reagan Revolution.

Shortly after leaving the Pentagon, she met David Horowitz and Peter Collier, two former Berkeley radicals who'd undergone a similar conversion to neoconservatism. Horowitz asked what she was interested in. "I want blood," she said. "I am so pissed. I can't live my life until I get even." They made Ledeen executive director of the Second Thoughts Project, a sort of support group they'd started for former leftists who'd seen the error of their ways. Ledeen grudgingly acknowledges that the Left made good on some of its promises. "There was no opportunity before, you could not bust through the top, and that was worth fighting for," she says. "But why can't they declare victory and fucking go home?"

IN 1986, DOUG Marlette and his wife had a son. The day after the birth, Bill Kovach, a former Washington bureau chief of the *New York Times* who'd just been made the editor of the *Atlanta Journal-Constitution*, called Marlette. Atlanta was the great city of the South, and Kovach said he wanted to make a great national newspaper and wanted Marlette to join him. "I told my wife I was going to win the Pulitzer Prize there," he says. Two years later he did.

It was a good time for cartooning. When Colorado senator Gary Hart (b. 1936), a veteran of the 1960s anti-war movement, pitched his 1988 presidential campaign at baby boomers by promising new ideas, then stumbled in a sex scandal, Marlette skewered him relentlessly, outraged by Hart's taunting the press to find him out. One cartoon, bannered "Front Runner," showed Hart with his pants around his ankles.

"It was good material in terms of the issues of restriction and restraint and indulgence and entitlement," he says. "That sense of entitlement was one of the terrible things with our generation. We were so self-righteous, so pious. And then we get caught in our contradictions and we're stunned. We thought we were invincible! And we wanted to tell everybody else how to live!" Hart was forced out of the race.

The Bush administration wasn't as sexy and fun as the election that led to it. "You're kind of held hostage to the headlines," Marlette says. As a newspaper employee, he was also held hostage to forces larger than himself. Bill Kovach resigned in November 1988, following an argument with his bosses about the paper's take-no-prisoners reporting style. Kovach had angered business leaders by challenging Atlanta's reputation as the city too busy to hate with a Pulitzer Prize-winning series about local banks refusing to make loans to blacks. Marlette was vocal in his disapproval of the ouster. His support of Kovach—he gave interviews and spoke out at a rally protesting the editor's departure—made Marlette's situation untenable, so he, too, left Atlanta, in February 1989. *Newsday,* a local newspaper on Long Island, was opening an edition in New York City and needed a cartoonist.

The move to liberal New York didn't keep Marlette out of trouble in the South. He'd been picking on Jesse Helms for years. Wall-eyed behind his horn-rims, the rabid conservative was a cartoonist's dream. At first, Helms had demoralized Marlette by requesting the original art whenever the cartoonist drew him, but eventually, he began complaining. When Helms attacked the idea of Martin Luther King Day, Marlette drew a cartoon suggesting that April Fool's Day be renamed in Helms's honor. In 1984, when Helms won a vicious reelection campaign, Marlette drew him with *his* pants around his ankles, sticking his rear end out a window toward the U.S. Capitol over the caption "Carolina Moon Keeps Shining . . ." The next day, Helms's office stopped returning the *Charlotte Observer*'s phone calls.

"I understood Jesse," Marlette says. "I can be self-righteous like that. I am Jesse Helms. That's why I get under his skin, and why he gets under my skin." So six years later, with Helms running for reelection again, Marlette wrote him into "Kudzu." In response to Helms's attacks on the National Endowments for the Arts and the Humanities, he drew a cartoon Helms, suffering from Cold War Separation Anxiety, finding a new enemy in the evil International Artistic Conspiracy. Those strips earned "Kudzu" an election-cycle exile to the op-ed pages of some North Carolina papers, and banishment from the *Raleigh News & Observer.* Only after hundreds of complaints did the paper agree to reinstate "Kudzu" and run the Helms strips—the day *after* the election.

INEVITABLY, DONALD TRUMP'S luck changed. In April 1985, he'd installed Ivana as president of his second Atlantic City casino-hotel, Trump Castle. After three children, the sexual energy in the Trump marriage had faltered. For the first time, the pair were not side by side. Several times a week, Ivana made the hourlong run to Atlantic City in the couple's sleek black Puma helicopter. Arriving at 9:30, she spent her days entertaining 10,000 visitors, supervising 4,000 employees, reviewing books and purchasing and marketing, signing checks, and getting a crash course in casino and hotel operations before flying back to New York at 4:30. In her spare time she planned benefits for causes like cerebral palsy and cancer research and managed the couple's homes and the kids.

Trump's eye started wandering. Friends heard rumors about Donald and a professional ice skater, several actresses and nouvelle socialites, and finally, Marla Maples (b. 1963), a beautiful model from Georgia. By spring 1988, when Trump bought New York's Plaza Hotel and brought Ivana back from Atlantic City to run it, stories linking Maples with Trump were common coin in insider circles. Ivana set to work renovating the Plaza and got herself spruced up as well. Sometime in the spring of 1989, she visited a cosmetic surgeon. A few months later, Ivana visited another expert, a divorce lawyer.

Then came Aspen, Colorado. On December 30, 1989, the Trump family was outside a restaurant halfway down Ajax Mountain when Maples approached Ivana and they had words. The children kept going, but Donald Trump joined the two women and asked what was going on. A few seconds later, Ivana and Donald skied off grim-faced. She pulled ahead of Donald, skiing backward. A few more words were exchanged. Back in New York, Ivana called Michael Kennedy, who started an intensive but fruitless negotiation to save the marriage.

Early in February 1990, when Trump flew to Tokyo for a Mike Tyson fight and to meet with bankers, Ivana's team went into action, going public with her legal arguments. By the end of that month, there was more trouble in Trump's world. Rumors began to spread that he was in a financial bind. The rumors were true. Suddenly Ivana Trump's biggest concern was establishing her place in the line of Trump's creditors.

Midas had lost his touch, disempowered by an economy souring in the early days of the Bush presidency. Real estate values in the Northeast and Southwest flattened and declined, and savings and loan institutions that had invested in that real estate were failing. In February 1989, inflation showed its biggest jump in two years. The Resolution Trust Corporation, set up by Bush that month, drove real estate prices down further by dumping the assets of troubled S&Ls it had seized at fire-sale prices.

Prosecutors had been on the trail of financial high fliers since the Ivan Boesky insider trading scandal broke open in 1986. In March 1989, Michael Milken was indicted in Manhattan on ninety-eight counts of fraud and securities violations stemming from the Boesky case. Though he pleaded not guilty, Drexel Burnham Lambert put him on leave and settled its own disputes with the government, plunging the junk bond market into a deep slump. Milken finally agreed to plead guilty to six felonies, to go to jail, and to pay $600 million in penalties. Stocks hit a new high that October, but took their second-worst hit in history a few days later, just after a proposed buyout of United Airlines collapsed. Japan's stock market tanked, too.[21] The go-go 1980s were gone-gone.

At first, it seemed Trump hadn't noticed. He played hardball with his wife and opened his third casino in Atlantic City, the opulent Taj Mahal. Just before the opening, though, a gambling analyst said the casino couldn't cover its costs. A month later, *Forbes* cast doubt on both Trump's net worth and his financial stability, claiming his properties, worth $3.7 billion, were encumbered by $3.2 billion of debt. His bankers were paying attention. Attempts to refinance the Grand Hyatt and Trump Tower failed. So, too, did the plans for Trump City. Environmental activists tied it up in knots, costing him millions. And no one would lend him the $20 million he needed to build penthouses atop the Plaza Hotel.

In June, for his forty-forth birthday, Trump missed a deadline for a $42 million payment on the bonds that financed another of his casinos, Trump Castle, and a $30 million payment on a personally guaranteed loan, and Moody's Investor Services downgraded the ratings of bonds for the Taj and Trump Plaza casinos. "The 1990s sure aren't anything like the 1980s," he reportedly said. He'd just returned from promoting his second book, *Trump: Surviving at the Top*, when the *Wall Street Journal* revealed that he'd begun negotiations a month earlier to restructure his debt.[22] In the cold light of the new decade, some of his deal-making no longer looked so artful. He'd paid top dollar and more for properties that, in the mean new economy, were no longer performing. The slowdown hit his hotels, casinos and airline, and real estate sales were especially hard hit by the credit crunch and the disappearance of Japanese capital.

Trump's bankers were in as much trouble as he was, with credit tight as a noose around all their necks.[23] The "workout" of Trump's debt, begun when banks loaned him an additional twenty million dollars to make the missed payments and avoid personal bankruptcy, continued for a year and provoked an avalanche of bad publicity. It was gleefully repeated that in December 1990, Trump's father bought $3.5 million in casino chips to give his son interest-free cash to pay his bills.

"The 1990s are a decade of de-leveraging," Trump told *Time* that spring. "I'm doing it too." In exchange for $65 million in new loans and an easing of the terms on old ones, Trump gave up control of his personal and business finances; brought in a bank-approved chief financial officer; handed over land in Atlantic City and hundreds of New York condominiums; sold his yacht, the Trump shuttle, his half-interest in the Grand Hyatt, and other properties; limited his household spending (to $450,000 a month in 1990, dropping to $300,000 by 1992); and agreed to submit monthly itemized business plans for his bankers' approval.[24] He got to keep Trump Tower, the Plaza, the Penn Central yard, Mar-a-Lago, and half of his three casinos, though he was forced to reorganize the finances of the Taj Mahal under bankruptcy protection and eventually traded most of his equity in the Penn Central property for release of personal loan guarantees. "I was in really deep shit," Trump says. "You know, publicity is a funny thing. It does create value. But if things go bad, you get it."

One day during the workout, Trump was walking in front of Tiffany & Co. with Marla Maples when he saw a beggar. "Look at that man over there," he said. "Do you know he's worth more than I am?"

"But he's a beggar!" Maples argued. "He's worth nothing."

"Right," Trump replied. "And I'm worth *minus* nine hundred million dollars."

THE COLLAPSE OF the Soviet Union after George Bush's ascension to the presidency stunned Mark Rudd. "Socialism ceased to exist," he says. "It had really ceased to exist decades before, but my illusion was there was an alternative somewhere." In 1990, his beloved Sandinistas were defeated in an election, and the Nicaraguan civil war ended. Finally, the January 1991 Gulf War, in which American troops liberated Kuwait from Iraqi invaders, threw Rudd into a deep depression.

"The Gulf War was kind of like the end of the sixties," he says. "My disillusion was over the ease with which the United States military and propaganda machine was able to whip up support. They were mouthing ridiculous slogans about Saddam Hussein being Hitler and not looking at the real causes of the war, which were economic and geopolitical control! And the inevitable outcome of beating down the Islamic world was that now we are hated by hundreds of millions."

What made it all worse was the assent of Rudd's age peers, the very people who'd fought the same process in Vietnam twenty-five years earlier. It all sent Rudd into a six-year tailspin. He broke up with a girlfriend he'd been with for years, "started a series of disastrous relationships, and went into my forms of therapy and healing," he says. He tried massage therapy, homeopathy, acupressure, psychic healing, cranial sacral massage, and Reiki, "looking to heal myself from pain and hurt," he says. Through it all, he stuck to his political guns, only now, instead of trying to change the world, he worked on his little corner of it.

Having returned to teaching at the junior college in Albuquerque, Rudd got involved in his union and in a national movement to make math education more accessible to minorities and working women, the sort of students who filled his classroom. "They are people who never got what they needed in high school—the basics," he says. "People who've come out of prison, who are disabled and want to reenter the workforce.

Community college is the streets of education. No pretension. And a massive life transformation. It was the continuation of my investigation into how people learn, develop their critical capacity, change their lives, and transform their consciousness. Social change of any sort is going to require enormous changes in consciousness."

SHORTLY AFTER THE 1988 Republican Convention, David McIntosh quit his White House post to run a congressional campaign in Southern California's Orange County—the conservative enclave where John Gage was born—for a colleague from the White House Counsel's office, Christopher Cox (b. 1952). "I knew nothing about running a campaign," he admits, "but he had won a tough primary so he felt safe having a friend who knew nothing about politics being his campaign manager."

Cox had a political consultant who took McIntosh under his wing and taught him the art of campaigning. Briefly, he considered staying in California and building a political career there, but he decided it wasn't where he wanted to raise a family. "Children were under enormous pressure to try the latest things, whether it's drugs or clothes," he says. Though his family was still hypothetical, "I didn't want to subject them to that."

He moved back to Washington at the start of the Bush administration and spent three months unemployed, reading William Manchester's biography of Winston Churchill and taking comfort from the fact that the British leader had spent time in the political wilderness himself. "I was running up against the fact that the Bush people didn't want to hire former Reagan people," he says. Finally, his experience in regulatory law attracted the attention of his fellow Hoosier Dan Quayle, and he was offered a job on the new vice president's staff.

His Reaganite friends advised him against working for a man whose stumbling inexperience had made him a national joke. But McIntosh, remembering the impression Quayle had made on him in high school, said yes. "And I think because of that general view, he worked harder as vice president than other people have and was willing to take on some tough issues because he had to prove he could," McIntosh says.

In 1990, when McIntosh first considered returning to Indiana and making a run for Congress, Quayle kept him in Washington by naming him deputy director of the Competitiveness Council, formed to assess and recommend reforms of government regulations. He soon got another promotion, and headed the council for the remainder of the Bush administration. Though it wasn't glamorous, regulatory reform was a bedrock issue to conservatives. A mole among moderates, McIntosh dug in and bided his time.

IN FEBRUARY 1987, Steve Ross, the former funeral home executive who'd built Warner Communications into one of the world's most powerful entertainment companies, was looking for ways to make it even stronger. Meanwhile, HBO chairman Michael Fuchs was worriedly watching John Malone, a cable system owner from the west whose growing Tele-Communications, Inc. empire threatened Time's. Fuchs and his employers also worried that Time, the third-largest wire owner in America, might become the target of a takeover. Though it had a tradition of feuding with Warner, the sixth-biggest cable outfit, Fuchs proposed that the two companies should band together with several other Eastern competitors against Malone. Thinking Steve Ross would like that idea, he suggested to his boss, Nick Nicholas, that he give Ross a call.

Fuchs wasn't only ambitious for his company; he really wanted to run a movie studio. HBO had invested in the startup of Orion Pictures, and he had discussed succeeding Arthur Krim, its chairman and an old friend of the Fuchs family, but finally decided he'd invested so many years in Time, he'd be better off staying put. Even though a faction on Time's board was anti-entertainment, Levin and Nicholas agreed that Time could better control its destiny if it expanded into Hollywood. When Ross and Nicholas started talking merger, it looked as if they would all get what they wanted.

By summer, serious talks with Warner were under way. Levin, the company's strategist, was promoting the idea of a "transforming transaction"—a consolidation of Time, Warner, and perhaps Ted Turner's Turner Broadcasting System—that would turn Time into an entertainment-oriented communications behemoth.[25] In August, Fuchs met the heads of the Warner Brothers movie studio, Robert Daly and Terry Semel, at a sit-down with Ross and Nicholas and suggested HBO make four or five low-budget youth films a year for them, leveraging its relationships with comedians. Instead of synergy, there was a clash of titanic egos. The Warner executives shot Fuchs down. Fuchs, who insists Daly and Semel "felt the only guy at Time who could rain on their parade was me," says he hadn't expected an agreement—but why not try?

The Time-Warner merger, creating the world's largest media company and greatly enriching the top executives of both firms, was announced in

March 1989. By that time, the deal had been restructured as a cash- and stock-backed purchase of Warner by Time following Paramount Communications' hostile all-cash offer for Time. Though the final transaction was neither leveraged nor hostile, it was still a perfect symbol of the ego-driven dealmaking that began at the end of the Reagan era and has continued ever since. In order to assuage the powers atop both companies, it was agreed that after the merger, Nicholas and Ross would be co-chief executives, with the younger Nicholas taking over after five years. Nicholas presumably knew a secret: Ross had cancer, although it was in remission.

Fuchs made no secret of his unhappiness with the final terms of the merger. "The Warner people got bought out, paid out, and then got control," he says. "Our people sold out our people." Even after he'd decided to support the deal, he still worried that instead of running and expanding a well-regarded if small operation within a large corporation, he'd be lost in an immense enterprise in which he was proportionately less important. He suddenly had to be concerned about his place in the pecking order as well as HBO's in the public eye. Which audience would be more fickle—cable viewers or his superiors—was a toss-up.

Daly and Semel were not going to let him grow. Indeed, some thought they might even try to take over his fiefdom. Rumors flew that Warner boss Steve Ross's fair-haired boy, Bob Pittman, who'd returned to the company after his brief sojourn on his own, would take over HBO. Fuchs felt his position was unique and defensible. After the merger, even Time Inc., people who'd long disdained HBO saw him as an ally, "someone who kept the religion, but could function in that other world," Fuchs says.

He'd convinced himself that "Time's class and intellectual curiosity would rub off on Warner's, and Warner's aggressiveness would rub off on Time." It didn't quite work out that way. "After the merger, the consensus was that HBO suffered the most. We lost our identity, our ability to grow, because many of the things we would have grown into were already being done at Warner." Steve Ross "was going to have the upper hand," Fuchs says, "and Steve favored the movie studio." Officially, Time had taken over Warner, but its executives "began to be treated like household help," Fuchs continues. "They were walking around saying how well they were all getting together, when we all knew it was just a fucking shitstorm."

Even before the merger, Fuchs had begun a multifront effort to strengthen and expand his domain. "Funny is money," he'd always said, so in 1989 he launched the Comedy Channel, an advertiser-supported basic (i.e., free) cable service that would give HBO access to a much larger audience and a much-longed-for presence in the only area of the cable business still promising explosive growth potential. It didn't hurt that he'd be aiming it straight at the audience of the wildly successful MTV, a basic service owned by HBO's rival, Viacom.

Within days of the announcement, Viacom fired back. First, it filed a $2.4 billion lawsuit against Time and HBO, alleging that by favoring HBO over Viacom's Showtime and The Movie Channel on its cable systems, Time had engaged in anticompetitive practices. A few weeks later, Viacom president and CEO Frank Biondi, Fuchs's former employee-turned-employer, announced that MTV would be launching its own comedy subsidiary, HA! It did not go unnoticed that Biondi and other Viacom executives had worked at HBO when the alleged monopolistic practices began.

"I thought my manifest destiny was to run a comedy channel," Fuchs says. "HBO's early years were comedy. I was best known for that. I thought comedy would be the rock 'n' roll of the '90s. And I'm still convinced I could have done it." He pushed to get his channel on the air first, but Viacom's maneuvers, which included offering cable operators discounts on license fees for MTV and VH1, spoiled his plans. Faced with a choice, many cable operators refused to make a decision.[26] The Comedy Channel, featuring an MTV-ish comedy-clip format, went on the air that November. HA!, offering reruns of old situation comedies and funny films, launched the following April Fool's Day. Faced with losing fortunes in a war of attrition, the two cable giants quickly began talking about merging the startups. With Viacom's lawsuit and a Time countersuit hovering in the background, arguments over which team would run the new channel almost derailed the talks. Finally, in December 1990, a compromise was reached and the two channels agreed to merge under neutral management. Aware that the suit would be ruinous even if Time won, Fuchs then sought to settle it. In August 1992, he succeeded with a complicated deal encompassing concessions estimated to be worth a mere $170 million, far less than the $800 million in actual damages originally claimed. "Considering our exposure, I'd have to say we ducked a bullet," Fuchs says. In the next several years, driven by the programming he excelled at creating, HBO regained its momentum. In 1993 it added a million subscribers. The next year, it posted profits of $257 million, making it America's most profitable television channel.

Fuchs also raised his personal profile. In August 1990, he threw the first of a series of summer parties to promote HBO original movies in East Hampton, Long Island, a patrician resort that had lately begun attracting the powerful and the press. "I once asked Simon Wiesenthal why he lived in Austria," Fuchs recalls. "He said, 'If you want to study malaria, go where the mosquitoes are.' We understood you had to program to opinion-makers."

Fuchs understood more than that. A generation that had disdained logos in its youth had evolved into a logocentric herd that had to be the first with the latest, whether it was a Dolce & Gabbana dress or an opinion on the latest HBO movie. Money and success didn't give boomers security; in fact, quite the opposite was true. "Marketing, branding, high pressure, high level," Fuchs recites. "By branding you could raise the prices, you could create economic value without any real cost appreciation. That's what we did in the Hamptons. Now branding has become generic. Everyone talks about it. There is this incredible need to belong. T-shirts with names on them are an easy way. Maybe that's the Baby Boom's ultimate gift, this branded world. We perfected it."

WHILE STEVE CAPPS was in Europe in the mid-1980s, writing music-editing software for the Mac and sending his work to his co-authors over an early modem, the PC landscape changed drastically. Microsoft released Windows—its PARC-like, Mac-like operating system—and began its slow, steady rise to dominance. To Capps, this was inevitable. Steve Jobs *was* a revolutionary, selling the cyber-lifestyle, not a device. Once the Mac had hit the market, he was no longer interested in fine-tuning it and helping it live up to its potential. "The world is a better place because Steve Jobs isn't as smart as Bill Gates, and Bill Gates does not have the charisma of Steve Jobs," Capps says. "It takes somebody to jostle people's thinking, and then other people benefit. We mocked Gates, but he's so smart. He said, 'Steady as she goes. I'll get there later, but I'll get there.'"

While Gates played catch-up, Capps played with toys. He worked on an interactive version of his sound-editing program, created a drawing program, and developed a chip-driven interactive book for kids, all the while fending off the entreaties of Jobs, who wanted Capps at his new company, NeXT. Instead, he and his wife, who'd become a digital artist, moved to San Francisco in 1986, continuing to work on various software products and freelancing for Apple.

Capps finished his book project, but the company that backed it went out of business. SoundEdit and another program, Jam Session, which allowed users to play the Mac keyboard like an instrument against famous rock tracks, accompanied by animation, did make it to market and are still in use today, as is the Jaminator, an "air guitar" toy Capps later created using the chip from his interactive books and Jam Session software. But by the end of 1987, with no payoff from his work in France in sight, Capps had been lured back to Apple with the promise that he could develop what came to be called Newton, a pocket-size computer that could read handwriting and send and receive electronic messages.

He returned to Apple at the start of a decade of failure and mismanagement at the company. For the next two years, Capps and about ten others were paid to think. Just think. "We were clueless," he says now. "We were off by ourselves, in our own building, not doing anything. We played a lot of basketball. We had a lot of ideas. We built prototypes, and we'd go to the board of directors and plead with them, or at least I did, saying, 'You've got to start up five or six of these projects; you've got to let a thousand flowers bloom.'" They wouldn't. Finally, Capps went to see Apple's CEO, John Sculley, and pleaded for the funding to make the handwriting machine real. Capps had learned one thing from Jobs: he was selling potential, not reality. "So I spun this vision." Sculley liked it and sent him to the board again. Capps mocked up a screen he could write on, tethered to a Macintosh. "All the smarts were on the Mac," he admits, but it didn't matter; he won permission to proceed with Newton.

In 1990, a marketing manager named Michael Tchao joined the Newton team as it "flailed, trying to get it done," Capps says. Finally Tchao put into words what Capps had only thought: the technology of the day wouldn't support the Newton. Together, they brainstormed a new product, a mini-Newton they called Sputnik, a satellite to a desktop computer, a halfway measure, but one that could be realized. They still had to fight in-house battles against the team assigned to the larger Newton, but they'd eventually win as surely as the Mac beat out Lisa. "Lisa was real, and Mac was the toy," Capps observes. "I'm convinced, absolutely, that the renegade toy projects are the ones that always win."

By January 1992, Sculley was confident enough to refer to the Newton in a speech at an electronics show in Las Vegas, coining the term "personal digital assistant" and predicting PDAs would become a $3.5 billion industry within ten years. His optimism was understandable. Apple needed to be in the lead of a business like that. Windows 3.1 had been introduced that April, confirming what many had long known: Microsoft had become the undisputed heavyweight champion of personal computing.

Sculley had gotten his first inkling of that then-not-quite-inevitability in fall 1985, when he first learned about Windows and threatened to sue to stop it. At that point, Microsoft—via its word processor and spreadsheet application software—controlled more than half the Macintosh software market. Though he's denied it, Bill Gates allegedly threatened to stop making new programs for Macs if Apple followed through on Sculley's threat.[27] Undisputed is the fact that Apple then inexplicably agreed in writing to license the Mac software's look to Microsoft in present and future versions of Windows. By spring 1988, Windows had evolved from a clunky clone to a robust competitor. Apple finally saw the threat it represented and sued for copyright infringement.

Since Capps was the only high-level Mac developer left at Apple, he became a key player in the lawsuit. Blunt, funny and an almost stereotypical nerd with his long hair, beard and eccentric uniform of white button-down shirts, black shorts, wool socks and black-and-white-checked Vans sneakers, Capps proved an ideal witness. Microsoft contended that the operating system design was obvious, like the steering wheel on a car, and couldn't be protected. "I got up there and said I'd spent hundreds of hours working on this, tried three dozen different designs, and it wasn't intuitive at all," Capps says. Apple lost the suit, but Capps emerged a winner. One of the junior lawyers on Apple's side was Marie D'Amico, who shortly thereafter became his second wife. He'd split with his first when he realized he wanted children and she didn't. "Sometimes, when you fall in love and you're young, you don't ask the right questions," he says.

As they fought the lawsuit, work on Newton continued. Capps demonstrated it in May 1992, at another Consumer Electronics Show. The demonstration "was total bullshit," he admits. The Newton simply wasn't good enough. "It didn't have modem support, printer support. I look at videotapes of that show, and I think I'm a walking advertisement for heart attacks. I'd had no sleep, I demo this total hack, the press just eats it up and I remember going, 'Oh, fuck.'" Apple had made another promise it couldn't keep.

Capps spent the next year in hell, "ramping up production for this thing," he says, he and his team working eighteen-hour days, out of his and D'Amico's home rather than in the demoralized atmosphere at Apple. "One guy committed suicide, and work pressures I'm sure contributed to his lack of judgment," Capps says.

Newton's launch was postponed to August 1993. Days before its introduction, complete with MTV-style videos at a Macintosh trade show, Capps and Tchao—well aware that the $700 gadget's central feature, its ability to recognize handwriting, was limited—argued that its release should be limited, too. They were ignored. Despite interim upgrades that addressed some of its problems, by year's end, Newton had been effectively declared a failure. It was telling that the same month Newton was introduced, Microsoft reported that for the first time, it had $1 billion in sales in a quarter-year. John Sculley left a few months later.[28] Despite one critical success—its PowerBook laptop computers—Apple looked rotten.

BY 1989, RUSSELL SIMMONS and Def Jam were an established brand in the music business. Rap may not have been loved, but it was accepted. With every record he released going gold, people were comparing Simmons to Berry Gordy, who'd created the Motown empire in the 1960s. The year before, Rick Rubin had left Def Jam, but Simmons replaced him with another Jewish music entrepreneur, Lyor Cohen, and kept signing new acts like Slick Rick, Method Man, D.J. Jazzy Jeff, the Fresh Prince (a/k/a Will Smith) and Public Enemy. But after a restructuring demanded by its distributor, CBS (by then a division of Sony), Def Jam ended up $20 million in debt.

Rap had evolved. In the mainstream, ersatz pop raps by artists like M. C. Hammer (b. 1962) and the white rapper Vanilla Ice (b. 1968) were selling in unprecedented numbers for major labels. On the streets, rap was anything but ersatz. In 1982, Carlton Ridenhour (b. 1960), a graphic design student, had recorded a rap called "Public Enemy No. 1." When Rick Rubin heard it, he began courting Ridenhour, who eventually formed a group called Public Enemy. Its second album, *It Takes a Nation of Millions to Hold Us Back*, was a huge success in 1988, driven by dense production and an equally novel point of view, informed by Ridenhour's membership in the Nation of Islam. Chuck D, as Ridenhour styled himself, wrote overtly political, rage-filled rhymes that condemned racism and police brutality and extolled black consciousness. But after the band endorsed the controversial Muslim leader Louis Farrakhan and several group members made statements deemed anti-Semitic, Public Enemy's sales headed south.

In the meantime, a new hip-hop avant-garde had emerged on the West Coast. Building on Public Enemy's collage of sound, a former drug dealer who'd funded a record label with his profits put together a band called N.W.A. (an acronym for Niggaz with Attitude) and introduced a new, violent, misogynistic genre, gangsta rap. N.W.A.'s 1989 album, *Straight Outta Compton*, named for the group's suburban ghetto hometown, got little radio play or press but became a cult phenomenon thanks to songs like "Fuck Tha Police," which earned N.W.A. a warning from the FBI. It was an omen. In 1992 another gangsta rapper would be dropped by his record label after making a record called "Cop Killer." With gangsta rap, the music business had finally found a sound guaranteed to grate on the ears of formerly all-accepting baby boomers—turning them into their parents every time a speaker-equipped "boom" car or boom box passed them by. Every fresh outrage gained the music new enemies. Every sneer from an aging boomer made new fans. Gangstas would rule rap straight through the 1990s.

Simmons liked the gangsta rappers, and added several to the Def Jam roster. "They borrowed a lot of Run-D.M.C.'s energy and attitude, and I understood immediately it was great," he says. "I didn't know the culture and lifestyle, but the more I started to know what that lifestyle was, the more engaging it was. Because it was so good and so honest. Honesty is the killer. And people really can feel authenticity. You don't have to live in Compton to know that shit's real."

While gangsta rap was taking shape, Simmons was getting his troubled business back on its feet, and then extending his valuable brand. He established Rush Communications as an umbrella over Def Jam Recordings, its music publishing arm, and Def Pictures, his film production company. He joined forces with several Hollywood pros to create a talent management company and Russell Simmons Television, which began developing its first show, a showcase for black comedians called *Def Comedy Jam*, which debuted on HBO in 1992. The show was so successful, it helped pulled Def Jam out of its jam and would eventually lead to a second program, *Russell Simmons' Oneworld Music Beat*.

The more the critics howled that his comedy, like rap music, was hateful or filthy or racist, the more money he made. "People are saying something legitimate that's coming out of their hearts," Simmons says. "When their fathers tell them niggers shouldn't say fuck the police, they say, 'Fuck you, Dad; give me a rap record.'" By 1998, rap would be selling in excess of eighty million albums a year, more than any other music genre.

THE FIRST FIFTEEN key employees of Sun Microsystems all got stock in the company, which skyrocketed in value, with annual sales hitting $1 billion in 1988. John Gage, among the oldest of the fifteen, had two kids and almost immediately cashed out a huge block of stock to buy a new house. Sun stock has increased in value 100 times since then, but Gage doesn't seem to mind. "I have the most expensive kitchen in Berkeley," he jokes dryly.

All that money was made before the idea of the network crossed over into consumer culture. When Joy and Gage coined the phrase "the network is the computer," Sun's mantra, only university and military types and computer sophisticates were on the biggest network of all, the Internet. "You have a couple of hundred thousand people using it," Gage remembers, "it's not very well known, and it's ugly. There were only three things the Internet could do: e-mail, transfer a file, link directly into another computer. And you had to learn commands to make it work. But for our community, the Internet was the heartbeat. We lived and died by communications."

That all changed with the World Wide Web. Suddenly Gage's little community opened its gates. The Web's inventor, Tim Berners-Lee (b. 1956), built his first computer while studying at Oxford University's Queens College. In 1980, while working as a consultant at CERN, the European Particle Physics Laboratory in Geneva, Switzerland, he wrote an information storage program that allowed for the programming of random links—i.e., mouse-click jumps that could take you from any word in a computer network's virtual "filing cabinet" to any other. That led to his 1989 proposal for a global web of documents, linked by something called hypertext, designed to let people collaborate by combining and interconnecting knowledge. Backed by CERN, Berners-Lee began writing what he now called the World Wide Web programs in 1990, and put them on the Internet a year later. "It was all open," says Gage. "The protocol to do this, the rules to make it all work were completely open. Nobody owned it. Put your community intellectual property in here and share with everybody."

Berners-Lee wrote an early rudimentary browser, and others followed. Consumer Internet service providers began to appear. Marc Andreessen (b. 1971), a coder at the National Center for Supercomputing Applications at the University of Illinois, began distributing a highly compatible, easily installed image-reading browser called Mosaic and the Internet and the value of networking spread to the world at large. The web was the public's map to the hidden treasures of the network. Even Sun's jaded employees responded to it. At one point, their Internet usage rose so precipitously that a company accountant threatened to make them pay for access. Finally "the entire company rose up as one and sent him insulting e-mail saying, 'You idiot, this allows everybody to share across all departments for the first time!'" Gage recalls.

It was all great news for Gage and Sun, whose top code-writer, Bill Joy, had worked on many of the protocols. "No matter what computer you were on, you had a piece of Joy's code that he gave away for free," Gage says. "By the time Mark Andreessen's sitting down in '91-'92, he's on Bill Joy's shoulders." Mosaic and its Andreessen-designed commercial successor, the wildly successful Netscape, followed the pattern of ETHERNET and of TCP/IP. "Give it away for free, and suddenly it runs on every machine," Gage crows. "And people loved it, because it was completely opposite to what Bill Gates did. And that made Gates mad." After ignoring networking for years, Gates suddenly found himself playing catch-up on the unfamiliar field of the Internet.

Gage was among the first to demonstrate the Web to the wider world at PC Forum, a spring 1994 conference in Phoenix, Arizona. Gage compared it to air, "the first essence of freedom," he says. "I breathe air, I don't need to ask if it's French air or Russian air. I assume it's going to work. It's instantly understandable." The audience "had a degree of skepticism." Most of them had never experienced the Internet, let alone the heretofore unseen Web. "But it was so simple, and the linkage thing was suddenly so apparently powerful," says Gage, who began his demonstration by holding up a telephone wire, making a call to Sun, and going online. Then he said, "You can do this."

He didn't tell them about Java, a new Sun programming language, but it was on his mind. He and Joy had come up with the idea on a plane flight in 1992. Gage was reading *Lignes d'Horizon* (Fayard, Paris, 1990), a treatise on geopolitics by Jacques Attali, an adviser to French President Francois Mitterand who predicted the emergence of a new "nomadic man," living in a future of fax machines, cellular telephones, biological implants and all-purpose smart cards. Gage translated sections of the book aloud to Joy, who made a prediction of his own: before the end of the century, people would be able to communicate, compute and issue electronic commands by carrying four electronic devices weighing a total of less than five pounds. Java software and its successor, Jini, were invented to make that prediction manifest.

Java works with what Joy called "virtual machine" software implanted within every browser to allow the movement of programs, not just data, around the Internet; the more ambitious Jini allows even home appliances to connect instantly to and to communicate with networks; both programs bypass operating systems, carrying with them an implicit threat to the Microsoft Windows monopoly. Sun was jubilant about that, but slow and steady Microsoft fought back, developing a web browser of its own and integrating it into Windows 95, then more tightly into Windows 98. Microsoft also adapted Java without sharing their improvements, violating the hacker rule book. When congressional and antitrust investigators began looking into Microsoft, studying whether it had abused its monopoly position in consumer operating systems, Sun executives, among the few in the industry with no ties to Gates (for by then even struggling Apple had made a strategic alliance with Microsoft), were among the first to speak out against the Redmond, Washington-based giant. Then it sued over Microsoft's Java "improvements."

Gage, ever the maverick, feels free to poke sticks in Bill Gates's cage. "Joy tried to give the networking code to Microsoft, offered to help make it fit in these little tiny, uninteresting junk machines"—PCs—"but Gates was too dumb to understand what networking is," Gage says, adding a prediction that this oversight will eventually kill Microsoft, which would be found to be a predatory monopoly by a Federal judge late in 1999. "When technology changes rapidly, anything closed and proprietary will die," Gage vows. "That's how we see Microsoft. They have a niche. The niche will go away."

IN 1987, TIM SCULLY had begun consulting for the primary supplier of software for computer-assisted graphic design, Autodesk, writing programs that allowed the company's programs to speak to and command attached, and often incompatible, devices like printers and pointing tools. He eventually learned to program for DOS, UNIX, and Windows machines. In 1989, he was made chief engineer and put in charge of a half-dozen programmers. "Since I spent a lot of years designing hardware and writing software, the interface between hardware and software is the place where my skills were best applied," he says, dismissing his work as "low-level bit-banging."

Scully's superiors at Autodesk know all about his arrest record but care more about his record of achievement. "There have been times when people were taken aback," he admits. "But really, people have been very nice. I've been lucky, but I also think people respond to the fact that I have no ill will toward anyone."

In recent years, computer culture has helped him incorporate his past into his present. As many programmers and computer pioneers came out of the drug culture as out of radical politics. One of Scully's programmers is married to a psychologist who's spent a half a decade studying the Deadhead colony of fans. Scully was delighted when she told him many of them were programmers, too. She'd also met Owsley, who'd survived his own two-year stint in jail, moved to Australia in 1982, became a sculptor, and now sometimes returns to Dead-related shows, where he sells gold, silver and cloisonné artwork, medallions and belt buckles. "I am back in touch," Scully says.

Owsley is disappointed that his ex-apprentice won't take drugs anymore. Though Scully says he suffers no ill effects from his drug days, he adds, "It certainly can be hazardous to your freedom!" Nowadays he sticks

to meditation, tai chi, and biofeedback, "doing various things to deliberately and consciously get into states that are in some ways similar to
being high," he says. Owsley sometimes argues that since they've both
"paid a lot of dues, we should be able to take all the acid we want," Scully
says with an indulgent smile.

Owsley, he adds, is also convinced that a new Ice Age is coming.

"HOW DO YOU think David Geffen, Barry Diller and Sandy Gallin
found out about this?" Marianne Williamson demands. "Through their
caterers, masseuses, lovers." By 1987, those servants and lovers, many of
them people getting sober, people with AIDS and people who loved
them, had passed the word that Williamson was delivering a message
worth hearing to Tinseltown boomers who'd lived their version of the
1960s in the discos and viper rooms of the 1970s and early 1980s. They
weren't just AIDS victims; they were "the addicted, or the obsessed and
compulsive," said *Time* magazine.[29] Williamson agrees. "You can't forget
Alcoholics Anonymous and twelve-step programs in all this. People
started getting sober. The party was over."

Many in Hollywood's power elite were looking for a reason to believe.
"For some people, the eighties were a total materialistic orgy," Williamson
says. "But most of those people finally got to the point where the rest of
our generation is now: Okay, now that I have two Ferraris, a house in Vail
and an apartment in Manhattan, now that I'm head of the studio, are you
telling me this is all there is?"

Williamson added her own spin to *A Course in Miracles;* her nonde-
nominational message combined Christ, Buddha, pop psychology, song
and movie references, and the tenets of twelve-step in lectures about
such hot-button topics as whether death exists, romantic delusions, fear
of intimacy and forgiving your parents. It was just the thing for bummed-
and burnt-out boomers who found the era's fundamentalist religious
alternative too small-minded and mean. Not only that, Williamson was a
performer in a town that had an insatiable appetite for them.

Four years after her first lecture, still barely supporting herself by selling audio- and videotapes and collecting a "suggested donation" of $5 dol-
lars at her lectures, Williamson was coming into her own. News of her
mystique had begun to spread. Not long after she began flying to New
York in 1986 to lecture once a month, David Geffen, the music and
movie mogul, heard her speak about her latest project, The Center for
Living. The facility offered nonmedical, nonresidential support services
(meals, housecleaning, discussion groups, yoga, massage and individual

and group prayer) to the "life-challenged," as the politically correct lingo of the moment termed it. The center was inspired by a friend with breast cancer who'd asked Williamson why there was no place she could go to be healed, and failing that, to be helped to die with dignity. Williamson not only got it started, she also contributed much of its budget. "We were holding the hands of dying people, and we didn't have any money," she says. When Geffen called to offer her $50,000 in 1987, "it was like we had won the lottery." Two years later, she opened Project Angel Food in Los Angeles, to provide hot meals for AIDS patients, and a second Center for Living in New York, backed by another $50,000 from Geffen.

Flying back and forth to New York every week, surrounded, in the papers at least, by a celebrity coterie, Williamson became a spiritual celebrity herself in 1991, a year that began with her blessing Geffen's star-studded birthday party and ended with her presiding over the wedding of Hollywood legend Elizabeth Taylor to her eighth husband, construction worker Larry Fortensky, at Michael Jackson's Neverland Ranch as media helicopters buzzed overhead. Ever since, Williamson has been on the defensive, accused of selling a shallow version of salvation to the self-obsessed, the materialistic and the driven, and of being part of the very idol worship and cultural blight she inveighs against in her books and lectures.

"Contrary to some of those caricatures, I am not a starfucker," she says flatly. "The vast majority of people who came to my lectures—or come now—were not connected to any of that." The same goes for some of the stars identified as devotees after they supported her AIDS efforts at Project Angel Food. "These people feel manipulated and used and I don't blame them," she says. "It was very embarrassing and it continues to be. I was never the guru to the stars. I was tarred with that."

But she was something to some stars. They liked Williamson's idea that it was okay to be *somewhat* enlightened. And there was no getting around the Taylor-Fortensky wedding, "the stupidest career mistake of all time," Williamson calls it. "Anybody who thinks I did that for career purposes should know, if you want a serious career in America, don't marry Elizabeth Taylor."

It got worse. Just as her first book, *A Return to Love*, was being published (kicked off at a party hosted by television producer Norman Lear), a series of exposés painted her as an abrasive, egomaniacal, publicity-obsessed hysteric just out for a buck. In the harsh climate of celebrity culture, she'd gone from flavor of the moment to target of media opportunity in a nanosecond.

A year after she started a support and prayer group for four pregnant girlfriends, Williamson had also become an unwed mother.[30] In the papers, that and the fact that she refused to identify the father of her daughter, conceived in 1989 and born in 1990, was made to seem sad and sordid. Though she saw herself as a feminist living an only slightly alternative lifestyle, she allows that others considered her "a terrible role model." Even worse were the tales of self-promotion, bullying and micro-management that emerged from her Centers for Living in 1992.

"We hear she yelled at a secretary when she was pregnant, so she must be the biggest bitch in the world," she repeats. "Yeah, I was pregnant and under unbelievable pressure and I'm not a perfect person." But still, this was juicy stuff. "I'm famous, I don't need this, damn it," she reportedly huffed at staffers after the *Los Angeles Times* reported that the Centers for Living were in turmoil.

Years later, Williamson is still wounded by the way a messy organizational conflict was used to diminish her. "You cross some line where your book is successful or you get a certain amount of press, you're the same person doing the same things, but the reaction turns from *Isn't she nice?* to *Who does she think she is?*" Williamson says. "Gay America gave me my career and opened the centers with me. Then a more glamorous element discovered AIDS as a cause and thought that they could take it from there. It's interesting. The myth about me is that I was horribly controlling. Having thought about this for many years, the problem was I was not controlling enough."

Yet she admits that for all the embellishment and distortion, the negative articles contained a grain of truth, and that she's since endeavored to take responsibility for her passions and her actions. "I'm real," she says. "I've never pretended to be anything I'm not, but I gave people the opportunity to imagine the worst. I've learned how dangerous attention is."

DOUG MARLETTE first met Bill Clinton at Renaissance Weekend, an event founded in 1981 by Philip Lader (b. 1946), a young college president (and later Clinton's ambassador to England) and his wife to bring accomplished baby boomers—especially Southern liberals—together with leaders of other generations. The touchy-feely invitation-only family get-togethers are held on Hilton Head Island, off South Carolina, each New Year's weekend.

Renaissance quickly became the power version of Jerry Rubin's networking salons, with a dash of New Age navel-gazing. ("Inward Bound," Marlette calls it.) Each year, personalities ranging from Supreme Court justices to folk singers would play golf, ride bicycles, and discuss everything from international policy to professional traumas and investment strategies. Seminars run the gamut from "Renaissance World Report: Commentaries on War Crimes, Human Rights and Refugees" to "Renaissance Quest: Stirring Waters of Belief" to "Renaissance Whispers: What My Spouse Is Wrong About."

Bill and Hillary Clinton and Marlette all attended their first Renaissance Weekend in 1984, when the guest list was still tiny. Arriving, Marlette spied a van with Arkansas plates pulling into the next parking space. Out popped the governor, his lawyer wife, and their young daughter, Chelsea. In an atmosphere at once democratic and elitist, Renaissance interwove all the dominant strains of baby boomerism: 1960s progressive politics, 1970s self-attuned spirituality, and the unchecked ambition of the 1980s, joined in a synergy that would define the 1990s. At one panel, Marlette's wife, Melinda, noted the disdain being heaped on newly named Yuppies and asked what was wrong with being young and ambitious. Clinton approached her afterward to say he agreed.

Another night, Clinton and Lader "tried to outdo each other with who would give the most moving and the most powerful speech," Marlette recalls. "They were doing this Yuppie Revivalism thing, these very successful people talking and bringing people to tears. Clinton talked about his brother being in prison. I'd been there before with the testimonies in Baptist church. This was in the service of political ambition, but it was the same thing as Youth for Christ." Driving home, Marlette said, "I would vote for him for President. I've never heard a politician that smart."

"Yeah," his wife said out of nowhere, "but he's a womanizer."

Marlette, who admits his cartoonist's instincts often run ahead of his consciousness, wasn't so sure. "He does it with everybody," he told Melinda. Over the years, the seduction continued. Clinton would write to compliment "Kudzu" strips. "I thought he was very likable," Marlette says. "I had an immediate affinity with him. His family was trailer trash, just like my family. So I got him from the get-go and thought he would do wonderful things." Something nagged, though, "something facile and glib. It's all there in your first encounters with people. He's doing that gaze and he's listening, he's holding my eyes, and talking, talking, talking, until there would come a moment at the end, when he saw he had me, the seduction had been successful, and the shades would go down, and he checked me off the list and moved on. You felt like Monica Lewinsky felt, and now the nation feels: used like a Kleenex and tossed aside."

Marlette felt it, but it didn't register yet. The enchantment of Clinton's attentive intelligence was overwhelming, and Marlette became one of a group of supporters known as Friends of Bill (FOB). "I'd tell friends, 'You've got to hear this guy Bill Clinton. This guy is the best speaker.'" When Clinton gave his famous, endless, awful speech at the 1988 Democratic Convention in Atlanta, introducing that year's presidential candidate, his fellow governor Michael Dukakis, "I had phone calls asking, 'What are you talking about! Are you crazy?'"

Marlette had moved to New York to work for *Newsday* that year and stayed two more before coming home to Hillsborough, North Carolina, where his father had been born. While in New York, other journalists, aware of his FOB status, asked him about Clinton, who'd gained a national profile. Marlette told them how profoundly he identified with the guy and how he was sure Clinton would do good things, especially on the issue of race, which continued to plague a nation that refused to address it.

By 1992, Reaganism had begun to infiltrate a Democratic Party desperate to move back to the political center after a dozen years out of power. That trend was embodied by Clinton, who'd established a base through the Democratic Leadership Council, a group formed in 1985 to revivify the party by selectively adopting conservative language and ideas. "The promise of America is equal opportunity, not equal outcomes," the group said in a declaration of principles at a March 1990 meeting at which Clinton was named its chairman. "The Democratic Party's fundamental mission is to expand opportunity, not government."

A few years later, Marlette didn't mind when Clinton, beginning his run for the presidency, claimed he had smoked marijuana but never inhaled. "I thought it was silly, but I understood. He was trying to win the election." It was different when Clinton began changing his story of how, out of college, he'd managed to avoid being drafted. At first, Clinton repeated the story he'd used since first running for governor of Arkansas in 1978: that he'd only been draft-eligible for a brief period in 1969 and had escaped the notice of the Selective Service. With a little help from the *Wall Street Journal*, it emerged that Clinton had received an induction notice, wangled himself an ROTC appointment to attend law school in Arkansas, and then reneged after pulling a draft lottery number high enough to eliminate worry about the draft. "I decided to accept the draft despite my political beliefs for one reason: to maintain my political viability within the system," Clinton had written to the head of the ROTC at the University of Arkansas. Then the twenty-three-year-old headed to law school—at Yale.

Marlette was incensed. "I give a lot of leeway. Those times were hideous. But when I think of anyone at that age writing and talking about his political viability, when people were dying and going to jail or Canada, that is so painful to me," Marlette says. "I can't imagine that calculation crossing my mind. It was a matter of how one lived and who one was. He was hollow and soulless, even then, and at such a young age."

Marlette smiles and adds, "I'm glad he was against the war."

BACK IN BOSTON after his trip to Ho Chi Minh City, early in 1985, Tommy Vallely declared himself a candidate for the Boston congressional seat occupied by the retiring Speaker of the House, Tip O'Neill. "I was a fairly popular legislator, I had my own money, I was going to play," says Vallely, who spent $200,000 on the run, which ended abruptly in December 1985, when Joseph P. Kennedy II, a son of Robert Kennedy, entered the Democratic primary. "I can't beat Joe Kennedy." Vallely decided not to seek reelection to the legislature, either. "I don't know what the fuck I'm going to do," he says. "My whole life just changed."

Having lost his seat to a Kennedy, he returned, appropriately enough, to Harvard's Kennedy School, as a researcher. He still dabbled in politics, playing a large role in Delaware Senator Joseph Biden's brief-lived presidential campaign in 1987. Biden (b. 1943) withdrew from the race following accusations that he'd plagiarized and inflated his academic credentials.

Back in Cambridge, Vallely, deciding to learn everything he could about the country he'd fought in two decades earlier, began reading about Vietnam and talking to experts at monthly discussions of Indochina sponsored by the Aspen Institute. At those meetings, he supported Arizona senator John McCain's proposal to set up an American diplomatic interest section in another government's embassy in Hanoi, and got to know the fellow vet in the process. Studying Vietnam, initially a hobby, became his raison d'être.

In Ho Chi Minh City four years earlier, Vallely had the idea of returning the funding he'd received to attend the Kennedy School in order to subsidize a scholarship for a Vietnamese student. In 1989, that fantasy came nearer to reality when he got a new job at the Harvard Institute for International Development as a research associate and director of a new Vietnam program. HIID, a think tank run by the university, is in effect a global management consulting service, working for governments and international organizations like the United Nations and the World Bank, running research and development projects around the world.

Vietnam was still a pariah nation to the America it defeated. Though the war had been over nearly fifteen years, remembering it—or at least its prisoners of war and soldiers missing in action—had become an American industry. Ronald Reagan had made POW politics a cornerstone of his presidential campaigns, but behind the scenes he'd begun the incremental process of reengagement with Vietnam.

Vallely didn't support Reagan ("I thought he was crazy") but has since changed his mind about the movie star president. "Reagan deserves credit for changing the way America thinks for the better," Vallely says. "I also think he did a very good job dealing with the dismantlement of the Soviet empire." In so doing, Reaganites changed the balance of power in the world and increased the geopolitical importance of Pacific Rim nations. As America's most knowledgeable behind-the-scenes proponent of a relationship with Vietnam, Vallely became an architect of policy toward the region. He argued that an opening to Vietnam would be good for U.S.

business and serve as a counterweight to Chinese influence. Even though three million Vietnamese had died in the war, shattering countless families, "they are very, very good at having relationships with people they were enemies with," Vallely notes. "That's how small countries survive."

The policy of resolving disputes and restoring ties to Vietnam, which was adopted by the Bush administration, got a boost following the 1991 Gulf War, when Senators McCain and Kerry went on a fact-finding mission to Kuwait and talked at length for the first time.[1] Shortly afterward, the two worked together on a newly created Senate Select Committee on POW/MIA Affairs—formed to investigate the fate of Americans unaccounted for since the war.

The Senate Select Committee built a relationship with the Vietnamese government. Kerry, the chairman, went there seven times in three years, and Vallely sometimes preceded or followed him. As the fact-finding mission proceeded, Bill Clinton's campaign against President Bush intruded. "I will always be a Democrat," says Vallely. "But I have voted for some Republicans." One was George Bush in 1992. Vallely just couldn't get past Clinton's draft antics. "He didn't want to go die," the ex-Marine says. "But some people got out of it by being honest. He got out by being himself, which is deceitful. I don't mind that he didn't go; I liked people that didn't go. But it's like his presidency. 'I can have everything I want.' Well, I don't think you can, Bill. He lacked character. And I voted for character, even though I didn't think George Bush understood America as well as Bill Clinton does."

The POW/MIA committee released a draft report a few days before Clinton's inauguration, concluding that while soldiers may have been left behind, there was no compelling evidence that any were still alive—or that the Vietnamese were holding any remains. Immediately, calls came to lift the eighteen-year-old U.S. trade embargo against Vietnam and to normalize relations.

Bill Clinton had a problem. His credibility on Vietnam-related issues had already been severely damaged—among vets like Vallely and beyond—by the draft revelations. On taking office, he'd stirred more bad feelings by immediately calling for an end to the ban on gays in the military. It was the first in a string of impolitic gaffes that by May 1993 had his poll numbers plunging. That month he began a campaign to repair his relationship with the military. On Memorial Day weekend, he gave a series of speeches setting the stage for reconciliation.

Clinton made a pitch for a strong military. In an interview before a speech at West Point, he said he'd secretly jogged by the Vietnam

Veteran's Memorial to look for the names of four friends from high school chiseled into it. On Memorial Day, he spoke at the wall after being introduced (and in effect inoculated) by the Chairman of the Joint Chiefs of Staff, Colin Powell. Though many jeered, the speech was a turning point, as pro- and antiwar forces alike realized the time had come to let old animosities go.

That happened fast. In June, several nations offered to refinance Vietnam's debts; a bipartisan delegation to Vietnam headed by former Secretary of State Edmund Muskie, issued a public call for normalization. Senator Kerry said it was time to stop spending $100 million annually in a futile search for POWs. To Vallely, it seemed silly to keep American companies from joining in the economic boom clearly beginning in Vietnam. Other countries were profiting by building hotels and golf courses. Six months later, when the President had yet to make a move, the odd couple of antiwar Kerry and pro-war McCain gave Clinton bipartisan cover with a Senate resolution to end the trade embargo. Finally, in February 1994, with the two heroes at his side, Clinton did so. In summer 1995, he restored diplomatic relations, "to bind up our own wounds," he said.

Some thought Vallely should be named the ambassador to Vietnam. Though Clinton passed him by, Vallely doesn't hold a grudge. "I was at the White House the day he normalized relations and I said, 'Mr. President, I apologize for underestimating you. I won't do it again.'" He could afford to be gracious. His dream was being realized.

Vallely had established a Fulbright exchange program to bring Vietnamese students to America in 1992 and quickly built it into the world's largest Fullbright program. He'd added an in-country teaching program in December 1994, after the trade embargo was lifted. In November 1995, he presided over the dedication of the Fulbright Center in Ho Chi Minh City. "Because of the war, the relationship between Vietnam and the United States remains tense, timid, and too often, bitter," he said that day. "But . . . it no longer matters what your position was during the war. We must think about the future . . . and reach out toward Vietnam in a peace of the brave."

BY 1991, WHEN her third child started school, Barbara Ledeen was ready for a new challenge. George Bush was beginning to campaign for a second term as President when Henry Hyde, a conservative congressman, came to dinner at the Ledeens' one night. She started badgering him about Bush's message to women. Though she knew she wouldn't vote for a Democrat, she still worried that the Republicans, in thrall to the Christian right and anti-abortion forces, had a problem. "What have you got for me?" she demanded of Hyde.

The answer came from another woman at the dinner. Ricky Silberman (b. 1937) had served as the vice chairman of Ronald Reagan's Economic Opportunity Commission under a younger conservative black lawyer named Clarence Thomas (b. 1948). Thomas had since been promoted first to the three-judge Federal Appeals Court—where he served with Silberman's husband, Laurence, and Douglas Ginsburg (b. 1946), whose nomination to the Supreme Court was derailed by his admission that he'd smoked marijuana—and then to the Supreme Court. But in his confirmation hearings that summer, Thomas had been accused of sexual harassment by a former protégé, Anita Hill (b. 1956). Hill's accusations caused a storm. The only counter was a group of 200 women Silberman organized to testify in Thomas's behalf. In doing so, they outraged the feminist establishment. Thomas's avowed opposition to affirmative action programs made him anathema to liberals.

After their evening with Hyde, Silberman and Ledeen sought out like-minded women. A former Pentagon co-worker, Lisa Schiffren (b. 1959)—who had gone on to write speeches for Dan Quayle, authoring his famous attack on television's Murphy Brown for having a child out of wedlock—asked Ledeen to lunch with "a nice bunch of Republican women who had not been radicalized," she says. Wendy Gramm, an economist, former head of the Commodity Futures Trading Commission, and wife of Senator Phil Gramm, liked Ledeen's idea of starting a conservative women's group. So did Anita Blair (b. 1959), a lawyer and member of The Federalist Society, who'd been politicized when she found herself afraid to admit she supported Quayle.

They all felt that traditional feminist organizations were too predictable, militant and concerned with divisive litmus-test issues, too interested in sustaining themselves, even if female equality was achieved, and too busy whining about how women were victimized to realize they didn't have to be anymore. Existing conservative women's organizations were too in thrall to the Christian right. "We could see there was an opening in the market," says Ledeen. An existing organization started by several Federalist Society lawyers was renamed IWF, the Independent Women's Forum, and Ledeen became executive director. She approached conservative foundations for seed money, and they were enthused at the prospect of a new women's group reflective of new times.[2]

Instead of building a grassroots organization, IWF's leaders decided to make its mark by providing the media with articulate women lawyers and writers, ready with cheeky quotes, provocative sound bites, op-ed pieces, congressional testimony, and *amicus* briefs on matters of law and public policy. The IWF program quickly attracted several hundred members and became a launchpad for conservative pundits like Danielle Crittenden (b. 1963), who edited IWF's cheeky magazine, *The Women's Quarterly;* Christina Hoff Sommers (b. 1950), a resident scholar at the American Enterprise Institute; and conservative sex symbol Laura Ingraham (b. 1964), the leopard-skirted lawyer and former Clarence Thomas clerk who gained fame by founding a conservative analogue to the liberal Renaissance Weekends. Demonstrating the new irreverence boomers brought to conservatism, she dubbed it the Dark Ages Weekend.

IN 1992, DAVID McIntosh decided that Bill Clinton had managed to pull off a neat trick, bridging the gap between the politics of the Baby Boom's youth and its middle-aged conservatism. "They liked Clinton and connected with him, and it's not because he protested the war or might have smoked pot," notes the congressman. "In the way he talked about things, he reached that stable American community, yet with a twinkle in his eye that said, 'I'm a rascal.' My brother-in-law, who went to Washington for antiwar protests, once said half the people were really there for free sex. And they saw Clinton, and thought, Yeah, here's somebody who's going to have fun."

Free sex had never been part of McIntosh's life. He was still a virgin at thirty-five. "I was always somewhat socially awkward and just had friends rather than steady girlfriends," he admits. But that summer, that all changed. He'd proposed marriage to a woman he'd met in the White House, Ruthie McManis, the director of First Lady Barbara Bush's Literacy Foundation. They married just after Clinton's 1993 inauguration. By then, McIntosh better understood the twinkle in Clinton's eye. "Ruthie was the first person I had been together with," he says.

At first, the newlyweds stayed in Washington; McIntosh worked with a group called Citizens for a Sound Economy, where he helped fight new taxes. When Dan Quayle settled into Indiana's conservative Hudson Institute, he offered McIntosh a job as an analyst there, and the McIntoshes moved back home. Meantime, Clinton's postelection leftward lurch hadn't gone unnoticed. In July 1993, McIntosh attended a town meeting with his local congressman, a moderate Democrat who'd been in office for years. "I'll never forget the union members, who had always been strong supporters of his, standing up and shouting, *Why did you vote for Bill Clinton's tax increase?"* Ruthie McIntosh whispered in his ear that since he'd fought that very tax increase, maybe he should run for Congress.

"I knew I wanted to," he says, "and that kind of clinched it." He announced his run before Thanksgiving. And again after. "I only had three or four people show up at each of the announcements," he says. "We didn't have any organization; I was still working at Hudson at the time." When a woman who'd interned in Quayle's office approached him and asked for a job, he says, "That made it real, because you had to get on the phone and raise money to make a payroll."

Lucky breaks gave the newcomer the Republican nomination—the incumbent pulled out of the race, and another likely opponent missed her filing deadline—but the general election against Indiana's pro-labor secretary of state, a close friend of the popular governor Evan Bayh, was hard-fought. McIntosh had to spend a lot of money "to let people know who I was," he says, "let them know about working for Quayle and Reagan" and then fight the charge that he was a Washington insider. In response, he played the Clinton card. Yes, he wanted to go back to Washington—to fight the liberals.

In Indiana in the summer, every little town has a parade. McIntosh and his wife marched in as many as they could, wearing matching American flag shirts—coopting a symbol usurped by radicals a quarter-century before. "Occasionally you'd get some people who were older and conservative saying, 'I like everything you do, David, but don't wear the flag as an article of clothing,'" he recalls. "They were thinking back to when Abbie Hoffman wore one. But for the average person, it was a positive symbol. The culture had changed from the sixties."

Though the district's voters were mostly Democrats, they were also Bible Belt traditionalists with a strong libertarian streak. McIntosh appealed to union members angry about gun control. While he was working in the Justice Department, he'd learned to shoot and bought a gun. The same voters loved it when McIntosh disparaged Clinton's crime legislation as a "hug a thug" bill. "That kind of summed up the problem, wanting to coddle the criminals and then taking away innocent people's firearms."

Election night, he was stunned, and not just by his own win. "I had no idea of the magnitude of change until late that night when someone said, you know, not only are you going to be a Congressman, you're going to be in the majority." The next morning he showed up at a foundry at 5:00 A.M. to thank the union men who'd voted for him. Then he joined the famous 1995 freshman class in Congress.

Early in McIntosh's term, it seemed as if those freshmen and their leader, Georgia congressman Newt Gingrich (b. 1943), were taking over the political world. Gingrich had joined the House in 1979 but through the 1980s was considered a noisy troublemaker, when considered at all. He'd started his local career as a liberal Republican who admitted smoking pot in college, but by the time he arrived in Congress he was a disciple of New Right guru Paul Weyrich. Branded a kook, he'd toss off futuristic ideas like privatizing space launches. When he and several other congressional outcasts formed the Conservative Opportunity Society, they proved themselves ready-made for the Reagan Revolution.

In 1986, Gingrich took over a political action committee that helped him build support for and among Republicans across the country. He came to national prominence two years later when he spearheaded an ethics investigation that drove then-Speaker of the House Jim Wright from his job. His reward: election as minority whip, the Number 2 party post in the House.[3] A series of ethics charges against him didn't stop Gingrich, who, in 1994, created the Contract with America, a campaign document that promised to restore traditional values and limit government with a balanced budget, tax cuts, term limits and welfare reform, and led to the first Republican-controlled House in forty years. He'd come to embody a new political paradigm for a generation that still fancied itself activist even as it courted certainty and stability. Gingrich had a perverse appeal to a generation raised to distrust and challenge the establishment.

In its first few heady months in office, the House Class of '95 set about to make revolution. They helped elect Gingrich speaker, and he put an end to years of tradition, remaking Congress so that ideology, expertise and energy, not seniority, determined who'd be running things. The newcomer McIntosh was made one of the freshmen Republicans' liaisons with the House leadership, the head of a new subcommittee on regulatory reform, and assistant Republican whip. It was a heady moment. "It quickly became apparent to me that everybody in our class felt we should push for the Contract to show we had kept our word," he says. "There was a real sense that we were change agents in the political process."

At first, the Republican-controlled House seemed unstoppable. It voted to cut taxes and institute regulatory reform, while Democrats fumbled a crime bill and health care reform. McIntosh's collegiate vision was becoming reality; conservatives were the new activists. "These guys are controlling the Republican Party, and the old-style Republicans who have been here for years have no voice," James Carville, the Clinton campaign strategist, complained. "They're true revolutionaries. They're serious."[4]

McIntosh epitomized their take-no-prisoners style. He quickly made his positions clear; he opposed retroactive liability on environmental protection, calling it "immoral,"[5] and was against national health care and lobbying by federal grant recipients. "In government, the people we hear from the most, the people asking for grants, are living off the taxpayer, using public funds for elaborate lobbying efforts to keep the programs going," he charged.

Though many of McIntosh's bills passed the House only to go down in defeat in the Senate, the 104th Congress was seen as a watershed in American politics. But just at the moment of their triumph, when Gingrich was named *Time* magazine's Man of the Year, he and his conservative cadre stumbled. In fall 1995, after Senate Majority Leader Bob Dole suggested that proposed Republican tax cuts be scaled back, McIntosh urged his fellow freshmen to oppose *any* decrease. He also favored a tactic that proved a Christmas present to Bill Clinton. At the end of 1995, the House freshmen shut down the federal government for weeks in what appeared to be a fit of partisan pique, refusing to pass a stopgap spending measure until the White House agreed to their plan to balance the federal budget.

"Closing down parts of the government isn't that much of a problem," McIntosh had predicted, incorrectly.[6] The public was outraged. When Gingrich eventually compromised and agreed to reopen the government, a handful of the conservatives, McIntosh among them, briefly revolted. McIntosh finally came around, voting to reopen the government. "Newt said, 'Look, you're part of my leadership team; I'm making the judgment call; fall in line,'" he explains. "I disagreed but chose to do that."

Ironically, right around then Clinton fell in line, too, lurching right as suddenly as he'd moved left after taking office. Clinton adopted the Republican budget, signed appropriations bills that cut government spending for the first time in a quarter-century, and embraced the conservatives' desire to end the welfare state. Meanwhile, Gingrich and the House freshmen alienated many supporters by guarding their right flank, refusing to compromise and pushing radical social measures far less popular than their economic fixes. By the end of 1996, Clinton was able to win reelection handily by running against an aged symbol of the Silent Generation, Dole, and against Gingrich, the unruly representative of the Baby Boom present. In May 1997, Clinton and the Republicans reached agreement on one of the key ideas of the Contract for America: a plan to enforce strict spending caps to balance the budget.

McIntosh had won reelection in 1996, too, by a wide margin, running campaign ads that personalized his fight against government regulation. He'd intervened on behalf of one five-year-old constituent to gain FDA approval for a life-saving drug, and had deleted funding for a regulation that required asphalt-layers to wear long pants during summer months. "The purpose was to show that the theoretical things I was working for had real consequences for people," he says.

Back in Washington, McIntosh played a leading role when the House Government Reform Oversight Committee started investigating fundraising illegalities in the 1996 election. More significantly, he played a leading role in an attempted coup d'etat in summer 1997, when eleven confrontational conservatives sought to topple Speaker Gingrich. The group, which eventually doubled in size, considered Gingrich too weakened by ethics charges, too willing to compromise with the Democrats, too unpopular, and too often outmaneuvered by the White House. They drafted a document to oust him, began collecting signatures, and approached the Republican leadership, but their brash move ended when those leaders tipped off Gingrich.

The Speaker survived. McIntosh, though chastened, was also disillusioned and continued to skirmish with Gingrich in the House and in the press over government spending and tax cuts. "I'm not sure Newt quite understood what he had accomplished," McIntosh says. "I think that's why his numbers inverted fairly quickly. He could have been a Reaganesque character had he had some core philosophy. Fundamental principles—individual freedom, smaller government, strengthening the family—are why I'm in politics. He ended up somebody who used positions to acquire power, when people wanted him to use power to forward ideas."

THOUGH SHE WAS lecturing to thousands every week, Marianne Williamson's life didn't go into overdrive until her first book, *A Return to Love*, topped the self-help bestseller list and stayed there for months following Oprah Winfrey's endorsement. "I have never been as moved by a book," the talk-show host said on the air. Williamson had been talked into writing it by a literary agent who went to one of her lectures in 1988 at a low point in his life. That serendipity changed her life as much as her mix of mysticism and self-help psychologizing changed his. Royalties from the tome and a multimillion-dollar deal for several more let her move with daughter, Emma, from a small West Hollywood condo into a house with a pool in the Hollywood Hills, and to trade in her nine-year-old Peugeot for a new Infiniti sedan.[7]

Although Williamson had stepped down as president of the board of the Center for Living, waves of bad press kept rolling in and "totally kept me off balance," she says. "I was profoundly hurt and left L.A." for Santa Barbara, where she lowered her profile, cut back her lecture schedule, and churned out more books. Her second, *A Woman's Worth*, earned nineteen weeks on the bestseller list with its advice that women should examine their inner selves, overcome damage done to them by their parents, give more value to their intuition, passion, receptivity, and nonviolence, and find the goddess, the Amazon, the mystical princess within, before trying to conquer the outer world. A third book, *Illuminata*, filled with Williamson-penned prayers (including pleas for forgiveness aimed at African-Americans and Native Americans), followed.

In the meantime, Williamson had come to the attention of Bill and Hillary Clinton. There was a natural bond with Hillary, who'd tried to do as an adult what Williamson had (somewhat more appropriately) claimed to have done as a child: channel Eleanor Roosevelt. At the end of 1994, Williamson was invited, along with the motivational author and hot-coal walker Tony Robbins and Stephen R. Covey, author of *Seven Habits of Highly Effective People*, to visit with the First Couple at Camp David. They seemed ready to anoint Williamson the Baby Boom's Billy Graham. "New Age guru-ism is mostly alien to Washington's practical political culture," the *Washington Post* observed archly, but it added that Williamson's writings on bucking the patriarchy probably appealed to the feminist First Lady.[8]

Williamson's politics certainly did. Like her father before her, she is "quite progressive," she says, although "the left is quicker to mock me than the right, because I have the audacity to talk in spiritual terms. The only reason a fear-based perspective has such power in this country is because a love-based perspective is not expressed so loudly. The Reaganites and born-again Christians had more chutzpah than we did. They don't have any problem stating their worldview. We talk too much, but we talk too little about things that matter. The problem is that the most narrow-minded people are the most organized, enthusiastic and efficient."

Williamson won't reveal what she told the Clintons at Camp David or subsequently, when she stayed overnight—"alone," she stresses—in the White House's Lincoln Bedroom, but she did have strong political opinions and an eagerness to share them. "There is no dearth of genius in this country," she says. "There are people in every area—mainly baby boomers—who have elucidated principles, theories and ideas that would make society work and are applying those ideas. However, at this particular moment the political dynamic is actually an obstruction, because the goal of the American government is not to make the country a better place. In the absence of campaign finance reform, our government is little more than a puppet whose strings are being pulled by corporate interests."

Clinton's strings, presumably, included.

Williamson has often said that after 1968, most of her fellow boomers moved upstairs in the house of American life, leaving the service floor—government—to people like Clinton who could stomach the compromises of politics. "Many of us were fine with that," she says. "We were looking at the stars, having a great time. But now we're looking down and saying, 'Shit, they're burning down the house.' All of a sudden it's not funny. The grace period for our generation is over. The universe is demanding that we state what we stand for. And not engaging in the democratic process out of disgust or some pseudo-rebellion is exactly what the most reactionary forces in America would have us do."

IN 1989, A DRUG gang called the Wild Cowboys had effectively taken over a neighborhood in northern Manhattan where they sold vials of crack with tiny red stoppers—their trademark. One night, when the gang engaged in a shootout with competitors selling yellow-topped crack vials, more than 200 rounds of ammunition were fired, but no one called the police. The Cowboys made an estimated $16 million a year, used juveniles as couriers, were known for their motto "Snitches get stitches," and slashed potential witnesses with knives.

Eventually, the police traced eleven murders during more than a half a decade to the Cowboys (many to the gang's hitman, who called himself Freddie Krueger, after the horror film *Nightmare on Elm Street*) and arrested forty-two members of the gang, most of whom testified for the prosecution. Finally, in May 1995, nine Wild Cowboys leaders were found guilty of conspiracy, murder, assault and drug and weapons charges. Though they maintained their innocence, Leslie Crocker Snyder sentenced the smirking drug dealers to a total of 868 1/3 years to life. They were put in holding pens where letters from the parole board are posted like big-game trophies, testifying to urban jackals Snyder has put away: a hit man for John Gotti's Mafia family, a drug dealer who lost a shootout with ten cops, the murderer of an elderly couple.

Snyder received death threats during the eight-month trial, and has lived with a twenty-four-hour police guard ever since. She neither downplays the danger nor dwells on it. "Judges get more threats than people realize," she says. "Most of the time you don't take them seriously. But when you're talking about the Mob, or a gang, they may have abilities individuals don't."

Though Snyder insists politics doesn't enter her courtroom, she makes hers clear in her sentences. She is a registered Democrat, but she admired the maverick mayor Ed Koch, who appointed her, more than she did his successor, the doctrinaire liberal David Dinkins. Dinkins became New York's first African-American mayor in 1989 in large part because he represented a last fling with the 1960s ethic of optimism about social change. His laissez-faire approach to public order caused many to rethink their political positions. Primary among them were boomers who, in New York, at least, were now comfortable if not wealthy, and beginning to live the cliché that links increasing age with growing conservatism. Storefronts closed with security glass, blaring car alarms, crack vials on the sidewalks, an epidemic of petty urban pathologies, and a record number of murders—2,245 in 1990—fueled their rightward turn.

"Many people were utterly disgusted with Dinkins," Snyder says. The prevailing attitude was that the city was ungovernable, "and he had no control over it. In terms of appointing judges, his criteria were ludicrous. All he was interested in was: Were you a minority? If you were a prosecutor, you couldn't possibly understand defendants."

To the New Deal-style progressives who supported Dinkins, Snyder probably seemed like some kind of throwback. But she was actually the near future in black robes and pearls—balancing the Bill of Rights against a culture of violence grown so extreme, some were calling for martial law. Faced with cases where witnesses were being threatened against testifying at preliminary hearings, she pioneered a new technique to conceal their identities from defendants *and* defense lawyers until trial, while revealing the gist of their testimony and their prior records. "This drove the defense bar crazy," she admits. "It's a very dramatic departure. I don't like doing this, I don't want to do this, but I don't see an alternative." Seeking a reversal, defense attorneys appealed all the way to the U.S. Supreme Court, expecting her to be overturned. She wasn't.

Snyder thinks that if Dinkins had won a second term as New York's mayor, she would not have been reappointed to the Court. But he was defeated in 1993 by a law-and-order candidate, the former U.S. Attorney and Justice Department official Rudolph Giuliani (b. 1944), who did reappoint her to a ten-year term in 1995. Giuliani's election, in the most liberal of American cities, symbolized a sea-change in American politics. He adopted the "broken-window theory" of policing, which argued that if police addressed petty but seemingly intractable problems like vandalism and panhandling, they would send a message that could alter civic society and halt chronic increases in crime. During his first two years in office, there was a nearly 30 percent drop in major felonies in New York.[9] The same trend was seen nationally. In 1998, violent and property crimes dropped by 7 percent, the largest annual decrease since those numbers had peaked in 1992.

Snyder is quick to point out that Giuliani benefited from programs begun under his predecessor, and from demographic changes. As the Baby Boom aged, its members were less likely to be aggressive or criminal. She does agree that his initiatives also had a great effect—practical and psychological. "He's a total control freak," she says. "I can relate to that."

Giuliani's programs failed to address one underlying problem: the pernicious effects of racism, festering throughout the 1990s and in no way limited to New York. The arrest and trial of O.J. Simpson (b. 1947), the black football star and celebrity, for the murder of his white wife reminded the country of the gaping chasm between white and black Americans when a mostly African-American jury acquitted the African-American defendant, and most whites considered it jury nullification—a decision based on emotion instead of facts.

Snyder had recently presided over a case with a similar dynamic, the shooting of an African-American undercover police officer by three African-American men. The predominately black jury acquitted the defendants after some of them were heard shouting "Cops are all racist pigs!" from behind the closed doors of the jury room. "I was shocked," Snyder says. "Your temptation is to excoriate them because it's such a ludicrous result. I didn't because I felt that (a) it's not going to accomplish anything, and (b) I would say something I would regret, and it would be on the record."

She would remember that verdict, though, when not long afterward a racially mixed group of third and fourth graders she mentors started telling her cops couldn't be trusted—the same sentiment she'd written in her diary years before. "Of course some cops are bad. But they were so young to be so negative," she says. "And that does go back to our failure as a society to address things on a longer-term basis." Suddenly, this modern Draco begins to sound like someone else, decrying the erosion of the family unit, and the way the problems of the 1960s, when many poor children lived with only one parent or grandparent, became pathology in the mid-1980s, when the parents discovered crack, the grandparents grew too old, and the children went wild. "Education is the key to everything," Snyder says. "We haven't addressed homelessness, joblessness, lack of equal opportunities, lack of adequate education for the under- or even middle-class. But that's not a popular political quick fix."

By 1999, despite continuing drastic drops in crime, many in New York had tired of Rudolph Giuliani, and his troubles, like his successes, became a national news story. When the aggressive police tactics of the city's Street Crime Unit led to the killing of an innocent black immigrant early in 1999, a small but significant protest movement rose up, modeled by the Reverend Al Sharpton (b. 1954) on the nonviolent civil rights protests of the early 1960s and aimed at Giuliani. The mayor's popularity sank just as he began maneuvering toward a run for the U.S. Senate. Snyder, too, has her detractors. Defense attorneys charged that Manhattan District Attorney Robert Morgenthau (b. 1921) was steering high-profile cases to her, avoiding the standard random selection process for judges. One reason for the vehemence may be that the judge makes no secret of her desire to run for District Attorney, the top law enforcement job in New York, when Morgenthau retires, perhaps as early as the end of his term in 2002.

When and if she does run for elected office, Snyder's first priority will be setting out a philosophy "not as one-dimensional as some members of the defense bar would like to make out," she says. "If you witness the kind of viciousness for which I give out what appear to be draconian sentences, you wouldn't think they were draconian. On the other hand, there are dozens of young people I've put on probation, into programs, on deferred sentence, to see if they'll do well. I believe in the concept of rehabilitation, and I think we've failed miserably at that, too. But take the top members of a drug gang who have killed people. Who cares what the root causes are at that point? Who cares whether they are rehabilitated?"

Snyder's judgment of Bill Clinton aptly demonstrates her ability to parse legal complexities—and oddly parallel comments made by the president's wife in summer 1999, as she positioned herself for a Senate run against Giuliani. Bill Clinton's "background is relevant," Snyder says. "His family was dysfunctional." Just like those she so often sees in her courtroom.

"I can look at him as representing the worst of baby boomer values or lack of values," she continues. "But I don't think being a baby boomer means that you turn out like Clinton, that you take an oath as lightly, that you feel entitled to whatever you wish. A whole lot of baby boomers are egomaniacal and feel they should make as much money as they want and buy everything they want, but they would hesitate at doing things he's done. You can't take some individual and say he represents a generation. You can say he represents the worst of a generation."

WHEN KATHRYN BOND Stockton left Brown University, she figured she and her fellow Theory followers would end up teaching in community colleges or even driving taxis. "But on the job market we are incredibly salable, because we know stuff most of our professors didn't know," she says. After considering several offers, she took a teaching post at the University of Utah.

All over the country, humanities and literature departments were racing to catch up with cutting-edge Theory. Adherents would soon be promoted into positions of prominence throughout academia, and put on the fast tenure track as they shaped a new canon. Initially, professors with "strong and precise political views" saw its promotion of multiple meaning as a threat to their agendas. But as they came to understand Theory, they grew to like it. "The political benefit of believing things are socially constructed, whether you're a sixties radical or a nineties feminist, is to believe that then things could be otherwise," Stockton says.

Since the early 1970s, many colleges had established multidisciplinary departments that taught through the lenses of Afrocentrism or gender. Now, as Theory became practice on campuses, they turned into cultural war zones. At Smith College in Massachusetts, for instance, the Office of Student Affairs prepared fliers to make students aware of such "manifestations of oppression" as ableism (discrimination against the "differently abled"); ageism; and lookism, the tyranny of beauty.[10] "Grievance," wrote the critic Robert Hughes, had been "elevated into automatic sanctity."[11]

These ideas weren't confined to colleges. In many urban areas, community activists forced political changes in elementary and secondary curriculums. And outside the education system, a parallel culture of victimization and entitlement rose up among those who defined themselves as dispossessed. Bans on the use of demeaning language spread across the country— except when those being demeaned were white males.

Though they sprang from the same impulse, Theory and political correctness weren't identical. Academic deconstructionists focused purely on language. Their real-world counterparts saw the deconstruction of language as a sociopolitical tool for the reconstruction of culture. It was no surprise, then, that conservative critics would soon equate academic deconstructionists with radical Afrocentrists claiming quantum physics had been invented in ancient Egypt, superfeminists like Andrea Dworkin claiming that all sex is rape, and the rising cadre of campus mind police out looking for speech code infractions and felonious flirting. (A professor was charged with sexual harassment after he explained simile by comparing belly-dancing to Jell-O on a plate with a vibrator beneath it; traffic signs reading SLOW CHILDREN were suddenly deemed insensitive to the mentally handicapped.[12])

At first, academic leftists were opposed only by Moral Majority leaders and populist demagogues like Senator Jesse Helms. But by the late 1980s, a more broad-based reaction had set in. The "oppressors" began standing up to this new mode of thought, belittling all pressure for change from below or outside mainstream culture, and ridiculing what they called the "P.C. crowd's" frequent excesses. Wielding anecdotes like swords, conservatives accused the politically correct of being closet authoritarians, attempting to reconstruct society into conformance with their vision, and Theory-heads of being closet careerists creating new disciplines, duchies and opportunities for themselves and like-minded friends.

The critics weren't entirely wrong. "There are massive differences between these people," Stockton says, though she adds they "are not necessarily antithetical." They fit under the same umbrella, albeit a large one. Proponents of change and Theory mavens could agree on one thing: there is no such thing as normality. "Look up *queer* in the dictionary, you get two different definitions," Stockton says. "The first is strange; anything strange. And the second is slang for homosexual. Now, take the most 'normal' people out there. Go into their lives in enough detail, and they will deconstruct themselves, in the sense that they will cease to be coherent and normal. So now, obviously, everybody is Queer. Because everyone is strange."

Stockton thinks Theory's critics went too far. Political correctness "did not stop people from being sexist," she says. "It did not stop men from raping women at fraternities. It just meant there was another discourse in play." A First Amendment absolutist, she thinks everything should be expressed—even hateful opinions, even kiddie porn. "It strikes me as a bad idea to censor anything. As a Queer, I will always and forever be against censorship of any form. No learning will take place where people do not say what they believe. I am a professor of literature; my work is words, pleasuring words, empowering words, dangerous words. To keep people from speaking is an incredibly bad idea."

More than a professor, Stockton is also a provocative writer. In her first book, *God Between Their Lips*, published after five years at Utah, she dips into psychology, intellectual history, philosophy and theology to find an unseen erotic dimension in a novel by Charlotte Brontë. In her reading, the spiritual autobiography of the central character—an older woman looking back at her life and an unrequited love—becomes a means for the Victorian-era writer to talk about taboo subjects like sexuality, auto-eroticism and desire between women. "Spiritual autobiography is a perfect form for speaking about women's desire, because you have a fall, and then you wander in sin and suffering and look for Christ to come again. So it's all about desire. It has to end in a state of desire, because this pleasure, Christ, has not yet come."

Though far less *outré* than a fellow Theorist's discovery of hidden references to fist-fucking in the notebooks of Henry James, Stockton's imposition on Brontë might be shocking to some. "Whatever you think about Theory's excesses," she says, "its power is that it has trained us to ask a different set of smart and crucial questions."

IN THE LATE 1980s, corporate America discovered gays as a niche market. Ironically, instead of making homosexuality untouchable, AIDS had made it more visible and, curiously, more acceptable to the American mainstream. People were sympathetic. Business saw an opportunity. AIDS focused a market. It also revitalized the gay movement and gave it a cause to organize around. "The downside was that everything became about AIDS," Jim Fouratt says. "But I remember going to an ACT-Up meeting very early on and being absolutely amazed that all these young people were out. I had this moment of joy, realizing that these were my children."

ACT-Up formed out of anger and need—yet by accident. In March 1987, Larry Kramer was called on as a last-minute replacement for the director Nora Ephron, who'd canceled a speech at the Gay & Lesbian Community Center in New York. Four years before, increasingly exasperated, not just with the press and politicians, but with colleagues who disagreed with his screeds against promiscuous sex, Kramer had quit GMHC's board, but continued his attacks on anyone he felt was impeding AIDS research and care. Now he was even angrier, and his speech was a call to arms that led to the instant formation of the AIDS Coalition to Unleash Power. The group's backbone was late-model boomers. "You had a lot of young men, people who would have been Club Kids, art students—very sexy and not political, just angry," says Fouratt. "And they were going to use any fuckin' tool that they had to make their point." They became the Yippies of the 1990s, even staging an action at the Stock Exchange.

ACT-Up was well-marketed, like all brands created by and for boomers. And ACT-Up gave gay and bisexual men and women a new form of social life, just like the peace movement before it. Gays had been scared out of clubs. "Drugs were really back and they were taking young gay men and other young people and destroying them," says Fouratt. "The decadence of nightlife was upon us." ACT-Up meetings became a replacement. "A lot of what motivates people to do things is the desire to have intercourse," Fouratt says. "And not necessarily sexual intercourse. Just intercourse with other human beings. In New York City, everyone lives in tiny apartments. So people go out."

Fouratt thinks ACT-Up's activism inspired the next gesture of gay anger, a controversial attempt to "out" closeted prominent gays. The leader of the outing movement was Michaelangelo Signorile (b. 1962), who headed ACT-Up's media committee and wrote a gossip column for *Outweek*, a gay magazine that regularly named names. "I don't think [back-end boomers] understood what coming out had meant," Fouratt says. "For most of us who came out in the sixties and seventies, we gave up power, access, the ability to do things we could have if we had stayed closeted." Though Fouratt approved of outing dead people, like Steve Rubell, whose death from AIDS-related causes in 1989 was covered up,[13] he thought the living should have the right to decide for themselves. "You don't punish people for being gay, which is essentially what they were doing," Fouratt says. "The process of coming out is painful and scary, and to force someone out is really self-centered."

Fouratt increasingly found himself out of step with his fellow activists. He moved out of the leadership of HEAL after the cause of AIDS, the HIV virus, was isolated, because he thought it was important to continue to talk about other factors—including lifestyle and genetics—that contributed to the collapse of people's immune systems. "The multifactorial position, which said you have to look at a lot of different things, was very unpopular in the late eighties," he says. "What if we get something that cures HIV and gay men go back to the same lifestyle? I was accused of being sex-phobic, but you have to be responsible. The victim mentality is wrong. We didn't cause AIDS. But if you say someone else did, it's wrong too. You have to look at your life."

Fouratt looked at his own. He'd already done a lot of self-examination in twelve-step programs, and he'd started therapy. "All that gave me some self-awareness so I could change certain things that made me sexy but didn't really help meacting out, being dramatic, confrontational," he says. "I made a decision I wasn't going to fight in ACT-Up with people who were dying. It wasn't worth being right."

* * *

IN 1989 A playwright named Billy Aronson had the idea of updating Puccini's opera *La Bohème*, moving it to the modern day, and replacing tuberculosis with AIDS. Seeking a composer with whom to work, he met Jonathan Larson, and they quickly wrote three songs together. Larson, who'd been waiting tables for years while waiting for a break, and volunteering at Marianne Williamson's Manhattan Center for Living, suggested an East Village milieu and the multiple-meaninged title *Rent*. He felt it could be a modern version of *Hair*, incorporating aspects—good and bad—of the new bohemian scene: heroin addiction and HIV, fashion and fame, performance art and the mainstreaming of what had once been considered sexual perversity in unconventional venues like artists' spaces and drag bars.

Two years later, in 1991, surrounded by friends all suffering with AIDS, Larson called Aronson and asked if he could take over the idea and pursue it on his own.[14] Larson was attending meetings at Friends in Deed, which spun off from the Manhattan Center after Williamson's fight with her board. The philosophy of both groups—that one can learn to live with terminal disease and still have a fulfilling life—had spurred Larson to return to *Rent*. That year, too, Victoria Leacock and Ali Gertz decided to form an organization to educate young people about HIV. After rejecting the names Rough Hope and Love Cures (because, unfortunately, it doesn't), they settled on Love Heals.

In the meantime, Leacock had decided to become a filmmaker like her father. Supporting herself by working for artists as a personal assistant, she began making videotapes and small films, including one that aired on MTV about Blondie, the Tom-Tom Club and the Ramones. After that, she got a job as the cinematographer on an AIDS documentary produced by director Jonathan Demme. Demme had been partly inspired to make a movie about AIDS, *Philadelphia*, by the story of Juan Botas, an artist friend of his wife who'd contracted HIV. Botas convinced Demme a movie could be made about a Greenwich Village clinic where groups of gay men living with AIDS received two-hour intravenous infusions of drugs. When Botas realized he couldn't film their conversations and take part in them, he brought in Leacock, who'd impressed Demme's assistant when she videotaped a charity function the director had organized.

She and Botas were busy filming when Ali Gertz died in August 1992. Botas died three weeks later. "I kept filming because I didn't know what else to do," says Leacock, who finally stopped three months after that when her grandmother died as well.[15] Leacock turned her attention to Love Heals, and along with several friends, got it up and running. They felt that the AIDS community, so tied up in gay issues, could benefit from an organization formed to tell the story of a girl who contracted HIV through heterosexual sex. Their experiences became part of the development of *Rent*. Larson and Leacock videotaped Gertz's memorial, inspiring the opening of the musical.

As Larson continued struggling with *Rent*, Leacock helped mount readings, workshops and backers' auditions. After she sold a house she'd inherited from her grandmother, she also financed and helped produce a recording session of songs he'd written. And she helped Larson earn money, getting him work scoring music for home movies she edited for *Rolling Stone* founder Jann Wenner.

In the early 1990s, Leacock's life was still consumed with illness. Her roommates, Gordon Rogers and Pam Shaw, kept getting sicker. There was one bright spot. In spring 1994, Larson got a grant to stage *Rent*. The ten performances that fall were sellouts. More important, they attracted backers. With a production now likely, Larson began adding songs and tightening the concept. Among many other changes, he incorporated ideas that came from Rogers, whose reaction to his illness was rage—not acceptance.

BY THE MID-1990S, yuppies were no longer scum, and ambition, for so long a quasi-dirty word, had become a given for most baby boomers. Those who had wanted more, and those who didn't wanted in. There were baby boomer billionaires out there! "Doing good" had taken on a whole new meaning.

For Michael Fuchs, the Time-Warner merger no longer seemed like a mess of broken eggs but an opportunity to make a golden corporate omelet. Even before the deal was concluded, Fuchs was operating behind the scenes. Feeling that Nick Nicholas had turned his back on his Time Inc. colleagues, Fuchs switched sides in what was still a secret corporate joust and began promoting Gerald Levin's ambition to take over the company. They talked a lot. Levin involved him at the boardroom level. Fuchs just didn't think Nicholas would be as effective.

In 1991, when Warner chairman Steve Ross began chemotherapy following a relapse of cancer, the maneuvering in the ranks grew fierce. Fuchs went to Levin and renegotiated his contract to become one of Time-Warner's three highest-paid executives, along with studio chiefs Bob Daly and Terry Semel—a fact soon trumpeted by a press corps that had turned corporate warriors into latter-day rock stars by chronicling their lives as intensely as it once had Keith Richards's drug use.

Fuchs wanted a bigger job, believing he deserved and had been promised one. In January 1992, Time-Warner's board fired Nicholas and made Levin co-CEO. When Ross died that December and Gerald Levin—the chief of Fuchs's tribe—took over, Fuchs expected a promotion, but it never happened. He was agitated, to say the least, and sometimes his feelings showed. Three years, another Oscar, and seventeen Emmys later, Fuchs let it be known he wanted out. "I was restless and bored, which is dangerous for me." In May 1995, Levin responded by asking him to take over Warner's music operation—the largest in the world, encompassing Warner Brothers, Elektra, and Atlantic Records.

Fuchs accepted. "I was clear in my own head that I would like to run Time-Warner some day," he says. "So when they handed me music, I thought, Maybe this is a step in the right direction. And I was enormously excited to do something new." Fuchs got rid of several executives. Before he got the chance to start rebuilding, though he sensed that the knives were out for him. He'd let Levin announce his new position before they settled on a contract. By summer, Levin was asking him to give up all his responsibilities at HBO. But Fuchs loved TV and movies. He didn't want to throw away twenty years of equity in those businesses. And that didn't please his rivals, Daly and Semel, who denied they had anything to do with his difficulties but were reported to be fretting over Fuchs's new job and unhappy with reports he was being positioned to take over post-Levin.[16] "All that mattered for those guys was the perception that that they were the most powerful people in the company," Fuchs says.

Daly and Semel may not have been the problem. When Levin started hearing the heir apparent talk, he apparently got nervous, too. In September, just after Time-Warner's $7.4 billion merger with TBS was announced, Fuchs was fired and his music job handed to Daly and Semel. A press report said his "blunt ambition" for Levin's job was a factor in his sudden skid from grace.[17] Although Levin had paid out millions to rid himself of a number of executives, the market applauded him. Time-Warner's stock price rose with the news of Fuchs's firing.

Fuchs won't comment on Levin's role in his dismissal, or speculate on whether his canny boss maneuvered him into a no-win situation. But in a speech not long afterward, he said, "There is such a thing as being too good and wanting to excel too much and having politics overwhelm performance." And he seems neither surprised nor sorry that in 1999, Gerald Levin skillfully eased Daly and Semel out of Time-Warner, too.

ON AUGUST 9, 1995, workers at a drug abuse treatment clinic in California discovered the body of Jerry Garcia in the room where he'd been staying while trying to kick his drug habit. The immediate cause of Garcia's death was a heart attack. But many blamed his death on thirty years of drug abuse. "Everybody I work with had a drug habit at some point—myself included," says Cameron Sears. "I'd smoke dope with the best of them. When I started working for the Grateful Dead, I had to stop, because I was the responsible adult."

Sears believes that while Garcia was hero to millions, he didn't want to be. "He just wanted to play guitar. He accepted his celebrity as a function of what he did, but as it got bigger and bigger, it got more difficult for him. He led a relatively insulated life. That connection with people was a very important thing to him, but it had gotten to the point where he didn't have it anymore. So he numbed out."

Garcia's death reawakened the activist impulses Sears had put on hold when he went to work for the band. In its wake, he redoubled efforts to communicate to grieving fans that drugs and decadence were not what the Dead had been about. Within the Dead community, Garcia's death was a wake-up call, too. "There was a deep regret at allowing it to get as out-of-hand as it did," Sears says. "That free spirit the band represented musically came back to haunt us."

STEVE CAPPS REFUSED to let go of the handheld computer called Newton. In September 1995, it was reintroduced and redeemed, at least among the cognoscenti. (When Steve Jobs returned to Apple in December 1996 and killed it, its fans let out a collective howl, but their numbers were so small they could be easily ignored.)

Meanwhile, the Internet had profoundly altered the world of computing. Capps, who'd been watching it out of the corner of his eye, was concerned. He saw it as a sprawling frontier ready to be tamed. And he feared that Microsoft-style capitalists, not Apple-style idealists, would get there first.

Capps had almost quit Apple in 1994, thinking to create an Internet company after having seen his first Web browser. To keep him, the company made him its fifth Apple Fellow, and gave him a substantial raise. Apple Fellows were the company's pie-in-the-sky types. "They basically sit around and pull lint out of their navels," Capps says. "I like to ship products. I don't like to sit around and think. I'd much rather be a shark and keep moving."

After Newton 2.0 shipped, Capps was given a sabbatical. He spent it playing basketball, trying to have a baby with wife Marie D'Amico (their daughter, Emma, was born in 1997), and thinking about his future. "Apple is in the doldrums," he says. Yet another CEO had been hired that February to turn the company around. "And I'm sitting there looking at the business and looking at browsers and asking myself what we should do to save the Macintosh."

In December 1995, Bill Gates had admitted he'd been wrong to dismiss the Internet and put the considerable resources of Microsoft behind a catchup strategy. Capps told management "that if Gates could admit he was wrong, so should they." He urged Apple to scrap a long-delayed new operating system, join forces with a network-based company like Sun, and "make Apple the 'Net cruiser of the nineties." When they wouldn't listen, he and two of his Newton colleagues went looking for a way out.[18]

As usual, Capps was bursting with ideas, but the venture capitalists he went to see wanted him to have one, not a dozen. "I don't understand their logic," Capps says, "but they're successful at making their money grow by a factor of ten, so I shouldn't question them too much." When one of his team accepted a corporate job, Capps and his remaining teammate began interviewing, too. "They're all kind of hankering for us, because there's very few people who really understand user interfaces," Capps says. Capps's Apple-bred idealism proved a tough fit, even at forward-thinking places like Netscape and Sun. For Capps, Sun's UNIX-based mentality— and its feeling that personal computers were junky, uninteresting little boxes—was too big a hurdle to get over. "UNIX people think software is a necessary evil to sell hardware," Capps says. "They think they're making this big locomotive and we're the guys that polish and wax it just before it leaves the factory. Whereas at Apple, the user experience was the way you thought about the world."

Microsoft, meanwhile, was looking at the Internet and thinking hard about how users experienced it. Capps got a warm welcome when he called an Apple executive from the Macintosh days who'd moved to Microsoft and recently been put in charge of its Internet strategy. "I told him the story about my ten ideas and he goes, 'If you have ten good ideas, we'll fund them all,'" says Capps. Having recently bought his first Windows machine, he threw down a gauntlet, telling the executive he thought Microsoft's Internet Explorer browser (which, mirroring the relationship of Macintosh and Windows, was based on the pioneering Netscape) was badly designed. When the executive asked him to explain instead of hanging up, Capps was intrigued. He flew to Redmond, Washington.

"What do you want to do?" a Microsoft vice president asked.

"I want to work real hard for another five years and then retire," Capps replied. The executive asked him to name his price. Capps did.

"We can do that," he said.

AFTER BILL CLINTON'S election, Doug Marlette had put together a book of cartoons on the First Couple and soon enough was summoned to the White House to present Clinton with a copy. Still hopeful about Clinton, he accepted, and watched proudly as the President leafed through it, laughing so loudly that Colin Powell, Secretary of Defense Les Aspin, and Clinton's secretary, Betty Currie, all rushed in to see what the ruckus was about. Looking at a cartoon of himself as a Bubba Yuppie schoolboy, crafting a crude Rolodex in wood shop, Clinton muttered, "Boy, that's really close to the bone."

Back then, Marlette was gentle with Clinton, but by mid-1993 he'd grown skeptical. He wrote a cover story for *Esquire* that summer called "Never Trust a Weeping Man," which described the Clintons as the "First Bacilli of the disease of our age . . . where narcissism meets obsessive compulsion." He compared the president to "the anchorman, the televangelist, the actor, the carnival sideshow snake-oil salesman," saying Clinton appealed to boomers because they'd lost the ability to feel.[19]

Shortly after writing that piece, Marlette became *Esquire*'s "Good Behavior" columnist, writing on topics like corporate backstabbing, commuter marriage, and staying friends with a former spouse. He took on the national impulse to share. "Why can't we all take our pain and suffering and our gotta-be-me-ness back into the closet? Closets are where we store valuable things." And most revealing of all, he wrote of his torment over what he would tell his son when the boy asked, inevitably, if his father ever took drugs. "For a generation so long defined by the media as 'the kids,' becoming parents, however long postponed, finally makes us put lives where our mouths were, raising all the questions we had successfully ignored, rubbing our noses in the shallowness of our cherished assumptions. We are responsible. We are accountable. And they are mirrors."

Marlette's new mood showed in his cartoons of the Clintons, too. Now, Clinton paddled in a canoe called Whitewater; his policy advisors stuck *Playboy* centerfolds in his briefing books; chameleons in the trees outside the Oval Office envied Clinton's ability to change his policies to fit his surroundings; and Hillary and Bill were perfecting their Nixon impressions. "We are not a crook," read that caption.

After Clinton's election, the Renaissance weekends had changed for

Marlette. They were studied and parsed and relentlessly publicized. One year, there were "huge crowds, huge panels, overorganized, a gazillion people, and all of a sudden, the program had gotten so big, every speaker's time was limited, and there was a lot of talk of people not being invited back," Marlette recalls. "The final night, Bill and Hillary talked off the record to the group. And I noticed—this is my gimlet eye—when Hillary introduced the President, she was sort of chilly. And then she gave a canned speech." The next morning, Marlette spoke at one of the last events of the weekend and made a crack about Hillary's boring speech and how someone had held up a two-minute warning sign to limit her—when he looked again, he continued, it turned out to be the President. The audience roared, and Marlette recalls that the person laughing loudest was the President. Later on, Kathleen Kennedy Townsend (b. 1951), the Lt. Governor of Maryland, asked him, "Did you realize they'd been fighting?"

At that same December 1997 event, in a panel discussing the Clinton legacy, Marlette told the crowd that he always applies a favorite Beatle test before judging anyone. "And it's been documented that the President's favorite Beatle was Paul McCartney, and we all wish that it was John Lennon." He paused for the laugh. "Hillary's favorite Beatle was Yoko Ono." The laughter wavered a bit; Hillary was in the room. He then described his cartoonist's vision of Clinton's legacy: a national monument portraying a giant zipper. "On the entire panel no one had mentioned anything about his problems in that area," Marlette says.

The next day, before leaving, Marlette thanked Clinton for some kind words he'd offered to Marlette's son. "He's usually very warm," Marlette says. "He's usually hugging. He turned and looked at me and hummingbirds would have frozen in midflight. It was nuclear winter. I could feel that Hillary had talked to him. There's not been any contact since then."

Less than a month later, Clinton had bigger problems than Marlette. They were named Monica Lewinsky and Kenneth Starr, the intern and the independent counsel. And they gave Marlette the best gift you can give to a cartoonist: a million opportunities for political incorrectness. "Hail to the Creep," said one Marlette cartoon. Another showed the White House as a trailer, decorated with a satellite dish, a lawn flamingo, and the legend *White Trash Legacy*. In the mailbox out in front are the November 1998 congressional election results. "Yeeehiiii, Hillary, we been vindicated!" read the caption. Standards had changed. When Marlette drew Saddam Hussein mooning Clinton while an aide observes,

"It's another stalker in a beret who wants to show you his thong," nobody tried to censor it.

Marlette regards his generation's post-scandal support of Bill and Hillary Clinton as deep mass denial. "There's something that's going on that we don't want to think about and that's why we focus on Ken Starr," he says. "I was feeling this before the speech and the confession. You cannot have the President, the nation's putative father, behave as an infant. It turns everything upside-down. And Hillary is practically his procurer. She never looks better than when he is screwing up. We cannot look too closely at Bill and Hillary, because they're us.

"The President of the United States, the Chief Executive Officer, is teaching my son—and a generation—that if he is caught with his hand in the cookie jar, he should say, 'Define hand,' 'define cookies.' This is where I will take it to the hoop with Bill and Hillary. I know they've read Orwell's essay on language. Nixon and Kissinger talked about 'pacification' when they were destroying villages, and about 'incursions' instead of invasions. Bill and Hillary, for the sake of his survival, have engaged in the same debasement and devaluation and weasel-wording. And then they waged war as distraction." Marlette shows me a cartoon of the President and First Lady looking at a chart of a cruise missile, smiling, over the caption, "It takes out a village."

"It's a long way from 1968, isn't it?" he says.

It all brings to mind another Southern leader. "Robert E. Lee took responsibility for Gettysburg," Marlette says. "He did not 'spin'; he was accountable. But we live in a time of polls and focus groups." Marlette hopes the Baby Boom will eventually tire of being spun and finally find itself desperate for authenticity. "It has been polled and market-researched to near-death," he says. "It is beating the life out of everything. All of it is the same—Clinton, Hollywood, market research, the Disneyfication of America—it is pushing things down people's throats, and there is a gag reflex. I embody the gag reflex. I am always throwing up."

ON A FREEZING cold morning early in 1997, as the Supreme Court began hearing arguments over whether Paula Corbin Jones should be allowed to pursue a sexual harassment lawsuit against President Clinton, a reporter approached a parka-clad demonstrator holding a sign supporting Jones's right to sue outside the courthouse.

"Do this often?" he asked

"Not in years," she replied.

"When was the last time you demonstrated?"

"Many years ago, in front of the Pentagon. I was doing the same thing I am now, exposing hypocrisy."

"You demonstrated during the war in Vietnam?"

She said she had. The reporter looked confused. Finally, he asked, "Which side were you on?"

The parka'ed picketer was Barbara Ledeen. In its brief existence, her organization, the Independent Women's Forum, had never shied away from controversy, but nothing prepared her for what would happen when the Jones sexual harassment lawsuit metastasized into 1998's consuming scandal. Initially, IWF's involvement was peripheral. Still when Bill Clinton's partisans launched their scorched-earth defense of the First Boomer, the flames licked Ledeen—and kicked off a bizarre volley of charge and countercharge.

On August 11, 1994, the Associated Press had reported that the IWF had approached Kenneth Starr to write a friend-of-the-court brief opposing President Clinton's claim of immunity from Jones's charge, and that Starr had agreed. A few days later, he was named independent counsel in the Whitewater investigation. For the next four years, the charge that Starr had worked for the IWF on behalf of Jones followed him, repeated everywhere from the *New York Times* editorial page to the floor of the U.S. Senate.

Starr hadn't actually crossed that line. He'd been approached, but was never hired, at least in part because the IWF's leaders were put off by Jones's belated claim. "We don't support the idea that years after the fact, somebody can whine and moan" about harassment, says Ledeen. Regardless, the ensuing controversy put IWF on the political map and gave the tiny group influence far beyond its size.

Barbara and Michael Ledeen were simultaneously embroiled in an explosive lawsuit brought by one of Michael's longtime ideological adversaries. On August 11, 1997, Sidney Blumenthal, once a journalist for the *New Republic* and *The New Yorker*, had gone to work at the White House as an assistant to the president. The day before, Matt Drudge (b. 1967), the World Wide Web gossip columnist and Clinton-antagonist, had printed an anonymously sourced item alleging that Blumenthal had committed acts of violence against his wife, who also worked in the White House. Two days later, in response to a letter from the Blumenthals' lawyer, Drudge apologized, issued a retraction, and admitted to reporters that he believed he'd been used by a politically motivated source.

Unsatisfied, the Blumenthals sued Drudge and America Online, which carried his reports, for $30 million.[20]

At first, the Ledeens were amused, since Blumenthal was among those who'd reprinted the old charges about Michael Ledeen when his name surfaced in the Iran-Contra investigation. "We're hysterical laughing; it's lovely to see that he who gives, gets," Barbara says. Two days later, she got a call from Drudge, who wondered if she could help confirm his story. She and her husband suggested instead that he apologize, even grovel, but they also helped him find a lawyer.

On January 27, 1998, in the wake of Drudge's biggest scoop yet, the exposure of the president's affair with a White House intern, Hillary Clinton appeared on the *Today* show and claimed there was a "vast right-wing conspiracy" dedicated to sliming her husband. A month later, White House aide Blumenthal—nicknamed Grassy Knoll for what the *New York Times* referred to as his "dark tales of right-wing cabals intent on bringing down President Clinton and Hillary Rodham Clinton"—was summoned to a grand jury Ken Starr had convened in his latest investigation, into Clinton's relationship with Monica Lewinsky.

Afterward, Blumenthal sputtered in his outrage at being "hauled before a federal grand jury to answer questions about my conversations with members of the media."[21] Yet that July, Ledeen and her husband were subpoenaed in the lawsuit by the Blumenthals, to testify about their conversations with various members of the media. Conservatives erupted over the subpoenas—and the hypocrisy they seemed to represent. The *National Review* even dug up an appropriate quote from Blumenthal, who'd once said, "I play by Chicago rules. You come after me with a knife, I come after you with a gun. You come after me with a gun, I come after you with a howitzer."[22] The White House had begun a battalion-strength counterattack against its perceived enemies, and Blumenthal's subpoenas were only a small part of it. IWF's links to the *American Spectator*—the conservative magazine that dragged Paula Jones into the spotlight—and to their conservative benefactor Richard Mellon Scaife were relentlessly publicized in following months. The attacks galvanized Ledeen's fury at Bill and Hillary Clinton.

Baby Boom voters who supported the Clintons in their dark hour in the November 1998 election were, says Ledeen, destructive "suckers" who are afraid to question the President's behavior because to do so would require taking a close look at their own. In Ledeen's eyes, Clinton's supporters thought 1960s protest was a party and couldn't "see past the entertainment value of the demonstrations to what they were really about." Their minds are clouded, too, she continues, only today their drug is prosperity instead of pot. Deeply defensive, they cling to the Clintons as life preservers, rare examples of boomers who appear to have held to their beliefs.

To Ledeen, the Clintons are dangerous authoritarians and Hillary Clinton's Senate run is the latest attempt to impose their program on America. "They *have* to make the world better," Ledeen says. "They have a utopian vision of improving mankind." The President is Hillary's stalking horse, "but he's not the one with the power right now," Ledeen says. "Hillary is the policy driver. She's known about his women for years but she always had some other deal in mind."

Ledeen snorts with derision when she recalls how the President wagged his finger at the public and said he'd never had sex with Monica Lewinsky. He did that while endorsing a $22 billion proposal for a national child care initiative—a pet program of the First Lady's—at a White House event held just hours after Hillary's "right-wing conspiracy" interview. "That was Hillary's payoff," Ledeen says flatly.

If the First Lady drops out of or loses her Senate race, Ledeen predicts the President will reward her with a lame-duck appointment to the World Bank. "The vision I have is of the moving trucks pulling up to the White House and Hillary grabbing onto the upholstery with her fingernails and not letting go."

THOUGH HE CAME into Congress as a firebrand, by 1998 David McIntosh was an established congressional leader. That February, he was elected chairman of the Conservative Action Team, a caucus of conservative congressmen who earned the nickname CATs because of their sharp claws. Though he vowed he would work with Republican leaders, in an attempt to tone down the CATs' image as confrontational reactionaries, he also warned the leaders that they would ignore the CAT agenda at their own peril.[23] Speculation arose that it was only a matter of time before McIntosh tried to replace House Speaker Gingrich or another member of the party leadership.

Within a month, he had set out a new CAT agenda calling for a balanced budget, tight controls on government spending, increased tax exemptions for dependent children, an eventual overhaul of the entire tax code, and parental oversight of educational curriculums as well as of medical, psychiatric and psychological testing or treatment of children. He also stood against the income tax marriage penalty, funding of the

National Endowment for the Arts, and the use of tax revenues to subsidize abortion.

Quietly, the CATs were positioning themselves for increased influence in the Republican leadership and maneuvering to push a tax cut through Congress to increase defense spending and find more budget cuts. McIntosh was, he says, consciously seeking to strike a reasonable balance and define issues that both social and economic conservatives could support, without venturing into territory like an abortion ban, where a broader consensus is difficult if not impossible to find.

As an example, McIntosh points to the Supreme Court's ban on prayer in schools. Though reversing that ban has been a conservative touchstone for years, McIntosh prefers to get around it. "Society will find its social moorings if we allow religious activities to occur in ways everybody in the community agrees with," he says. "You won't have the Bible being taught in schools, because very few communities actually want that. But you won't have ridiculous prohibitions on students saying a prayer at a graduation. Freedom is not only the key to economic success and individual happiness, but also to allowing moral values to be taught—outside of government—in the community, whether it's in the church or the Boy Scouts or community organizations."

As McIntosh was establishing that agenda, Bill Clinton became the nation's biggest issue. For McIntosh, the link between the President's new problems and previous ones, such as the fundraising abuses he'd investigated, were clear. "Clinton and Gore bent the rules," he says. "They used government resources to woo donors. And that approach applied across the board. The place Clinton ended up getting caught was in his personal life. He cheated on his wife, who obviously knew he had been doing this and was reconciled to it because she enjoyed the power of being First Lady." To McIntosh's credit, he kept his eye on the big picture, and let others wallow in the dirty laundry.

In the wake of the Lewinsky revelations, House conservatives started getting uppity again. McIntosh even threatened to force another government shutdown if the President didn't negotiate in good faith over how to prioritize federal spending. House leaders and Republican moderates immediately voiced their fear that the politically adept Clinton would use the conservatives' threats to divert attention from the sex scandal. The CATs then issued assurances that they'd be willing to negotiate, and even lose on some issues, as long as their suggestions were considered.

In an interview that September, just after the President admitted he'd been lying about his affair, McIntosh disputed Clinton's contention that it was a private matter ("It happened in the Oval Office," the congressman said bluntly), but nonetheless issued a warning to the special prosecutor investigating the President that would prove to be prophetic. Focus on law, not sex, McIntosh told Ken Starr, noting that at a recent Rotary Club meeting in his district, only a quarter of those attending raised their hands when asked if the president should be impeached.[24]

Unfortunately for moderate Republicans in Congress, they didn't heed the young politician's warnings, and instead angered the CATs by delaying discussions of spending in hope that the President would be further weakened by Starr, which caused them to be outmaneuvered and forced to compromise on the budget. Though the Republicans still held a majority in Congress and the President was wounded, the $580 billion spending bill that passed that October allowed surplus funds intended to shore up Social Security to be used for other spending measures, failed to limit abortion, and offered no tax relief. McIntosh sneered afterward that it was "a terrible bill . . . a Great Society bill" and faulted Republican leaders for a distressing lack of vision.

A month before the November 1998 election, the House voted to hold an impeachment inquiry. McIntosh voted with the majority because he felt he had no choice. "It was a classic replay of what got Nixon—the coverup," he says. "And I was surprised as I was watching this, because Hillary was there during Watergate. Why didn't Clinton just say 'Yes, I did it, but Hillary's forgiven me?'

"Ultimately," he continues, "they made that appeal to the American public," but by dodging that admission for months, the Clintons "left everybody else in government with a choice: Do we pretend it didn't happen? Do we seem to condone it? And this is where my legal training really set my antennae going, realizing that that would totally undermine the judicial branch of government."

At home in Indiana, they must have liked what they saw. Though Republican losses in the congressional election that November were significant, and the election was seen as a punishment to the party trying to impeach the President over his Oval Office peccadilloes, McIntosh won reelection easily. During the next few days, he moved against Gingrich, briefly seeking a leadership job himself, then backing off slightly in order to achieve the larger goal of getting rid of the Speaker. Gingrich (who, it was later revealed, was having an extramarital affair of his own at the time) made that easy by resigning. McIntosh suffered a setback when another man he considered an appeaser, Robert Livingston, was made Speaker. Soon he, too, admitted he'd committed adultery and quit the House.

Despite his brashness and obvious ambition, the upright McIntosh remained standing, with a higher national profile than he'd ever had before. Although he knew it wouldn't be popular, he voted in Washington that December to send three of four impeachment charges to the Senate for trial. "I concluded we had to, even knowing it was very unlikely the Senate would actually impeach," he says. He doesn't regret doing so. "Watching what went on in the Senate, I had the sense that the Republicans were uncomfortable because the polls were against them. But the Democrats were also very uncomfortable because although the polls were with Clinton, so politically they to stand with him, they *knew* something was wrong."

IN 1994 RUSSELL Simmons bought back the distribution rights to his Def Jam record label and sold them (and a stake in the company) to the Dutch conglomerate Polygram for $33 million. Soon afterward, he turned Def Jam's music operation over to his partner Lyor Cohen and began living in Hollywood, where he produced several films. But movies weren't enough to occupy the ambitious entrepreneur. Simmons founded a charity, Rush Philanthropic Arts Foundation, focusing on the career needs of inner-city youth; started a magazine, *Oneworld*, to promote his vision of a new multiracial youth culture; and opened an advertising and promotion agency specializing in urban markets. After two years in Los Angeles, he returned to New York in 1998, determined to expand Phat Farm, a line of clothing he'd begun as a hobby in 1992.

For many boomers, fashion had come to fill the slot in their lives once occupied by drugs and rock music. Just as those enthusiasms made promises they couldn't quite keep, so fashion's trappings seemed to carry with them the aura of affluence. To understand the boom's fashion fascination, you have to return to when it was young, and anti-fashion was the fashion.

It all began with blue jeans. Denim's progress from totem of rebellion to status symbol charted the generation's progression. In the early 1970s, fashionable hippies were showing the first signs of premature yuppiedom. New York's Serendipity boutique offered "Lifestyle" jeans for $45 to $500, depending upon their level of "distress," a sort of prefabricated personalization meant to evoke walking (if ghost-written) autobiographies. And in the mid-seventies, Sasson introduced the status jeans, engendering back pockets bearing the *haute* signatures of baby boomer Diane von Furstenberg (b. 1946) and the older American aristocrats Charlotte Ford and Gloria Vanderbilt. The latter, backed by an Indian apparel manufacturer who owned garment factories in Hong Kong, can be credited with the unlikely synthesis of mass market designer fashion.

For the first time, fashion manufacturers were approaching the public directly, without the mediation of the previously dominant conduits, stores and fashion magazines. A whole new phenomenon of mass expansion and diffusion of high-fashion followed. Here were "name" designer goods one could buy for as little as 30 dollars. The status that attached to a signature brand was now available to all comers, never mind the fact that their status was diluted since everyone was wearing them.

It wasn't so much the jeans as the way they were sold that made designers rock star replacements. They began plowing jean profits into advertising featuring their own faces. "I've made a lot of money because people are fascinated with designers," Calvin Klein told a reporter. "I never would have run a portrait if people hadn't wanted to know who Calvin Klein was." The next step was television. Klein's multimillion-dollar TV campaign introduced in 1980 and starring Brooke Shields (b. 1965) and a group of other models mewling about their prolonged adolescence—was influential and copied far beyond the fashion business.

In exchange for their fame, designers offered concrete expressions of fantasy and dreams to people yearning for clues about how to live. They preyed on the baby boom's vulnerabilities, its desire for more, whether that was Ralph Lauren's forward-looking desire for money and status or Klein's nostalgic clinging to sex and irresponsible fun. Image manipulation, as much as any particular talent for design, put Lauren (b. 1939) into *Forbes* magazine's listing of the richest Americans, and paid Klein's 1987 take-home check of some $12 million a year.

Eventually, jean sales started slipping, but boomers were by then used to wanting and paying for labels. Designers were, in the words of art critic John Russell, mining a "vein of understated democratic poetry." Their clothes, beauty products and accessories became the tools of a participatory art. Now anyone could play at visual expression through appearance, expressing parallel yearnings for definition and status.

As wealth crept out of the closet in the anti-egalitarian Reagan years, hedonism, luxury and self-display became permissible again; indeed, they seemed to be encouraged by the new politics of self-indulgence. Baby boomers finally accepted the idea that the world was competitive and that in order to live in it, they had to worry about standing out for the right reasons. Fashion was there to serve. By the mid-1980s, when inflation was checked, affluence was on the rise, and a new sense of economic optimism set in, it was natural for fashion's stars to extend their lines—

first into image-management clothing, then into more permanent signifiers of style—designer "home" collections.

What might be called the fashion decade lasted from 1977, when
designer jeans first became popular, to late 1987, when the stock market
crash threw most high-end garment makers into a tizzy that lasted well into
the next decade. Some, like Calvin Klein, went into personal tailspins. Other
just suffered through business reverses. But the genie of democratized style
would not be put back in the bottle. In the early 1990s, when a new generation of fashion consumers reached free-spending age, older designers
scrambled to adapt (often selling the looks of their youths back to their children via 1960s and 1970s revivals promoted by boomer magazine editors
and photographers), while new designers carved out new markets.

Primary among them was Tommy Hilfiger (b. 1952), the second of nine
children born into a suburban family in Elmira, a small city in upstate
New York. A frustrated athlete, he was a ripe candidate for the counterculture when he encountered it in summer 1969. That's when Tommy
got a job in a boutique selling posters, candles and incense, grew his hair,
and started wearing bell bottoms and sandals, which promptly got him
thrown out of high school. So he and a partner invested $150 each,
bought a batch of earrings, candles and jeans, and set up shop in a fifty
dollar-a-month storefront they painted black, curtained in burlap, and
called The People's Place. Soon he owned eight branches and had started
designing clothes. By the early 1990s, backed by the same financier who'd
put Gloria Vanderbilt in the jeans business, Hilfiger's sales had hit $50
million in a year. In 1992, Tommy Hilfiger went public, offering shares on
the stock exchange.

Then, in 1994, came the accident that made Hilfiger truly famous. One
of his partners was a Formula One racing fanatic and convinced Hilfiger
to sponsor a race car and design uniforms for its team. After he saw how
people reacted to the logo-splattered shirts he created, Hilfiger designed a
nautical line, oversized as was his fashion, but with one added attraction:
huge logos. Urban youth began buying them in job lots. Those in-your-
face logos carried a big message; they said, "I can afford anything you
have."

One day shortly thereafter, Hilfiger's brother spied a rapper, Grand
Puba, in a Hilfiger shirt and dragged Tommy over the racial divide, introducing the ultra-white designer to the ultra-black hip-hop star. Now, he
was "my nigga, Hilfiger," and designers like Ralph Lauren and Donna
Karan soon followed suit, making clothes for the rising urban elite. The
inheritors of integration were coming into their own and wanted to wave

their success, just as their parents and grandparents had waved picket signs. More rappers soon came into Hilfiger's orbit, among them Russell Simmons, who offered Hilfiger his knowledge of the urban street scene and access to more rap artists in return for advice on his own clothing line. The cross-marketing of music and clothing proved an astonishing success. Hilfiger now sells nearly a billion dollars in clothes a year. Soon, to the distress of some admirers, Simmons looked to be more interested in clothes than in music.

In fact, it wasn't clothes that caught his attention—at first. "It was models, to be real honest," he admits. Although he'd given up drugs in 1989 (and, after taking up yoga and vegetarianism, would forswear cigarettes and alcohol for nine months every year), he never gave up his habit of going out until all hours with beautiful women. Only now he fished in a bigger pond. "I started to have an interest in people other than Alternative Outlaws," he says. "It was a more affluent, different world. I really didn't get to know the mainstream. But I wanted to know people who moved things, people who were about culture and change and were either powerful in some way or interesting." He laughs. "I always thought I'd know everybody."

First among these new faces were young fashion models, who flocked to the latest clubs and loved clothes and music. The hip young fashion crowd "brought me to fashion shows, and fashion shows brought me to a different world," Simmons says.

Simmons was still deeply involved with rap—even helping organize a rappers' summit meeting at the Chicago home of Louis Farrakhan, when disputes between rival factions of East and West Coast rappers led to murder and mayhem, culminating in the 1997 shootings of rappers Tupac Shakur (b. 1971), whose mother, Afeni, was one of the Panther 21, and The Notorious B.I.G. (b. 1972).[25] Simmons's vision of a multicultural universe had grown beyond the confines of rap's corner of the world.

In 1998, Def Jam grossed almost $200 million, making it the second-largest black-owned entertainment company after the cable channel Black Entertainment Television. When Seagram Co.'s CEO Edgar Bronfman Jr. (b. 1955) bought Def Jam's parent, Polygram Records the following year, Simmons's 40 percent stake in Def Jam was said to be worth in excess of $100 million. Phat Farm made only $17 million that year. Determined to build the business, Simmons vowed to triple that in 1999, and he has no intention of stopping there. He'll tell anyone who'll listen that he wants to make the kind of money Klein, Lauren and Hilfiger do. "They can't out-market me in my own market," he told *USA Today*.[26]

What makes Russell Simmons run? The same desires that have motivated upward mobility since time immemorial, multiplied by the power
of modern media to communicate all there is in the world to want. "It's
not rebellion for the sake of it," he says. "I've been watching TV, and I
want every fucking thing on the screen. Rap is about getting money. Rap
is about 'I don't give a fuck. I'm takin' it. If you don't have it for me, I'm
gon' rob you.' Niggers have a different agenda because they come from
the ghetto. This is not rock 'n' roll for the fun of it. The idea is, get yours
and *don't* be angry. Even though you can't get a cab, you can get a Rolls-
Royce."

Simmons had crossed a great divide and become a celebrity himself.
He'd undergone another change, too, when he married a model, Kimora
Lee, late in 1998, on the celebrity isle of St. Barth. "I think I'm growing
up a little bit," he says. "I can't do all the things I used to do. It's not as
much fun. I'm an adult." He settled down a bit; after years of play, he was
ready to climb mountains again. "Now I feel very much motivated to
work. I think that now we can do some more legitimate things from a
business standpoint with the culture and how it's evolving. The ball is in
our court to do a lot of things we want to do, including the clothing and
more films. The television arena is becoming really open. I always looked
ahead one day—to get the record finished, get it out on time, get the
spring collection done. Now I'm thinking about the overall plan, which I
never thought about before."

That plan is based on the simple fact of society's homogenization. "The
backdrop of urban culture is black music," Simmons says. "But the rest of
it is a free-for-all." He hoists a copy of *Oneworld* magazine. Lauryn Hill,
the singer whose rap-R&B fusion won multiple Grammy Awards in 1998,
is on the cover. But Leonardo DiCaprio, the star of *Titanic*, is profiled
inside. "He's a star," says Simmons. "Black girls want to fuck him.
Oneworld exists."

There are still battles to be fought against the old way of thinking that
tries to minimize urban culture. "They'll stick you in a hole today,"
Simmons says. "I'm dealing with it everywhere." His ad agency does work
for Coca-Cola. "My commercials are the number-one testing in the mainstream, but they still got me on a nigger budget," he complains. "You're
told, 'This is what your space is.' The ethnic clothing business; I don't
want to be in the ethnic clothing business. Fuck you. You don't get my
clothes. It's not about color. It's who's got the same interests as you,
who's interesting and fun to be around, and that's the end of it."

* * *

THERE IS A vague sense of sadness about Cynthia Bowman as she talks about recent times. When you've flown with Jefferson Starship, it's hard to come down. With rock, drugs and sex eliminated from her life, Bowman was left with her somewhat unconventional family—she, Grace Slick, Paul Kantner, their children and assorted significant others—and a thriving career. "I got lucky again," Bowman says. She began with people she knew—Bill Graham, whose company gave her a number of projects to publicize, including several Vietnam veterans' benefits and a concert for Earthquake relief; Boz Scaggs, whose restaurant account led to others; the symphony. "What I did I did well," she says. "And I made enough money to sustain myself and keep a decent lifestyle, and I kept moving forward."

Though she still worked with celebrities—particularly when their presence could attract attention to such good causes as afterschool programs for children—she disdained the burgeoning field of "suppress agentry," which sprang up in the mid-1970s, when rock stars needed protection from themselves, and by the celebrity-centric 1990s had PR people dictating content to editors of glossy magazines desperate to get stars on their covers and at their promotional parties. "I'm way too old for the celebrity crap that goes along with working with 'stars,'" Bowman says. "So unless there's a ton of money involved, I stay clear of them."

By the mid-1990s, her accounts ranged from established radicals like Bread and Roses, which produces performances in prisons, hospitals and other institutions, and the Haight-Ashbury Free Clinic to mainline institutions like the Fairmont Hotel and the San Francisco Museum of Art. She handled Willie L. Brown's mayoral inauguration in 1996 and in 1998 got a contract to publicize Sony's Metreon, a massive entertainment complex in downtown San Francisco—a deal that helped pay for her house, the first property she's ever owned. "My piece of the planet," she says. "I'd started realizing, wait a minute, where are you going to be in fifteen years? You don't have a husband, a retirement plan, a Keogh plan. Here's God's way of letting you secure your future. I'm not going to blow it again."

She's feeling her age. "I'm entering my twilight years here," she says. "There's no going back now. I'm in the second half of my life. I still don't feel grown up. I see that reflection of myself and I think, My god, that's me? I'm going to be fifty years old: that is hard to fathom, but that's reality. What's the alternative?"

Bowman's son is going to college in fall 2000. She plans to keep working until he's graduated and then to reinvent herself. "I am going to devote the second half of my life to something else," she vows. "Maybe go back to school and become a nurse. I haven't identified what it's going to be, but it's going to be community service. I have a little bit of power in this city because I've been here for so long, and I can refocus my power and use it in a different way. I'm tired of making everybody in the world look good when they're not."

Bill Clinton's impeachment made Bowman see that the world of image, privilege and self-indulgence is not where she wants to live anymore. "We thought he was the figurehead for our generation," she says. "Well, it turned out that like the rest of us, he's got a tarnished record. Only most of us weren't that bad. Clinton was hurting his wife and his daughter. We weren't hurting anybody. We were smoking pot. The only people we hurt were ourselves. It impacted our health, probably our productivity. But we weren't lying. I don't lie. I get in a lot of trouble because I *don't* lie. There's something wrong with a country where everybody is lying all the time. I don't even think a rock star would have done it in the Oval Office. That part of it really offends me. The kind of crap that goes on backstage or on a tour bus shouldn't go on in the White House."

A DECADE AFTER arriving in Salt Lake City, Kathryn Bond Stockton was named the University of Utah's director of graduate studies in English. Though it sounds strange that a lesbian feminist would find a warm welcome in the heart of Mormon country, she thinks it makes a queer kind of sense. "What you realize living in this environment, where there truly are guys called Patriarchs and they live downtown, is that you don't have to prove to anybody that there is a patriarchy. The very people who started being persecuted as sexual queers because of their polygamy now stand for family values and American normativity."

Even in Utah, there are people "who are hungry to hear something other than that message," Stockton continues. "Obviously, there are Mormon colleges, so if a student is devoutly Mormon they tend not to go to the University of Utah; it's considered to be the radical bastion. So we get students who have grown up in Mormon families and yet they may be gay, they may be feminists, and they are desperate to take classes called Feminist Theory, Deconstruction, the whole shebang. And you still have Shakespeare and Milton being taught, so I would hardly say that Theory rules the day."

As her appointment attests, it has become the latest thing. In the 1990s, a new offshoot, Queer Theory, stormed many campuses, examining marginalized, "transgressive" sexualities, and lauding them precisely because they disrupt the traditions and norms of the patriarchy. "I think we are seen as fashion hounds," Stockton admits, "but just remember, fashion is not necessarily a bad thing." Often, it's a mirror on society.

The baby boom specialized in raising the bar of outrage, so it was no surprise that the advent of Queer Theory caused shrill, anguished howls. The phrase first appeared in the press in 1992, in a report on the first semester of the University of Buffalo's Queer Theory Study Group.[27] Rutgers also introduced a "queer" specialization in its English department that year, and it attracted more students than Marxism and deconstruction combined. Queer Theory—propelled by off-campus movements like AIDS activism and its politicization of sexuality, Queer Nation (formed in 1990 to combat anti-gay violence), and pro-sex feminism and its sexualization of politics—took off like wildfire, just as gay people were gaining a measure of acceptance at the movies (*Philadelphia*), on Broadway (*Angels in America*), in medicine (the AMA finally gave up the idea of curing homosexuality), and in public education (Massachusetts passed a law to protect gay students, and a Los Angeles school held the first gay prom).

In spring 1994, the twenty-fifth anniversary of Hillary Rodham's graduation from Wellesley College, the *Boston Herald* reported on the latest trends at her alma mater, where orientation week now began with "intercultural awareness" sessions featuring readings from a tract called *Unpacking the White Privileged Backpack*; white students who showed insufficient sensitivity were urged to take African studies courses, such as one where students were assigned a book on the slave trade asserting that Simon Legree, the wicked slave owner of *Uncle Tom's Cabin*, was really named Seymour Saperstein; and dormitory resident assistants were given a masturbation orientation, including a demonstration of a vibrator, in order to help students overcome sexual repression.[28]

By 1997, the year lesbian comedian Ellen DeGeneres (b. 1958) "came out" on her television sitcom, the cutting edge had already sliced far past her. That fall, the State University of New York at New Paltz came under fire after it hosted a women's studies conference titled "Revolting Behavior: The Challenges of Women's Sexual Freedom" that included (among more conventional offerings) a sex toy demonstration; a workshop on "safe, sane and consensual" sadism and masochism; a performance in which an ex-stripper mounted and whipped a colleague dressed as a Hasidic Jew; the distribution of instructions on how to dispose of razor blades following "bloodletting sexual activities"; and, for lesbians, a step-by-step guide to using "a slippery, lubed-up latex glove" to "safely rock [their partners] into a frenzy."

Stockton is not shocked by any of this, but is herself shocking when she claims it's not political. "I don't really think our job is politics," she says. "I honestly believe our job is pleasure. What we're really trying to do is have pleasure with something that calls itself a literary text, and that is a luxury. Politics will be involved in that, because to read them we have to make interpretations, we have to make certain decisions that are full of bias and assumption. And what we need to realize is that the very luxuries that we pursue will end up puncturing our politics."

Pleasure? Luxuries? Though she's been good about avoiding the impenetrable jargon most Theorists hide behind, she's lost me there. It turns out she's arguing for instant gratification, for Peter Pan, for all those things the Baby Boom has supposedly left behind. "We learned from the fall of communism that nothing is more necessary than luxuries," she says. "Nobody needs literature, but nobody wants to live without it. Communism fell because it had no answer to pleasure. This is what makes queer politics different than African-American politics and a lot of the other identity formations. Queers are problems because of their pleasures."

Although many people say they don't like gays because they believe the gay lifestyle is unnatural, "I don't think anybody in their heart of hearts really believes that," Stockton continues. "I think what they're saying is, 'It's unfair. We cannot allow that form of pleasure to take place. If I am disciplining myself, I don't want to see you indulging yourself.' The heart of that argument is that queer pleasure is not about productive use. We bow to the god of productive use. We cannot allow for reckless expenditure. And that's what gay life is seen as."

The pathological view of homosexuality considered it a symptom of arrested development. "You don't grow up," Stockton explains. Growing up is a vertical concept, and vertical, logical, goal-attaining reason is another of those patriarchal apple carts Queer Theory seeks to upset. Horizontal thinking is feminine, sensitive, intuitive and a perfect fit for a postmodern baby boomer. "'Growing up' presumes I was this and now I have changed," says Stockton. "Yes, time is upon my body, my life has extended in these many ways. But that's very different than growing up, which presumes leaving certain things behind that are of childhood, and taking responsibility, and finding my place in a vertical chain."

That brings her back to her politics of luxury, which she holds up in opposition to the ticking of the career clock, the ticking of her biological clock. "Show me the person who does not have as their goal to waste time," she commands. "The evangelical is about deferred pleasure. You are waiting for the day when the true story begins, the Book of Revelations, the wedding banquet in Heaven, the streets paved with jewels. The most disciplined Marxists will not allow themselves any pleasure until the Revolution has begun, and all people drink good wine. Still, the goal is to bring pleasure to people. That's the story of the twentieth century. It's all about pleasure in the end."

So it fits that Stockton thinks that somehow, Bill and Hillary Clinton are queer. "Bill Clinton must be profoundly propelled in many directions," Stockton says. "He is probably deeply concerned about people. He needs to be popular in such a lethal way that that's his greatest fault as a human being. He got into politics to get things done and to be popular. And sexuality is very much a part of his person, one he never found a way to put a brake on. A queer reading sees the bind that he's in." But "the official discourse of the day is still the discourse of heteronormativity," Stockton continues. "In other words, you have to be normal. It doesn't matter who you are. You're going to have to talk about family values."

Baby boomers have created a society where monogamy is not what it once was, if it ever was, where divorce is a norm, where families are redefined daily. "Who knows what goes on in private relationships?" Stockton asks. "There is no normative pattern of pleasure-taking. So whatever arrangement the Clintons had strikes me as a very intricate one. I don't think Hillary was a person who, in some straightforward way, closed her eyes and stood by her man. Whatever he was doing in the White House, that's just the tip of the iceberg. So they have some understanding, some deal we cannot be told as a country, because that would be far more troubling to people."

Daughter Chelsea gives Stockton a bit more trouble. "But maybe she knows of her parents' agreement. Until we know that part, I don't see what we could possibly hold against him. What did he do that the country should be concerned about? Nothing. If he's sexually harassing people, which he may have along the way, that's a bad thing. But that didn't come into the Monica Lewinsky stuff. The story he was impeached over is just profound and utter nonsense."

NINA HARTLEY'S CAREER in porn hit a slump in the late 1980s. Luckily, a revival of burlesque in upscale strip clubs, where porn stars appear as featured attractions, allowed her to raise her income just as her onscreen activity dropped off. There were also social changes in the wind. Although aging baby boomers were behaving less promiscuously, it soon turned out they were not, as some claimed, turned off to sex. They were simply finding new outlets for their urges. Even as political correctness was being promoted by unreconstructed 1960s radicals grown up into tenured New Puritans on college campuses, their younger brothers and sisters from the back end of the baby boom were finding new ways to outrage the uptight and rebel against the prevailing repression.

By the time of Bill Clinton's election in 1992, sex was back in a big way. "The anti-pornography push eased considerably," Hartley says. "We started going mainstream." MTV was offering sexual suggestion twenty-four hours a day, and "people had gotten desensitized," says Hartley. So the latest wrinkle in porn was called gonzo, "sweat flying, makeup running, in your face, stripped of all pretense, anything to get a rise out of people." Mainstream sexuality wasn't so extreme, but it, too, was pushing the boundaries. Chastity had proved untenable; the sex drive couldn't be rebottled. With gay men leading the way, sex was passing through the valley of death to make real if tentative inroads into a brave new AIDS-aware world. "AIDS was a boon on one level," Hartley says. "Now we *have* to talk about this. I don't care if your mama don't like it."

Jesse Helms and the Moral Majority notwithstanding, sex had come back out in the open, forced there by discussions of the disease. Even kids knew all about *it*, and they were not only learning it in school, but from Clarence Thomas, whose Supreme Court confirmation hearings—with their talk of harassment by pubic hair and Long Dong Silver—exposed how extremes had become mainstream long before Bill and Monica.

Sexual freedom wasn't absolute. In 1993 Hartley and ten other women were arrested at a lingerie show in an adult video store in Las Vegas benefiting the Free Speech Coalition, the adult film industry's anti-censorship group. But Hartley has had the last laugh, as her brand of sexual liberation becomes increasingly mainstream. Porn is now estimated to be an $8 billion industry; video porn represents 25 percent of the home video market. Hard core is celebrated and emulated on the airwaves by Howard Stern and Jerry Springer, hard-core performers are crossing into the mainstream, and mainstream stars are doing porn, apparently without shame. Tommy Lee and Pamela Anderson appear in the best-selling porn tape of all time. In 1999, Paul Weyrich wrote a letter admitting that the Moral Majority had lost its crusade to de-liberate America.

Two years before that, Hartley appeared in *Boogie Nights*, a film made by a director who'd watched her videos as a high school student. Then, in 1998, she spoke at the World Pornography Conference in Los Angeles, sponsored by California State University, alongside college professors and the president of the ACLU. Andrea Dworkin and Catharine MacKinnon were invited but declined to participate, dissing the conference in print instead. "People . . . don't seem to care," Dworkin told *Time* magazine. "It makes me ill." MacKinnon agreed: "Society has made the decision they want the abuse to continue."[29]

"Give it up, girls," Hartley responds. "The truth has come out. You can read what Dworkin and MacKinnon have to say and what I have to say and make your own decisions based on your own experience. I won't say we've won. We've made significant strides. There is porn by women out there. Young women have more of a sense of themselves as sexual creatures. Younger folk are making their own families and their own tribes that cross gender and racial boundaries. Baby boomers set the example."

Hartley now hopes she'll be able to live out her dream of growing old as a sex educator, doing for the young what the authors of *Our Bodies, Our Selves* did for her. "Of course you can get old in this business," she insists. "I'm at the top of my game. I pretty much still have my looks. I don't know how I'll feel the first time a boy in his twenties looks at me and doesn't think I'm sexy. But the Baby Boom needs to see women getting older, it needs to see older women with younger men, so I think I have a glorious future. You have to be a certain age to be a healer. That's what I wanted to be from the first."

THE FALL OF 1995 was a series of crises for Victoria Leacock. Her best friend, Gordon Rogers, died of AIDS that September, her latest boyfriend broke up with her, she was evicted from the borrowed apartment in which she was living, her godmother Maxene Andrews died, and then her roommate, Pam Shaw, died of AIDS, all within ten weeks. Though Jonathan Larson was in the midst of rewriting *Rent*, he stopped work to speak at the two AIDS memorials, videotaped the memorial for Andrews, helped Leacock move out, and did his best to convince her that her ex was a jerk.

Rehearsals of *Rent* began in December. Larson wanted Leacock to be there with him, but without a role to play, she was unwilling. Previews of *Rent* were to begin a few days before an apartment she'd rented would be available to her, so Leacock decided to leave town until then. After videotaping Larson's last day as a waiter (he'd finally quit his job after nine years), she spent December with family in Barbados. "Eight years of my life had been devoted to people with AIDS, one after the other, and they'd all died horrible, agonizing deaths," she said. "The sun was so good for me. And I remember someone made me laugh, and I felt I hadn't laughed in years."

In January, Leacock's father invited her to join him in Siberia, where he was making a movie. She called Larson to apologize that she was going to miss his first preview, but said she'd be home for his thirty-sixth birthday a week later. He lied and told her things were fantastic—in fact, he was fighting with his director and the producers, plus he was broke and stressed to the breaking point. Unaware, Leacock flew to Siberia as *Rent* went into final rehearsals.

Four days before the previews began, Larson felt a pain in his chest. Taken to the hospital, he was diagnosed with food poisoning and sent home. On January 23, he went back to the hospital. This time he was told he had the flu. The next night, Larson attended the final dress rehearsal, which got a standing ovation. A reporter from the *New York Times* was there. Larson gave a brief interview, saying the show was inspired by friends who'd died of AIDS, and that its message was that what matters isn't how long you live, but what you do. Afterward, Larson went home and before going to bed, put water on the stove to make a cup of tea.[30]

In Siberia, Leacock and her father were "staying in a rathole, which is a nice apartment in Siberia," she says. They'd been unable to get the phone to work, but suddenly it started ringing. Richard Leacock answered. When he said the name Jonathan Larson aloud, Victoria knew something was wrong. "I thought, 'Oh my god, his show's been canceled.' That was the worst thing I could think of," she says. "I looked at Dad and said, 'Did Jonathan die?' so when I found out his show was canceled, it wouldn't be as awful." It was just that awful. Larson's chest pains had been a unheeded warning sign. On the evening of January 24, 1996, the young playwright/composer died of an aortic aneurysm while boiling water for tea.[31]

Leacock was bereft. She changed her flight plans in order to get home in time for Larson's memorial service, the day before his birthday, but weather caused delays. By the time she got to the theater, 400 of Larson's friends had already gathered. "In a way, the saddest part and the end of the story is, Pam Shaw's family was there and the Rogers were there," Leacock says. "All the parents felt like they'd lost another child. And then I went home, and I had sacks of mail. There were two things from Jonathan—the invitation to opening night and his Christmas card. I opened the Christmas card and it said, 'Dearest Vic: May '96 be our year. (And no more funerals.) Love, Jon.'"

Two days before the show's official opening, the *New York Times* ran its article featuring Larson's last interview. Then, on Valentine's Day, a *Times* review compared *Rent* to *Hair* for giving "a pulsing, unexpectedly catchy voice to one generation's confusion, anger and anarchic, pleasure-seeking vitality." The show sold out the next day, was extended, sold out again, and moved to Broadway in a matter of weeks.[32] Leacock was featured in many of the articles about Larson, she thinks, "because he'd died at a young age unexpectedly, and so a tremendous amount of people assumed he really died of AIDS—which he didn't. They were interviewing me so they could say 'his ex-girlfriend' and identify him as a heterosexual."

Leacock's connection to Larson and *Rent* continued. She became part of the small group that dealt with his property and archived the music and plays he'd left behind—a few of which she still hopes to produce. She'd given the composer close to $8,000 during his lean years, and he'd promised her a cut of *Rent* royalties in return. When his parents learned that, they told her they'd always suspected there had been "another bank," and soon weekly checks started to arrive. "My job became Jonathan Larson," she says. "And it was a good thing because I needed something to do, but it was also a bad thing because it kept me in permanent grief for a long time, and having the money to support me also meant I didn't have to get my head together." But the money also paid for her next short film, which has won awards, been shown at several film festivals, and raised her hopes that she has a future as a filmmaker.

DONALD TRUMP CALLS the years 1990 to 1994 the most interesting of his life. "Not necessarily the best time of my life, because it certainly wasn't, but I learned more about myself during those years than any other time," he says. "I had never had adversity, and all of a sudden, I am being fuckin' creamed. It was a bad time, obviously, for the country. It was a bad time for New York. And I was the symbol. So they wouldn't do a story that real estate in New York was doing terribly. They'd do a story that Trump is doing terribly."

In fact, as the same people who'd cheered his noisy rise jeered at his fall, he was setting the stage for a comeback. In March 1991, he settled with his ex-wife Ivana. Though she and her lawyer, Michael Kennedy, had sought as much as $2.5 billion—half of Trump's presumed assets—she eventually settled for exactly what her several ante-nuptial agreements promised her, about $14 million, child support, and their Connecticut mansion.

A year later, Trump filed prepackaged bankruptcy plans, approved by most of his bondholders, for the Trump Castle and Trump Plaza casinos, relinquishing half-ownership of one in exchange for lower interest rates.[33] If he met specified financial performance goals and made interest payments on time, his stake could rise again—up to 80 percent. Nine days later, he agreed to give his bankers 49 percent of the Plaza Hotel (which had gone into bankruptcy at the beginning of 1992), canceling $125 million in debt and gaining more favorable terms on a $300 million mortgage. At the same time, Trump finally won a crucial approval to develop his remaining Penn Central yard. By the end of 1992, the *New York Times* was reporting: "Wall Street clearly sees Mr. Trump in a new light."[34]

Trump kept fine-tuning his various deals, restructuring his debts, reducing interest payments, and reclaiming his equity. He was regaining his bravado. That spring, he sued the federal government, claiming that allowing Native Americans to run casinos without paying taxes discriminated against casino owners. The suit went nowhere, but indicated that his brief spell of uncharacteristic humility was over. On firmer financial footing, he finally married Marla Maples, two years after announcing their engagement, and two months after she gave birth to a daughter they named Tiffany. The ceremony was held at the Plaza Hotel in the presence of guests like radio shock jock Howard Stern and boxer Evander Holyfield.

In 1994, Trump tried to take his casinos public, but failed when he found he couldn't refinance and regain control of the Taj Mahal. A little more than a year later, Trump put together an initial public offering to sell stock in the holding company that owned the Trump Plaza, his least debt-ridden Atlantic City property. He used the proceeds to enlarge its casino, buy back two properties he'd lost to banks, get into riverboat gambling in Indiana, and reduce his personal loan guarantees. By October 1995, he was being hailed by politicians and businessmen at a luncheon in New York for pulling off "the comeback of the decade."

Trump's trick wasn't easy, but it was clever. "I now have an advantage I didn't have then—experience," he says. "I never saw a crash before." Now he is more cautious. He began selling his services and his name to others, forming partnerships in which he worked as pitchman, negotiator and construction manager. He made a deal that paid him $50 million to oversee the renovation and sale of apartments in the former Gulf & Western Building overlooking New York's Columbus Circle and Central Park. The building was renamed Trump International Hotel and Tower, even though others owned the building and paid the redevelopment bills. When apartments there went on sale in 1997, they included eight of the city's ten top apartment sale prices. Then, backed by a Hong Kong holding company, Trump began to build a scaled-down and environmentally friendly version of Trump City—first renamed Riverside South, then Trump Place—with 5,700 apartments in sixteen high-rise buildings and 1.8 million square feet of commercial space. Trump retained a 30 percent share of the seventy-five-acre site. Finally, after more negotiations and restructurings, Trump folded all of his casinos into Trump Hotels and Casino Resorts and ended up with 37 percent of its stock.

In summer 1998, just turned fifty-two, Trump was back. In partnership with an insurance company, he bought the General Motors building, a landmark overlooking Central Park, a few blocks from Trump Tower; his Trump Place apartments were selling rapidly, and he was refurbishing 40 Wall Street, which he bought for $5 million and subsequently mortgaged for $125 million. "I didn't appreciate my success in the eighties," he says, "because it just seemed natural. Now I appreciate it because I know the perils."

Unfortunately, his refound sense of security spelled the end of his brief second marriage. After months of rumors, Trump and wife Marla announced their separation that spring. "I don't know if I'd call it a midlife crisis," he says. Then he adds, "It could be. Certainly I'm having a good time with it." He felt he'd never had the chance to enjoy the fruits of his success. "I went from one marriage to another, which was a mistake. Marla's a good girl, and I had a good marriage with her, but it's just that I get fuckin' bored. One of those little things. Work to me is going on a vacation and sitting around going nuts, because there's no telephone. So I'm still young enough, and I want to have a good time for a while. I deserve it." Asked if he regrets not playing more when he was younger, he quotes John Paul Getty: "A lot of people have a happy marriage, but there's only one John Paul Getty."

Trump says he feels a closer bond to Getty than he does to his own generation. "I have absolutely no consciousness of my generation," he says, but he admits that like many his age, he doesn't want to get old. "I think you always want to fight it," he says. "I'm not a huge fan of the aging process. And I can't believe that too many people are. But I've seen people who fight it, and it doesn't work. People with facelifts look like they have facelifts. In many cases, they look a helluva lot worse."

Asked what he's proudest of, Trump points to photos of his four children lined up in ranks near his desk. "I wouldn't be happy not having children," he says. "There's something nice when a kid calls up and starts blabbing. Having children is a little bit of a hedge against age. A lot of my friends don't, and they regret it more now than they did when they were thirty and forty. But you can't beat the clock."

Trump keeps trying. After leaving his second wife, he's dated a series of beauties and opened a modeling agency, but he admits that can't go on forever. "I used to hate it, at Le Club, when I'd see a seventy-five-year-old guy walk in with two twenty-year-old girls," he says. "I'm conscious of that. And if you look at most of the girls I'm seeing, they're in their thirties, I'm very proud to tell you. This is a positive thing, okay? Is it a hedge, though?" Trump pauses and gestures at a copy of the *National Enquirer* sitting on his desk, open to a poll of young women, who'd been asked which billionaire they'd most like to date. As he reads the headline—TRUMP'S NEW JACKPOT: HE WINS SEXIEST DREAM MAN TITLE—he smiles to himself. "I think it's just like buildings," he says. "If I didn't like it, I wouldn't do it."

In fall 1999, as dot.com mania swept the country and instant Internet millionaires became common coin, rendering the 1980s the garish displays of wealth small-time in comparison, this baby boom P. T. Barnum took his show on the road again, this time with his girlfriend du jour, a 26-year-old Slovenian lingerie model, by his side, in order to seek the presidential nomination of the insurgent Reform Party, founded earlier in the decade by fellow billionaire, Ross Perot, and headed by wrestler-turned-governor Jesse Ventura (b. 1951).

Although that put him up against seasoned politicians Al Gore, Bill Bradley (b. 1943) and George W. Bush (b. 1946), and despite his warning that he wouldn't run if—as seemed inevitable—he didn't think he could win, some in both the public and press actually took Trump's posturing as something more than mere publicity-seeking. If it was, then his egocentric grandiosity likely served as a stand-in for the sort of self-indulgence his fellow boomers no longer allow themselves.

AT FIFTY-TWO, Mark Rudd is no longer a firebrand. "Political change takes much longer than I thought," he says. "I've developed a kind of existential point of view; you just keep plugging away and over time it accretes." In 1997, he met Marla Painter, an anti-military activist and environmental educator who advises philanthropists working with community organizers. When they married in June 1998, Rudd got a conciliatory note from his old comrade-adversary, Bernadine Dohrn.

"My view of my youthful idealism is bittersweet," he says, "but the basic analysis is still right. U.S. imperialism sucks bad. We've created a militarized world, and now it and global capital, which goes along with it, have created a world of haves and slaves. We are the haves and the Third World are the slaves.

"It's comforting to think it's human nature—then you can't do anything about it, you might as well just go enjoy your sport utility vehicle. I'm not saying I don't enjoy my pickup; I don't have a sport utility vehicle yet, but if I needed one, I'd probably go get one. But the world can't keep going at this level of imbalance. We live in a town in which five percent of the people live up on the hill and eat really well, and ninety-five percent are down below, inundated with toxins, eating next to nothing, slaving away twelve hours a day. It's an unstable situation, and there has to be some reaction, either disaster or rebellion or both."

Rudd's kids, both college-age now, know his stories and his worldview. "They think we tried to do too much, and failed," he says. "I don't think they have a clear sense of the euphoria and feeling of power you get when you're in a true mass movement."

The absence of young people in politics depresses him. The foot troops are "by and large people our age," Rudd says. "I kind of wish more of us had committed suicide politically so young people wouldn't be burdened by the heavy hand of the past. Youth energy is the sine qua non. The New Left got as far as it did because we rejected our elders. And we did accomplish something: the antiwar movement, the rise of the women's movement, the gay movement. When else has a foreign military adventure been successfully opposed by a movement in this country? But young people have got to just forget about it. They are constantly having to compare themselves to us."

Rudd, too, is condemned to keep comparing himself to the myth of Media Mark, which almost overwhelmed him, and the reality of who he was, which, try as he might, he can't push away. Toward the end of our talk he says something about the 1960s, but I get the sense he's really talking about himself. "I just want the thing to die so that nobody has to live up to it anymore," Mark Rudd pleads.

FOR MANY, THE Internet represents the best of everything the Baby Boom stood for in its youth. It's a place where artists, scientists, and just plain folks share wisdom, humor, sorrows and joys inexpensively and instantaneously. It expedites instant communication, not just with family and friends but with cultures around the world. It is nibbling away at the sense of the Other, which has caused racial, national and religious strife since time began. It embodies the values of grass-roots empowerment, speeding the decentralization of power. John Gage created Net Day in 1995, a national volunteer project to wire every classroom and library in America, and then the world, to the Internet so that "the same conversation reaches everybody and you can't exclude anyone," he exults. "The boundaries of the village encompass the world. And the kids think it's normal! They have not learned that this is not the way human history has been."

The rage of the 1960s was directed against centralized, indifferent power. "The Internet is the antithesis," Gage continues. "I can e-mail Bill Clinton. I can touch the levers of the machinery he also touches. The Internet allows all of us to reach hundreds of millions of people with no investment in machinery. The idea is loose and can never be controlled again."

The boomers were privileged kids and "much of what we were able to do was because we were privileged," Gage says. "Out of privilege came our sense of entitlement and freedom. That has now found expression in the Internet. And I think most of the people of our generation are deeply committed to extending this entitlement to every kid everywhere. The Internet will become a chaos of languages and cults, a means of community conversation. In the past, cinema opened a window. Now the windows are being opened everywhere and the people opening them are six, seven, eight years old. A natural justice will emerge from the great deal of human experience visible for the first time. We've put windows in walls. And we should be proud of it."

TIM SCULLY HAS some regrets about his role in opening windows of consciousness with LSD, but they don't color his forward vision, whether looking in or outward. "In the psychedelic years we had the fantasy of a commune where craftspeople and scientists and engineers would get together and have really good facilities and tools and raw materials so if you had an idea, you could materialize it quickly and be able to share it," he says. "We had a fantasy of being able to access the world's knowledge base by computer. And those fantasies have materialized on the Internet."

Having applied for a presidential pardon in 1994, Scully is understandably reluctant to talk about the politician who didn't inhale. He'd rather discuss his work with the Mendocino government, with his local airport's advisory committee (he still flies the plane Billy Hitchcock gave him), and with the local Grange, where he's assistant steward and where members well into their eighties "still feel very much the way they did when they were young," he says. "I don't think we lose that sense of who we were when we were fifteen or twenty."

Scully thinks the people we were have helped make a better world. "Women's rights, racial issues, and environmental issues are being worked on much more consciously," he says. "Those were special-interest issues that have now become central to our culture. Our attitudes about starting wars have changed quite a bit, too. There's a lot more tendency to question and be cautious. We may not be doing perfectly, but we're sure doing a heck of a lot better than we were thirty or forty years ago."

Scully won't condemn drug use, even if he no longer promotes it. "The goals of being more conscious and of becoming more integrated with the universe are valid and always have been," he says. "There are lots of traditions—meditation, yoga, religious disciplines—for pursuing those goals. Most people who follow those disciplines see taking drugs as cheating. But I think it's useful to be able to go to the back of the book, see what the experience is like, and know it's worth putting some real work into learning how to get there on your own."

He, for one, is happy to admit what he did and where it got him. "That time is still part of who I am," he says. "Pretty frequently I'll stop and remember there's more to life than just work, remember to be conscious and gentle, and remember how it felt to be really connected to everyone else. Every year or two, and sometimes a lot more often, I see a gleam in people's eye when they tell me that they tried acid. I think that everybody was changed in some way by the experience. Fortunately, most people feel that they were changed in a positive way." He gives me one last twinkling smile. "That, of course, was what we had in mind."

JONATHAN LARSON WROTE one character into *Rent* who reminds Victoria Leacock of herself. Mark, the narrator, is always filming things, and bemoaning that he's the one who survives while all around him die. "I think Jonathan was concerned that I couldn't get my eyes out of the grave," she says. She wonders if he wasn't trying to warn her not to be consumed by the sadness around her.

"To me everything was tainted by AIDS," she says. "And you know what, baby? It ain't over yet. Two weeks ago, for the first time in a long time, I had a friend tell me that he'd just found out he's HIV-positive."

Leacock, who still lectures to thousands of students each year about AIDS, has continued working on Larson's behalf, serving on the board of the foundation set up to give away the money he earned with *Rent* to, as she puts it, "encourage future Jonathan Larsons." She's followed his advice: taking the overwhelming sadness that has burdened her—and many of her peers at the tail end of the Baby Boom—and trying to turn it into something constructive. In 1998, she published a book of celebrity drawings, *Signature Flowers*, with 30 percent of the proceeds going to AIDS charities. And she still hopes one day to make films as good as her father's.

Where does she go from here? She's thirty-five and single. "I want to take one step at a time," she says carefully. Despite it all, she's cautiously optimistic. "I ask myself, What can I leave on this planet? I can hopefully fall in love, have some children, and learn to be happy. I still speak to kids because I figure if one person doesn't get infected, the world is changed forever. You know, everyone who lives changes the world."

BY 1999, DAVID McIntosh was chafing in Congress. He was still having fun, being a rabid partisan, mocking vice president Al Gore (b. 1948) on the floor of the house for predicting that internal combustion engines would disappear by 2025, and knocking $32 million out of a spending bill to pay for a pet Gore project: a live Internet image of the earth spinning in space. It didn't pass unnoticed that in the process, he was getting revenge for the ruthless mockery of his sometime mentor Dan Quayle.

That spring, he acknowledged year-old reports that he was considering a run for the governorship of Indiana in the November 2000 election. In fact, since 1997, he'd been campaigning and raising political action committee funds for Republicans in state legislative races, building a base for a statewide run. He said he wanted influence over matters that have been transferred to localities, like welfare, education and health care. It may well have been the failed effort to impeach Bill Clinton, and its fallout in Congress, that finally made the choice for him.

Though the Republicans lost the political battle, McIntosh thinks the aftermath of impeachment will include self-examination and remorse on the part of those who backed Clinton and a strengthening of the base of support for conservative politicians. "The people who wanted us to stand up for conservative principles are happy," he says. "We've now got to show that our agenda is good for everybody else." That may not include the baby boom. "Boomers tried to fashion new moral standards," says McIntosh. "This whole episode made it harder for the generation to be the guardians of a new morality." It's Monica Lewinsky's generation that gives *him* hope. "The next generation is what the battle is all about." In retreating to Indiana, McIntosh is cleaving to fellow believers, with whom he can safely wait to see if the rest of the country will come around. "What will tell is what happens in the next two to ten years. Do people run away and say the lesson of Clinton is, 'Don't talk about it and don't ask'? Or do they tell their children, 'It's wrong to cheat on your wife'?"

In July 1999, McIntosh announced his decision to quit Congress and run for governor of Indiana, promising to concentrate his efforts on education, tax-cutting and attracting high-tech jobs to the Hoosier state. Though he faces both a primary and a fierce battle against an incumbent who is likely to portray him as a dangerous extremist, his rock-solid Midwestern virtues are a significant strength. And McIntosh's decision, implicitly criticizing a Congress mired in minutiae and partisan spitballing, may reflect more than a local mood. Intelligent, lucky, fearless and thus far undefeated, McIntosh is reaching for a political synthesis from the right like the one on the left that gave Bill Clinton his weightless approval ratings. "We have to think about moral values," he says. "We have to wake people up."

DAVE McINTOSH THINKS the way to the future lies within; Tommy Vallely thinks we need to look outward. "This country is not challenged enough, and when you're not challenged, you don't know what you have to give up," he says. "After the Second World War, America didn't get strong by making Idaho strong. It got strong by making Japan strong, by rebuilding Europe."

Vallely's involvement in Vietnam today is not a matter of making reparations, but of understanding the larger lessons of that divisive conflict. "What the United States got from Vietnam is what I got: self-knowledge," he says. "And self-knowledge is worth a lot. I certainly didn't go to Vietnam to get it. I went to Vietnam as a curious kid who felt, somewhat ideologically, that when America went somewhere, it did good."

That was the legacy of the boom's parents—the World War II generation—which, at the end of the 20th century, was hailed by many as the "greatest" generation in history. Vallely doesn't agree. "I don't think that generation has the self-knowledge my generation has," he says. "This generation knows more about humanity than that one did. Because that generation created Vietnam. D-Day—that's the day America went to Vietnam. That's the mentality. They landed in Normandy to do good. They wanted to defeat the Nazis. But when it's over, you think that all your actions create good. And what Vietnam teaches you is that sometimes when you think you're doing good, you do evil. Vietnam is not the first war that was the wrong war. It's much more than that. It's the maturing of America."

With a mindset forged by that war, Valley knows the new challenge facing America is how to get along with the rest of the world. Unlike many, he's come to respect Bill Clinton. "He's not somebody that I think the generation should be ashamed of. He does understand race. And he did change the Democratic Party. He eliminated a lot of the domination of the special-interest groups, because he's comfortable with black people, he's not afraid of them." But, Vallely adds, Clinton "doesn't understand the future, he's a short-term guy" who learned the wrong lesson from Vietnam.

"We can do good everywhere in the world?" Vallely scoffs, irony on full. "We're the most powerful country in the world with the best economy, the best military, but we haven't figured out a way to turn military and economic power into influence. We want influence on the cheap. Openness is our new value. Let's go to Russia and have democracy. Let's go to Cambodia and have democracy. But it's not working. And that's what America has to figure out, how to take the power it has and keep humanity from killing itself."

Vietnam is his model. "My relationship to Vietnam is clearly related to the future," he says. "I became interested in Vietnam, because I learned something there—that humankind can do really bad things to each other, and you need a certain amount of civilization to prevent it. That's the issue that I care about. How is humanity going to govern itself?" To answer that, Vallely has developed his own global philosophy, "which is," he says, "that there's not a big difference between Western values and Eastern values. I have as many Vietnamese friends as American. They want their kids to obey their parents, to have the identical value system we have, to go to Harvard. If we knew more about the world, it wouldn't seem as complicated."

To Vallely, hope lies with the Vietnam veterans in politics who've spent the years since the war trying to figure out what happened and how to prevent it happening again. "Their self-doubt, their conflicts, make them interesting and more understanding of other people and other ideas," says Vallely. "Americans are still the richest people in the world, but we can't live in this world unless poor countries do better."

It's an uphill battle, but the Silver Star winner believes it must be won. Surveying the field from age forty-nine, he hopes he'll be part of it. He's a little bit bored, he says, and he wonders whether any contenders for the presidency in 2000 will put him to work. He grins when asked what he'll do if they don't. "Retirement?" he says. "Golf?" Then he shakes his head and admits he may not be ready to give up just yet. "If you're not conflicted," Vallely says with a laugh, "you just don't know shit."

THOUGH IT RETAINED its hippie image, by 1995 the Grateful Dead had become a moveable corporation, traveling in rented Boeing 727 jets, crashing in luxury hotels. After Jerry Garcia died that summer, Cameron Sears had to help supervise the retrenchment and restructuring of Grateful Dead Productions.

Its small record label and large merchandising operation kept the business going, but its collective wisdom was that the band could no longer tour under its old name. Some members had gotten out of the rock business altogether. Two, Bob Weir and Mickey Hart, formed bands of their own, and toured the next two summers with like-minded musicians under the banner of the Furthur Festival, named for Ken Kesey's magic bus, "in an effort to keep the Dead community and spirit together," Sears says. In summer 1998, most of the surviving Dead members toured again as The Other Ones. "Life without Jerry was a daunting prospect, but it was important they be able to perform," Sears says. They toured in buses and stayed at Radissons. "On a comfort level, it was a sacrifice," Sears says. "But at the same time, it reconnected them with their audience in a very tactile way. We were all traveling the same roads."

Where once the Dead might have spent its off-hours tripping, now they arranged private trips to art museums and the White House and dinners with fans like Al Gore. They didn't miss their old life. "When you've been up the mountain a hundred times, it doesn't have the same fascination," Sears says. "And thanks to their wives and families, they finally began experiencing things most people take for granted." They'd also begun to think of their legacy, announcing plans to build Terrapin Station, a $60 million multimedia concert hall, museum and counterculture complex in San Francisco.

Unregenerate Deadheads quickly denounced the place as an attempt by the band to erect a monument to itself and, as a writer in the *San Francisco Chronicle* put it, "cash in on the Golden Age of Greed."[35] Sears mounted their defense. "People wanted to think of it as some sort of Planet Hollywood, but I explained that the intent is completely the opposite," he says. "Terrapin will show how the tradition that gave the Dead life has evolved as well as where it came from. We want to go back and celebrate the Beats, the Free Speech Movement, the social awareness movements that evolved out of that, and the music that was their backdrop."

Despite its influence and wealth, the Dead remains a lively part of a renegade movement survives lives thirty years after its moment. In that time, the band contributed in many extra-musical ways, often focusing on the environmental concerns that led Sears to them in the first place. It biggest splash was made in 1988, when the Dead played a benefit in New York for groups like Rainforest Action Network and Greenpeace. Afterward, it set up its own philanthropic organization, the Rex Foundation, to "look for and fund organizations that might otherwise fall through the cracks," says Sears, "not the big Sierra Clubs, but grassroots groups" like Friends of the River, organic farming groups, a coalition working to save California's last remaining old-growth virgin redwood groves from timber companies, a monitoring group that operates emission-monitoring sensors downwind of Pennsylvania's still-operating Three Mile

Island nuclear power plant, and a solo activist who spends his time sniffing out pollution in San Francisco Bay.

The idealistic fervor that turned Earth Day into a mass movement in the 1970s is a thing of the past, a luxury most boomers say they can no longer afford, even as they accumulate luxury cars, computers, cell phones and summer houses. "Everyone's gotten too comfortable and they've stopped paying attention," admits Sears, who himself drives a BMW. "We're all working more, and we want to spend what time is left with our families. I have not been on the front line like I was, but a lot of very dedicated people are still fighting the good fight."

Even activists have come to see the shades of gray in what were once deemed black-or-white conflicts. "The debate pitting jobs against the environment is very divisive," Sears says. "You've got vocal young hippie kids arguing with hard-working guys, basically. And the environmental movement has also always suffered from the fact that the places most at risk are extremely remote. But though we may never see them, we still take solace from their existence."

Sears isn't surprised that many dismiss the staged calls to arms issued by environmentally conscious politicians like Al Gore. "He has conviction; you can't quibble with his motivations," Sears insists. "But the fact is, people are less concerned about the environment than whether they're going to get in on next week's IPO."

It's enough to send any right-thinking boomer into paroxysms of guilt. Sears knows that running benefits and writing checks isn't enough. "The status quo won't suffice in the long run. We have the knowledge, technology, information and wealth to make things better. Take San Francisco. People can't eat fish out of the Bay. The wetlands are disappearing, and yet they're debating building a new airport runway through them. We're all driving around in gas-guzzling SUVs; it's like nobody remembers the gas crisis. But the challenge is to do something about it, to maintain the idealism we had at nineteen. I'm just afraid that until we get a radical wake-up call, the vast majority won't be motivated."

Sears sees a glimmer of hope in the scattered victories environmentalists still win. With contributions from thousands paying for the work of a highly motivated handful, he says, redwoods do get saved, organic farms stay in business, and endangered species are restored to viability. "None of us can afford to lose the roof over our heads to protect the coho salmon, but we can all do a little bit to spread the gospel and reaffirm our commitment to things that are important," he says. "You can be comfortable without forgetting who you were."

Sears wants to emulate boomer-led companies like Patagonia, the out-doors supplier, and Ben & Jerry's Ice Cream. "A percentage of their profits go back to the community," he says, "and lots of us can do that now. There's a reason the church got so powerful. People gave a percentage of their income to it. Why can't we do that for the environmental move-ment? The problem is, it doesn't have a product to sell. What value do we place on the air we breathe?"

WHILE ON TOUR for *A Return to Love* in 1992, Marianne Williamson conceived what would become her fourth book, *The Healing of America*. She said she'd sensed a collective despair in the country and wanted to suggest a radical, spiritual cure for what ailed the body politic. In the mid-1990s, she returned to that book, a call to spiritually motivated, non-denominational civic activism. Williamson describes the book as a last-ditch attempt to win her father's approval. He died in 1995.

Williamson found her political roots in a nineteenth-century philoso-phy propounded by Ralph Waldo Emerson and Henry Thoreau. Transcendentalism says that there are ideas, ideals and spiritual truths that exist apart from experience, and that they are where the individual and the universal meet and resolve their contradictions. Transcendentalism val-ues the reality of the spirit over the illusion of the material. Williamson, who sees democracy as transcendental, urges her readers to use the power of love to better the world. Like the boomer rock stars who said war would end if we all woke up one morning and declared it obsolete, her prescrip-tion for social injustice is, "Think the following thought: This should not be happening in America." Though it was hardly an earth-shattering notion, at least she was asking her followers to go beyond *me*-ism, to think and care about something bigger than themselves.

The response was predictable. She was accused of being a typical spoiled boomer, putting her self and its spiritual needs above even rational discourse. Decrying her "ersatz universalism," her tenuous grasp of history and her obsession with thinness and dieting, the *New Republic*'s Margaret Talbot denounced the "pious book" as a "delegitimation of judgment and a delegitimation of conflict; a promiscuous intermingling of the personal and spiritual realms with the public and political realms; a dalliance with conspiracy theories; and a distrust of rationality and the intellect that would make democratic deliberation meaningless." Finally, Talbot warned that Williamson's proposal to incorporate magical thinking into politics smacked of "fascist government, which always prefers charisma to law, and ecstasy to decency."[36]

Williamson is no proto-fascist. Her political views are decent, if naive. Though she's not a knee-jerk progressive (she allows that dismantling the welfare system was "not the worst thing in the world"), neither is she terribly practical. She is given to grand statements, both sweeping ("We have the information right now if we wanted to solve the problems of the world") and empty ("A young child in the inner city of the United States is an American citizen with the same rights and opportunities as a corporate CEO"). She is adamant in her dedication to inclusion, social justice, putting people before profit. She believes in the power of government to ameliorate social ills. "We'll spend billions of dollars on a war against drugs when, for a fraction of that, we could provide sustenance that would drastically reduce crime because people would not be in such despair," she says. "Do you know building prisons is our single largest urban industry? We've made big business out of misery."

To Williamson, the answer to America's dilemma won't be found until the new ruling class of baby boomers "goes back to the moment we were wounded," she says. "That's going back to Martin Luther King and Bobby Kennedy. Those voices expressed a higher philosophical vision within the political domain. There's a huge group of Americans for whom the over-secularization of the left has left them feeling very dry." The tough-minded lack heart, she continues, while loving hearts "need to read a book or two" and toughen up.

For her part, in 1998, Williamson went back to Detroit, Michigan, the town where her father was born. That March, feeling the need "to have dirt under my fingernails," she took over the Church of Today, in a Detroit suburb. The congregation is associated with the Unity Church, a Christian Science-like group founded in 1889 by two faith healers, Charles and Myrtle Fillmore, who considered Jesus an exemplar of a divinity available to any believer. Williamson had spoken at the Detroit church and, after its founding minister died, proposed herself as a replacement. The racially mixed congregation gave her the chance to put into practice ideas she'd propounded in her books, such as having white people apologize to blacks for the way they've been treated in America. "Racial issues are the hippopotamus on America's coffee table that none of us are talking about," she says. "So Detroit is perfect for me. I'm real big on applying the principles of personal healing to the collective psyche. You have to atone for mistakes before you're freed from their consequences. I don't know where white America gets off thinking we don't owe anything to these people."

That same spring, Williamson co-founded a group called the Global

Renaissance Alliance and recruited a board of directors that includes New Age and self-help celebrities like Deepak Chopra (b. 1946), Wayne Dyer (b. 1946) and Jean Houston (b. 1939), an early advocate of LSD, who turned to nondrug exploration of the inner-self after the drug was banned.[37] The Alliance's goal is "to provide a context for people to reengage in the democratic process and promulgate compassion and sharing and reverence for life as dominant political values," Williamson says. Its World Wide Web site (www.renaissancealliance.org, which is linked to www.marianne.com, on which Williamson touts her books, videotapes and spiritual vacation tours to Bali) explains that the alliance is based on "citizens' circles" of two or more people who agree to meet regularly and meditate on bettering the world. "These are open, emotionally safe forums," the web site says, "in which people join together to not only expand their political awareness but to also take action to help make manifest the most compassionate society."

Although Williamson won't reveal what was discussed with the August 1998 "spirit healing team" that ministered to Bill Clinton after his admission of Oval Office adultery, she thinks that the protracted impeachment process opened new avenues of awareness for Clinton's fellow baby boomers. "We are reaching a climax of disgust and the eye-opening realization that politics as we now know it is a completely corrupt mental, spiritual and emotional environment. People are going to be open to new voices and possibilities in a way they haven't been in a long time," she says.

The Baby Boom has come to a fork in the road, rather as Clinton did. "We were a narcissistic generation, but when things get really tough and you're a grown-up, you remember who you are," Williamson says. "Despite everything, despite the mistakes of this country and despite our own mistakes, at the deepest level we have a cellular recognition that this country is one of the great radical experiments in ultimate good on this planet."

The challenge ahead is to "marry the material mastery we achieved in our yuppiedom to the idealism we had before we made it in the world," Williamson continues. "If we can pull off that synthesis, future generations will bless us. Either way, they will remember us. But will we be known as those who woke up before it was too late, or will we be remembered as those bastards who used up all the resources and left an unsustainable planet? The reason we haven't had meaningful answers in America is that we have not been asking meaningful questions. The most meaningful questions are not *How do I get laid?* and *How do I make more money?* What's happening to the baby boomers now is that they're realizing they have more yesterdays than tomorrows. When you start combining questions about your own mortality with questions like *What did I contribute in my life?*, then a major, major earthquake will take place.

"Our generation had the longest postadolescent period in the history of the world," Williamson notes. "Most people hit puberty, take ten years and then they're grown-ups. But because of the traumas we experienced, we got frozen and created a culture that claimed maturity was something to be averted at all costs. We're now at the point where we have to make a choice. Are we going to actually have an adulthood? The idea that we haven't gone for it is scarier than the thought that they might kill us if we do. This is the last window of opportunity for this generation."

Rejecting pessimism as immoral, Williamson thinks her generation "yearns to get it right before we die," she says. "The wall in front of us now is personal courage. We know about global warming. We know there's an environmental crisis. The only way we will move forward as a generation is if we have the courage to do what it takes to change things. Otherwise we will go down as a generation of great shame because we will go down as a generation that knew and didn't do."

IT'S BEEN SAID that Michael Fuchs earned $50 million getting fired by Time-Warner. "I wanted revenge," he admits.

For months afterward, he believed he was up for a job running Sony in America, "but they never contacted me," he says. He was briefly considered for a job at Universal. It went to Frank Biondi, who'd lost his job at Viacom. "Then comes the great test of no longer belonging, no longer having the vehicle, and having risen to a certain height where jobs are not so easily available—and also being considered one of the more aggressive and difficult-to-manage executives in the business, although smart and successful," Fuchs says. "I was afraid to think of what it would be like without a job. I found out it could be pretty good."

There were some adjustments. He'd been a CEO so long, he'd forgotten how much was done for him. He'd never used a cash machine; HBO had a cash window. "But quite honestly, I've been able to master the acquisition of cash," he says laughing.

In 1999, Fuchs was still looking for a job. Just not very hard. Between tennis games, race car lessons and plane trips, he sits on the boards of several small companies he's invested in and works for cultural institutions like the avant-garde Brooklyn Academy of Music and for charitable foundations.

Fuchs has always criticized his colleagues in entertainment, so the fact that he still does is no surprise. Coming from a man who dodged Vietnam if not the draft, who chose the law over protest, who climbed the corporate ladder while his peers were listening to "Stairway to Heaven," and who made millions in the cutthroat climate of the 1980s and 1990s, what he has to say is as radical as it is surprising. For here in his lavish penthouse, Fuchs is railing against empty entertainment and shortsighted greed, two things he knows something about.

"Big companies clearly make creative decisions for business reasons and the bigger these companies get, the more they have at stake, the more that's going to happen," Fuchs says. "I always liked to go against the stream. I feel the stream increasing in speed in the opposite direction from where I want to go. Hollywood is one of the most greedy places on earth. Look at what people get paid, and the accumulation of money, and the quality of the product that results from all of that."

Fuchs fumes that these days, your job is to keep your job, even if that means fitting in, acting safe, and not challenging your superiors. To his former colleagues, he offers a challenge: "You are so lucky to be in a position where you can communicate to tens of millions of people. Wouldn't it be nice if you said something a little smarter, more irreverent, relevant or enduring?"

If they don't, Fuchs might. "I'm not dying to get back into big corporations. I am excessively prideful and would never come back unless I had the kind of authority I feel I'm entitled to. So I've scaled down my ambitions." But starting a small movie company is "not out of the question," Fuchs says. "I don't think I would have trouble raising the money or attracting the talent." So retirement may be just a way station. "At fifty-two, I still feel like a kid," he says. "Maybe I am Peter Pan."

JIM FOURATT RETURNED to the music business in 1991. "It's nice to make money," he says. "I've been able to save money, which I never did before. And I made a deal with myself that no matter what the provocation was, I wasn't going to quit. I think that is being adult and self-preservationist."

Fouratt sounds curiously conservative as he decries the factionalism he believes has destroyed the commonality popular music gave his generation. Punk, once the last best hope of cultural activists, degenerated into style and a nihilism that "takes kids who want to be outside society into darkness," he says, adding that the same goes for gangsta rap. "They're marketing nihilism, and they're co-opting and sucking the vitality out of any of these movements, just so they can sell. Rap was about how black kids survive in this culture without killing each other, without becoming drug addicts. It was about finding poetry within yourself, and trying to get that message out and have some kind of dignity. But gangsta rap is materialistic. It completely denies there is any other way to be a black kid. And no matter what anybody says, two or three black entrepreneurs were allowed to become heads of companies but the profits were made by white industry people."

Fouratt still attends political rallies and gay protests, and still votes in every election. "I have opinions," he says. "I engage people. Most of my friends don't vote. I think this is crazy. This is why we have the governments that we have now. Do I believe in Clinton? I voted for Bill Clinton. I'd probably vote for him again. He's been an enormous disappointment to me. But I'm not devastated like some people are. I learned long ago not to be a true believer. I have no illusions about Clinton. He's not a hero, so therefore he doesn't fall from grace for me."

Early in 1999, Fouratt lost his job at Mercury Records after it was taken over by Universal, which had itself been bought by Seagram. He was given back the name of his record imprint, Beauty, but none of its records or musicians. Nowadays he spends his days writing record reviews and consulting for various musicians and record companies, and his nights on the Internet, where he's gathered old cronies onto a mailing list he uses to provoke discussion. "Most of them have not given up on what they believe in," he says. "I've gathered other like-minded people of my generation to talk about what we can do. I want to provoke. One of the patterns we deal with in the late nineties is lethargy. So I try to prick, scratch, do something to get someone to take some kind of personal action. Because I really believe personal action is what makes the difference. Doing something that matters, that helps make a better world, that helps another individual to understand that they are powerful and meaningful. My goal is to say we're all part of the human society. Identity politics was important: to know how you're different. But it's not an end in itself. The end is, now that I know how we're different, what do you and I have in common?"

Fouratt cringes when I ask about getting older. "Our culture does not endorse getting older. This is what I talk about with my friends of a certain age. If we can figure out how to be vital and share our experience and be creative whatever age we are, that's the way we combat it. Boomers are a huge population, and the AARP is going to be transformed by the influx of boomers who are not willing to be old.

"I don't want to be old," Fouratt adds, shaking his head sharply, then shooting me an arch smile. "Whatever 'old' means."

* * *

IN MAY 1996, when Steve Capps quit Apple for Microsoft, it was national news. People hissed at him on the streets of Silicon Valley. He'd gone over to the dark side. But it wasn't really that simple.

Twenty years after finding his first desktop computer in a Xerox closet, Capps remained an idealist. He'd identified a job that needed to be done—distilling the miasma of the World Wide Web to a home computer's desktop. When he tried to sell the idea, it was as if the fabled library of Alexandria was sitting on a barge just offshore, he'd offered to build a bridge to it, and the Pharaohs of Egypt had told him to scram. He'd offered his scheme to Apple, to Sun, and to Netscape, and had been shown the door. Yet the allegedly evil empire welcomed him.

Capps came to Microsoft with a vague idea of developing a new computing paradigm that would make the Internet and the home computer more consistent and reliable, less chaotic, and easier to use. In his first few months at the company, he played freelance troubleshooter and idea generator, suggesting refinements to make its web browser, Internet Explorer, more user-friendly. "Then my desire to ship products came back," he says, and he started work on what will eventually be the first version of Windows for the new millennium, not Windows 2000, which will have the same basic user interface as the 1995 and 1998 versions, but a total redesign that will provide the one thing computers—even the ultra-simple, toylike iMacs with which Steve Jobs restarted Apple in 1998—still lack.

"When you buy a cell phone, you're handed a functioning thing," Capps says. "You don't even need to know your phone number to make a call. Today, if you're not a nerd, you still need a friend to set your computer up for you and even then, it's way too hard. There's no reason a computer can't be much simpler. The technology is all there; it's nothing new. We'd like you to be able to buy your eighty-two-year-old mother a computer, have it configured for bad eyesight and loaded up with your e-mail address and her investments, so she can turn it on and check how they're doing, and then brag to you about it."

Microsoft has finally realized what Apple always knew. "We want to make customers smile," Capps says. He knows it won't be easy. "There's lofty goals and then there's the reality of markets," he says. "In this economy, it's easy to have high ideals." Too easy sometimes. Time and again, Capps comes back to the hypocrisy he finds rampant in Silicon Valley. Capps admires the founders of Sun Microsystems, for instance, but he condemns their attacks on Microsoft, which escalated after the Justice

Department sued the company for antitrust violations and continued when America Online bought Netscape in November 1998, simultaneously forming an alliance with Sun. "It's so easy for the guys at Sun to be purists and say they believe in open source," Capps says. "Then they get in their Porsches and drive home to their big houses. Meanwhile, the guys who haven't made it yet, the guys who are doing startups and mortgaging their houses, are the ones being innovative."

It's more than innovation driving cyber-business today; Capps compares the atmosphere in Silicon Valley—and beyond—to a riot. "All these nerds are looting," he says. "He got his. I gotta get mine. I'm susceptible to it also. In the old days we worked crazy hours for our salaries. Now it's more like, we deserve to get rich. I know people who are turning venture capital away. It's a mob scene, and if you don't take advantage, you're kind of stupid."

Capps chose security over startup roulette. With an eye toward planning a family, going to work for Microsoft, even under the shadow of an anti-trust lawsuit, struck him as a sure bet. And he has nothing but disdain for those who say he's gone to work for Satan's son. "Everyone thinks Bill Gates is the Wizard of Oz, controlling everything. But the conspiracy theory is a joke. Gates monitors and gives feedback, but people do what they want." Microsoft's great success was happenstance, he thinks. "The world had to settle on one operating system just like it had to have one phone system," Capps says. "Microsoft lucked out with the right products at the right time. Serendipity played a large part here."

With age, Capps has come to realize that every revolution gets coopted eventually. Though ideals are fundamental, they exist in the real world. "Go back to the *Whole Earth Catalogue*," he says. "The commune that started weaving rope hammocks got into the business of rope hammocks, and then it broke up when capitalism got involved." The Internet and the hacker-driven open-source movement, with its talk of idealism, sharing and free exchange of information, "is a rebound from the sixties," Capps says. "But people also like to have five million dollars in the bank. Money will change open-source. It will be commercialized."

Economic realism and his own accumulation of capital aside, Capps remains the closet liberal he was when he argued with his parents about Watergate. Not that he does much about it. He grew up in "dropout mode, not go-march mode," he admits. "I haven't been mugged yet, so I haven't turned Republican." But neither does he play the cyber-mogul game of gladhanding liberal politicians. "My cynicism is such, I'd know they were there for wrong reasons, and I would be, too," he says. "I was a big Clinton fan, and I still like him, even though his libido got the best of him. I know he's totally fake; he's just fake in a way that aligns with my beliefs, the same way Reagan aligned with my mother's."

Like many boomers, Capps thinks the Internet has the potential to change things, but only if it doesn't drown in the noise of millions of know-it-alls chattering about nothing. "In our lifetimes, the Internet will have a lot of impact," he says, "but over my daughter's lifetime, who knows. The Net is a revolution that isn't over. Our kids will still be inventing it. Where we are now is equivalent to the telephone in the nineteen-twenties."

Capps's daughter is two and a half—and her impact on him has been incalculable. "The first time you yell at kids in a playground to settle down, you feel bizarre," Capps says. "But then you realize you're a grown-up in their eyes." When he looks in the mirror, he's not so sure. "I've been very blessed. When you think about it, I've never had a real job, I've always been able to do what I wanted, I've looked forward to work. I'll look forward to it even more when I'm totally in control."

When will that be? When he retires, though he has no plans to stop working. He figures instead that in a couple of years, he'll be able to quit "worrying about money," he says. "I want freedom, basically. Everybody around here is rich, but I still can't walk up to Bill Gates and say, 'Fuck you.' There are people who've quit Microsoft with a million dollars and think they've got it made." He snickers. "Maybe if they moved back to Idaho." What does he plan to do? "I've never had a deficit of ideas," he says. "I've got a list ten pages long of things I've invented." When he does quit Microsoft, one thing is sure: whatever he does will be "completely altruistic; it will make somebody smile."

Capps doesn't mind if people think he wants to stay a child. "What's wrong with that?" he says. "I haven't gotten to the point where I'm taking fifty pills to increase my sexual power and brain power. Will I? Who knows."

From the way he talks, it seems as if Capps will be content when age finally gets the better of him. "Our grandchildren will then have to find the next revolution," he says. He's thrilled to have played a small role in the second one in his generation's lifetime. Once not long ago, in bed late at night, he told his wife how cool it is that he's been part of it all. Marie D'Amico started to laugh.

"Go to sleep," she said.

Hereafter

"ISN'T THIS . . . UNNATURAL?"

We are in a corridor of the Alexis Park, a hotel in Las Vegas that has not a single slot machine or craps table. That's unnatural enough, but it's not what the reporter facing down Ronald M. Klatz, D.O., at an impromptu press conference is so upset about. Dr. Klatz (b. 1955), a bearded, bespectacled osteopath with shoulder-length black hair and a sloping, almost simian forehead, dressed in a black windowpane suit and cowboy boots, is president of the American Academy of Anti-Aging Medicine, sponsor of this Sixth International Congress on Anti-Aging & Bio-Medical Technologies. A4M, as his group is known, was founded in 1993 with the mission of slowing and eventually eradicating what it deems the disorder of aging.

Klatz, his own best patient, plans to live to 150. Think that's unnatural? "So is electric lighting, so are glasses, cell phones, synthetic clothing," he says. "Our lives are so good because we control our environment. We've controlled polio, diphtheria, whooping cough, extending life expectancy to seventy-seven years. But hormone replacement that increases life expectancy from seventy-seven to one hundred and seven isn't okay? I'm not okay with that."

Klatz is on to something. A4M's prescription for aging includes old-fashioned exercise and nutrition, cutting-edge detection of degenerative diseases, preventive measures from simple antioxidants to complex hormone therapies, and neo-sci-fi stuff like genetic engineering and human cloning. "When these come out of lab and into the real world, all bets are off in terms of lifespan," Klatz says. "We believe that half the healthy baby boomers will live to one hundred and beyond."

He's talking to you. An A4M handout, "Facts About the Demographics of Aging," makes its target audience evident, stating that in 1996, baby boomers comprised 29 percent of the U.S. population and that every 7.7 seconds a boomer turns fifty. When the first boomers were born, the pamphlet says, most people in the world died before age fifty; by 2025, when the last boomers are closing in on sixty-five, life expectancy will pass 100. Americans over fifty eat out three times a week, own 77 percent of the nation's assets, purchase 43 percent of cars, account for 90 percent of all travel, and spend a total of about $1 trillion a year, claims A4M. The number of cosmetic surgery procedures in the U.S. increased 75 percent between 1993 and 1997, with boomers accounting for much of the increase. Between 1992 and 1998, sales of fitness equipment doubled to $3.1 billion. More than $20 billion per year is spent developing—and $1 billion marketing—new products for boomers, all told a $300 billion industry. In its first three months on the market, 2.9 million prescriptions were written for Viagra, representing almost $260 million in sales.

Marketers, start your engines. It's the same old song with a different beat now that we're getting on. Klatz and his crew are busy turning the ultimate rebellion—against death—into money.

This convocation divides neatly in half; realists, medical researchers, and doctors in $3,000 suits on one side, wild-eyed health zealots and wishful thinkers, even one turbaned like a swami, on the other. The Alexis Park's large auditorium is hosting medical and scientific presentations, many by scientists with strong credentials. The rest of the hotel's facilities are so laden with bizarre promises of youth, Ponce de Leon would think he'd found his fabled fountain.

In the auditorium, they're talking about advances in imaging diagnosis of cancer, glutathione as a naturally occurring anti-aging protectant, the role of exercise in retaining competence in old age, the treatment of Alzheimer's disease, and the effect of nutrition on brain function. A few feet away, though, they're talking lifestyle. "I've got proteins that are profound," a voice proclaims. "I'm selling libido," extols another.

A lot of this is standard stuff, alternative medicine to some, quackery to others: nutritional supplements to promote brain function and blood flow; vitamins, minerals, melatonin and echinacea; blackberry-flavored Siberian Ginseng, Fo-Ti and Ginkgo smartness-enhancing drinks; books singing the praises of garlic; booths touting Laetrile and other ostensibly nontoxic cancer therapies; pain-relieving magnetized bracelets; $129 pendants with copper coil antennae to neutralize electromagnetic fields and enhance the bioenergy the Chinese call *chi* and Indians, *prana;* and a doctor who claims he can restore your cellular pulse by sending current through your DNA in search of your second genetic code—the one that stores energy, not information. "The theory is larger than any particular medicine," he patiently explains.

Some of the offerings are familiar to readers of supermarket tabloids. The spirits of Peter Pan and Michael Jackson hover over the Hyperbaric Oxygen Therapy booth. "I'm gonna force so much oxygen into you, you're gonna feel like a spring chicken," promises salesman Roland Cordova. "They've proven all degenerative disease from cancer to retinitis pigmentosa *and* all premature aging starts with a low oxygen level in the body." Who is *they?* Cordova has a leafletful of quotes purportedly from Nobel Prize winners. "Oxygen is affordable," he says. "You can have it in your home!"

Keep moving, I think, past skin creams fortified with immune-system boosters, pituitary-stimulating amino acids, energy-enhancing crystals, Trim Patches for homeopathic weight loss, rectal rockets, nonsurgical body-sculptors, Libidoplex Virility Enhancing Formula for Men (a "recreational vitamin" with "guaranteed potency"), the Posture Pump Spine Trainer. Rheotherapy, a sort of oil filter for the blood, is proffered as a cure for macular degeneration. "This is real medicine," says Dr. Richard Davis. "Some of this other stuff is, uh . . ." At the booth for the O'Neil Center for Skin Rejuvenation, the magic is "a chemical, kind of like a peel; it's a secret," explains Clara Asimakopoulos, who adds that in the last few years the average age of its customers has plummeted by twenty years. "You have to look younger to compete," she says, "even if you're experienced and knowledgeable."

Life Enhancement representative Will Block is touting smart drugs, "the zenith of the scientific aspect of the drug culture," he says. "It's not kids whipping up batches on street corners." Nearby, David Butler is defending an illegal substance called GHB, which induces sleep; he sells a legal precursor. Seems GHB is so effective it's been used for date rape. "It has been demonized," he complains. "It's dose-sensitive." He leans forward to confide, "This would put sleeping drug companies out of business, it's so powerful."

Theories of aging abound. "Tension makes you older," says Buddy Macy, who's touting a magnetic massager. "I'm not a doctor," he adds thoughtfully. "Medicine tells you disease and aging is from an imbalance and lack of enzymes," thinks Dr. Dic Qie Fuller, explaining his system of advanced enzyme formula nutritional support. "When people age it's because they don't make the right enzymes to digest their food. Our experience is, you have to balance the gut before you can do anything for the immune system or anti-aging."

Once you understand why you don't *need* to age, you can explore why you don't want to. John G. Scott, forty-nine, marketing director for three cosmetic surgery concerns, shows me plastic sleeves with before-and-after photos of his own face and torso surgery—he had liposuction to get rid of his potbelly and flanks, pseudo-gynocomastia on his breasts, an endoscopic brow lift, in which muscles are removed from the forehead, and an upper and lower blepharoplasty—to rid the face of drooping eyelids. "We can make you look better than you feel," he says. "Most people say they don't feel fifty. Well, they sure *look* fifty. The baby boomers aren't reluctant to indulge their vanity. It's no longer one of the seven sins; it's one of the keys to health. Youthfulness is intrinsic to their identity. They feel depersonalized growing older, being someone else—being their parents—and they're not comfortable with that."

"Baby boomers look at their parents and grandparents and don't want to go down that road," agrees Frank Scaraggi, president and CEO of Longevity Institute International, which trains doctors to manage the aging process using the company's Internet-ready Bio-Marker Matrix software, which helps diagnose the disease of aging and produces a multi-page personalized aging blueprint for prostate, mood, bone, joint, brain, memory and sleep support. ("Our goal is to help you die fast; no slow, lingering diseases," Bio-Marker Matrix promises.)

"They do not want to end up in a nursing home," Scaraggi says. "They do not want to be a burden to their kids. They want to contract for eighty good years, grow old gracefully, and then see Dr. Kevorkian. The problem is, they'd feel good at seventy-nine and want to break that contract. I'm forty-eight, I've invested well; I have ten to fifteen million dollars; I don't have to work anymore. Now it's time to live, and I don't want my money to outlive me. That's the pot of gold. That's our market segment."

How far will boomers go? At a large stand in the corner of one of the showrooms, I meet Dr. Barbara Brewitt, founder and chief scientific officer of Biomed Comm, Inc., which sells recombinant Human Growth Hormone, or hGH. Natural hGH is produced in and secreted by the pituitary gland, but production declines with age. Its proponents say hGH replacement slows the aging process at a cellular level, promotes muscle tissue, decreases body fat, strengthens bones, skin and the immune system, optimizes mental and physical well-being, strength, endurance, libido, appetite and quality of sleep, and even increases penis size.

Unfortunately, the only way to get the stuff is by prescription, which can cost more than $1,000 monthly, or via a black market that may have harvested it from human cadavers frequently contaminated with tiny particles that can cause neural degenerative disease.

Brewitt says her lab-made, recombinant, reformulated, homeopathic versions, created using technology that inserts the DNA codes for hGH into natural organisms like yeast and bacteria, cost only $49 a month. This over-the-counter version is "the same stuff," she assures me, pointing to the results of double-blind placebo-controlled studies that show many of the same results as the prescription hormone. "I'm not saying it does the same thing," she adds carefully. So how do you tell the difference? "Buyer beware," she says. "Your desires may lead you astray."

Kathleen Slaven of the Pharmaceutical Corporation of America knows whereof Brewitt speaks. She shows me her gray hairs and says the hGH precursors she's selling for a mere $10 a dose have raised her energy level—a little too much. "Unfortunately, my libido increased, too," she complains. "I'm single, but I won't jump around with just anybody."

THE BABY BOOM'S interest in health may well have begun in the days when boomers *did* jump around with anybody. For many if not most, sex was intimately tied to pharmacology. One of the baby boom's bibles was the *Physicians Desk Reference*, an encyclopedic directory of drugs, more often consulted for illicit reasons than licit ones. Though many scoffed at the domino theory of drug use—which held that one puff of pot led straight to heroin addiction—a well-trodden path emerged from illegal substances to prescription pharmaceuticals like Quaaludes to ever-harder and more exotic drugs, like cocaine and the synthetic opiate Dilaudid. Often, when a boomer died of a drug overdose, autopsies would reveal they'd treated their bodies like experiments in recreational polypharmacy.

Drug use led to indiscriminate sex, too, which led in turn to venereal disease and the doctor's office. For many, too much fun turned sour and caused breakdowns, mental and physical. Younger boomers gained a rare advantage in that arena; they could see the bad examples set by their older brothers and sisters. It was someone even older, boomer role model Jane Fonda, who first propelled the generation toward healthier pursuits.

The daughter of actor Henry and sister of *Easy Rider* auteur Peter, Jane began her career as a fashion model, but by 1968 had gained fame as a sex kitten via the films of her then-husband, Roger Vadim. Uncomfortable in her objectification, she set about reinventing herself as the personification of the antiwar movement, championing the Black Panthers and Native Americans, and visiting Hanoi, the capital of North Vietnam, where she made antiwar broadcasts in 1972, earning herself the eternal enmity of American conservatives and the nickname Hanoi Jane. The following year, divorced from Vadim, she married the former SDS leader Tom Hayden.

After two decades of bingeing, dieting and amphetamine use, Fonda became concerned about her health after giving birth to a daughter in 1968. In 1974, she founded her own movie company with Hayden, I.P.C. (for Indo-China Peace Campaign), which produced movies with progressive themes to raise money for the couple's political campaigns. Five years later, after proving that a woman in her forties could still look buff by baring almost all in bikinis in her films *California Suite* and *On Golden Pond*, Fonda went into the aerobic exercise business, founding a company called Workout Inc. and opening her first aerobic studio, with all profits being funneled into Hayden's political action group, Campaign for Economic Democracy. By 1983, Workout Inc. was minting money from *Jane Fonda's Workout*, the videocassette industry's all-time bestseller, books, records and a line of clothing. Urging her followers to "feel the burn," Fonda helped the baby boom find a new kind of healthy high.

That year, working out got the Counterculture Seal of Approval when Jann Wenner's *Rolling Stone* put the health club craze on its cover in a story that called the fitness clubs the latest thing on the singles scene. With drugs fading fast as a tool of seduction and the baby boom's youth slipping away, too, exercise proved an apt Rx.

Around the same time, another healthy hippie offshoot sprang up. The alternative health movement, a conglomeration of New Age therapies and traditional medicines, "goes back to Watergate," says Ron Tepper, editor of the *Journal of Longevity*. "Watergate was the turning point when they questioned all the traditional things. You didn't do what the doctor said anymore."

Allopathic, or conventional, crisis-oriented medicine seemed like a branch of the same establishment that believed the war in Vietnam was necessary and smoking pot led to addiction. Facing the inevitability of middle age, the baby boom wanted more than a ten-minute consultation with a man in a white coat offering a fistful of prescriptions. Wanting what they presumed was the due of Dr. Spock-coddled babies—attentive, politically correct care—they were inevitably dissatisfied with a medical establishment just beginning to feel the pinch of spiraling costs and declining profitability, and went out to find an alternative. The advent of AIDS in the mid-eighties, and the long failure of traditional medicine to address it, supercharged that sometimes-desperate search.

As it turned out, Holy Grails were easy to come by. All over America, 1960s types had spent their adult lives becoming expert in a bouillabaisse of unconventional therapies, quackeries, and ancient disciplines: acupuncture, biofeedback, aromatherapy, homeopathy, craniosacral therapy, chelation therapy, relaxation-response therapy, mind-body medicine, mental imagery, naturopathy, energy healing, crystal healing, reflexology, guided imagery, hands-on healing, hypnosis, Chinese herbs, qi gong and tai chi, therapeutic detoxification, deep tissue massage, meditation, group support and stress reduction.

The New Age movement had grown in tandem with the baby boom ever since its precursor, the Age of Aquarius, dawned. The same phenomena that characterized the fabled apotheosis of Aquarius at Woodstock '69 wound their way through all the "isms" of the 1970s to find a new host in the yearning for health and wellness among aging boomers in the 1990s. Even if they weren't all they were cracked up to be, they offered things boomers had long felt entitled to: instant gratification, escapism, empowerment, self-indulgence, empathy, pleasure, vanity and even the sense of still being subversive.

Most of the superstars of alternative health come from the boom generation. Several spring out of its very core. Andrew Weil, M.D. (b. 1942), whose books on natural medicine and optimizing health typically top bestseller lists, was the reporter at the *Harvard Crimson* whose exposés of Timothy Leary and Richard Alpert's experiments with LSD led to their ouster from the university. Oddly, Weil ended up following their path and becoming friendly with both.

After earning a B.A. in botany, Weil, the son of millinery retailers, entered Harvard Medical School in 1964 with the express purpose of avoiding the draft. In his second year there, he led a student revolt against attending classes. In 1968, he won permission and funding for the first double-blind human study of the effects of pot-smoking. He concluded that the weed was a mild intoxicant with few side effects. The next year, he worked at Haight-Ashbury's infamous Free Clinic. Then he traveled through South America and Africa, studying shamanism, natural healing and the effects of medicinal plants, eventually founding a group to study "beneficial plants" and an annual symposium on the medical and psychoactive effects of mushrooms. His first book, *The Natural Mind*, argued against outlawing drugs, and a later one, *From Chocolate to Morphine*, was a controversial and oft-banned consumer guide to getting high.[1] A dozen years later, Weil had reinvented himself as the multimedia guru of natural healing, a field he's dubbed "integrative medicine," and teaches in a post-doctoral program at the University of Arizona.

As Weil rose up out of the boomer drug culture, Deepak Chopra, M.D., emerged from the post-drug mind-expansion fashion of transcendental meditation. Born in New Delhi, the son of a cardiologist, Chopra was a doctor in India, where he was introduced to the subcontinent's ancient healing tradition, ayurveda, which blends diet, herbs, yoga, breathing exercises, meditation, massages, purges, enemas and aromatherapy. After moving to America in 1970, Chopra studied endocrinology and eventually became chief of staff at a Massachusetts hospital where, stressed out, smoking, and drinking, he turned to TM for help. In 1985, after meeting the Beatles' old guru, Maharishi Mahesh Yogi, he was named head of the Maharishi's ayurvedic clinic and helped establish Ayurveda Products, to make and sell medicines. Lectures and articles raised Chopra's profile and, in 1991, immersed him in a scandal, when he was accused of deception after his commercial ties to the products he'd extolled in a medical journal were revealed. As with Weil, controversy propelled his career. By the end of the 1990s, he'd become an acclaimed spiritual leader, bestselling writer, television personality and, along with Marianne Williamson, counselor to President Clinton.

As Weil and Chopra have raised the popular profile of alternative medicine, Dr. Dean Ornish (b. 1953) has given it scientific credibility. The Sausalito, California-based cardiac specialist and nutrition expert, funded by private contributions from real estate and oil tycoons, amassed scientific evidence indicating that mental attitude adjustments, meditation and support groups, combined with more basic techniques like a low-fat diet and exercise, not only stop heart disease but can reverse damage caused by it.[2]

Thanks to his research—carried out despite initial opposition from the American Heart Institute—health insurance companies around the country began to cover "alternative" providers. By the mid–1990s, the work of Weil, Chopra, Ornish and others like them brought about a paradigm shift in the medical establishment. In 1992, the National Institutes of Health opened an Office of Alternative Medicine. And after a 1993 study published in the *New England Journal of Medicine* showed that millions of American were spending billions of dollars on unconventional treatments, doctors began to incorporate alternative techniques in their practices, and top medical schools rushed to study and teach them.

* * *

AGE IS THE Baby Boom's last new frontier, but will the fight to conquer it be the generation's last tilt at a windmill? Even though anti-authoritarians like Andrew Weil disdain it ("I take a dim view of anti-aging medicine," he says. "The goal is to accept aging and adapt to it, not try to reverse or defeat it, which is impossible."), boomers seem willing to spend fortunes in a hedge against the ultimate authority, mortality. More than a few of their fellows are eager to pander to them.

The most impressive exhibit at the A4M conference belongs to a company called Cenegenics, which bills itself as "the medical life-enhancement company." Open since 1997, Cenegenics claims to have signed up about 150 patients in its first year of operation. Cenegenics sells its services with stylish ads that could be peddling polo shirts as easily as Human Growth Hormone therapy. The headline "Coming of Age" appears next to the ever-so-slightly-wrinkled-with-worry foreheads of beautiful youngish boomers with $150 haircuts in the company's pair of print ads, one aimed at each sex. "It comes as a sense of disbelief and subtle betrayal," the copy reads. "The knowledge that the hands of time have turned against you, silently stealing your thunder and slowly weakening your grasp on the good life. Will you accept this news?"

Hell no, we won't go!

In keeping with the baby boom's addiction to image, everything about Cenegenics ("dedicated to the science of youthful aging") is cloaked in studied style. Its convention booth staff wears black suits that match the company's furniture and violet T-shirts the same shade as the clinic's wall-to-wall carpet. Clutching a bottle of water, bodybuilder's arms nearly exploding the sleeves of his black Italian suit, John E. Adams, the company's president, separates himself from a pack of similarly clad bruisers and describes a comprehensive program of exercise physiology, hormone management and nutrition, before issuing an invitation for a shuttle bus tour to the company's nearby $5 million headquarters.

Two patients a day fly into the Cenegenics facility in a neoclassical office complex, set behind a golf course and surrounded by developments of $90,000 condominiums, a half-hour's drive northwest of the Las Vegas Strip. Though hardly homey, the clinic is a family affair. Alan P. Mintz, a six-tyish Chicago radiologist, created Cenegenics; paintings by a relative decorate the walls, and one office sports a photo of his mother running a marathon on her eightieth birthday. After touring the facility, customers fill in a 480-item multiple-choice questionnaire before undergoing a six-hour evaluation that gauges what Mintz calls age bio-markers: measurements of bone density, body fat, skin thickness, lung capacity, sight, hearing, strength, mental and physical response time, flexibility, speed, stability and memory, to document the subject's current status and biological, as opposed to actual, age. With its mauve examination tables, Cybex and video-game-style testing equipment and computerized gadgetry spitting out multicolored charts, Cenegenics is MTV medicine.

Results in, company doctors design a personalized program of exercise, neutraceuticals, and hormone management. In exchange for a monthly charge, patients get automatic vitamin and supplement refills, regular lab follow-ups conducted by physician partners near their homes, and telephone tracking of results. The Cenegenics program seeks to increase muscle and bone density, decrease fat, ameliorate sleep disorders, and elevate sexual performance. Such improvements don't come cheap—and they're not covered by medical insurance. Patients pay $1,300 for their initial visit. Follow-up charges are determined by age. The youngest boomers are charged about $200 per month. The older you get, the more you pay. And if you include Federal Express deliveries of injectible Human Growth Hormone—which come with self-injection kits complete with tiny needles "you just pop in your leg," Adams says—the cost escalates rapidly to as much as $1,800 a month. "It's an affluent demographic—business executives and entertainers born between 1946 and 1964—that can afford the program," Adams says.

The incentive to stay with the program is obvious. As someone on my tour mutters as we drive back into Vegas, "Once you stop, it's Dorian Gray time." An A4M panel on the ethics of anti-aging medicine, held just after we get back, raises the ghosts of more pertinent literary characters. The panel includes Fred Chamberlain, president of a company engaged in cryopreservation, the freezing technique he contends will "change death from near-term certainty to profound long-term uncertainty" (before admitting that currently, freezing the recently deceased causes irreparable damage to the corpse); and Richard Seed, Ph.D., a bearded, bombastic Old Testament type who insists, to many snickers, that by decade's end he will have cloned himself.

Other, calmer voices offer a reality check. Vernon Howard, co-director of Harvard's Philosophy of Education Research Center, reads a paper entitled "Body Parts and Tainted Blood," a look at medical ethics through the lens of Mary Shelley's *Frankenstein* and Bram Stoker's *Dracula*. Howard contends that the first, concerned with "creation and regeneration," and the second, immersed in "sex and contagion," have much to say to modern times. In Howard's reading, the story of Count Dracula and the undead becomes a poignant metaphor for AIDS. But it is Dr.

Frankenstein, defined by his overweening ambition, awful self-absorption and utter irresponsibility who speaks to the Baby Boom.

Victor Frankenstein represents the "threat of a medical technology whose reach has exceeded its moral grasp," Howard says. "This is perhaps a philosophical diagnosis one doesn't want to hear. But can we afford to ignore it when the market in pirated organs, often from underdeveloped countries, for recipients who can afford them, is now a fact? Can we ignore it now that researchers in Scotland and Hawaii have cloned sheep and mice from adult animal's cells?" Railing against the "egotistical pretentiousness" of those who would posit cloning as an acceptable path to immortality, Howard condemns the quest for longevity as an end in itself. "That way lies self-deception."

Finally, Dr. Thomas Wesley Allen, dean of the College of Osteopathic Medicine at Oklahoma State University, steps to the podium and compares the assembled anti-aging advocates and their customers to Prometheus, the thief who stole fire and was punished by Zeus by being chained to a rock where vultures fed on his immortal liver afresh each day. "Wouldn't it be great if our wisdom doubled as frequently as our knowledge?" Allen asks. "Is it for the body or the spirit that we seek immortality? What is it we are prolonging? I simply suggest we heed the words of the preacher in Ecclesiastes, 'For God shall bring every work into judgment. . . .' I hope that we will see to it that all our work can be judged as good."

As the Baby Boom hits the far turn in its race through life, haunted by its youthful ideals and chastened by experience, we would do well to hope for the same.

Acknowledgments

THE ORIGINS OF this book are explained in the text. But it would not have happened without Ellen Levine, a model of support, belief and perseverance for more than two decades. She introduced me to my inspiring editor, Diane Reverand of Cliff Street Books, who took a bad idea for a different book and turned it into *The More Things Change*.

I relied on the sage advice of several trusted friends while trying to distill the story of the baby boom into a narrative that would reduce, if not entirely eliminate, the accompanying noise and chaos. My most profound thanks go to my colleagues and friends, Peter Herbst, Stephen Demorest, Alan Deutschman, and Eric Pooley. Lanny Jones, Killian Jordan, Camille Paglia, Todd Gitlin of New York University, Peter Collier of the Center for the Study of Popular Culture, David L. Schalk of Vassar College, and Richard Esposito also gave invaluable advice and encouragement.

Carrie Schneider's editorial surgery and Lazar Bloch's persistence in tracking down photos made my life much easier and this book much better. My transcribers, Ted Panken and Jean Brown, are both treasures. Thanks to David Bailey and his assistant Andrew Brooke for making me look good and Chip Kidd and Joseph Montebello for doing the same for this book. And I can't give enough praise to my interns, Ananda Chaudhuri, Catherine "Cat" Connell, and Stacy Lavin, or enough thanks to Nancy Hass of New York University, who helped me find them.

This book rests on the foundation of nineteen extraordinary lives. But a number of other people were interviewed and then not included for various reasons. I want to thank each of them, for they nonetheless helped shape everything I wrote. They are venture capitalist Ann Winblad of

Hummer-Winblad Associates, Senator Robert Torricelli of New Jersey, defense lawyer Gerald Lefcourt, hacker extraordinaire Richard Stallman, Robert Stiller and Burt Rubin, the co-inventors of EZ Wider rolling paper, psychologist and drug evangelist Bruce Ehrlich, entrepreneur Mark Rennie, and Dr. Ronald Klatz of the American Academy of Anti-Aging Medicine. I am immensely grateful to all of my interviewees for giving me so many hours of their time. Transcripts of the additional conversations— along with other material on the Baby Boom—can be found on the World Wide Web at www.mgross.com.

At various points, dozens of individuals helped me find a stray fact, straighten out a historical tangle, reach out to a necessary source, or sim- ply grow smarter. In no particular order, I would like to thank Vicki Joy; Marie D'Amico; Sam Magee; Peter Coyote; Molly Irani; John Markoff; Norma Foederer; Mary Hamilton; Jo Schuman; Roy Eisenhardt; Lee Felsenstein; Andy Hertzfeld; Bill Joy; Vinod Khosla; Arianna Huffington; Darryl Inaba; Joel Selvin; Barney Hoskyns; Simone Reyes and Cassandra Julme at Rush Communications; Larry Kramer; Michael Ledeen; Lorraine Spurge; Chris Jones and Angie Orem of Rep. David McIntosh's staff; Lona Valmorro, Joy Howell and Linda Baruchi of Senator Torricelli's office; Theresa Matushaj at New York Supreme Court; Allison Kelley; Linda Gage; Marie Koenig; May Goh; Jeremy Barnish; Patricia Fitzgerald; Susanne Vagadori; Sandy Mendelsohn; Kate Coleman; Linnea Due; Dennis McNally; Susie Bright; Candida Royalle; Jon Maynard of CSPAN; Michael Tomasky; Ray Brown of Court TV; Karen Ames; Bruce Raben; Brian Rohan; Andrew Weil; Anne Doyle; Edward Harrington; Owsley Stanley; Peggy and Billy Hitchcock; Hillard Elkins; Vernon Howard; Bob Strang; Cynthia Robbins; Dale Kern; Carol Queen; Garry Trudeau; Bernadine Dohrn; Edwin Moise; Elyn Wollensky; Eric Foner; Fred Baker; George Emery; Richard Bernstein; Dr. Barbara Brewitt; Ivy McClure; David Talbot; Robert A. McCaughey; Paul Berman; William Frederic Starr; Jennifer Mertz; Terry Housholder; Judith C. Bailey; Kat Sunlove; Michelle Wallace; Kath Weston; Danny Fields; Lewis Cole; Mareev Zehavi; Bobby Lilly; Randall Rothenberg; Michael Parker; and Alex Perry.

At the Ellen Levine Literary Agency, my thanks to Diana Finch, Louise Quayle, Bob Simpson, Deborah Clifford, Jay Rogers, Claudia Mooser, Brigit Dermott and Tom Dickson. At Cliff Street Books, I am grateful to Janet Dery, Margaret Meacham, Pamela Pfeifer, Robin Artz and Matthew Guma. At News Corp., my thanks to Anthea Disney. At *New York* maga- zine, thanks to Caroline Miller, John Homans and Maer Roshan; and

Dany Levy; Brett Kelly, Sam Grobart, Ariel Levy, Deb Slater, Michael Steele and Nick Meyer, who were always helpful, even when I wasn't. At *Travel & Leisure*, thanks to Nancy Novogrod and Laura Begley. At GQ, I am grateful to Art Cooper, Martin Beiser and Merv Kaiser.

For tea, sympathy and shelter from various storms, thanks to Kee Tan; to Lori Levin-Hyams, Debbie Dar and Richard Branson of Virgin Group; to Holly Solomon; to Guy Garcia; to John Weitz; to Melissa Olds; to Anita Sarko; to Susan Blond; to Dan Carlinsky; to Andrew Stengel; to Patrick McMullen; to Victor Kerpel; to Jackie Lividini; to Jim Haynes and Jack Moore; to Christine Biddle; to Dr. Gerald Imber and Catherine Collins; to Janis Kaye; to Marla Maples; to Brian Saltzman; to Matthew Snyder of Creative Artists Agency; to Keith Fleer; to Ken Norwick; to Chuck Roven, Doug Segal and the late Dawn Steel of Atlas Entertainment; to Jaan Uhelszki and Matthew Kauffman; to cousins Jimmy and Pammie; to Matthew and Louise Evins; to Judy Green; to Randy and Maya Gurley; to Stèphane and Bernard; to Fran Curtis and Jami Farbstein at Rogers & Cowan; to Tony Cacace; to Mary Goggin; to Zachary Bregman; to Dale Rubin; to Sharyn Rosenblum; to Silvano Marchetto of Da Silvano, Patricia and Michel Jean of Provence, Michael McCarty of Michael's and Elaine Kaufman of Elaine's; to Drew Kerr; and to whoever I haven't remembered and will always regret not mentioning.

Jane Gross was the first baby boomer I ever met, and has always stood by me—even when she thought better of it. For her constant encouragement, my special gratitude also goes to Denise Hale.

And finally, all my love goes to Messalina and Barbara, who share their house with me, keep me sane, and remind me that every once in a while, a little insanity is good for the soul.

Source Notes

CONCEPTION

1. Readers interested in generational theory, demography and the origins of the Baby Boom—none of which are covered in any depth here—should seek out two previous books that focused on the generation. *Great Expectations* by Landon Y. Jones (Coward, McCann & Geoghegan, New York, 1980) is a landmark demographic study with a significant focus on the period before the generation came to consciousness, when America had to adjust itself to make room for the boom. *Generations* by William Strauss and Neil Howe (William Morrow, New York, 1991), is a profound retelling of the history of America through a generational lens. Jones uses the demographic definition of the Baby Boom. Strauss and Howe define a generation as "a cohort-group . . . whose boundaries are fixed by peer personalities," and set the boom's beginning in 1943 and its end in January 1961, on the day of John Kennedy's inaugural. *The More Things Change* accepts aspects of both definitions in order to paint the fullest possible portrait of the generation's life and times.

2. *Great Expectations*, p. 4. Jones calls this elite the main agent of social change.

3. Which is not to say that front-end African-American boomers have not had both the kind of symbolic experiences this book focuses on, and the achievements its structure demands. Two such individuals, Thomas Jones, who was a leader of the black student takeover at Cornell University in 1969 and is now a top executive at Citicorp, and Cicero Wilson, a student leader at Columbia University in 1968 and later a fellow at the Conservative American Enterprise Institute, were approached for interviews but, regrettably, declined to participate.

4. Bennet, James, "At 50, a Rock-and-roll President Acts His Age in a Cable Special." *New York Times*, March 3, 1997.

5. Morse, Rob, "It's Not My Fault, Ken Started It," *San Francisco Examiner*, August 18, 1998.

6. From *Remarks of Hillary D. Rodham*, President of the Wellesley College Government Association, at Wellesley's commencement ceremony on May 31, 1969. I requested an interview with the First Lady for this book in September 1998. Her press secretary, Marsha Berry, responded that there were certain "legal contraints"against the First Family's cooperation with "commercial projects." I asked how then Mrs. Clinton was able to apear at the premiere of a film produced by one of her husband's political contributors, and to pose for the cover of the fashion

magazine *Vogue*. Berry cited the difference between a "personal project"—i.e., a book by a sole author—and "the media." I suggested that movies, books and magazines were all products of a free press. Berry responded that, "the point of difference is personal profit." I asked under what legal principle an individual author's profits were deemed different from those of a privately owned magazine or a movie studio. Berry referred that question to the White House Counsel's office. Despite repeated requests for clarification, it has not, as of the publication date of this book, responded.

7. Wenner, Jann S. "The National Affair," *Rolling Stone*, November 12, 1998.

8. Dowd, Maureen, "Liberties: An American Tragedy," *New York Times*, July 29, 1998.

CHILDHOOD

1. Fouratt refuses to confirm his birthdate. "You can't ask a gay man his age!" he says.

2. Jackson, Kenneth T. (ed.), *The Encyclopedia of New York City*, Yale University Press, New Haven, Connecticut, 1995.

3. Belis, Gary, "Donald Trump Explained," *Fortune*, January 4, 1988.

4. Robinson, John, "Marianne Williamson: A New Age Oracle Comes Down to Earth," *Boston Globe*, May 20, 1993.

5. Mills, David, "The Vision Thing; New Age Guru Looks to Heal What Ails Us," *Washington Post*, July 7, 1993.

6. Oumano, Elena, *Marianne Williamson* (St. Martin's Paperbacks, 1992), p. 44.

7. Bernstein, Richard, *Dictatorship of Virtue* (Vintage Books, 1995), p. 7.

8. When the Supreme Court overturned the conviction in 1962, Grady was indicted again. When the new indictment was thrown out a year later, the government appealed. It finally dropped the case six years after it began.

9. Sears left his job in 1999 to manage the solo career of Bob Weir, a member of the Dead.

10. Stafford, P. G. and Golightly, B. H., *LSD: The Problem-Solving Psychedelic*, (Award, New York, 1967), p. 31.

11. Stevens, Jay, *Storming Heaven: LSD and the American Dream*, (Grove, New York, 1987), p. 45.

12. Ibid, p. 150–51.

13. Ibid, pp. 162–63.

14. Tendler, Stewart and May, David, *The Brotherhood of Eternal Love*, (Panther, 1984), p. 49.

15. Leary, Timothy, *Flashbacks*, (Jeremy P Tarcher, LA, 1990), p. 131.

16. Stevens, p. 182.

17. In a telephone interview with the author on July 12, 1999, Haworth confirmed the episode. "It's absolutely true," she said. "I'm quite proud of it." She remembers Fouratt less well, but confirmed that "somebody" took her to the concert.

18. Sewall-Ruskin, Yvonne, *High on Rebellion*, (Thunder's Mouth, NY, 1998), p. 19.

19. Warhol, Andy and Hackett, Pat, *Popism: The Warhol '60s*, (Harcourt Brace & Jovanocich, NY, 1980), p. 185.

ADOLESCENCE

1. Stevens, Jay, *Storming Heaven: LSD and The American Dream*, (Grove, NY, 1987), p. 192.

2. Ibid, p. 195.

3. Tendler, Steward and May, David, *The Brotherhood of Eternal Love*, (Granada, London, 1984), p. 58.

4. Hersh, Burton, *The Mellon Family: A Fortune in History*, (William Morrow, New York, 1978), p. 479.

5. Billy Hitchcock replied to various questions posed by the author in a fax dated April 19, 1999.

6. Wolfe, Tom, *The Electric Kool-Aid Acid Test* (Bantam, 1969), pp. 120–21.

7. Ibid, p. 210.

8. Hersh, p. 480.

9. Ibid, p. 484.

10. Ibid, p. 485.

11. Stevens, p. 273.

12. Anthony, Gene, *The Summer of Love*, (Celestial Arts, Berkeley, CA, 1980), p. 53.

13. E-mail to author from Owsley Stanley, May 16, 1999.

14. Wolfe, p. 243.

15. In e-mail to the author, Owsley dismisses Scully's claims of collaboration in the process as "nonsense." "I guess Bear doesn't think I contributed anything to the work and I think I did," Scully counters.

16. Trump, Donald J., with Tony Schwartz, *The Art of the Deal* (Random House, 1988), p. 58.

17. Raskin, Jonah, *For the Hell of It* (University of California Press, CA, 1996), p. 108; and *WIN*, September 15, 1967, pp. 8–10.

18. "We knew what the FBI had done to Martin Luther King," says Jim Fouratt. "We knew about the mistress. We had our own sources of information. So when King died, it had a profound effect on us. We thought the government killed him."

19. McNeil, Don, *Moving Through Here* (Knopf, 1970), p. 23.

20. Ibid, p. 6

21. Ibid, pp. 8–10.

22. Ibid, p. 25.

23. Gitlin, Todd, The Sixties: Years of Hope, Days of Rage, (Bantam, New York, 1987), p. 192.

24. Wells, Tom, *The War Within*, (University of Chicago Press, Berkeley, CA, 1994) p. 214.

25. In his e-mail to the author, Owsley claimed he never intended to give Scully his remaining raw materials, but only to train him in acid manufacture.

26. Tendler, p. 353.

27. Slick, Grace, *Somebody to Love*, (Warner, New York, 1998), p. 103.

28. Hersh, pp. 486–87; in his April 19, 1999, fax, Hitchcock denied setting up offshore accounts for Sand and Owsley, but admitted he introduced the pair to a Swiss bank.

29. In his e-mail, Owsley alleges that 27 grams of the seized LSD disappeared from police custody before trial and were eventually sold on "the street, where it belonged."

30. Hersh, p. 489.

31. Tendler, pp. 90–91.

32. Hitchcock says the money was in the form of a loan to Scully.

33. Hersh, p. 489.

34. Tender, p. 152.

35. Avorn, Jerry, L., *Up Against the Ivy Wall: A History of the Columbia Crisis*, (H. Wolff, New York, 1968), p. 32.

36. Ibid, pp. 25–27.

37. Ibid, p. 35.

38. Avorn, pp. 42–48.

39. Ibid, p. 88.

40. Ibid, p. 227.

41. Threatened with immediate conscription by his draft board, Rudd sought—unsuccessfully—an occupational deferment as a revolutionary, and was finally deferred on medical grounds.

42. Although he didn't attend the convention, Jim Fouratt proudly notes that he was named an un-indicated co-conspirator.

43. Leary, Timothy, *Flashbacks*, (Jeremy P. Tarcher, LA, 1990), p. 278.

44. Tendler, p. 166.

45. Gitlin, p. 387; Sale, Kirkpatrick, *SDS*, (Random House, New York, 1973), p. 468.

46. Collier, Peter and Horowitz, David, *Destructive Generation*, (Summit, New York, 1989), pp. 74–76.

47. Gitlin, p. 388.

48. After one of the defendants Black Panther Bobby Seale, was ordered tried separately, the group became known as The Chicago Seven. The designations are interchangeable.

49. Wells, p. 336.

50. Sale, p. 587.

51. Bender, Marilyn, "The Empire and Ego of Donald Trump," *New York Times*, August 7, 1983.

52. Gitlin, p. 367.

53. Martin Duberman, *Stonewall*, (Plume, New York, 1994), pp. 211–12.

54. Spitz, Bob, *Barefoot in Babylon*, (Norton, New York, 1989), p. 168.

55. Ibid, p. 452.

56. Sale, p. 595.

57. Collier and Horowitz, pp. 85–86.

58. Wells, p. 337.

59. Ibid, p. 85.

60. Alpert, Jane, *Growing Up Underground*, (William Morrow, New York, 1981), pp. 240–45.

61. Sale, p. 627.

62. Ibid, p. 627n.

63. Gitlin, p. 400.

64. Wells, p. 371.

65. Ibid, p. 372.

EXTENDED ADOLESCENCE

1. www.wholeearthmag.com.

2. Collier, Peter and Horowitz, David, *Destructive Generation*, (Summit, New York, 1989), p. 102.

3. Jacobs, Ron, *The Way the Wind Blew: A History of the Weather Underground*, (London, Verso, 1997) p. 137.

4. Ibid, p. 142.

5. Collier and Horowitz, p. 106.

6. Sale, Kirkpatrick, *SDS*, (Random House, New York, 1973) p. 644–45.

7. Kevin Gillies, "The Last Radical." In *Vancouver*, November 1998. J. J. wandered the West Coast for years and ended up in Vancouver, where he worked as a gardener, day laborer, and marijuana dealer, and never gave up his political beliefs or fugitive status. "The last Weatherman," as Rudd called him, died of cancer in 1977.

8. Duberman, Martin, *Stonewall*, (Plume, New York, 1994), pp. 226–32.

9. Rubin, Jerry, *Growing (Up) at 37*, (M. Evans, New York, 1976), p. 20.

10. Hersh, Burton, The Mellon Family: A Fortune in History, (William Morrow, New York, 1978), p. 490.

11. In an e-mail to the author, Owsley says the money belonged "to the community I was serving." He claims that Hitchcock ignored his instruction to invest those funds in gold and put them in speculative stocks instead. "The stocks which went up were put into Billy's accounts, the ones which fell were put into Tim's, Nick's and my accounts. Pretty soon there was no money in our accounts and one of Billy's schemes took down the little Swiss bank," Owsley writes.

12. In a fax to the author, Hitchcock says the Swiss bank invested Owsley's funds and "may have lost some but not all of it." Despite repeated requests, he declined to elaborate.

13. Interview with Timothy Leary by the author, January 1991.

14. Jonnes, Jill, *Hep-Cats, Narcs and Pipe Dreams*, (Scribner, New York, 1996), p. 261.

15. Eisner, Bruce, "LSD Purity," *High Times*, January 1977.

16. Leary testified against Mark Rudd, among others. "But he was Leary, so his evidence was worthless," Rudd says.

17. Wells, p. 491.

18. Trump bought the two yards for a small option payment against an ultimate purchase price variously reported as $62 to $100 million. The money came from his tax shelter proceeds.

19. Blum, Howard, "Trump: Development of a Manhattan Developer," *New York Times*, August 26, 1980; Bender, Marilyn, "The Empire and Ego of Donald Trump," *New York Times*, August 7, 1983.

20. According to Burton Hersh's *The Mellon Family*, Hitchcock would later be given a suspended sentence of five years with probation and be ordered to consult a psychotherapist. At the sentencing, Judge Morris Lasker commented on the irony that being rich is sometimes as much a burden as being poor. Hitchcock blamed his misbehavior on the death of his father in a military plane crash in 1944, and "the insane fucking war."

21. Scully was also fined and hit with a back tax bill. He later negotiated those down to $10,000 in taxes and penalties, and the IRS agreed that his bail and legal fees were deductible business expenses. He made time payments to the IRS for many years until the bill was paid.

22. In 1985, with enrollment declining, *est* morphed into the Forum, a less authoritarian training, and in 1991, plagued by controversy, and charges he was leading a cult, Erhard sold it and dropped from view. But *est*'s ideas ("Master the possibilities," "Be all that you can be") lived on.

23. Heidenry, John, *What Wild Ecstasy: The Rise and Fall of the Sexual Revolution*, (Simon & Schuster, New York, 1997), p. 32.

24. Hubner, John, *Bottom Feeders*, (Doubleday, New York, 1993), p. 99.

25. Often busted, they shared a lawyer, Michael Kennedy, with Timothy Leary and the Weather Bureau.

26. Kristof, Nicholas, D., "X-Rated Industry in a Slump," *New York Times*, October 5, 1986.

27. Michael Ledeen to author in telephone call, June 11, 1999.

28. Draper, Robert, *Rolling Stone: The Uncensored History*, (Doubleday, New York, 1990), p. 34.

29. Ibid, p. 44.

30. Ibid, p. 52.

31. Ibid, p. 67.

32. Say what you will about Wenner, no matter how classy the crowd he ran

with, there was nothing traditional about him. For the next decade, he swanned with the swells, while *Rolling Stone* lurched among caretaker editors, and finally started gathering moss as an advertising vehicle for youth marketers. Into the breach stole Bob Guccione Jr., the first credible threat to Wenner's place at the top of the pops. The son of *Penthouse* publisher Bob Guccione, Bobby Jr. conceived of *Spin* in 1983, counterprogramming against Wenner the same way his dad had done in 1969 when he pitted *Penthouse* (and the pubic hair of its Pets) against *Playboy*'s airbrushed-to-perfection Playmates. Branding Wenner an aging, atrophied sellout, "the Dr. Faustus of the yuppie generation," he promised to "kick *Rolling Stone*'s ass." Guccione had presciently identified the emerging market that would come to be called Gen X—and set out to serve it with a magazine modeled on—what else?— *Rolling Stone*, which suddenly found itself fighting to retain its prominence in a market that called boomers Mom and Dad. But Wenner's flagship took the hits and kept sailing; by the late 1990s, it was *Spin* that was flailing in the face of the rap revolution, while *Rolling Stone* had found stability as the magazine equivalent of a national monument, an integral, if oft-underestimated, part of the landscape.

33. Slick, Grace, *Somebody to Love*, (Warner, New York, 1998), p. 169.
34. Clurman, Richard M., *To the End of Time* (Simon & Schuster, 1992), p. 39.

YOUNG ADULTHOOD

1. Cringley, Robert X., *Accidental Empires*, (HarperBusiness, New York, 1996), pp. 82–84.
2. Levy, Steven, *Hackers: Heroes of the Computer Revolution*, (Delta, New York, 1994), p. 23.
3. Ibid, p. 52.
4. Ibid, p. 71.
5. Ibid, p. 131.
6. Available at various places on the Internet, The Jargon File, v. 4.0.0. A "comprehensive compendium of hacker slang," it is also an invaluable resource concerning the history of computing.
7. Levy, p. 143.
8. The National Science Foundation's NSFnet, a separate "pipeline," eventually replaced ARPAnet, which was shut down in 1990. By 1994, NSFnet had been broken up and sold to commercial concerns.
9. Levy, pp. 213–14.
10. Carlton, Jim, *Apple: The Inside Story of Intrigue, Egomania and Business Blunders*, (Times Business, New York, 1997), pp. 8–9.
11. Cooker, Chet H., "What a Rush," *Vibe*, December 1995.
12. Simmons, Sheila, "Pioneer Herc as Big as His Music Reputation," *The Plain-Dealer*, August 13, 1995.
13. Leland, John, "When Rap Meets Reggae," *Newsweek*, September 7, 1992.
14. Ibid.
15. Cringley, Robert X., pp. 132–33.
16. Gorov, Lynda, "Faith, Marianne Williamson is Full of It," *Mother Jones*, November 1997.
17. Servin, James, "Prophet of Love has the Timing of a Comedian," *New York Times*, February 19, 1992.
18. Oumano, Elena, *Marianne Williamson*, (St. Martin's Paperbacks, New York, 1992), p. 78.
19. The marriage lasted three months, according to Oumano.
20. Oumano, p. 84.
21. Author unknown, "Slick and Surviving," *Washington Post*, July 3, 1981.
22. The first mention of Ledeen as "a long time agent and disinformant for the

CIA" in the Nexis database of international news articles is in a BBC Summary of World Broadcasts on September 27, 1984, repeating charges made two days earlier in a Bulgarian publication, *Rabotnichesko Delo.*

23. Cockburn, Andrew, "Beat the Devil: the History of Hot Air," *The Nation,* August 17, 1985.

24. In a telephone interview on June 25, 1999, Rudolf confirmed that he'd taken down the Haring. "I took down a Basquiat, too, to put up other artists," he says.

25. Haden-Guest, Anthony, *The Last Party,* (William Morrow, New York, 1997), p. 224.

26. Rubin, Jerry, "Guess Who's Coming to Wall Street?" *New York Times,* July 30, 1980.

27. Haden-Guest, p. 226.

28. Studio 54 was rented out to a series of independent promoters. One night, when it was transformed into a black after-hours club, Jim Fouratt showed up with a man named Barry Freed, actually the fugitive Abbie Hoffman, who'd become an environmental activist under his new name, but was still curious about the cultural cutting edge.

29. Haden-Guest, p. 226.

30. Adler, Jerry, et al., "The Year of the Yuppie," *Newsweek,* December 31, 1984.

31. Hoffman returned to his career as a radical, community organizer, writer and counterculture comedian after he was released from jail. He was arrested, along with President Carter's daughter, Amy, at a protest against the Central Intelligence Agency in 1987. A chronic manic-depressive, he committed suicide with barbiturates and alcohol in April 1989.

32. Taylor, Alexander, "Bad Days at the Box Office," *Time,* June 1, 1981.

33. *The Christian Science Monitor,* July 3, 1981.

34. Bruck, Connie, *Master of the Game* (Simon & Schuster, New York, 1994), p. 252.

35. Smothers, Ronald, "Ex-Television Evangelist Bakker Ends Prison Sentence for Fraud," *New York Times,* December 2, 1994.

36. Levy, p. 384.

37. It would be settled in 1984 for $180 million.

38. Kempster, Norman, "Vietnam War Leaves Legacy of Anguish," *Los Angeles Times,* April 28, 1985.

39. www.friendsoftheriver.org.

40. Cringley, p. 190.

41. Quittner, Joshua, "A Crisis of Faith," *Time,* March 17, 1997.

MATURITY

1. Area, the "downtown"-style megaclub for big-spending uptown types, inspired the most mega club of them all, Palladium, the last disco created by Steve Rubell and Ian Schrager, along with the post-Fouratt Rudolf Pieper. Palladium opened in 1985, incorporating and commercializing many of the ideas that had been floating around bohemia during the preceding half-decade; it was the quintessential Postmodern nightclub. Jim Fouratt hated it. "They took a little, special thing and blew it up too big," he says.

2. Although the possibility of a coup was not mentioned in press reports at the time, Michael Ledeen confirmed his wife's account in a telephone interview with the author on June 11, 1999.

3. Chapple, Steve and Talbot, David, "The Changing of the Feminist Guard; Burning Desires," *Playboy,* June 1989.

4. Peterson, James R., "Politically Correct Sex," *Playboy,* November, 1986.

5. Bennett, Catherine, "Portrait: A Prophet and Porn," *The Guardian* (London), May 27, 1994.

6. Clymer, Adam, "Poll Finds Nation is Becoming Increasingly Republican," *New York Times*, May 3, 1981.

7. Dugggan, Lisa, "Pornography Makes Strange Bedfellows," *Bergen Record*, September 15, 1985.

8. Leo, John, "The New Scarlet Letter," *Time*, August 2, 1982.

9. Heidenry, John, *What Wild Ecstasy: The Rise and Fall of the Sexual Revolution*, (Simon & Schuster, New York, 1997), p. 330.

10. Haley, Kathy, "On Top of the Mountain," *Multichannel News*, July 28, 1997.

11. Carter, Bill, "No Laughing Matter," *New York Times Magazine*, November 5, 1989.

12. Shilts, Randy, *And the Band Played On*, (St. Martin's, New York, 1987), p. 68.

13. Altman, Lawrence K., "Rare Cancer Seen in 41 Homosexuals," *New York Times*, July 3, 1981.

14. In an unhappy irony, Poststructuralism's leading voice, Michel Foucault, would succumb to the new disease in 1984, and his death would be followed by rumors that he'd continued to have unprotected anonymous sex in bathhouses after his diagnosis.

15. Flanders's brother Howard Weintraub had once been Jim Fouratt's boyfriend.

16. www.allmusic.com: from the site's Grateful Dead biography page.

17. No Byline, "Judge Scalia's Cheerleaders," *New York Times*, July 23, 1986.

18. Moss, Debra Cassens, "The Policy and the Rhetoric of Ed Meese," *ABA Journal*, February 1, 1987.

19. Under threat of libel,North's source for that allegation—an Israeli—later admitted it wasn't true, according to and article in the *New York Times*, "On the Ledeen Case," March 23, 1987, no byline.

20. Exactly 51 years after Kristallnacht.

21. No Byline, "The Morning After," *Institutional Investor*, July 1992, p. 171.

22. Reibstein, Larry, et al., "Trump: The Fall," *Newsweek*, June 18, 1990.

23. Sherman, Stratford P., "Donald Trump Just Won't Die," *Fortune*, August 13, 1990, and Castro, Janice, "Trump Trips Up," *Time*, May 6, 1991.

24. Ibid, and Hylton, Richard D., "Banks Approve Loans for Trump But Take Control of His Finances," *New York Times*, June 27, 1990.

25. Clurman, Richard M., *The End of Time*, (Simon & Schuster, New York, 1992), p. 147.

26. Carter, Bill, "No Laughing Matter," *New York Times Magazine*, November 5, 1989.

27. Carlton, Jim, *Apple: The Inside Story of Intrigue, Egomania and Business Blunders*," (Times Business, New York, 1997), p. 54.

28. No Byline, "Timeline," *Infoworld*, January 31, 1994.

29. Smileis, Martha, "Mother Teresa for the '90s?," *Time*, July 29, 1991.

30. Oumano, Elena, *Marianne Williamson*, (St. Martin's Paperbacks, New York, 1992), p. 201.

PRIME TIME

1. Carroll, James, "The Friendship that Ended the Wark, *The New Yorker*, October 21, 1996.

2. One IWF backer is a foundation run by Richard Mellon Scaife, whose funds, curiously, come from the same Mellon fortune as those of Tim Scully's benefactor, Billy Hitchcock.

3. Morrow, Lance, "Newt's World," *Time*, December 25, 1995.

4. Shribman, David M., "The People to See," *Boston Globe*, January 28, 1996.

5. Browning, Graeme, "The Fire Brand," *National Journal*, January 27, 1996.

6. Ibid.

7. Robinson, Hohn, "Marianne Williamson: A New Age Oracle Comes Down to Earth," *Boston Globe*, May 20, 1993.

8. Devroy, Ann, "New Age 'Guru to the Glitterati' Advised Clintons," *Washington Post*, January 11, 1995.

9. Krauss, Clifford, "New York Crime Rate Plummets to Levels Not Seen in 30 Years," *New York Times*, December 20, 1996.

10. Taylor, John, "Are You Politically Correct?" *New York*, January 21, 1991.

11. Hughes, Robert, "The Fraying of America," *Time*, February 3, 1992.

12. Leo, John, "Looking Back at a PC Extravaganza," *U.S. News & World Report*, January 31, 1994.

13. Rubell's aged parents were alive and unaware that he was gay.

14. Larson, Jonathon, *Rent* (Morrow, New York, 1997), pp. 19–20.

15. The clinic film, titled *One Foot on a Banana Peel, The Other Foot in the Grave: Secrets From the Dolly Madison Room*, was completed by another director and eventually played on the documentary circuit.

16. Eller, Claudia, "Masters at Expressing Brotherly Love," *Los Angeles Times*, June 27, 1995.

17. Roberts, Johnnie L., "One More Stab At It," *Newsweek*, November 27, 1995.

18. Quittner, Joshua, "A Crisis of Faith," *Time*, March 17, 1997.

19. Marlette, Doug, "Never Trust a Weeping Man," *Esquire*, October, 1993.

20. AOL was eventually severed from the suit, after claiming that although it provides "media content," it is not a "publisher."

21. Broader, John M., "A Clinton Adviser Details Testimony," *New York Times*, February 27, 1998.

22. Lowry, Richard, "Sins of Sid," *National Review*, August 17, 1998.

23. VandeHei, Jim, "McIntosh Now Leader of House GOP Rebels," *Roll Call*, February 12, 1998.

24. Ferguson, Ellyn, "McIntosh Hopes Lawmakers focus on Budget, Tax Cuts," *Gannett* News Service, September 3, 1998.

25. "He called them to his house," Simmons says. "You think anybody else could make them go? No one else could make them go. No one in the world could call them niggers and have them go to his house. And it changed everything. People who had a problem with each other listened and talked, and everybody hugged — and that was it."

26. Wells, Melanie, "Urban Outfitter Picks Up the Tempo," *USA Today*, October 5, 1998.

27. Montgomery, David, "The 'Queer Theory' Connection," *Buffalo News*, December 6, 1992.

28. Feder, Don, "Many Faces of PC at Dear Wellesley," *Boston Herald*, May 26, 1994.

29. Stein, Joel, "Porn Goes Mainstream," *Time*, September 7, 1998.

30. Larson, pp. 49–50.

31. Ibid, pp. 51–52, 56.

32. Brantley, Ben, "Rock Opera à la 'Boheme' and 'Hair,'" *New York Times*, February 14, 1996.

33. Hylton, Richard D. "Trumps Settle; She Gets $14 Million Plus," *New York Times*, March 21, 1991, Associated Press, "Two Trump Bankruptcies," March 10, 1992.

34. Henriques, Diana B., "Trump's Back and May Be Bankable," *New York Times*, December 16, 1992.

35. Garcia, Ken, "The Dead's Unseemly Greedy Grab," *San Francisco Chronicle*, January 17, 1998.

36. Talbot, Margaret, "The Healing of America," *New Republic*, December 8, 1997.

37. Gardiner, Marin, "Jean Houston: Guru of Human Potential," *Skeptical Inquirer*, January 1997.

HEREAFTER
1. Weil, Andrew and Betzold, Michael, *Newsmakers 1997* (Gale Research, 1997).
2. Wallis, Claudia, "Why New Age Medicine is Catching On," *Time*, November 4, 1991.

Bibliography

Acton, Jay, Alan LeMond, and Parker Hodges. *Mug Shots: Who's Who in the New Earth.* New York: World, 1972.

Anderson, Patrick. *High in America.* New York: Viking, 1981.

Anthony, Gene. *The Summer of Love.* Berkeley: Celestial Arts, 1980.

Avorn, Jerry L. *Up Against the Ivy Wall: A History of the Columbia Crisis.* New York: H. Wolff, 1968.

Barr, Ann and Peter York. *The Official Sloane Ranger Handbook.* London: Ebury Press, 1982.

Bernstein, Richard. *Dictatorship of Virtue.* New York: Vintage, 1995.

Birnbach, Lisa (ed.). *The Preppy Handbook.* New York, Workman, 1980.

Bruck, Connie. *Master of the Game.* New York, Simon & Schuster, 1994.

Burkett, Elinor. *The Right Women.* New York, Scribner, 1998.

Carlton, Jim. *Apple: The Inside Story of Intrigue, Egomania and Business Blunders.* New York: Times Business, 1997.

Casale, Anthony M. and Philip Lerman., *Where Have All The Flowers Gone?* Kansas City: Andrews and McMeel, 1989.

Charters, Ann (ed.). *The Portable Beat Reader.* New York: Penguin, 1992.

Clurman, Richard M. *To the End of Time.* New York: Simon & Schuster, 1992.

Collier, Peter, and David Horowitz. *Destructive Generation.* New York: Summit, 1989.

Coyote, Peter. *Sleeping Where I Fall.* Washington: Counterpoint, 1998.

Cringely, Robert X. *Accidental Empires.* New York: HarperBusiness, 1996.

Crouse, Timothy. *The Boys on the Bus.* New York: Ballantine, 1973.

Davies, Hunter. *The Beatles: The Authorized Biography.* New York: McGraw Hill, 1968.

Delacoste, Frédérique, and Priscilla Alexander (eds.). *Sex Work.* Pittsburgh: Cleis Press, 1987.

Dickstein, Morris. *Gates of Eden.* New York: Basic, 1977.

Draper, Robert. *Rolling Stone Magazine: The Uncensored History.* New York: Doubleday, 1990.

Duberman, Martin. *Stonewall.* New York: Plume, 1994.

Gitlin, Todd. *The Sixties: Years of Hope, Days of Rage.* New York: Bantam, 1987.

Goldsmith, Judith. *A Biased Timeline of the Counterculture,* (unfinished project);

posted on the *well.com* gopher site and available via ftp (file transfer protocol).

Goodman, Fred. *The Mansion on the Hill.* New York: Vintage, 1998.

Gottlieb, Annie. *Do You Believe in Magic?* New York: Times Books, 1987.

Grathwold, Larry, as told to Frank Reagan, *Bringing Down America: An FBI Informer with the Weathermen.* New Rochelle, N.Y.: Arlington House, 1976.

Grogan, Emmet. *Ringolevio: A Life Played for Keeps.* Boston: Little Brown, 1972.

Haden-Guest, Anthony. *The Last Party.* New York: William Morrow, 1997.

Heidenry, John. *What Wild Ecstasy: The Rise and Fall of the Sexual Revolution.* New York: Simon & Schuster, 1997.

Henke, James, with Parke Puterbaugh (eds.). *I Want to Take You Higher.* San Francisco: Chronicle, 1997.

Hersh, Burton. *The Mellon Family: A Fortune in History.* New York: William Morrow, 1978.

Hiltzik, Michael. *Dealers of Lightning.* New York: HarperBusiness, 1999.

Hoffman, Abbie (as Free). *Revolution for the Hell of It.* New York: Dial Press, 1968.

———. *Steal This Book.* New York: Pirate Editions, 1971.

Hoffman, Jack, and Daniel Simon. *Run Run Run: The Lives of Abbie Hoffman.* New York: Tarcher/Putnam, 1996.

Hoskyns, Barney. *Beneath the Diamond Sky.* New York: Simon & Schuster, 1997.

Hubner, John. *Bottom Feeders.* New York: Doubleday, 1993.

Jacobs, Ron. *The Way the Wind Blew: A History of the Weather Underground.* London: Verso, 1997.

Jay, Karla. *Tales of the Lavender Menace.* New York: Basic, 1999.

Jones, Landon Y. *Great Expectations.* New York: Coward, McCann & Geoghegan, 1980.

Jonnes, Jill. *Hep-Cats, Narcs and Pipe Dreams.* New York: Scribner, 1996.

Kaiser, Charles. *1968.* New York: Weidenfeld and Nicholson, 1988.

———. *The Gay Metropolis.* New York: Harcourt Brace, 1997.

Klatz, Ronald, and Robert Goldman. *Stopping the Clock.* New Canaan, Connecticut: Keats, 1996.

Larson, Jonathan. *Rent.* New York: William Morrow, 1997.

Leacock, Victoria. *Signature Flowers.* New York: Melcher Media, 1998.

Leary, Timothy. *Flashbacks.* Los Angeles: Jeremy P. Tarcher, 1990.

Levy, Steven. *Hackers: Heroes of the Computer Revolution.* New York: Delta, 1994.

Marlette, Doug. *Drawing Blood.* Washington D.C.: Graphic Press, 1980.

———. *In Your Face.* Boston: Houghton Mifflin, 1991.

McNeil, Don. *Moving Through Here.* New York: Knopf, 1970.

Miller, James. *"Democracy Is in the Streets."* New York: Simon & Schuster, 1987.

Mills, D. Quinn. *Not Like Our Parents.* New York: William Morrow, 1987.

Mungo, Raymond. *Famous Long Ago.* Boston: Beacon Press, 1970.

Musto, Michael. *Downtown.* New York: Vintage, 1986.

Nagle, Jill (ed.). *Whores and Other Feminists.* New York: Routledge, 1997.

Oumano, Elena. *Marianne Williamson.* New York: St. Martin's Paperbacks, 1992.

Patterson, James T. *Grand Expectations.* New York: Oxford, 1996.

Pressman, Steven. *Outrageous Betrayal: The Dark Journey of Werner Erhard from est to Exile.* New York: St. Martin's Press, 1993.

Raskin, Jonah. *For the Hell of It.* Berkeley: University of California Press, 1996.

Rubin, Jerry. *Do It!* New York: Simon & Schuster, 1970.

———. *Growing Up at 37.* New York: M. Evans, 1976.

Sale, Kirkpatrick. *SDS.* New York: Random House, 1973.

Sann, Paul. *The Angry Decade: The Sixties.* New York: Crown, 1979.

Schlesinger, Arthur M., Jr. *The Almanac of American History.* New York: Putnam, 1983.

Sedgwick, Eve Kosofsky. *Novel Gazing.* Durham, N.C.: Duke University Press, 1997.

Sewall-Ruskin, Yvonne. *High on Rebellion.* New York: Thunder's Mouth, 1998.

Sheehy, Gail. *New Passages.* New York: Ballantine, 1996.

Shilts, Randy. *And the Band Played On.* New York: St. Martin's Press, 1987.

Slick, Grace. *Somebody to Love.* New York: Warner, 1998.

Sloman, Larry. *Steal This Dream.* New York: Doubleday, 1998.

Solomon, David (ed.). *The Marihuana Papers.* New York: Signet, 1966.

Spitz, Bob. *Barefoot in Babylon.* New York: Norton, 1989.

Stafford, P.G., and B.H. Golightly. *LSD: The Problem-Solving Psychedelic.* New York: Award, 1967.

Stevens, Jay. *Storming Heaven: LSD and the American Dream.* New York: Grove, 1987.

Stockton, Kathryn Bond. *God Between Their Lips.* Stanford, Calif.: Stanford University Press, 1994.

Strauss, William and Neil Howe. *Generations.* New York: William Morrow, 1991.

Tendler, Stewart, and David May. *The Brotherhood of Eternal Love.* London: Granada, 1984.

Wells, Tom. *The War Within.* Berkeley, Calif.: University of California Press, 1994.

Williamson, Marianne. *A Return To Love.* New York: HarperCollins, 1992.

———. *A Woman's Worth.* New York: Random House, 1993.

———. *The Healing of America.* New York: Simon & Schuster, 1997.

Index